D1538671

POPULATION GROWTH

AND AGRICULTURAL

CHANGE IN AFRICA

✦

CENTER FOR AFRICAN STUDIES
UNIVERSITY OF FLORIDA

CARTER LECTURE SERIES
Center for African Studies, University of Florida

Structural Adjustment and African Woman Farmers,
edited by Christina H. Gladwin (1991)

Apartheid Unravels,
edited by R. Hunt Davis, Jr. (1991)

Human Rights and Governance in Africa,
edited by Ronald Cohen, Goran Hyden, and Winston P. Nagan (1993)

Population Growth and Agricultural Change in Africa,
edited by B.L. Turner II, Goran Hyden, and Robert Kates (1993)

POPULATION GROWTH AND AGRICULTURAL CHANGE IN AFRICA

✦ ✦ ✦ ✦ ✦ ✦ ✦ ✦

Edited by B. L. Turner II,
Goran Hyden, and Robert W. Kates

UNIVERSITY PRESS OF FLORIDA
Gainesville   Tallahassee   Tampa   Boca Raton
Pensacola   Orlando   Miami   Jacksonville

Library of Congress Cataloging-in-Publication Data

Population growth and agricultural change in Africa / edited by B.L. Turner II,
    Goran Hyden, and Robert Kates.
       p.   cm.
    "Carter lectures on Africa."
    Includes index.
    ISBN 0-8130-1219-8 (acid-free paper)
    1. Food supply—Africa, Sub-Saharan—Congresses. 2. Agricultural productivity—Africa,
Sub-Saharan—Congresses. 3. Africa, Sub-Saharan—Population—Congresses. I. Turner,
B.L. (Billie Lee), 1945-. II. Hyden, Goran, 1938-. III. Kates, Robert William.
HD9017.S82P66   1993
338.1'96—dc20   93-2860
               CIP

The University Press of Florida is the scholarly publishing agency for the State University
System of Florida, comprised of Florida A & M University, Florida Atlantic University,
Florida International University, Florida State University, University of Central Florida,
University of Florida, University of North Florida, University of South Florida, and University
of West Florida.

University Press of Florida
15 Northwest 15th Street
Gainesville, FL 32611

CONTENTS ✦

ILLUSTRATIONS ✦

TABLES   ✦

FOREWORD ✦

The question of population growth looms large in the future of Africa. The editors of *Population Growth and Agricultural Change in Africa* observe in their introductory chapter that the estimated population of 530 million people in 1989 will double by the year 2015. This increase will take place within a context of decreasing per capita food production over the last several decades. What does the future hold with these two trends in play? While noting that both technical and political causes explain decreasing productivity, the editors are more interested in understanding the processes that lead to intensification of agriculture, for it is by intensification that most increases in agricultural productivity will occur.

The contributors examine the relationship between population growth and agricultural intensification through a case study approach that is sensitive to historical data. Through an examination of different high-density populations in Nigeria, Rwanda, Tanzania, Uganda, and Kenya, it is possible to see changes in technology and productivity over time and to isolate the conditions under which agricultural intensification follows population growth and is sustainable in the long term. In this approach the book offers concrete examples of positive relationships between population growth and agricultural intensification, examples with important implications for policy and land-use planning. It is encouraging to see that agricultural histories, especially those that capture processes of rapid population growth that imitate today's trends, can have a positive impact for planning to meet the future needs of African peoples.

The Center for African Studies sponsors the annual Carter Lecture Series, which are devoted to critical issues facing Africa today. It hosted and helped to sponsor the workshop/conference at which the papers in this volume were discussed and reviewed by the authors and several outside discussants. These papers address two of the most important and interrelated problems on the continent today.

The center is grateful for the administrative support provided by University of Florida Provost Andrew Sorensen. Thanks go as well to George Bedell and Walda Metcalf at the University Press of Florida, who encouraged publication of this volume when financial conditions and reorganization of the press seemed to dim the possibility that it would be a book. We are also grateful to Billie Turner and Robert Kates for their willingness to support Goran Hyden's suggestion that the center undertake this important publication project.

Peter Schmidt,
Director,
Center for African Studies,
University of Florida

PREFACE   ✦

Perhaps nowhere in the world does the relationship between population growth and agricultural change currently seem so important as in sub-Saharan Africa. The two trajectories appear to be on a course for disaster in this subcontinental region; population growth is the most rapid in the world with little sign of abating in the near future, while per capita food production continues to decline. In both its present-day and its pending magnitude, the widening gap between population and production has been of central concern in policy analysis and academic research alike. Numerous factors have been invoked to explain the problem: the subcontinent has a disproportionate amount of marginal or fragile land for cultivation; it has not received sufficient funding directed at enhancing food production; it is woefully lacking in rural infrastructure; it is suffering from underdevelopment, and so on. The evidence supporting any of these arguments is surprisingly slim, however; few systematic and comparative treatments have been carried out in Africa. Moreover, many of these arguments are grounded in the major theoretical perspectives on population-agriculture relationships. Some see the African case as supporting Malthusian-like principles of rapid population growth outstripping growth in agriculture. An alternative position, supported by a considerable body of data drawn from around the world, posits population growth as a prerequisite for agricultural growth (measured by the intensity of cultivation). Interestingly, several studies indicate a positive relationship between population growth and agricultural intensification in African farming communities.

The basic question of this study is whether population growth in densely settled areas of rural Africa has led to the intensification of agriculture. Densely settled areas are examined because they offer examples of the land-pressure conditions that are to be expected throughout much of Africa if population growth does not abate. Hence they may offer many insights into the future of African agriculture. This basic question is then used to explore those factors that influence the population-agriculture relationship and its consequences for environmental and economic sustainability.

This question and its implications are addressed through existing data as interpreted by the experts who provided them, operating under a common protocol of study. The editors commissioned ten case studies on the basis of background work defining and identifying areas of high rural population in sub-Saharan Africa and matched these areas with researchers who had studied them in relation to the themes of the volume. The resulting papers were presented at a workshop at the University of Florida, Gainesville, April 30–May 2, 1988. The workshop focused on lengthy discussion of individual papers and "break-out" groups assigned to address common themes and lessons that might be drawn from the papers. Joining the authors at the workshop were the editors and a select group of commentators, all long and intimately acquainted with issues of population and agriculture in the subcontinent: Richard Bilsborrow, University of North Carolina, Chapel Hill; Ronald Cohen, University of Florida; Gregory Knight, Pennsylvania State University; Philip Porter, University of Minnesota; and Donald Vermeer, George Washington University. All papers were redrafted after the workshop.

Full compliance with the data demands of the protocol proved difficult for each case study. The data gaps that result, as well as the varying quality of the data that were obtained, inhibit strict quantitative analyses and leave a number of questions unanswered. These problems noted, the individual chapters provide empirically rich assessments of the population-agriculture relationship, and comparisons among them provide important insights to the suite of questions posed about the population-agriculture relationship and their meaning for the subcontinent in general. We believe that they offer a base from which further studies can be launched and further insights gained.

This effort was sponsored by a grant from the Rockefeller Foundation. Financial assistance for various facets of the project was also provided by the Center for African Studies, University of Florida, the Alan Shawn Feinstein World Hunger Program, Brown University, and the Graduate School of Geography and the George Perkins Marsh Institute, Clark University. We thank the various individuals in these programs who assisted the project during its preparation and implementation, especially David Mazambani, Mark Johnson, and Richard Nolan. Viola Haarmann deserves special recognition for her assistance during the editing phase of the project. The graphics were prepared by Margaret Pearce and Anne Gibson of the Clark Cartography Lab.

B. L. Turner II
Worcester, Massachusetts

Goran Hyden
Gainesville, Florida

Robert W. Kates
Providence, Rhode Island

1 / Theory, Evidence, Study Design

Robert W. Kates, Goran Hyden, and
B. L. Turner II

Over the next century, Africa's population may increase fourfold before stabilizing, creating densities of population unprecedented on the continent. Many expect that this situation will severely compound the current agricultural crisis; others believe that it will stimulate agricultural growth through the intensification of agriculture, leading to improvements in food availability and to general economic development. Evidence for both views has been found. Throughout most of the developing world, the intensity of agriculture and greater land productivity is broadly associated with higher population densities. Against this generality, however, are many instances in which the intensification process has not led to the types of adjustments in agriculture that improve food availability or general quality of well-being. Indeed, stagnation, involution, and environmental deterioration may be equally associated with increasing population density and related agricultural practices. Given the seeming inevitability of rapid population growth in Africa, therefore, it is particularly important to understand those situations that lead to positive conditions of intensification—improved food supply, well-being, and sustainable agriculture—and those that lead to negative conditions of stagnation and of environmental degradation.

There are at least four theoretical traditions that yield differing expectations of the relationship between population and agricultural growth. Broadly interpreted, they view the relationship optimistically or pessimistically and ground much of the argument within the roles played by population pressures or economic development (fig. 1.1). Seen as a localized process, especially among subsistence-oriented economies, *neo-Malthusians* have negative expectations—population has the potential to outstrip agricultural change, inducing land fragmentation, environmental deterioration, poverty, and famine (MacDonald 1989). In contrast, *Boserupians* (following Boserup [1965 and 1981] and others) have positive expectations—population growth is a stimulus for an intensification

1

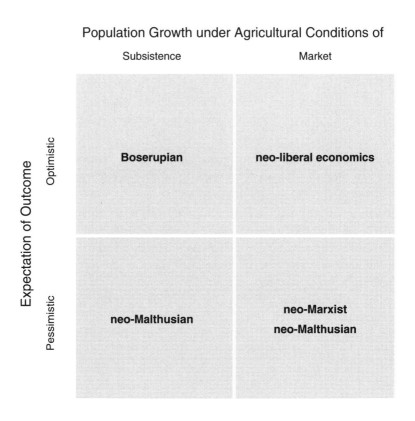

Fig. 1.1. Expectations of the population-agricultural growth relationship: theoretical traditions

of agriculture, which is the triggering mechanism for higher levels of productivity owing to the technological change and division of labor that accompany the process. This view blends into the larger context of markets and external relations of the *neoliberal* economists who posit outcomes dependent on an appropriate economic structure that provides rewards to the individual farmer for intensifying production, encourages specialization, and facilitates entry into "free" markets (see Schultz 1964; Mellor 1966). Finally, the market context also gives rise to two pessimistic views. *Neo-Marxist* social scientists argue that the colonial legacy, the current international reach of capitalism, and class-based national politics have created political and economic conditions that inhibit the development spinoffs of intensification, even if they were to occur (see Watts 1989; Bernstein et al. 1990). Alternatively, neo-Malthusians warn that rapid population growth, even in well-developed market economies, leads to pressures on world resources that potentially threaten the global carrying capacity (see Ehrlich and Ehrlich 1990).

Fortunately, we do not need to rely solely on generalized observations or on speculative theory to ask whether the extraordinary population changes currently taking place in Africa offer opportunities for encouraging production or simply compound existing problems. There are today, in many parts of Africa, areas of rapid population growth and high population density that can serve as case studies or "natural experiments" for examining this question. In this volume, we select a set of such high-density population areas and examine how, over time, the intensity of agriculture changed, how such changes came about, and what have been the immediate and longer-term consequences of such changes.

No study can provide equal weight to all elements of a theme as complex as this one, and we make no attempt to do so here. Our primary objective is to begin at the beginning, so to speak, focusing on the first issue through two principal queries. Has population growth in densely settled areas of sub-Saharan Africa led to agricultural intensification, and, if so, under what local environmental and socioeconomic conditions? Issues of the larger national and international socioeconomic orders are not explored in as much detail, although their importance emerges in several of the case studies and is discussed in the concluding section of this book. Our approach thus counters the emphasis of the general literature on sub-Saharan Africa that has articulated the impact on agriculture of the sociopolitical history of the subcontinent and has paid less attention to local and regional comparisons or to the local dynamics of agricultural change (see MacDonald 1989: 207).

Population Growth

Africa, south of the Sahara, is composed of 47 countries, whose 1992 population is estimated at 507 million people with an overall density of 23 people per square kilometer, and growing at a rate of 2.9 percent per annum (Population Reference Bureau 1992). This population is expected to double by 2010 and to reach 1.7 billion by 2055 before leveling off, according to World Bank projections that assume a universally declining fertility rate beginning in 1995. Using other assumptions, the population in 2055 may be 25 percent lower or higher (Chen 1989: 2–3). Nonetheless all projections agree that, barring major catastrophes, over a period when the world population will probably double, African population will grow twice as fast—a rate of change unprecedented for any continent within human history that places unprecedented demands on the growth of African agriculture.

By the middle of the next century, six African nations may have populations greater than 100 million, larger than any of the major European powers today, and the population of Nigeria alone may exceed that today of all of North America. Africa's population density, however, will still be relatively low compared to that of Asia: about 75 people/km^2, about the density of Greece today (Chen 1989). The great growth in African population, then, is taking place on a continent that is still relatively sparsely populated.

The Crisis in Agriculture

Between 1965 and 1985, food production grew in sub-Saharan Africa by 54 percent, but per capita food production declined by 12 percent according to standard sources (WRI 1988–89). Although the accuracy of such estimates is questioned, there is a general consensus that the aggregate data used to estimate continentwide production trends indicate circumstances that do not bode well for the future (see Singh 1983; Ho 1985). The African case, then, stands in stark contrast to the remainder of the developing world where per capita food production at the international scale has risen dramatically in Asia, and maintained itself in the Near East and Latin America (fig. 1.2).

Many causes for this lag in agricultural production have been suggested. They can be divided into two categories, the technical and the political, dominated by the international development and the academic communities, respectively. New technologies were emphasized in international development circles in Africa during the 1960s and early 1970s in an attempt to replicate the "green revolution" successes of Asia. This approach largely failed, and alternatives were sought. One alternative concentrated on developing a better understanding of Africa's indigenous farming systems (see Harwood 1979; Moock 1986; Dommen 1988), including its environmental basis (Porter 1979); another focused

Index numbers

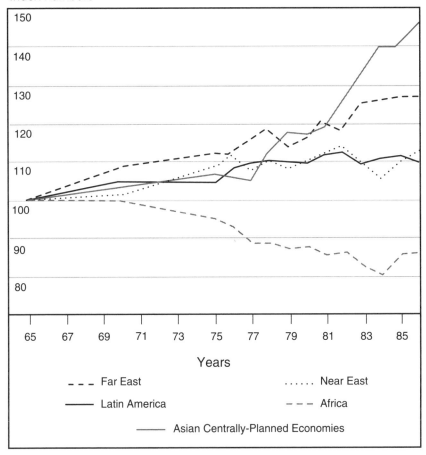

Fig. 1.2. Index of per capita food production. Figure adapted from *World Resources* 1988–89. Copyright 1988 by the World Resources Institute and the International Institute for Environment and Development in collaboration with the United Nations Environmental Program. Reprinted by permission of Basic Books, a division of HarperCollins Publishers, Inc.

on strengthening its physical and economic infrastructure (see Mellor 1984). During the 1980s, these approaches were complemented by exploration of Africa's complicated and multifaceted land-tenure systems (see Noronha 1988) and by a strong plea for the importance of the long-term development of the continent's own research system (see Eicher 1988). Subsequently, interests have shifted toward support of Africa's low-resource farmers (Office of Technology Assessment 1988)—the unimodal approach advocated for a long time by Johnston and his colleagues (see Johnston and Clark 1982)—and this shift has been paralleled by assessments of past practices by the poorest farmers (see Lipton 1989). These approaches have fed back to farmers and communities through projects emphasizing low-capital technology and labor-based land improvements (see Rocheleau, Weber, and Field-Juma 1988). These approaches have also been viewed in a population-resource perspective (Ho 1985; Lele and Stone 1989), leading to recommendations that emphasize the targeting of regions with high agricultural potential for the development of high-yielding and high-valued crops.

Much of academic debate has been dominated by economists and political economists. The latter have consistently argued that Africa's agriculture suffers because of the structure of the global economy and the exploitation that it gives rise to, by both the rich over the poor nations and the privileged over the underprivileged classes (see Dumont 1962; Wisner 1988). In the 1980s, this approach ventured beyond these concerns, focusing on gender relations, household-labor processes, and resource management (Watts 1989).

The former, or neoliberal economic perspective, has explained the situation in African agriculture in terms of the pace of demands on food production outstripping the ability of farmers to make technological and procedural adjustments (see Pingali, Bigot, and Binswanger 1987); the parallel slow response of "induced innovation" owing to the rather late development of large-scale, intensive pressures on agriculture; or the use of inappropriate or alienating technologies introduced from abroad and not adapted to African conditions (Levi and Havinden 1982:16; Mellor 1984; Dommen 1988). Others emphasize the disincentives to African farmers, such as the complicated and multifaceted land-tenure systems (see Netting 1968; Noronha 1988) that may inhibit land improvements; the artificially low prices paid for staples, a policy followed by local governments to ensure "stability" in urban areas (see Schultz 1978); the negative impacts of inadequate infrastructure on agricultural behavior in general (Lele 1988); and the variable and generally low market value of many African staples (World Bank 1984).

Cross-cutting these explanations have been the contradictory "lessons" derived from the African experience (Huss-Ashmore and Katz 1989). These demonstrate the resilience, flexibility, and "successes" of some groups of African farmers through adaptation strategies (see Hill

1963; Netting 1968; Coulibaly 1978; Mortimore 1989) and the role of local institutions (see Harrison 1987) that allow resistance to negative forces of change (see Scott 1985).

Although we do not reject any of the broad or specific explanations noted above, our experience suggests a number of population-related factors impeding the development of agriculture in Africa that recur across multiple cases. These include the overall low density of population and dispersed settlement patterns, the general absence of effective localized markets for both inputs and outputs, the rudimentary transportation network that connects a diffusely settled population, the inadequate incentives to adopt more demanding (in time and risk) technologies, and the existence of large areas of potential agricultural and pastoral lands denied by eradicable disease, such as onchocerciasis or trypanosomiasis, that could be made productive by higher population through sustained land use. Such factors have not been thoroughly addressed or developed into a multicausal framework.

In short, we enter the 1990s with no macrotheory or approach to explain the agricultural crisis. Africa and the world have come to recognize that there is no single solution to the crisis in Africa's agriculture, just as there is no concise or simple theory to guide that solution. One avenue that deserves further investigation is the role of the intensification of agriculture in African farming and food crisis. Intensification is fundamental to increase agricultural production, which is a critical component of the crisis.

Agricultural Intensification

Agricultural growth takes place either through expansion—the extension of land under cultivation—or intensification—the increased utilization or productivity of land currently under production. About 80 percent of the growth in African agriculture has come from the extension of the area under cultivation (Paulino 1987), much of it on lands once considered too marginal to cultivate. If Africa is to feed its growing population and retain its much-needed agricultural export trade, a better balance will be needed between production gains from the expansion and intensification of agriculture; and surely most of future agricultural growth will come from more intensive use of the prime agricultural lands (see also Lele and Stone 1989).

Theories of Intensification

Theories and themes that seek to explain agricultural intensification can be placed in two broad categories: those that relate production to household needs and wants (usually population-driven) under conditions of "subsistence" and those that relate production to demands from the market. These theories and themes are potentially complementary, as each emphasizes one part of the reality experienced by most African farmers; production for both direct consumption and commodity sale (see Brush and Turner 1987).

Much of contemporary consumption-based or "needs" theory has its origins in the works of Chayanov (1966) and Boserup (1965, 1981). It asserts that farmers are responsive primarily to the biological needs of the immediate population that they must feed, defined, of course, by cultural standards of acceptable consumption. Output is achieved through the least-effort means perceived by the farmer and is limited by the immediate need. As the population-land ratio increases, farmers are "forced" to employ greater labor and technical inputs to achieve greater production. In this case, output per unit of area land grows (a reverse process is possible, however). This growth does not necessarily improve per capita production. For improvement to take place, technological change is normally required. In the early or extensive phases of a growth trajectory, these changes may involve "traditional" land improvements (for example, irrigation or drainage) in which land transformation takes place; in the later phases they involve modern bioscience-derived inputs (for example, high-yielding varieties). Importantly, these technological changes do not necessarily take place in a linear or uniform phasing in response to demands, particularly for those changes that require large investments in labor. Rather, thresholds of demand must be met before the investment is made, and this leads to a stair-step growth pattern in agriculture (see Robinson and Schutjer 1984). Each "stair step" in agricultural growth involves major improvements in land productivity and, presumably, improvement in per capita production. Continued pressures on the new agricultural system result in diminishing returns until a new threshold level is reached, leading to a new technological system.

This segment of the theory—an elaboration of Boserup's original thesis—focuses on the behavior of farmers in consumption production and explains why total output is increased in relation to population stresses placed on the farmer. As such, it can be seen as a subsistence or, perhaps more accurately, a "need" theme. In this case, need refers to biological and social factors that set, for example, the expected standards of consumption, combined with satisfying redistribution and survival insurance responsibilities. The less-developed segment (see Boserup 1965, chap. 12; 1981) of the theory asserts that the intensification process leads to specialization in labor and preconditions for "exchange" and market production. This stage of "growth" presumably moves behavior more toward that described in the neoclassical tradition involving the "market" theme of demand on agriculture.

The market or commodity theory applied to Third World farmers has its modern origins in the pioneering works of Tax (1953), Schultz (1964), Wharton (1969), and other agricultural economists and economic anthropologists. It asserts that once farmers accept commodity production, they respond to market demand within the constraints placed upon them, maximizing production to the level of maximum reward. This theory has been modified through the critiques of Lipton (1968), Collinson (1972), Scott (1976), and others, who demonstrate that economic efficiency in the allocation of resources, strictly defined, cannot be achieved by such farmers. Rather, farmers tend to be risk averse, at least in regard to some minimum production needed for survival (see Levi and Havinden 1982) and, therefore, respond in a "proficient" manner (Schluter and Mount 1976). These behavioral themes are linked to a large number of broader economic and agricultural models (for growth stage or conservation models, see Hayami and Ruttan 1985), leading to specific views about the trajectories that agriculture will take. These have been merged into a theory of "induced innovation," in which technological and institutional changes required to develop agriculture are endogenously derived as a result of changes in resource endowments and demand (Binswanger and Ruttan 1978; Hayami and Ruttan 1985).

Pure applications of each theory have largely ignored the others. Those interested in the consumption or needs side have emphasized its elaboration; many working on the commodity or market side have assumed that even the slightest market engagement makes farming behavior, and hence agricultural development, subject to commodity theory. Yet many instances have been documented in which household agricultural functions are divided between consumption and commodity crops and fields, presumably with different motivations involved in each (see Gray 1988). And this logic can be extended to the multitude of "deviations" recognized between the commodity theory and the reality of the farming unit—that is, these deviations follow from not only constraints on farmers but also a behavior that is fully predicated neither on the commodity nor on consumption theories. This has led to a consumption-commodity or "induced-intensification" theory (see Ali and Turner n.d.), particularly among those outside economics; it asserts that farming behavior for most Third World farmers is predicated on a composite of the consumption and commodity rationales (see Fisk 1964; Grossman 1985; Turner and Brush 1987) and that agricultural change, including technological and institutional changes, is driven by the joint demands placed on it. On the consumption side, intensification is induced largely through mechanisms endogenous to the farmer and, therefore, is the product of indigenous experimentation and accumulated wisdom. On the commodity side, however, intensification is induced by mechanisms exogenous to the farmer and ultimately is largely associated with technological changes from commercial and public experimental institutions, following the induced-innovation theme. Drawing upon themes that focus on these attributes of agricultural behavior in the face of increasing demand seems particularly appropriate for our study; most African smallholders who produce directly for their own needs and for markets have demonstrated considerable resilience to constraints and demands (Pingali, Bigot, and Binswanger 1987) and have "innovated" changes in agriculture through landscape transformations as a response to local demands and, more recently, through other types of technological and institutional changes as a response to market demands.

Measures of Density and Intensification

Characterizing the relationship between population growth and agricultural intensification often involves comparing measures of population per unit area for a given period of time. Population density is usually expressed as the number of persons per unit area of land, of potential arable land, or of land employed in agriculture. The measure of agricultural intensification has taken on a rather precise meaning as the total production per unit area and time (typically per hectare and year). Its obvious measure, therefore, should be that of total output. Owing to several complications and to the paucity of data at the local level, surrogate measures are commonly employed. The most common two are the frequency of cultivation and the type and number of agrotechnologies (Turner and Doolittle 1978).

Study of the relationship between population density and agricultural intensification is complicated by several problems, most of which

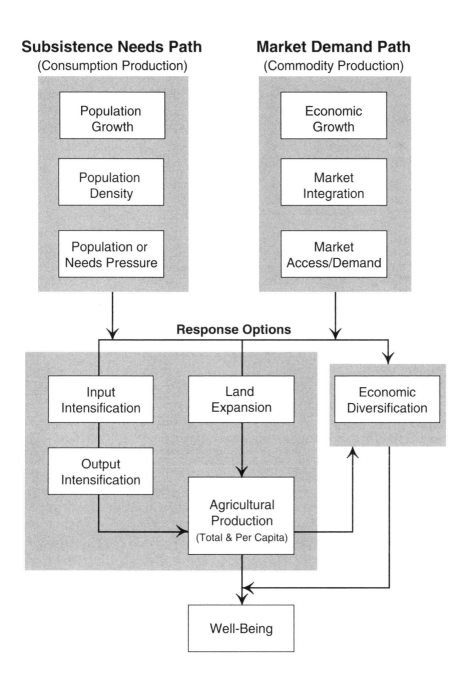

Fig. 1.3. Pathways from agricultural growth to improved well-being

involve the pros and cons of the measure used and, for Africa, the quality of the data on which they may be based. For a measure of *population density*, "raw" density or population per total area in question (for example, village or district) fails to account for the great range in land quality and use that may occur within the area. A low "raw" density may be generated by the presence of much land highly unsuited for cultivation, and therefore, the "pressures" on the cultivated lands are not adequately captured. "Relative" density, population per selected area thought relevant to agricultural production (often expressed as arable or cultivated land), is an improvement but also can be deceiving. What constitutes arable land (or cultivated land) varies by changes in technology and need. Of the measures, data for the calculation of "raw" density are typically the easiest to obtain, but the "relative" measure per cultivated land may best reflect agricultural pressures if cultivation is fundamental to the household economy.

The best direct measures of agricultural intensity in terms of *total output per unit area and time* also have problems related to the multiplicity of products, times, and conversion measures used to equate them. Data for systems of mixed cropping (numerous species in one plot) and for multiple functioning fields, orchards, and livestock zones are difficult to obtain. Various means can be used to create an overall set of output figures, but these then require reduction to a common denominator for effective comparisons. Cultigens vary from food to fiber to condiments and are produced for both direct consumption and sale. Energy measures (kilocalories produced) are inappropriate for fiber crops, and weight or volume measures say little about the value of production. Root crops, for example, produce much more weight per hectare than do cereals, but the caloric value of cereals may be much greater. Monetary measures, of course, are strongly affected by the vagaries of the market, including instances in which major differences exist in the worth of the same produce depending upon its use: for instance, the amount of food purchased with the cash obtained from the sale of the harvest is usually not equivalent to the amount of food sold. This said, an adequate measure may be obtained by standardizing the entire harvest to a staple-food equivalent (for example, maize, sorghum, or rice).

Because good production data are so difficult to obtain, the conventional surrogate measure of agricultural intensity is the frequency of cultivation (after Boserup 1965) as shown on the top line of figure 1.4. Calculating the frequency of cultivation—the number of harvests per plot over a standard time frame—is complicated by the prevalence of

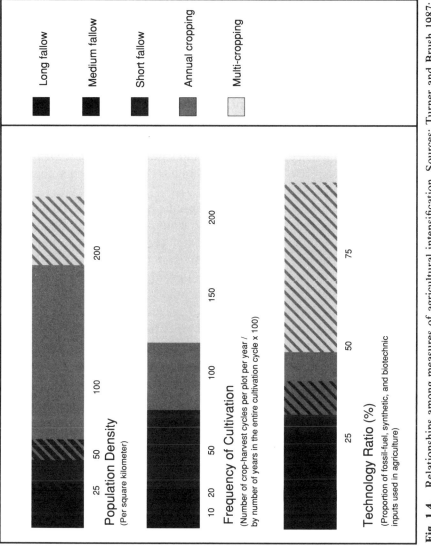

Fig. 1.4. Relationships among measures of agricultural intensification. Sources: Turner and Brush 1987; Pingalli 1987:27.

multiple cropping (more than one harvest per plot per year), the simultaneous employment of various fallow practices within the same system, and the use of species that need not be planted and harvested within a single cultivation cycle or season (for example, manioc/cassava). Although descriptive categories can be used—for instance, long fallow or multiple cropping—they are imprecise measures and are not well suited for comparative analysis. Typically, then, frequency is calculated in terms of a percent of time that a plot of land is under cultivation. Despite its problems, the frequency measure is popular because of the broad correspondence between total land productivity (not yield) and cultivation frequency, especially if similar levels of technology are involved.

Beyond frequency of cultivation, specific mixes of technologies have been used as surrogate measures. For example, one study on African agriculture has compared operations employed in different farming systems with increasing frequency of cultivation (Pingali, Bigot, and Binswanger 1987). The use of these operations and their implied technologies as indicators of intensification is complicated by the disputed role such technologies are seen to play within extensive agriculture. This is so because high amounts of labor and procedures can be used as substitutes for technology in some systems; some low-tech systems are more land-intensive than are high-tech ones (see Turner and Brush 1987: 7). Even such commonly accepted indicators of intensification as the irrigation works and agricultural terracing found in historical and archaeological studies do not necessarily imply widespread intensification in the African context (Sutton 1984). Within "low-resource" agriculture, subtle procedures and technologies, constituting creative recombinations of existing productive inputs, are commonly employed (Richards 1985; Dommen 1988; Office of Technology Assessment 1988), and these types of "technology" are not readily accountable in technological measures.

Evidence of Intensification with Increasing Population Density

Consistent relationships between population density and agricultural intensity (measured through either the frequency of cultivation or output per unit area or time) have been demonstrated for many parts of the world (Brush and Turner 1987). These include village- or regional level comparisons in the tropics (Dalrymple 1971; Turner, Hanham, and Portararo 1977) and highland New Guinea (Brookfield 1962; Brown and Podolefsky 1976), and intra-village comparisons in Central America

(Bartlett 1976) and Southeast Asia (Sahlins 1971). Also, although not addressing the intensification theme per se, other studies have produced comparative evidence that strongly supports the general trends between population density and agricultural intensity (see Ruthenberg 1980).

Few comparative studies have found the relationship lacking, and those that have are controversial because of methodological and other problems; for example, Metzner's (1982) findings on the Isla de Flores involved perennial tree crops, a situation in which the relationship was never intended. In an interesting alternative, Richards (1985, 1987) has shown that loss of population has led to intensification in parts of West Africa. This situation results from the migration of males—those who clear the forests for extensive systems—and the increased significance of female labor, which is employed to increase output on land already cleared for cultivation.

A number of studies have identified positive relationships between increased population (or agricultural demand) and agricultural intensification in Africa, especially in West Africa, and at least four general treatments of the subject exist: Cleave (1974) and Pingali, Bigot, Binswanger (1987) for pan-Africa, and Gleave and White (1969) and Netting, Cleveland, and Steir (1980) for West Africa. Examinations in the Sahelian zones have been made by Haswell (1953), Grove (1961), Mortimore (1967), Benneh (1972), and Norman (1974). Other support comes from Vermeer (1970) for the Tiv of Nigeria and Basehart (1973) for the Matengo of Tanzania. The most detailed treatment of the subject, however, is of the Jos Plateau of Nigeria, where Netting (1968) found population density to be strongly associated with the intensity of cultivation.

One of the few contrary interpretations has been offered by Datoo (1976) for agriculture in the Uluguru Mountains of Tanzania. It is not clear, however, whether his specific argument employs too narrow an interpretation of intensification or is a case of agricultural involution as discussed below. More recently, Lele and Stone (1989) have examined agricultural change in six African nations—Cameroon, Tanzania, Senegal, Kenya, Malawi, and Nigeria—and have concluded that population growth has not led to agricultural growth because it requires evolutionary processes under conditions of low population density and slow population growth, while these nations, and most of Africa, are experiencing very rapid population growth. They do not reject the overall Boserup theme but argue for two conditions of intensification: an evolutionary condition (the Boserup and other demand themes) and a policy-driven condition of high population density and growth.

The general thesis raised by Lele and Stone is an important one, essentially addressing cases of agricultural involution and stagnation (see Geertz 1966). They capture many of the mediating factors that can deflect or alter the trajectories of agricultural change in the modified-demand theme. Several of their conceptual interpretations and the logic employed are somewhat confusing to us, however, making their findings unclear and, therefore, questionable. For example, much of their skepticism is based on the original Boserup (1965) argument, not on its many elaborations (as noted above), which can account for the adjustments in definitions and measure they use (Lele and Stone 1989: 5).

More important, Lele and Stone must reconcile their interpretive base—the impact of conditions of high population-density growth rates on agricultural change—with the fact that most of Africa is sparsely populated by world standards. To do this, they interpret population pressure in the African context in terms of population per unit of arable land, accepting the premise that sub-Saharan Africa is dominated by marginal agricultural lands and that, therefore, overall low "raw" population densities are relatively high. We suggest that this and other such environmental premises must be weighed cautiously. Cultivation in the tropics in general offers both constraints and opportunities, and we are unaware of any comparative studies documenting that, on a subcontinental basis, sub-Saharan Africa fares more poorly than any other tropical area in terms of agricultural environments. Indeed, now, as in the past, numerous cases of "undersettled" prime agricultural lands and densely settled lands of lesser intrinsic agricultural quality can be found in sub-Saharan Africa (Dommen 1988: 115–17). What must be recognized is that the quality of an agricultural environment is as much a product of its use, including landscape transformations, as of "raw" nature: the polders of the Netherlands (below sea level), Andean terracing on extreme slopes, the raised fields throughout the wetlands of highland New Guinea, and the wheat fields on the arid Great Plains of North America are examples. The case for Africa is commonly biased toward undocumented explanations of environmental constraints to cultivation rather than understanding why these environments have not been "reshaped" to be upgraded.

Finally, Lele and Stone ignore the extensive literature supporting the rudiments of the demand themes for African agriculture, including cases from the very countries considered in their study. These have been detailed above.

These problems aside, Lele and Stone also confront the second phase of the intensification theme—the movement or absence of movement from increased food production to increased standard of consumption or well-being—and detail some of the shortcomings of the evidence for it in the six nations that they examine. Here they recall a commonly overlooked statement by Boserup (1965: 118) that the intensification process may not work under conditions of high population densities and rapid population growth, the very conditions that we address in this book. Such conclusions have also been implied in recent studies of South Asia (see Rodgers 1989), although studies by Boyce (1987) and Ali and Turner (n.d.) have demonstrated that agricultural intensification has kept pace with population growth in parts of this region. Ho's (1985) interpretation of regional and national data from sub-Saharan Africa concludes that the frequency of cropping has increased but that the technological changes (substitutes) required to sustain this trend have been inadequate, contributing to environmental degradation. Like Lele and Stone, Ho suggests that this lag in technological development is associated with the extremely high rates of increase in population.

Market Access

At this juncture, we can only speculate on how to weigh the relative importance of population and market access in the light of the induced intensification theme (see Pingali, Bigot and Binswanger 1987). There is clearly some positive density feedback between the two—market access invites immigrants to an area, and high population density encourages the development of a marketing infrastructure. Recent studies from Kenya (Goldman 1987) and Zimbabwe (Gray 1988; Rohrbach 1988) underscore the positive interplay between the two forces of market and population, with a developed infrastructure for commodity production accelerating efforts to intensify agriculture in response to increasing population density. Thus commodity production surely modifies the simple relationship between population density and agricultural intensification.

Environmental Conditions

Environment also modifies the relationship. Levi (1976), preceding Lele and Stone, challenged the positive relationship between population pressure and agricultural intensity as long as pressure is dependent solely on population density, not density as mediated by environmental conditions (land quality). Brookfield (1962, 1984) and Turner, Hanham, and Portararo (1977) have shown that the density-intensity relationship is strongest where environmental constraints to land quality are moderate— perhaps most cultivated lands. Extremely severe constraints either impede agricultural growth or require such high levels of inputs (landscape changes) to overcome them that the resulting intensity is higher than the population density warrants (Turner, Hanham, and Portararo 1977; Pingali 1987). Conversely, optimal, highly productive environments exaggerate intensity, if measured as output or frequency. Pingali, Bigot, and Binswanger (1987) show that, at the extremes, intensification in Africa is inversely related to rainfall. Maintaining agriculture in low-rainfall areas (<750 mm) requires the use of intensive and expensive (in labor or capital) technologies. Conversely, the lowland high-rainfall areas (>1200 mm) suffer from thin soils, leaching, and acidification that inhibit continuous cultivation. Lele and Stone (1989: 16–17) argue that both rainfall and soil conditions throughout much of sub-Saharan Africa are constraints to agricultural improvement. But although environment undoubtedly affects the demand-agriculture relationship, African farmers have demonstrated an ability to support substantial populations in conditions described by some (see Matlon 1987) as especially susceptible to degradation. Indeed, high population densities have been sustained longer in parts of Nigeria and West Africa on soils thought to be especially constraining to cultivation than almost anywhere else in the subcontinent.

Summary

In sum, there is ample evidence to conclude that the seemingly inevitable population increases in sub-Saharan Africa can play a forcing role for the needed intensification of agriculture. But to do so does not necessarily lead to the adoption of the pronatalist stance of Simon (1981) that sees in population increase the growth of "the ultimate resource." The ideal conditions on which the demand themes (fig. 1.3) are based are not the only operating conditions, as we detail below. Therefore, although population growth and increasing density seem inevitable in sub-Saharan Africa, a beneficial density-intensity development is not.

Involution, Diminished Well-Being, and Environmental Degradation

Intensification can lead to involution and the diminution of economic and social well-being or threaten the long-term sustainability of agriculture through environmental deterioration. The theory of involution, proposed by Geertz in 1963, characterized the condition in which increasing demand is met by output intensification but at the costs of decreasing or small marginal and average returns to inputs. In addition to the original studies on Java, conditions that are involution-like have been found in South Asian systems characterized by extremely high densities, intensities, and environmental constraints (Ahmad 1985; Ali 1987). In Bangladesh, for example, population pressures have induced extremely high frequencies of cultivation, but the combination of rapid population growth and extreme environmental problems (for example, deep and prolonged flooding) that cannot always be countered by the farmer or village has led to "food" stagnation—a case in which output increases may not match increases in demand (Boyce 1987; Ali and Turner n.d.). For Africa, Martin's (1987) historical assessment for parts of Nigeria and Rwanda, where population densities are high and have been so for a long time, asserts that involution and perhaps stagnation is evident. Involution-like or stagnating conditions also follow from the recent interpretations of Ho (1985) and Lele and Stone (1989) for sub-Saharan Africa in general (also Datoo 1976, 1978; Jewswiecki and Chrétien 1984).

Similarly, intensification can lead to real losses of social, cultural, and economic well-being (Johnston and Kilby 1975; Heyer, Roberts, and Williams 1981; Hart 1982; Berry 1984). In Africa, more intensive systems almost always mean more work for the individual farmer, often female, in contrast to South Asia, where the higher labor requirements may offer employment to the rural landless. Compared to other peoples, Africans, especially in their indigenous systems, have had a high degree of equitable access to resources, especially the common property resource of land. With population growth and new, intensive land uses, competition and conflict over land are growing rapidly, especially in areas of high density (see Bassett 1988). Credit, technological inputs, and market opportunities are not equitably distributed and may lead to systematic differentiation based on class, ethnic origin, or locale (see Watts and Bassett 1986; Wisner 1988; Lipton 1989). Women farmers in particular seem to be at a disadvantage in access to the new technologies and inputs (Mackintosh 1989; Stamp 1989). Also added to the traditional risks of pest and climate are new social and economic risks of price fluctuation, the dependability of input supplies, and the availability and price of purchased foods. New dependencies and relationships are created that are far beyond the ken and control of African farmers (Watts 1983, 1989; Wisner 1988).

Illiffe (1987), in a recent study, argues that African poverty is different in land-rich and land-scarce societies. In the former, poverty arises from a shortage of labor needed to exploit the land, and the incapacitated, elderly, young, and isolated suffer most. In the latter, these groups also suffer, but added to these are those able-bodied persons without access to land resources or the ability to get a good return for their wage labor. As people in some places experience land scarcity, Illiffe foresees an increase in poverty, as "only slowly [does] possession of a family, rather than lack of one, become a cause of structural poverty" (p. 6).

Equally important are the negative impacts of intensive agricultural activities and technologies on the long-term sustainability of the agricultural resource base (Farvar and Milton 1972; Clark and Munn 1986; Lewis and Berry 1988). Usually, more frequent cropping and less fallow reduce soil fertility and increase soil loss. These problems can be countered by the addition of procedural and technical inputs (such as fertilizers, ground-covering cultigens, and terraces), but the degree to which these inputs have compensated for the decrease in fallow has been questioned by Ho (1985) and Lele and Stone (1989). In some documented cases, diminished returns to these inputs, nitrogen, for example, appear after a number of years, requiring additional nutrients to restore productivity (Lal 1987). Irrigation, poorly designed or managed, can lead to salinization and waterlogging of soils and, even when well managed, to toxic-material accumulation, to an increase in human disease habitats such as schistomiasis, and to a decrease in natural soil fertility. The use of herbicides promises to ease the intense seasonal shortages of labor in African agricultural systems but at high costs, both economically and environmentally. Similarly, pesticide usage to control ample tropical pest populations leaves residues on food, threatens the health of applicators, and leads to pesticide-resistant species (Tait and Napompeth 1987).

Lee (1986) has provided the conceptual groundwork for understanding the trajectories of the interactions among population, technology, and environment, with an implied outcome of development or well-being. His conclusion is that the trajectories do not grow forever (in our case, intensification) but show spurts of acceleration and deceleration until a "high-technological–high-population stable equilibrium" is reached, unless preventive checks arrest growth at some lower level of the population-technology ratio.

The lesson from this brief survey of population-intensification relationships and Lee's broader thesis is simple. Long-term population growth and economic development usually do not take place without intensification and agricultural growth, although intensification and agricultural growth do not inevitably follow population growth and are not necessarily beneficial or sustainable Thus it is critical to identify the conditions under which agricultural intensification does follow population growth, benefits its practitioners, and is sustainable for the long term.

Case Studies of Growth and Intensification

Design of a Natural Experiment

Toward this objective, our basic strategy was to use the existing areas of high density in sub-Saharan Africa as "natural experiments" through which to examine in detail the chain of relationships among population growth, increased density, and the intensification of agriculture and, in less detail, the consequences for well-being and the sustainability of agriculture. To explore this strategy, we drew upon previous fieldwork and knowledge, identifying researchers with field experience in high-density areas, and commissioning case studies from them, prepared with a common, mutually agreed upon protocol.

In developing and carrying out the study design, the following steps were begun in 1986: (1) identifying existing high-density areas in sub-Saharan Africa, particularly that large expanse of land falling within the tropics; (2) identifying researchers with field experience in these areas, preferably those having published on agricultural issues; (3) developing a draft protocol for case studies; (4) commissioning case studies and convening a workshop to review and compare draft studies in light of the common protocol; (5) preparing and publishing the case studies and assessments of their implications.

This approach was taken for several important reasons. We sought a comparative study of regional cases through the use of a "natural experimental" approach, therefore examining the proposed relationships between population growth and agricultural intensification across a number of cases and through the complexity of the situations in which they occur. Unfortunately, standardized data of the kind needed to make this assessment for the regions in question are simply unavailable, and time and funding constraints would not permit extended field studies to produce them. Therefore, we drew upon commissioned case studies prepared by highly knowledgeable field-workers who were familiar with the data for particular regions and could also provide a depth of analysis and understanding of the situations that could not be generated from a "synthesis" of the data, even if they were available. These experts used a common protocol, thus facilitating comparisons among the cases not found in isolated village or regional case studies, and were brought together to assist in the interpretations of their own and other cases.

Drawing and building on their work, understanding, and guidance proved to be a highly economical method, bringing together what was already known without embarking on expensive field study. In this manner, we sought to illuminate the commonalities and differences among cases of long-term population growth and agricultural intensification in sub-Saharan Africa in order to explore these linkages. We use the insights gained as lessons for understanding agriculture change and policies geared to improve well-being in terms of food production and consumption.

Existing High-Density "Rural" Areas within Sub-Saharan Africa

In Africa, population data are of highly variable quality and typically out-of-date; data for small spatial units are particularly difficult to obtain. This posed a problem for the identification of high-density zones or regions of "rural" occupation that was fundamental to our undertaking. The rationale for the rural criterion is simple; we seek populations of farmers responding to major increases in agricultural demand, particularly that emanating from local population growth. Eliminated from consideration, then, were districts with high densities created by the count of the urban (largely nonfarming) populace.

The next issue focused on the size of the rural area in question. The microspatial scale—village or small clusters of villages—was eliminated;

innumerable anomalies can be found at this level, and the small size of the unit would not necessarily capture the dynamics in question. Macro-scale spatial units—ecological zones, states, and nations—were eliminated because of the great variability of population densities and other conditions within them. The midscale was sought through the use of the administrative unit "district." But it is precisely this unit for which adequate population information is so difficult to obtain. As we were lacking a central data source, Johnson (1987) created one for us. He examined census data sources in various North American archives and agencies for district-level data for forty-eight countries in sub-Saharan Africa, excluding the Republic of South Africa, which was eliminated from consideration. No data or suspicious data were located for nine of the countries, although three—Lesotho, Togo, and Zaire—may include districts with relatively high densities. For the remaining thirty-nine countries, censuses were located dating back to the 1960s in five cases, as current as the 1980s in eight cases, and with the remainder from the 1970s. He then crudely projected all data to an assumed 1985 base, using the current estimate of national growth rate by the Population Reference Bureau.

Based on the results, four "high" population-density categories were established (people/km^2): $>100-<200$; $>200-<300$; $>300-<400$; and >400. Omitting four small island countries and districts, and excluding small districts centered on major urban concentrations, 14 countries were found to contain 112 districts with densities >100 (people/km^2), and 9 contained 55 districts with densities >200 (people/km^2).

Attention was focused on those districts with "rural" densities >200 people/km^2, modifying the list in an effort to account for districts whose ranking in this density category was due primarily to urban populations. In so doing, thirty-nine districts in eight countries were identified as maintaining the required density level (table 1.1). Of these, however, twenty-one are suspected to be influenced significantly by urban populations, and further study may demonstrate that their true rural population is not >200 people/km^2.

Identifying Potential Collaborators with Field Experience

After this exercise, we searched the literature, doctoral abstracts, and agency papers to identify, first, authors of field studies especially related to the issue at hand in the previously targeted districts and, second, au-

Table 1.1. Districts with Rural Population Densities in Excess of 200/km²

Country (census data)	District[a]	Population density (/km²)	Suspected urban influence[b]
Burundi (1976)	Ngozi	390	x
	Bujumbura	385	x
	Muramvya	378	x
	Gitenga	261	
Cameroon (1976)	Mifi	265	x
Kenya (1979)	Kisii	505	x
	Kakamega	376	x
	Kiambu	358	x
	Muranga	334	
	Kisumu	294	
	Kirinyaga	258	
	Siaya	240	
	Busia	234	
	Bungoma	208	
	Kericho	206	
Malawi (1977)	Chiradzulu	300	x
	Blantyre	262	x
	Thyolo	240	x
Nigeria (1963)	Uyo	585	x
	Umahia	373	x
	Enugu	365	x
	Abakaliki	272	
	Kano	268	x
	Ondo	258	
	Degema	248	
	Katsina	208	
Rwanda (1978)	Kibuye	416	
	Ruhengeri	375	x
	Gitarama	335	x
	Gisenyi	315	x
	Kigali	262	x
	Gikongora	210	
	Cyangugu	202	
Tanzania (1978)	Moshi	291	x
	Ukerewe	270	x
	Mwanza	236	x
Uganda (1980)	Mable	261	
	Kabale	230	
	Tororo	200	
Totals	39		

[a]Island districts and countries omitted.

[b]Urban areas probably contribute significantly to the district's overall population density.

thors of studies anywhere in sub-Saharan Africa addressing the population density–agricultural intensity question. Of the fifty-five densely settled districts originally identified, we located only a handful of studies dealing with any of these districts, and these studies were not necessarily of the type needed for our purposes.

With this extensive search but sparse yield, we sought further to increase the number of potential case study authors based on our own knowledge of African scholarship and our extensive network of colleagues. Overall, fifteen potential collaborators were identified with extensive field experience in high-density areas, ten of whom were able to undertake the preparation of case studies.

The Draft Protocol for Case Studies

The ten collaborators were asked to select a site or area with a current "rural" population of about 200 people/km² or above for which they had primary or "first-hand" microlevel data on the dynamics of agriculture. The site could range in area size from a village to a small region or district. If a village was selected, household data could be used; if a district, village-level data were to be employed. In all cases, authors were able to address the issue at the district or subdistrict (region within a district). In most cases, household-level data were employed, usually based on samples taken throughout the area in question. The time depth suggested for the studies varied within a ten- to fifty-year range: flexibility was required, depending on the data source. The key was to capture a period in which the dynamics of population could be assessed against the dynamics of agriculture.

For comparative purposes, case study authors were requested to provide information, where possible, on seven key items: the site; its environmental setting; the nature of population change; the nature of agricultural change; changes in external forces of production; the consequences of the various changes; and near-future trajectories of change (table 1.2). In addition to this common core, they were encouraged to share their own unique data and insights as they related to the broad theme.

Natural experiments or field tests are by definition imperfect, depending as they do on the happenstance of nature and society rather than on the careful controls of the laboratory. And when the experiment is undertaken in this collaborative mode, depending on insights and data

Table 1.2. Case Study Protocol

Items	Characteristics
Site definition	Agricultural base
	Approaching or above 200 people/km²
Environmental setting	Basic soil groups
	Elevation
	Precipitation patterns
	Devegetation problems
	Flooding and drainage problems
	Common crop pathogens and pests
Population changes	Density
	Age and sex structure
	Migration
Agricultural change: inputs and outputs	Labor
	Procedures
	Technologies
	Frequency of cultivation
	Cultigens
	Yields (per harvest)
	Land productivity (per unit area and time)
	Value of production
External forces of production	Nonfarm sources of food, labor, and capital
	Markets
	Government policies
	International agency activity
Consequences of change	Environmental
	Economic
	Social
	Quality of life/welfare
Future trajectories of change	Population
	Agriculture
	External forces
	Consequences

drawn from the work of diverse scholars—often collected for other purposes—the common protocol becomes a statement of aspirations rather than a table of contents. Thus, none of the studies was able to provide the complete set of data deemed desirable, although each offered invaluable insights into the population-agriculture relationship.

Our natural experiment also omits, as do most such efforts, the important component of genuine controls—sites similar in most respects to those studied, except for the high levels of population density. If we could find "all other things being equal" situations, we would have had an effective set of controls for our natural experiment. We would also be able to balance the bias toward "successful" cases, places where large densities, once achieved, are sustained. The great failures, places where large densities were not sustained, if they existed, are by definition missing from our density-defined criterion for case studies. Thus although we found identifying criteria eminently desirable, we had difficulty in establishing criteria from which to compare "all other things" and in obtaining the information that would allow comparisons between our case study sites and possible control sites. But beyond these difficulties, we speculate that such sites may not exist because nature and society interact so as to fill common human-ecological niches. Over time, environments suitable for high population densities fill up.

Ten Case Studies

The selected case studies explore densities that range in size from less than 150 km^2 to more than 10,000 km^2. With one exception, they involve district or district-like units. They cluster in the highlands of East Africa (Kenya, Rwanda, Tanzania, and Uganda) and in Nigeria (fig. 1.5). This clustering follows from both the population geography of sub-Saharan Africa and the happenstance of regional expertise. Although other highly populated rural zones exist in sub-Saharan Africa, field-workers and field studies devoted to population-agriculture relationships are undoubtedly concentrated in certain areas.

East Africa

Throughout their history, the highlands of East Africa have been densely populated compared with the regions that surround them and with most of sub-Saharan Africa. The highlands offer a multitude of habitats, most of which have long been filled by different economic adaptations—agriculture, pastoralism, and mixes of the two. For the most part these habitats include some combination of rainfall, soils, or pest/disease absence that offers less resistance to occupation than do the surrounding lowlands, although exceptions exist (Lewis and Berry 1988). The highlands were favored during colonial occupation of Africa, and more recently the region has experienced rapid population growth, some of the highest in the world.

BUSHENYI CASE (UGANDA). Bushenyi is an administrative district in southwestern Uganda, an area of high rainfall and numerous lakes and wetlands. Bushenyi has experienced the political turmoil and dis-

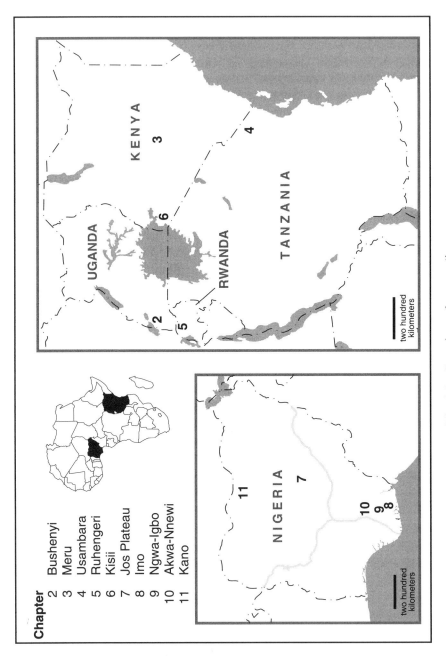

Fig. 1.5. Locations of case studies

Chapter	
2	Bushenyi
3	Meru
4	Usambara
5	Ruhengeri
6	Kisii
7	Jos Plateau
8	Imo
9	Ngwa-Igbo
10	Akwa-Nnewi
11	Kano

ruption of warfare that the rest of Uganda has incurred over the last twenty years. Despite this, population appears to have grown rapidly, now approaching 150 people/km². This growth, a series of changes in land tenure, including the ability to cultivate wetlands that were once common grazing lands, combined with a major shift to market cultivation, has been related to the intensification of agriculture and to increased agricultural production in a zone of relatively good soils. This increase has followed minimal capital inputs but major increases in labor, with most indicators of agricultural growth up (e.g., increased yields and market value). These changes have been accompanied by economic diversification.

MERU CASE (KENYA). Centered on the slopes of Mt. Meru in the heart of Kenya, Meru exhibits rather diverse environmental conditions from the temperate and well-watered upper slopes with good soils to the tropical and arid foothills where drought is a problem. The better agricultural lands in the district, mostly in the temperate zone, have long sustained relatively dense populations. Recently, densities have approached 190 people/km², exacerbating land pressures and leading to intensification in the uplands and to cultivation of precarious lands in the dry foothills below. In this respect, Meru may be seen as two cases: agricultural growth in the temperate uplands, complete with government inducements for market crops, and "frontier" farming in the foothills. The upland case is one of near-annual cultivation, significant increases in market production, and a rise in capital inputs to cultivation, primarily hybrid crops and synthetic pesticides and fertilizers; this has been accompanied by major social changes in economic diversification. The frontier case has been much more problematic.

USAMBARA CASE (TANZANIA). The Usambara case focuses on a mountainous region in northeastern Tanzania. Historic evidence suggests relatively large populations and intensive agriculture, much of it on steeply sloping lands with soils that are not exceptional for cultivation. Its modern population-agriculture history is a puzzle. During a time of rapid population growth—now approaching 190 people/km²—the intensification of agriculture has apparently been sporadic, perhaps showing an overall increase but with major deviations from this trend. This situation seems to be related to a number of social and economic conditions that have acted as disincentives not only to intensification but to agricultural expansion as well. Although market cultivation was not important at the time of the study, the needs pressures were leading to increased migration and economic diversification in the face of an overall decline in food availability.

RUHENGERI CASE (RWANDA). An administrative prefectorate within the northern portion of Rwanda, Ruhengeri is a high-altitude, well-watered mountainous zone of steep slopes and wetlands, with variable soil suitability for cultivation. Historically, it has been one of the most densely occupied regions in all of Africa, with current populations over $400/km^2$. Agriculture has historically kept pace with demand, perhaps facilitated by policies that have promoted small-scale farming and, in many instances, without major landscape capital (e.g., terracing, irrigation) that might otherwise be expected from labor-intensive farming. Recently, land stress has become increasingly evident, and agriculture has expanded into wetlands. Cropping frequency is rising while yields have been more or less stable. Market cultivation has become important, as have outmigration and economic diversification. Overall, food availability seems to have kept pace roughly with demand, and economic well-being has been relatively stable.

KISII CASE (KENYA). Kisii District, southwestern Kenya, is another case of a high-rainfall upland with good agricultural soils. During colonial and more recent times, it has been a focus of significant effort for "modern" development, complete with research, planning, and funding. This effort has been matched by rapid population growth. Densities now approach $500/km^2$, not including the population of cities and towns. Agriculture, much of which is multicropping, has become strongly market oriented and has shown remarkable growth, in part because of the flexibility of the tenure system. Nevertheless, recently there has been evidence of slowing agricultural growth and environmental stress. Outmigration is significant, and most farming units are involved in some type of nonfarming enterprise or wage labor.

West Africa—Nigeria

West Africa has historically been the most populated large-scale region in tropical Africa, despite the demographic effects of intensive slaving in the past. In contrast to East Africa, much of its population has been supported along major river drainages within lowland wet-dry forest zones and in pockets along the Sahelian fringe. Therefore, broadly speaking, it represents high population densities in environments that are, perhaps, more common throughout sub-Saharan Africa than are the mountains of East Africa. Nigeria alone has long sustained the largest population of any sub-Saharan country, even on soils thought to be marginal at best. With some exceptions, agriculture has grown in response to demand.

JOS PLATEAU CASE (CENTRAL NIGERIA). The Jos Plateau consumes most of the Plateau District of central Nigeria, a transition zone between wet and dry climates. High density growth, ranging from 90 to 300 people/km², has been a recent phenomenon, and agricultural growth has been a product of both intensification and land expansion. The Kofyar people of the plateau, with minimal formal inducements, have responded to the opening of new lands for major entry into market cultivation by adapting their long-developed cultivation practices to the Benue Valley lands. Their success may be unparalleled in most of tropical Africa. Cropping frequency, yields, and the market value of produce are rising, through increases both in labor and in capital, primarily biotechnic inputs. To date, social changes may have been minimal, as is economic diversification. Most important, food availability and economic well-being are increasing, on average.

IMO CASE (EASTERN NIGERIA). Sample districts in Imo State, Nigeria, long one of the major centers of population concentrations in a lowland tropical setting, show population densities that range from 200 to 1,000 people/km² throughout the area, the higher densities affected by urban populations. It is situated in the heart of the oil palm production zone, and long-term intensification has taken the form of intensive compound gardens with increasingly intensifying outfields. From a purely agricultural perspective, much of the area may have reached a condition of involution, and farming units have diversified their internal economies accordingly. Nevertheless, the multicropping systems and yields have increased, as has market cultivation. Biotechnic inputs are on the rise. Despite these changes, land pressures are so great as to lead to major outmigration.

NGWA-IGBO CASE (EASTERN NIGERIA). The Ngwa region is also situated in Imo State, and its rural population densities have exceeded 200 people/km² for some time. In the first half of this century, the region witnessed agricultural diversification and commercialization through oil palm cultivation, despite relatively poor agricultural soils. These changes, perhaps motivated by desires to increase standards of living rather than by population pressures per se, then stimulated further population growth. The latter half of this century has witnessed rapid population growth, land degradation, and switches to cassava production as a means to sustain ouput in the face of involution or stagnation in agriculture. This study adds historical depth to the broader case study of the Imo State.

AWKA-NNEWI CASE (EASTERN NIGERIA). This region is situated within Anambra State, Nigeria. Located immediately north of Imo State, its environment and socioeconomic history share many commonalities with the previous two case studies. Awka-Nnewi has a long history of dense occupation, its settlement pattern described by some as an extended "suburbia," owing to population densities exceeding $500/km^2$ throughout. Few opportunities exist for agricultural expansion, and efforts to intensify may have slowed, becoming more difficult. Market cultivation is significant, but total production is apparently dropping. Environmental degradation is increasing, and household-diversification strategies have been substituted as alternatives to cultivation. Food availability may be on the decline.

KANO CASE (NORTHERN NIGERIA). The area studied is not Kano city, northern Nigeria, but its immediate hinterlands referred to as the Close-Settled Zone. In this Sahelian fringe land of variable soil quality and major drought episodes, purely "rural" populations exceed $500/km^2$. Agriculture has intensified largely through major infusions of labor into a market-gardening system marked by diversification through livestock and agroforestry. Currently cropping frequency and yields are stable, while the value of production is increasing. With the addition of household diversification off the farm, food availability and economic well-being are apparently stable now and into the near future.

Population Growth and Agricultural Change Workshop

The authors of the commissioned case studies were brought together in the spring of 1988 at the Center for African Studies, University of Florida, Gainesville. With the assistance of invited commentators (Richard

Bilsborrow, Ronald Cohen, Gregory Knight, Phil Porter, and Donald Vermeer), the workshop reviewed the draft studies, suggesting revisions and identifying new issues that the authors were able to address in their revisions; the gathering was also used to brainstorm the subject of population growth and agriculture, leading to various revised interpretations about the critical elements of agricultural change in Africa. Revisions of the papers were undertaken through 1988–89, and they constitute the bulk of this volume.

In what follows, we move through individual case studies beginning with those from East Africa. The sequencing of the cases for each of the two clusters largely follows from the less to most densely occupied situation. The final chapter returns to the central questions of this endeavor, addressing them through a synthesis and comparison of the case studies and based upon the themes that were identified during the 1988 workshop.

The individual studies provide a wealth of insight in their own right. They are rooted in the colonial period, and they bridge what a recent workshop of African scholars (Achebe et al. 1990) has called the "times of euphoria" of nation-creating and nation-building and the current "times of troubles" of the sustained agricultural, economic, and welfare crises. The very presence of these densely occupied farming regions calls into question the numerous perspectives on these issues, and the case studies here provide evidence illustrating the rudiments of the apparent transformations of conditions in such regions now under way. They also speak to the great variation in African agriculture and indigenous innovation and adaptation. The case assessments, therefore, testify to how Africans survive, subsist, and occasionally prosper at population densities comparable to extremes found in Asia and Europe.

References

Achebe, C. G., G. Hyden, C. Magadza, and A. P. O. Keyo, eds. 1990. *Beyond Hunger in Africa: Conventional Wisdom and an African Vision.* Nairobi: Heinemann Kenya. London: James Currey.

Ahmad, A. 1985. "The Effect of Population Growth on a Peasant Economy: The Case of Bangladesh." In *The Primary Sector in Economic Development,* ed. M. Lundahl. London: Croom Helm.

Ali, A. M. S. 1987. "Intensive Paddy Agriculture in Shyampur, Bangladesh." In *Comparative Farming Systems,* ed. B. L. Turner II and S. B. Brush. New York: Guilford.

Ali, A.M.S., and B.L. Turner II. n.d. Stagnation or Growth in Bangladesh Agriculture, 1950–1986. Manuscript.

Barlett, P.F. 1976. "Labor Efficiency and the Mechanics of Agricultural Evolution." *Journal of Anthropological Research* 32: 124–40.

Basehart, H.W. 1973. "Cultivation Intensity, Settlement Patterns, and Homestead Forms among the Matengo of Tanzania." *Ethnology* 7: 57–73.

Bassett, T. 1988. "The Political Ecology of Peasant-Herder Conflicts." *Annals of the Association of American Geographers* 78: 453–72.

Benneh, G. 1972. "Population Growth and Food Supply in Ghana." *Peasant Studies Newsletter* 4: 17–22.

Bernstein, H., B. Crow, M. Mackintosh, and C. Martin. 1990. *The Food Question: Profit versus People?* London: Earthscan.

Berry, S. 1984. "The Food Crisis and Agrarian Change in Africa: A Review Essay." *African Studies Review* 27(2): 59–112.

Binswanger, H.P., and V. Ruttan. 1978. *Induced Innovation: Technology, Institutions and Development.* Baltimore: Johns Hopkins University Press.

Boserup, E. 1965. *The Conditions of Agricultural Growth.* Chicago: Aldine.

———. 1981. *Population and Technological Change.* Chicago: University of Chicago Press.

Boyce, J. 1987. *Agrarian Impasse in Bengal: Institutional Constraints to Technological Change.* Oxford: Oxford University Press.

Brookfield, H.C. 1962. "Local Study and Comparative Method: An Example from Central New Guinea." *Annals of the Association of American Geographers* 52: 242–54.

———. 1984. "Intensification Revisited." *Pacific Viewpoint* 25: 15–44.

Brown, P., and A. Podolefsky. 1976. "Population Density, Agricultural Intensity, Land Tenure, and Group Size in the New Guinea Highlands." *Ethnology* 15: 211–38.

Brush, S.B., and B.L. Turner II. 1987. "The Nature of Farming Systems and Views of Their Change." In *Comparative Farming Systems*, ed. B.L. Turner II and S.B. Brush, pp. 11–48. New York: Guilford Press.

Chayanov, A.V. 1966. "Peasant Farm Organization." In *A.V. Chayanov on the Theory of Peasant Economy*, ed. D. Thorner, B. Kerblay, and R.E.F. Smith. Homewood, Ill: R.D. Irwin.

Chen, R.S. 1989. Current Perspectives on Africa's Future, 1957–2057. Alan Shawn Feinstein World Hunger Program Research Report, RR 89-3. Providence, R.I.: World Hunger Program, Brown University.

Clark, W., and R.E. Munn, eds. 1986. *Sustainable Development of the Biosphere.* Cambridge: Cambridge University Press.

Cleave, J. 1974. *African Farmers: Labor Use in the Development of Smallholder Agriculture.* New York: Praeger.

Collinson, M. 1972. *Farm Management in Peasant Agriculture.* New York: Praeger.

Coulibaly, S. 1978. *Le Paysan Senoufo.* Abidjan and Dakar: Les Nouvelles Editions Africaines.

Dalrymple, D. G. 1971. *Survey of Multiple Cropping in Less Developed Nations.* Washington, D.C.: Foreign Economic Development Service, USDA.

Datoo, B. A. 1976. "Relationship between Population Density and Agricultural Systems in the Uluguru Mountains, Tanzania." *Journal of Tropical Geography* 42: 1–12.

_____. 1978. "Toward a Reformation of Boserup's Theory of Agricultural Change." *Economic Geography* 54: 133–44.

Dommen, A. J. 1988. *Innovation in African Agriculture.* Boulder, Colo.: Westview Press.

Dumont, R. 1962. *L'Afrique noire est mal partie.* Paris: Editions du Seuil.

Ehrlich, P. R., and A. H. Ehrlich. 1990. *The Population Explosion.* New York: Simon & Schuster.

Eicher, C. 1988. Sustainable Institutions for African Agricultural Development. Paper for seminar on "The Changing Dynamics of Global Agriculture: Research Policy Implications for National Agricultural Research Systems." ISNAR, CTA and DSE, Feldafing, Germany, September 22–28.

Farvar, M. T., and J. P. Milton, eds. 1972. *The Careless Technology: Ecology and International Development.* Garden City, N.Y.: The Natural History Press.

Fisk, E. H. 1964. "Planning in a Primitive Economy: From Pure Subsistence to the Production of Market Surplus." *Economic Record* 40: 156–74.

Geertz, C. 1963. *Agricultural Involution: The Process of Ecological Change in Indonesia.* Berkeley: University of California Press.

Gleave, M. B., and H. P. White. 1969. "Population Density and Agricultural Systems in West Africa." In *Environment and Land Use*, ed. M. F. Thomas and G. W. Whittington. London: Methuen.

Goldman, A. 1987. Agricultural Innovation in Three Areas of Kenya. Paper presented at annual meeting of the Association of American Geographers, Portland, Oregon.

Gray, A. L. 1988. "The Relationship of Production Type to Resource Stock Manipulation in Chipinge District, Zimbabwe: A Micro-Agricultural Geography." Ph.D. dissertation, Clark University.

Grossman, L. S. 1985. *Peasants, Subsistence Ecology, and Development in the Highlands of Papua New Guinea.* Princeton: Princeton University Press.

Grove, A. T. 1961. "Population and Agriculture in Northern Nigeria." In *Essays on African Population*, ed. K. M. Barbour and R. M. Prothero. London: Routledge and Kegan Paul.

Harrison, P. 1987. *The Greening of Africa: Breaking through the Battle for Land and Food.* London: Penguin/IIED.

Hart, K. 1982. *The Political Economy of West African Agriculture.* Cambridge: Cambridge University Press.

Harwood, R.R. 1979. *Small Farm Development: Understanding and Improving Farming Systems in the Tropics*. Boulder, Colo.: Westview Press.

Haswell, M.R. 1953. *Economics of Agriculture in a Savannah Village*. London: The Colonial Office, Her Majesty's Stationery Office.

Hayami, Y., and V. Ruttan. 1985. *Agricultural Development: An International Perspective*. Baltimore: Johns Hopkins University Press.

Heyer, J., P. Roberts, and G. Williams. 1981. *Rural Development in Tropical Africa*. London: Macmillan.

Hill, P. 1963. *The Migrant Cocoa Farmers in Southern Ghana: A Study in Rural Capitalism*. London: Cambridge University Press.

Ho, T.J. 1985. "Population Growth and Agricultural Productivity in Sub-Saharan Africa." In *Proceedings of the Fifth Agricultural Sector Symposium: Population and Food*, ed. T.J. Davis. Washington, D.C.: World Bank.

Huss-Ashmore, R., and S.H. Katz, eds. 1989. *African Food Systems in Crisis. Part One: Microperspectives. Part Two: Contending with Change*. New York: Gordon and Breach.

Illiffe, J. 1987. *The African Poor: A History*. Cambridge: Cambridge University Press.

Jewswiecki, B., and J.P. Chrétien, eds. 1984. *Ambiguités de l'innovation. Sociétés rurales et technologies en Afrique centrale et occidentale au xxe siècle*. Ste Foy, France: Editions SAFI.

Johnson, M. 1987. Report of Densely Settled Districts of Sub-Saharan Africa. Manuscript, Providence, R.I.: Alan Shawn Feinstein World Hunger Program, Brown University.

Johnston, B.F., and W.C. Clark. 1982. *Redesigning Rural Development: An Adaptive Perspective*. Baltimore: Johns Hopkins University Press.

Johnston, B.F., and P. Kilby. 1975. *Agricultural and Structural Transformation: Economic Strategies in Late-Developing Countries*. New York: Oxford University Press.

Lal, R. 1987. "Managing the Soils of Sub-Saharan Africa." *Science* 236: 1069–76.

Lee, R.D. 1986. "Malthus and Boserup: A Dynamic Synthesis." In *The State of Population Theory: Forward from Malthus*, ed. D. Coleman and R. Schofield, pp. 96–130. Oxford: Basil Blackwell.

Lele, U. 1988. "Comparative Advantage and Structural Transformation: A Review of Africa's Economic Development Experience." In *The State of Development Economics: Progress and Perspectives*, ed. G. Ranis and P.T. Schultz. New York: Blackwell.

Lele, U., and S.B. Stone. 1989. *Population Pressure, the Environment, and Agricultural Intensification: Variations on the Boserup Hypothesis*. Managing Agricultural Development in Africa (MADIA) Symposium.

Levi, J. F. S. 1976. "Population Pressure and Agricultural Change in the Land-Intensive Economy." *Journal of Development Studies* 13: 61–78.

Levi, J., and M. Havinden. 1982. *Economics of African Agriculture.* Harlow, U.K.: Longman.

Lewis, L., and L. Berry. 1988. *African Environments and Resources.* Boston: Unwin Hyman.

Lipton, M. 1968. "The Theory of the Optimizing Peasant." *Journal of Development Studies* 4: 327–51.

———. 1989. *New Seeds and Poor People.* Baltimore: Johns Hopkins University Press.

MacDonald, Andrew S. 1989. *Nowhere to Go but Down? Peasant Farming and the International Development Game.* London: Unwin Hyman.

Mackintosh, M. 1989. *Gender, Class and Rural Transition: Agribusiness and the Food Crisis in Senegal.* London: Zed Books.

Martin, S. D. 1987. "Boserup Revisited: Population and Technology in Tropical African Agriculture, 1900–1940." *Journal of Imperial and Commonwealth History* 16(10): 109–23.

Matlon, P. J. 1987. "The West African Semiarid Tropics." In *Accelerating Food Production in Sub-Saharan Africa*, ed. J. W. Mellor, C. L. Delgado, and M. J. Blackie. Baltimore: Johns Hopkins Univerity Press.

Mellor, J. W. 1966. *The Economics of Agricultural Development.* Ithaca, N.Y.: Cornell University Press.

———. 1984. *The Economics of Agricultural Development.* Ithaca, N.Y.: Cornell University Press.

Metzner, J. K. 1982. *Agriculture and Population Pressure in Sikka, Isle de Flores.* Development Studies Center, Monograph No. 28. Canberra: Australian National University Press.

Moock, J., ed. 1986. *Understanding Africa's Rural Households and Farming Systems.* Boulder, Colo.: Westview Press.

Mortimore, M. J. 1967. "Land and Population Pressure in the Kano Close-Settled Zone, Northern Nigeria." *The Advancement of Science* 23: 677–88.

———. 1989. *Adapting to Drought: Farmers, Famines and Desertification in West Africa.* Cambridge: Cambridge University Press.

Netting, R. McC. 1968. *Hill Farmers of Nigeria. Cultural Ecology of the Kofyar of the Jos Plateau.* Seattle: University of Washington Press.

Netting, R. McC., D. Cleveland, and F. Steir. 1980. "The Conditions of Agricultural Intensification in the West African Savannah." In *Sahelian Social Development.* Abidjan: USAID, Regional Economic Development Service Office, West Africa.

Norman, D. W. 1974. "An Economic Study of Three Villages in Zaria Province, Part 1, Land and Labour Relationships." *Samaru Miscellaneous Paper 19.*

Samaru, Nigeria: Institute for Agricultural Research, Ahmadu Bello University.

Noronha, R. 1988. *Land-Tenure in Sub-Saharan Africa*. Baltimore: Johns Hopkins University Press.

Office of Technology Assessment. 1988. *Enhancing Agriculture in Africa*. Washington, D.C.: OTA.

Paulino, L.A. 1987. "The Evolving Food Situation." In *Accelerating Food Production in Sub-Saharan Africa*, ed. J.W. Mellor, C.L. Delgado, and M.J. Blackie. Baltimore: Johns Hopkins University Press.

Pingali, P. 1987. Institutional and Agro-Climatic Constraints to Agricultural Intensification in Sub-Saharan Africa. Paper presented at Expert Consultation on Population and Agricultural and Rural Development: Institutions and Policy, Rome June 29–July 1.

Pingali, P., Y. Bigot, and H.P. Binswanger. 1987. *Agricultural Mechanization and the Evolution of Farming Systems in Sub-Saharan Africa*. Baltimore: Johns Hopkins University Press.

Population Reference Bureau. 1992. 1992 World Population Data Sheet. Washington: PRB.

Porter, P.W. 1979. *Food and Development in the Semi-Arid Zone of East Africa*. Foreign and Comparative Studies No. 32. Syracuse: Maxwell School of Citizenship and Public Affairs, Syracuse University.

Richards, P. 1985. *Indigenous Agricultural Revolution: Ecology and Food Production in West Africa*. London: Hutchinson.

———. 1987. "Upland and Swamp Rice Farming Systems in Sierra Leone: An Evolutionary Transition?" In *Comparative Farming Systems*, ed. B.L. Turner II and S.B. Brush, pp. 156–87. New York: Guilford Press.

Robinson, W., and W. Schutjer. 1984. "Agricultural Development and Demographic Change: A Generalization of the Boserup Model." *Economic Development and Cultural Change* 32: 355–66.

Rocheleau, D., F. Weber, and A. Field-Juma. 1988. *Agroforestry in Dryland Africa*. Nairobi: International Council for Research in Agroforestry.

Rodgers, G., ed. 1989. *Population Growth and Poverty in Rural South Asia*. London: Sage.

Rohrbach, David D. 1988. "The Growth of Smallholder Maize Production in Zimbabwe: Causes and Implications for Food Security." Ph.D. dissertation. Michigan State University.

Ruthenberg, H. 1980. *Farming Systems in the Tropics*. 3d ed. Oxford: Oxford University Press.

Sahlins, M.D. 1971. "The Intensity of Domestic Production in Primitive Societies: Social Inflections of the Chayanovian Slope." In *Studies in Economic Anthropology*, ed. G. Dalton. Washington, D.C.: American Anthropology Society.

Schluter, M. G. G., and T. D. Mount. 1976. "Some Management Objectives for the Peasant Farmer: An Analysis of Risk Aversion in the Choice of Cropping Patterns." *Journal of Development Studies* 12: 246–67.

Schultz, T. W. 1964. *Transforming Traditional Agriculture.* New Haven: Yale University Press.

————, ed. 1978. *Distortions of Agricultural Incentives.* Bloomington: Indiana University Press.

Scott, J. C. 1976. *The Moral Economy of the Peasant: Rebellion and Subsistence in Southeast Asia.* New Haven: Yale University Press.

————. 1985. *Weapons of the Weak: Everyday Forms of Peasant Resistance.* New Haven: Yale University Press.

Simon, J. 1981. *The Ultimate Resource.* Princeton, N.J.: Princeton University Press.

Singh, S. 1983. *Sub-Saharan Agriculture—Synthesis and Trade Prospects.* World Bank Staff Working Papers, No. 608. Washington, D.C.: World Bank.

Stamp, Patricia. 1989. *Technology, Gender, and Power in Africa.* Technical Study 6e, International Development Research Centre. Ottawa, Canada.

Sutton, J. E. G. 1984. "Irrigation and Soil-Conservation in Agricultural History: With a Reconsideration of the Inyanga Terracing (Zimbabwe) and Engaruka Irrigation Works (Tanzania)." *Journal of African History* 25: 25–41.

Tait, J., and B. Napompeth. 1987. *Management of Pests and Pesticides: Farmers' Perceptions and Practices.* Boulder, Colo.: Westview Press.

Tax, S. 1953. *Penny Capitalism.* Smithsonian Institution, Institute of Social Anthropology, Publ. no. 16. Washington, D.C.: U.S. Government Printing Office.

Thomas-Slatyer, B. P., and R. Ford. 1990. "Water, Soils, Food and Rural Development: Examining Institutional Frameworks in Kathetka." *Canadian Journal of African Studies*, 23: 250–71.

Turner, B. L. II. 1987. "Purpose, Classification, and Organization." In *Comparative Farming Systems*, ed. B. L. Turner II and S. B. Brush. New York: Guilford Press.

Turner, B. L. II, and S. B. Brush, eds. 1987. *Comparative Farming Systems.* New York: Guilford Press.

Turner, B. L. II, and W. Doolittle. 1978. "The Concept and Measure of Agricultural Intensity." *Professional Geographer* 30: 297–301.

Turner, B. L. II, R. Q. Hanham, and A. V. Portararo. 1977. "Population Pressure and Agricultural Intensity." *Annals of the Association of American Geographers* 67: 384–96.

Vermeer, D. 1970. "Population Pressure and Crop Rotational Changes among the Tiv of Nigeria." *Annals of the Association of American Geographers* 60: 384–96.

Watts, M.J. 1983. *Silent Violence: Food, Famine, and Peasantry in Northern Nigeria*. Berkeley: University of California Press.

———. 1989. "The Agrarian Crisis in Africa: Debating the Crisis." *Progress in Human Geography* 13: 1–41.

Watts, M.J., and T. Bassett. 1986. "Politics, the State and Agrarian Development: A Comparative Study of Nigeria and the Ivory Coast." *Political Geography Quarterly* 5: 103–25.

Wharton, C.R., Jr., ed. 1969. *Subsistence Agriculture and Economic Development*. Chicago: Aldine.

Wisner, B. 1988. *Power and Need in Africa*. London: Earthscan.

World Resources 1988–89. New York: Basic Books.

World Bank. 1984. *Toward Sustained Development in Sub-Saharan Africa: A Joint Program of Action*. Washington, D.C.: World Bank.

World Resources Institute (WRI). 1989. *World Resources 1988–89*. New York: Basic Books.

2 / Agricultural Transformation in the Robusta Coffee/Banana Zone of Bushenyi, Uganda

Nelson Kasfir

Bushenyi District in southwestern Uganda has experienced significant agricultural change in the past two decades (fig. 2.1). This change must be understood within the context of the even greater and ongoing transformation in agriculture created by the colonial political economy since 1900. The most important changes have been the closing of the land frontier due to increasing population growth and changes in land-tenure policies and the incapacity of the state to stimulate production of export crops and maintain basic levels of political security and economic certainty. Together these factors poise the district on the edge of significant changes in agricultural practices that will require more effective use of the land in order to feed its inhabitants and to earn them adequate incomes. But few postindependence changes in production techniques, use of labor, or cropping intensity appear to have been widely adopted in the district thus far.

Population pressure on the land has turned a district considered lightly populated at independence into one in which the sons of many poor farmers will not inherit enough land to grow crops sufficient to feed their families. Nor will they be able to move onto unused public land, the conventional solution to this problem in both the precolonial and colonial periods. Since the 1960s, changes in land tenure and rapidly rising land values have caused all the remaining public land to be fenced and converted into private farms.

The change in relations between the state and farmers has been equally dramatic. The state has always attempted to promote and control the production of export crops. During the colonial and early independence periods, government officials maintained this vital function by creating close contacts with farmers through by-laws, taxes, cooperatives, extension advice, provision of seeds, and production subsidies. The

Fig. 2.1. Uganda districts, 1993

most important connection was the insistence of the state on setting producer prices for all important export crops and requiring farmers to sell them to the state. Subsequently, the state lost the capacity to implement policies to help farmers, even though its coercive capabilities remained relatively effective and often intrusive.

Casual observers of Uganda are often surprised to discover that Bushenyi continued to enjoy a period of dynamic commercial agricultural growth after Idi Amin came to power in 1971. This agricultural growth has spanned the political and economic uncertainties that Amin's government introduced, the upheavals of two wars fought near this area, which disrupted transport and communication, and the continuing decay of the national economy. Agricultural changes have been most noticeable in the increasing shift toward the production of milk and food crops for domestic markets rather than export crops for overseas sale. The transition has produced wealth for enterprising farmers and poverty for others, rapidly increasing the economic differentiation among farmers in the district. The virtual disappearance of government support and subsidies for agricultural production and marketing has not hindered this process.

Measuring changes in agricultural practices and investigating their relation to population and economic trends is difficult anywhere in Africa. In Bushenyi only those few farmers who hold leases have had their land surveyed. The rest, who hold by customary tenure, generally have an approximate idea of how much land they have but not its precise measurements. Few of these farmers keep accounts. Typically they account for their output in terms of locally available, nonstandardized containers, designed for entirely different purposes.

Precise measurement requires so intrusive and time-intensive an inquiry that the numbers of farmers examined will necessarily be few, and the risk of altering their behavior will always be present. In addition, for the past decade and a half in Uganda the accurate collection and publication of population, economic, or agricultural statistics have been as difficult to produce as any other state service. Civil servants and academics who might have engaged in farm research have had to take second jobs and trade on the black market in order to survive. That leaves little time for data collection and analysis. Published statistics are much less reliable than they were two decades ago.[1]

Basic Features of the Study Site

The area selected for inquiry here consists of the robusta coffee/banana zone (fig. 2.2), including most of the counties of Igara, Sheema, and, to a lesser extent, Ruhinda in Bushenyi District (Planning Unit of the Ministry of Agriculture, Forestry and Cooperatives [PUMAFC] 1972: 17–20).[2] This heavily populated area was part of Ankole District until 1974. Warnings about pressure on available land have been sounded periodically since the 1960s. However, it also is a food-surplus area able to service urban markets as far away as Kampala. In 1964 Ankole farmers

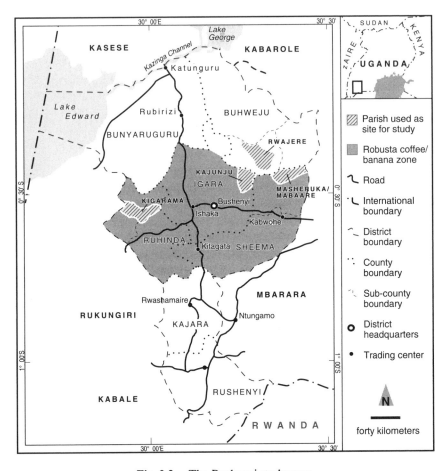

Fig. 2.2. The Bushenyi study area

accounted for only 6.4 percent of Ugandan land devoted to robusta coffee, but 70 percent of them had already adopted it (MAC 1966: 66, 70). By this time, Ankole already accounted for 12 percent of the banana hectarage, third in size behind Busoga and Masaka districts (MAC 1966: 99). Coffee production from Ankole increased until the middle 1970s and then stagnated when sales fell. Banana production has steadily risen.

The creation of this robusta coffee/banana zone was the most profound agricultural transformation to occur in this area during the twentieth century. Robusta coffee was not cultivated when colonial rule began. Bananas may have been grown for food, but were not widely cultivated and were not produced for the market. Thus, the time frame for this study begins with the institution of colonial rule early in the twentieth century but focuses more on the period since widespread adoption of coffee in the 1950s.

On the basis of its precolonial royal heritage, but with an expanded territory that for the first time included the area now in Bushenyi District, Ankole was established as a kingdom during the protectorate period on the basis of an agreement between the king (*Omugabe*) and the British authorities. During colonial rule, British colonial authorities continued to recognize the existing chiefly elite, Bahima by ethnic identification, as the legitimate rulers. By custom the Bahima are a pastoral people and consist of roughly 5 percent of the people living in Ankole. The Bairu, customarily agriculturalists, amount to about 90 percent (Doornbos 1977: 53). Bahima and Bairu are related to each other through a stratified class system that became a subject of political contention as independence neared. With the arrival of democratic elections in the 1950s, the Bairu united to overturn Bahima dominance and eventually to take control of most elective offices (Doornbos 1970: 1096–1109). In addition, political parties competed on the basis of existing rivalries between Protestants and Catholics. The complex interactions of religious and ethnic rivalries caused factionalism to become institutionalized in the politics of Ankole (Doornbos 1977: 72). That pattern has continued into the 1980s in the two new districts.

In the administrative reorganization of 1974, the five western counties of Ankole District (formerly Kingdom) became Bushenyi District (then called West Ankole). The area of the new district is 5,395 km², of which 4,905 km² are land. By 1986 the original five counties had been reconstituted into seven. The census population of this area rose from 299,832 in 1959 to 410,683 in 1969 and then to 524,669 in 1980. The 1980 Population Census (COMPED 1982: 234, 235) thus reported the overall population-to-land densities as 84/km² in 1969 and 107/km² in 1980 as compared to the rise in reported Ugandan population density from 48/km² in 1969 to 64/km² in 1980. However, there are several difficulties with these figures that suggest that the actual ratios are far higher.

Enormous problems of transport result from lack of maintenance of the roads, another state function that has been performed quite intermittently since the 1960s. The main road to Kampala is paved, although in

1989 it had become so pitted with potholes that it drastically shortened the life of the reduced number of vehicles that continued to provide the main economic connection to the capital. The interior roads are mostly *murram* (unpaved) and impassable during the rainy seasons. Many villages are sufficiently far from the paved road to make it impossible for them to enter the banana trade. Indeed, Ugandan agricultural officials distinguished two different robusta coffee/banana zones for just this reason, despite similar ecological conditions (PUMAFC 1972: 19–20). A later study confirms that farmers with the largest banana hectarage in this area live in villages close to paved roads (Kyeyune-Ssentongo 1985: 31).

Oberg states that there were no markets before the protectorate government was established (1943: 575), but there had been extensive barter locally and long-distance trade in salt for at least two centuries before that (Good 1970: 149–69). The first official market in Ankole, located in Mbarara, was established in 1902 (Good 1970: 180). There are biweekly markets throughout the area attended by itinerant traders selling textiles and other consumer goods and small weekly (and in some places daily) markets in which the chief merchandise is agricultural produce traded among farmers (Kyeyune-Ssentongo 1985: 64–65).

Environmental Setting

Using Chenery's productivity ratings, Langlands and Mbakyenga (1974), following the procedure described in Langlands (1974c: 1–5), judge the soils of the robusta coffee/banana zone (fig. 2.2) in Bushenyi as medium in productivity in Igara County and medium to fair in Sheema County. In Igara, the soil is characterized as latosols loam, typically a red-clay loam, occurring from the weathering of schist and phyllites in Precambrian rocks (Langlands and Mbakyenga 1974; Langlands 1974c: 13). The soils in Sheema are a complex mixture of six types. The largest area (44 percent) contains sandy loams developed on schists and phyllites on Precambrian rocks (Langlands and Mbakyenga 1974; Langlands 1974c: 16). Another sixth of the area is the same type of more productive soil found in Igara. Harrop (1967: 26) points out that "the heavier textured soils are the more fertile" and adds that characteristic soils of Bushenyi "have a well developed humic topsoil together with a distinct humic horizon at some depth in the soil profile."

The topography consists of a plateau at an elevation of about 1,200 m with gently rolling country generally without steep slopes but interspersed with small, highly eroded stony and steep ridges up to 300 m high and often 25 to 50 km long with narrow and deep river courses at their base. The Rwizi River is the largest and longest of these. The valley bottoms often contained papyrus swamps, which are now being drained by their new owners. Though perhaps not well-founded, there are widespread fears among farmers and local officials that the drainage of swamps will lower the water table and may even change the weather pattern.

Precipitation occurs throughout the year in a bimodal pattern with the "long" rainy season from March to May and the "short" rains from September to November. The former season is less reliable, however, so most annual crops, particularly millet, are grown during the latter. Rainfall ranges from 100 to 125 cm per annum with the total greater in the West. There are typically 90 to 120 days of rain per year (Kyeyune-Ssentongo 1985: 6–7). Rain is least likely in January and February. Drought occurs rarely, but part of the area did experience one in 1980. The mean minimum temperature ranges between 12.5°C and 15°C, whereas the mean maximum varies between 20°C and 27.5°C. The western areas of Bushenyi are cooler and more humid than the eastern.

The chief pest of the banana (*Musa* spp.) is the weevil (*Cosmopolites sordida*) (Ingram 1970). Banana wilt (*Fusarium oxysporum* var. *cubense*) was first found in Ankole in 1952 (McMaster 1962: 43). But the banana's ecological suitability has been demonstrated by its success in resisting both. Much research has been done on diseases and pests affecting robusta coffee (*Coffea canephora*). The most significant disease appears to be Red Blister Disease caused by a strain of *Cercospora coffeicola*. The coffee-berry borer (*Hypothenemus hampei*) is a worrisome pest (Butt et al. 1970: 201–5). Finger millet (*Eleusine coracana*) has been relatively free from disease (McMaster 1962: 50). The main pests are birds and the infrequent invasions of locusts. Cassava (*Manihot esculenta*) suffers most frequently from mosaic, spread by a virus (McMaster 1962: 69)—its most common pests are monkeys. Beans (*Phaseolus vulgaris and P. lunatus*) are attacked by anthracnose. Sweet potatoes (*Ipomoea batatas*) are most affected by a virus disease first recognized in southwestern Uganda in 1944 but now becoming more serious, as well as by rats and moles (McMaster 1962: 74). Diseases and pests attacking groundnuts (*Arachis hypogaea*) are not numerous; the most widespread disease is rosette (McMaster 1962: 77), although crested cranes and crows sometimes destroy entire gardens.

Changes in Population and Land Tenure

Over the last two decades all unused public land has disappeared in re- sponse to changes in rural-population density, land-tenure legislation, and economic insecurity caused by rapid inflation. The three factors have combined to place farmers in this agricultural zone on the brink of a very serious situation. In my own surveys during 1984 and 1986, I found few people who were already landless, although several poor farmers did not have enough land of their own to supply the subsistence needs of their families.[3]

The population densities reported for Bushenyi District in the 1980 census (COMPED 1982: 234) were derived by measuring the land avail- able by simply subtracting the area of open water. A more useful mea- sure is the ratio of population to cultivable area defined as total land area excluding open water, permanent swamps, lands over 2,000 m and all lands legally designated for a specific nonagricultural use, such as forest reserves, national parks, and game reserves (Langlands 1974d: 55, and see Langlands 1974a). On this basis, Langlands (1974d: 63) calcu- lated the total cultivable land in each of the counties now comprising Bushenyi. The cultivable area of the district amounts to 3,559 km², which yields a districtwide population density of 85/km² for 1959 and a rural population density of 115/km² for 1969 (calculated from Lang- lands 1974d: 63).[4] On this basis the rural population density of Bushenyi in 1980 rose to 147/km², about three-eighths higher than the density the census reported.

But there are other problems with the 1980 census. Much of its origi- nal data was lost, although almost all the population records for Bushenyi survived. In a recent re-analysis of these surviving records, it became clear that children under one year were almost totally ignored by the census takers (MPED 1988: 22–24). Correcting for this error increases Bushenyi's total population by about 4 percent and provides a 1980 rural-population density of 153/km² of cultivable land. In addition, it is reasonable to assume that in general there was an undercount by the 1980 census takers, given the extremely difficult and insecure conditions of the transitional political regime just following the overthrow of Amin.

Within Bushenyi the robusta coffee/banana zone has a higher population than the rest of the district. Unfortunately, Langlands's calculations of cultivable area are determined at the county level only and based on those counties existing at the time of the 1969 census. Since Ruhinda County was created out of subcounties taken from both Igara and Sheema counties, it is impossible to determine the 1980 rural-population density based on cultivable areas within each of those three counties, or within subcounties or parishes in them. Nevertheless, a 1980 rural-population density can be established for Igara and Sheema counties taken together as they existed in 1969. That figure provides a good estimate of the population density of the Bushenyi portion of the robusta coffee/banana zone, even though these county boundaries do not entirely coincide with those of the zone.

The population density of Igara County grew from $78/km^2$ in 1959 to $110/km^2$ in 1969, while that of Sheema increased from 95 to $137/km^2$ over the same period (Langlands, 1974d: 63).[5] Combining Igara and Sheema as they existed in 1969 (i.e., including Ruhinda), the 1980 population figures give a rural density of $152/km^2$.[6] When 4 percent is added to correct for the error in the 1980 census, the rural-density figure becomes $158/km^2$.[7] I have no reason to assume that subcounty rural-density figures are much different from the county figures. Nevertheless, the hue and cry in the area about land scarcity indicates that access to land has become much more unequal, which means that rural density is significantly higher than even this figure in parts of the zone.

Migration patterns—both temporary and permanent—contribute to the explanation of population density, the availability of adult agricultural labor, and the gender balance on local farms. Data on changes in age and sex structure for the population of this zone, from which migration patterns could be inferred, do not exist. The absence of county-level breakdowns in the 1959 census requires that any comparisons over time be made at the level of the former Ankole District. The absence of any breakdown by age in the 1980 census further inhibits analysis.

Nevertheless, some explanation is possible. The agricultural and population census data show that from 1959 to 1969 male to female population ratios by age group for Ankole follow the conventional pattern of more males than females leaving the area during their most productive years. The necessity to produce a cash income spurred temporary migrants to seek employment on the farms of Buganda or in urban occupations in Kampala and then to return home, sometimes after a season and sometimes after many years. Thus, Ankole served to some extent as a labor reserve for Buganda during this period, reducing the agricultural labor available for production in the district. In addition, there was greater reliance on female laborers remaining on their farms.

The *Report on Uganda Census of Agriculture* (MAC 1965: 44) shows that in 1963 there was a surplus of 106 males for each 100 females up to the age of 16, 86 males for 100 females between the ages of 16 and 45 and an equal number of males and females over 45. A roughly similar figure occurs in the analysis of the 1959 population census. There, the number of males falls below the number of females between the ages of 10 and 14, reaching a low point of 71 males for every 100 females between the ages of 25 and 29, and rises to 100 for the ages of 45 to 49 (SBMEA 1961: 72). In the 1969 census the number of males falls below that of females in the 15–19-year category, reaches a low of 75 males for every 100 females at 25–29 years, and rises to 91 at the ages of 45–49 (SDPO, Statistics Division, President's Office 1976: 2). The changes in these ratios over this ten-year period suggest a trend for agricultural labor in Ankole to become more balanced by gender in the first decade after independence.

Over this period there may also have been a reduction in the proportion of the total population that migrated, as agriculture in Bushenyi became more commercial. It would be reasonable to anticipate such a trend to accelerate (or else to begin) in the 1970s and 1980s. The sharp rise of food prices and insecurity in urban areas made life in the countryside far more attractive. In addition, rising urban food prices provided a remarkable reversal in income opportunities favoring farmers over civil-service employees for the first time since the establishment of a monetary economy.

The 1980 population census, however, suggests that the same level of gender imbalance in outmigration continued through the 1970s. It provides a breakdown between the sexes but no division into age categories. For Sheema it reports 89 males for every 100 females, for Igara 92 males and for Ruhinda 88 males (COMPED 1982: 32, 33, 39). That compares to the 1969 figures of 89 males for every 100 females in Sheema and 92 in Igara (SDMPED, Statistics Division, Ministry of Planning and Economic Development 1971: 292, 312). Since the differential favoring agricultural over civil service income increased even more rapidly during the 1980s, the effect may merely have been delayed. Therefore, one would expect the next census to show a closer balance between males and females living in rural areas. There has probably also been a decline in temporary outmigration from Bushenyi for the purpose of earning a cash income, but I have no data to demonstrate it.

Inmigration during the 1950s and 1960s came primarily from the inhabitants of Rukungiri and Kabale districts where a period of land scarcity had begun a generation earlier than it did for Bushenyi residents, and from Rwanda where the overthrow of the Watutsi monarchy led to a large number of refugees. In the 1969 census Ankole showed a net increase of 38,000 migrants, about 4 percent of its total population (SDPO 1976: 37). There are no data on migration per se in the 1980 census. However, the annual rates of population growth from 1969 to 1980 between Bushenyi and Mbarara districts differ considerably, 2.3 percent and 4.2 percent respectively. The most plausible explanation is net permanent outmigration from Bushenyi where population is more dense and land is more expensive and net inmigration into Mbarara, although not necessarily from Bushenyi only (Ntozi and Gasana 1980: 3).

Within the zone, chiefs in Bushenyi subcounties where land is expensive report an excess of people selling their land and leaving over new arrivals buying farms (Kasfir 1984–86). But where land is cheaper, chiefs report the reverse. The rapidly rising price of land in the robusta coffee/banana zone is one of the most frequent reasons farmers give to explain outmigration from this area (Kasfir 1984–86). In a shameful episode, with overtones of tensions over land, about 80,000 people, identified ethnically as Rwandans but including many Ugandan citizens, were uprooted from their homes, deprived of much of their property, and forced into Rwanda or make-shift refugee camps near the border by popular action orchestrated by local political officials (Clay 1984). In general, migration trends are not so distinct that they can be drawn from existing data, but the patterns becoming apparent indicate that responses to overcrowding are beginning to appear in this zone.

The implications of growing rural-population density in Bushenyi for agricultural change revolve to a very large extent around the recent disappearance of public land (*karandaranda*). Only thirty years ago there were enormous stretches of Crown or public land, particularly in the eastern part of Ankole, but also in what is now Bushenyi. This explains why McMaster (1962: 35) estimates that in 1958 only 11 percent of available land was in use. According to the agricultural census, in 1964 only 18.8 percent of Ankole's land was claimed as part of private holdings.[8] Even as late as 1970 the Department of Land and Surveys still regarded 76 percent of agricultural land in Sheema and 60 percent in Igara as "unused" (Kyeyune-Ssentongo 1985: 18).

But starting in the late 1960s, "in West and East Ankole, there [was] . . . a rush for people to fence their land" (Muwonge 1978: 168). Now, as Kyeyune-Ssentongo (1985: 18) tartly points out, "in spite of the abundance of land, there is no land which is free. All land which is not gazetted as Forest Reserve, National Park or controlled hunting area in Ankole, is occupied by somebody." In Bushenyi and Mbarara districts, the land frontier has closed (Kasfir 1988). Long gone are the days when "as a rule a peasant could cultivate any piece of land he liked and there were no restrictions on his breaking up new land except previous occupation" (Roscoe 1923: 95). The grandchildren of many of those "peasants," who continue to hold their land in customary tenure, are considerably more at risk. It is not just a matter of reduction in available land, but of profound changes in the land-tenure system during both the colonial and independent periods.

Since customary tenure is based on occupation and use, the availability of land to which no one has legal title is essential to permit the system to adapt to population growth. During the colonial period the contradiction between the European conception that all land must be owned by someone and the local notion of customary tenure was neatly solved through the fiction that the state owned all land not held privately in freehold or leasehold but exercised no incidents of ownership. In Bushenyi, only a small amount of the land was ever alienated in freehold. Early in the colonial period, chiefs were given freehold estates (*mailo*) as a reward for agreeing to British overrule, and, in a short-lived experimental scheme at the end of the colonial period, enterprising farmers were permitted to apply for "adjudicated freehold" for farms they already held in customary tenure as an incentive to improve productivity (Doornbos 1975). Since government policy was generally opposed to freehold, most grants of land to individuals by the Land Board since independence have been leaseholds. Nevertheless, most farmers probably still hold their land by customary tenure.

When the Land Reform Decree was passed in 1975, it "nationalized" all land, vesting freehold in the state alone. Since then, nothing more than a long-term renewable leasehold can be privately owned in Uganda. Mailo and adjudicated freehold estates were automatically converted to leasehold, although technically the land had to be surveyed and plans for economic development had to be submitted. Since the leases could be held for up to ninety-nine years and are then renewable, the owner loses little. But customary tenants on former mailo land as well as customary holders on public land on which a lease is acquired lose the security of tenure that the law previously gave them. They may be dispossessed, although they must be given six months' notice and adequate compensation. In theory the Land Board must also resettle them on comparable public land. But this assumes that there remains such land, and even then there is no guarantee that someone else might not lease that public land and start eviction proceedings all over again (Nabudere 1980: 205).

Nonetheless, the lack of government capacity since the Land Reform Decree was promulgated to survey lease applications rapidly, or to review lessee plans for economic development, has caused great uncertainty over whether the decree will actually be applied. In such circumstances, uncertainty frequently works in favor of those who have connections to state notables. Generally speaking, all a powerful political figure had to do was convince a court or a land board that he had a plan to develop the area. As one Lands Officer (DLS, Department of Lands and Surveys 1980: 18) wryly noted: "Such a situation has not proved satisfactory as hundreds of customary tenants have had their bibanjas [customary holdings] leased to influential persons without reasonable excuse." Many of those displaced during the Amin regime, he added, received no compensation at all. Other observers point to the same practice in the 1980s under the Obote government.

Thus, in the late 1960s when rising coffee income made land a valuable commodity in Bushenyi, wealthy people began to invest their money in it. Unused public land provided a windfall profit, because it had always been free so long as no one had put it into use. Now merely for the price of a survey and legal fees, it could be held as a long-term lease. Nor was evidence of use essential to ownership. Public land soon disappeared.

Fencing was a reliable method for indicating boundaries to newly acquired land that no longer had to be occupied and farmed to be owned. Since the government subsidized fencing materials in the 1960s, the growth of enclosed farms increased all the more rapidly (Muwonge 1978: 182). Fencing is, of course, important for improving the productivity of a farm. Good dairy practice requires separating paddocks, and fences allow cropland to lie fallow without ambiguity over ownership

(Muwonge 1978: 180). But for the most part what was fenced was simply the perimeter.

The combination of increased human and livestock populations (Muwonge 1978: 178–79), the dizzying rate of monetary inflation, and the high returns to food and dairy agriculture made investment in land extraordinarily compelling. For the first time it became an attractive investment to lease and drain swamps in order to turn them into private pasture. According to custom, a swamp had always been considered communal property that could not be held even by customary tenure. Instead, they were available to all who lived nearby for planting sweet potatoes (on large dirt mounds), for collecting clay for pots (Roscoe 1923: 103), and for gathering thatch for roofs. Now they are private property complete with perimeter fences to keep out neighbors. It is not surprising to discover reports of violent land disputes in the district commissioner's files (Kasfir 1988: 170–71). In addition, out of 59 farmers in my 1984 sample, 22 reported that their families had experienced seasonal hunger, and 19 others said they had not but knew of families that had. Frequently, poor peasants sell their farms and migrate, often to Mbarara District where land prices are lower (Muwonge 1978: 181; Ntozi and Gasana 1980: 3).

Whether or not "fencing out" the rapidly increasing rural population was the cause, it is clear that by the mid-1970s the average holding of farmers in the robusta coffee/banana zone was smaller than might be expected from earlier reports of vast amounts of unused land and considerably smaller than the fenced farms. The agricultural census (MAC 1966: 20) found that the median holding of farmers in Ankole in 1964 was 1.8 ha (corrected to size of cultivated area).[9] The average farmer in the 1974 sample from the robusta coffee/banana zone held 2 ha, whereas only 8 percent had more than 4 ha. Two-fifths of these farmers had 0.8 to 1.6 ha, while two-thirds had between 0.4 and 2.4 ha (Kyeyune-Ssentongo 1985: 21, 22).

One indication of the coming land squeeze is the suprisingly low proportion of inheritance of the original farmstead in the 1974 survey. Only 57 percent of the respondents reported they inherited their first parcel. Almost one-quarter said they started out by purchasing their first plot (Kyeyune-Ssentongo 1985: 19). Of the 28 percent of farmers who added more land, 82 percent did so by purchasing it. Indeed, for these respondents the purchase of land was the second largest farm expense after hired labor (Kyeyune-Ssentongo 1985: 68–69). In comparison Muwonge (1978: 175) discovered for the same counties in 1973 that Sheema contained 283 farms that had been fenced, averaging 30.43 ha, whereas Igara had 232, averaging 38.34 ha.

All local observers say the trend to buy and fence large farms throughout Bushenyi District has continued to accelerate. Knowledgeable local observers estimate that the increase in land values over the past two decades has gone up several hundredfold (Kasfir 1988: 166). It is hard to be sure that the real value of land has risen much, given the disastrous decline in the shilling. But this is beside the point. Land was where rational Ugandan investors who could not export their capital ought to have stored their money. The general consequence has been to raise effective rural-population densities—that is, the density of accessible land—to a far higher, if presently unknown, level.

The Nature of Agricultural Change

The typical farming system in the robusta coffee/banana zone (fig. 2.3) in Bushenyi consists of one or a few nearby plots, on which the homestead is located. Villages therefore comprise dispersed settlements. The farmer uses a few simple tools, particularly the hoe, makes few capital investments in his land, relies primarily on family labor, although frequently labor also is hired or hired out, and has received virtually no direct government assistance for the past fifteen years. Almost all farmers grow a mix of similar cultigens for subsistence and cash income, but these cultigens have changed significantly over the past eighty years. Within the general framework proposed by Turner and Brush (1987: 6–8), these farming systems would be characterized by low but probably increasing output intensity, relatively static paleotechnic rather than neotechnic inputs, and mixed production for both direct consumption and, increasingly, market sales.

The most important agricultural changes in this zone have been the shift from finger millet to bananas and the introduction of robusta coffee. Widespread ownership of cattle by the nonpastoral Bairu for dairy and meat production also has been a significant innovation. These changes were largely the consequence of the spread of the monetary economy from Buganda following the imposition of colonial rule. Cash became increasingly indispensable for taxes and for school fees, as well as for purchasing first imported commodities and eventually even locally grown food crops. Farmers became increasingly market oriented.

Finger millet was "the main crop" during the earlier colonial period,

Fig. 2.3. Farm with three buildings (including granary), Igara County, Bushenyi District, 1989. Bananas in foreground and background surround open pasture. Young cassava below granary and pineapples below cassava. Fence in field used to spray cattle.

although it was supplemented with bananas, sweet potatoes, peas, beans, groundnuts and marrows (Roscoe 1923: 96, 100; Oberg 1943: 573, see Thomas 1970). Williams (1936: 203) calls attention to "the supreme importance attached to the performance of all that is humanly possible to ensure the successful harvesting of the staff of life—millet, called *buro*." Its use in sealing blood brotherhood indicates its symbolic importance (Williams 1934). Oberg (1943: 573) found that "elaborate magical practices" were used to protect the millet crop, but not others. It was usually the first cultigen planted on new land (Taylor 1969: 105). Even today when it is no longer the subsistence staple of the Bairu, discussions of millet generally evoke palpable enthusiasm. Despite their overwhelming importance bananas have not replaced millet as a symbol of ethnic identification.

Considerable expansion of banana cultivation occurred after 1952 (McMaster 1962: 52; Mukasa 1970: 139). By 1965, 97 percent of Ankole farmers grew bananas, whereas only 65 percent grew millet (MAC, 1966: 46). In 1972 agricultural officials reported that "finger millet . . . [had] lost its dominant place as the major food crop" in the robusta coffee/banana zone (PUMAFC 1972: 18). In 1974 bananas provided over one-half of the total available food for farmers in the zone, whereas millet provided only 4 percent (Kyeyune-Ssentongo 1985: 28–29). A little later bananas replaced coffee as a cash crop in some areas, primarily in Sheema county, but more typically they were combined with coffee and either replaced annual crops or were planted on previously unused land. Further expansion of banana production occurred as the urban market price of bananas inflated at a dizzying rate—over two hundredfold between 1970 and 1984 and 150 times again by 1988.

Good (1970: 178) attributes the change from millet to bananas to the cultural prestige of the Baganda.[10] Practical advantages, however, may better explain this shift. In comparison to millet, bananas have lower labor requirements, greater reliability, and year-round availability, although millet can be stored for a long time. The shift to bananas may have been further reinforced by the importance of planting a permanent crop in order to demonstrate ownership in times of increasing land scarcity. If coffee was considered undesirable for this purpose, bananas would be the most logical substitute.

Arabica coffee was planted by local Bushenyi farmers in the late 1920s, as the Ugandan experiment with coffee as a plantation cultigen grown by settlers was coming to an end. The pace of adoption was slow because arabica was susceptible to disease. In the 1930s arabica trees were uprooted and replaced with robusta, except in Bunyaruguru County. Kyeyune-Ssentongo (1985: 91) suggests that poor farmers who worked on coffee farms in Buganda introduced coffee into Ankole. Land planted to coffee in Western Province (which includes Bushenyi) has always lagged behind Buganda—in the 1930s about one-third as much land was used for coffee.

"Really phenomenal growth in the Uganda coffee industry has occurred only since the war" (Uganda Government 1967: 2). Nevertheless, as late as 1951 production in Ankole remained trivial, amounting to less than 200 metric tons. A year after independence, the whole kingdom still produced only a little over 5,000 metric tons a year. Coffee adoption expanded sharply in the 1950s and after, so much so that the agricultural census reported that by 1965, 70 percent of the farmers in Ankole had some coffee trees (MAC 1966: 70). In 1974, 92 percent of the farmers sampled in this zone had some trees (Kyeyune-Ssentongo 1985: 30). Because of the coffee quota, little new planting occurred after the mid-1960s. Nevertheless, coffee had become the main source of cash income for these farmers in Kyeyune-Ssentongo's sample in 1973–74, providing 62 percent of total income (1985: 41).

By the 1980s the decline in returns to coffee and the rise in the value of sales of bananas, other food crops, and milk had again altered farmers' production preferences. Economic incentives must be quite significant before farmers will uproot coffee trees that have taken three to four years to mature in order to plant bananas or introduce pasture for livestock. Good (1970: 26) reports that some farmers were already uprooting their coffee trees in the 1960s with the encouragement of local agricultural officials.[11] However, the practice did not become noticeable until 1975 when farmers were not paid for their coffee by the government (Kasfir 1984–86). Uprooting trees seems to have occurred primarily in areas of Sheema in which bananas do particularly well, but it also took place in Igara. Elsewhere in this agricultural zone coffee was given little attention or investment from the mid-1970s, but the trees were left standing. Yields fell, but the reduced crop was usually harvested and sold. Energies went instead into clearance of unused land for the expansion of banana plantations for market production and for pasture for dairy cattle (Kasfir 1984–86).

By traditional preference the Bairu, the predominant inhabitants of this zone, were agriculturalists, whereas the Bahima, about 5 percent of the population, were nomadic cattle herders. However, in a cattle census conducted in 1937 Bairu owned two-thirds as many head of cattle in Ankole as the Bahima and had achieved the same rate of increase with only half the number of breeding cows (Mackintosh 1938: 29). In the 1970s Bairu owned two-thirds of the cattle in Bushenyi (Muwonge 1978: 170). With the startling rise in the price of milk and spread of its consumption in urban areas, profits from dairy herds frequently exceed coffee and rival bananas. The indigenous long-horned Ankole cow (*sanga*) successfully resists local diseases, but it is a poor milk (and beef) producer. Exotic dairy cows give far more milk (up to twenty liters a day) but are highly susceptible to East Coast Fever, unless protected with acaricides. Exotic cattle, Guernsey and Friesian, were first introduced into Bushenyi in 1965. Despite the extraordinary difficulties involved in importing drugs on a reliable basis, dairy herds of up to sixty head, generally crossbred but in a few cases entirely purebred, have been maintained throughout all the difficulties of the Amin and subsequent periods (Kasfir 1984–86).[12]

Inputs

With a few notable exceptions, particularly dairy production, Uganda's economic and political difficulties have made it impossible for most farmers to move away from paleotechnic systems using little energy, emphasizing primarily manual labor, and introducing few chemical or mechanical improvements into the production process. Precolonial farming in this zone was based on a hoe culture, and "no source of power other than the human arm and back was utilized" (Oberg 1943: 573). Hoes and knives were produced by local blacksmiths. The land was cleared and prepared by shallow turning of the soil in each of the dry seasons, followed by deeper cultivation at the beginning of the rains. A bush fallow system was followed with cultivation for approximately three years before the land was left fallow. No fertilizer or artificial irrigation was used (Taylor 1969: 105). The situation today remains virtually the same.

Hand labor is still the most important agricultural input; neither oxen, nor tractors, nor fertilizer, nor pesticides, nor improved seeds are used regularly (Kyeyune-Ssentongo 1985: 47). Thus, the hoe remains by far the most important and widely used farming implement. Cheap and widely available up to the early 1970s, it is not so easily replaced today because of the production problems in Uganda's factories and of the disappearance of local blacksmiths a generation ago. Nevertheless, all households have at least one hoe, three-quarters possess a *panga* (machete), and almost half have a long-handled pruning knife (Kasfir 1984–86). Richer farmers frequently own six to ten hoes, though only one or two pangas and pruning knives. What is more important, however, is that these rich farmers rarely own any other tools that are technologically superior to those of poor farmers (Kasfir 1984–86). Wealth or size of farm, then, seems to have virtually no effect on the kind of tools owned by these farmers. This is a significant indicator that technological changes in farming—outside the dairy industry—are not presently occurring.

Ox plowing has not been adopted in Bushenyi, although it has spread widely over the past seventy-five years in other parts of Uganda, particularly in the cotton-growing areas in the east (Uchendu and Anthony 1975: 36–38).[13] The reasons for not moving from the hoe to ox plowing in Bushenyi are based on environmental constraints, choice of cultigens, and plot size, in addition to the difficulties of introducing technological innovation in the midst of political and economic instabilities. Even where population density is relatively high, there often is no comparative advantage of the ox plow over the hoe where plots are small, the terrain is steep and much of the land is devoted to tree crops (Pingali et al. 1987: 7). All three factors are characteristic of Bushenyi. In addition, only sixty kilometers south and east of the robusta coffee/banana zone efforts to eradicate animal trypanosomiasis transmitted by the tsetse fly (*Glossina* sp.) that had been relatively effective in the 1960s have been losing ground since then.

The family continues to be the most important source of farm labor. The 1964 agricultural census (MAC 1965: 56) found that only 20 percent of land holders in Ankole hired labor, a little more than half the national average. It also indicated that the percentage of holdings employing laborers increased with size but only to 28 percent of holdings of more than 4 ha (MAC 1966: 36). In the robusta coffee/banana zone in 1974 almost half of the farmers hired labor, which provided only 7 percent of the average monthly input on all farms (Kyeyune-Ssentongo 1985: 47–48, 55).[14] Most hired laborers were not permanent, but worked at times of peak labor demand. Nevertheless, hired labor was the largest average expenditure for these farmers (Kyeyune-Ssentongo 1985: 68).

A decade later rich farmers in this zone were found employing up to seven laborers full time, although many were retreating to family labor, using hired labor only for short-term contracts for specific projects such as land clearance (Kasfir 1984–86). Rapidly increasing inflation made hiring permanent labor unprofitable even for most wealthy farmers. However, in another respect hired labor has greatly increased since independence, although to what extent is unknown. Population pressure and fenced property have led to the practice of borrowing land—almost unheard of a generation earlier. Since the "rent" for such land is not paid in cash but consists of clearing it and providing a small part (8–15 percent) of the harvest, farmers who own such land usually do not think of this labor as "hired." Consequently, there is reason to think that the amount of hired labor, although still limited, is growing. Population pressure on the land is likely to cause it to increase more rapidly during the next generation.

Kyeyune-Ssentongo (1985: 47, 49, 52) found that family-labor use in this area was lower than in other nearby agricultural zones, with a modal average of 600 to 800 hours per year per husband and per wife. On average, women provided 14 percent more hours of labor on the farm— in addition, of course, to their work in the home.[15] The farmer provided 35 percent, his wives 40 percent, and children provided about 10 percent of average total annual farm labor input (Kyeyune-Ssentongo 1985: 54). Women missed fewer days and worked longer hours.

However, he adds that "the days of sex specialization by crop or by type of operation—if they ever existed—are gone in Central Ankole" (1985: 54).[16] Both husbands and wives contribute labor to every task in growing each crop. Husbands contributed more than half the labor of pruning and mulching bananas and coffee, and of harvesting coffee, but provided almost no labor toward sowing and weeding millet (Kyeyune-Ssentongo 1985: 45, 55). Bananas and coffee received 80 percent of total farm-labor input. He found that for both crops the marginal value of labor was well above zero, indicating that farmers could significantly raise their income by intensifying their use of labor (1985: 59). He also found that the amount of family labor was relatively constant throughout the year, and that the higher the labor input on a farm, the larger the share of labor contributed by children and hired labor (1985: 48, 50).

The most important land modification has been swamp drainage that is the product of the hunger for land described above. As noted, custom used to treat swamps as public land that could not be privately held. But postindependence laws permitting leaseholds over formerly public land did not distinguish between swamps and dry land. Thus, as land became more desirable, people filed to lease swamps and then drained them for crops or pasture. Local fears that this might lead to a fall in the water table and to a growth in tensions between the new holders and former users led to an informal administrative ban on further drainage of swamps (BDG 1982). There is very little terracing or other forms of soil protection on hillsides, unlike the steeper and universally terraced slopes of neighboring Kabale District. Coffee and particularly bananas are frequently mulched, a practice which protects against erosion.

In the 1950s and 1960s the government enthusiastically promoted new, largely imported, technologies to improve agriculture. These inputs—the use of fertilizer, pesticides, better seeds and tractors—were made available to the fortunate few "progressive farmers" in the hope that their use would create knowledge of their benefits and demand for further distribution by other farmers. Today, however, availability of these inputs depends on the spasmodic generosity of international agencies.

The few tractors still in working order are more profitably used for transportation than for farming. Many farmers insist they would use fertilizer and spray pesticides on their coffee trees if the real price of coffee were more attractive. However, even if there were a demand for fertilizer and pesticides neither the government nor private channels could presently supply them in adequate quantities. Throughout the 1980s, hoes have been in short supply, and expensive when available in markets. Use of improved seeds has never been widespread. Farmers rely on the previous year's harvest for their seed (Kyeyune-Ssentongo 1985: 47). In the 1980s, however, demand for new coffee seedlings surfaced intermittently when the government price stayed ahead of inflation (Kasfir 1984–86).

The question of measuring increased frequency of cultivation in response to increased population and land pressures is complicated by the shift to perennial crops grown partly for subsistence and partly for the market. Schemes for measuring agricultural intensification by multiplying the number of times a particular crop is cultivated during a specific time period, such as the scheme proposed by Turner and Doolittle (1978), cannot account for reliance on perennial crops. Improved techniques can increase yields, but—by definition—not the frequency of perennial crops. That makes it more difficult to assess agricultural intensification in this zone where bananas, coffee, and pasture account for over four-fifths of the area of the average farm and most of the typical farmer's subsistence staple and cash income.

Other cultigens are planted either once or twice a year at the onset of each rainy season with almost double the area devoted to crops planted in the second rains. Beans, peas, groundnuts, sorghum, and sweet potatoes are generally planted twice, whereas millet is usually planted once during the more reliable second rains (Kyeyune-Ssentongo 1985: 24). Quickly maturing cultigens, such as peas, beans, and drought-resistant sweet potatoes and sorghum, are more likely to be planted in the more unpredictable first rains (Kyeyune-Ssentongo 1985: 24–25). Cassava and to a lesser extent pineapples have become widespread in the 1980s. Maize, pumpkins, yams, Irish potatoes, and sugarcane also are grown. However, the Bushenyi Agricultural Officer reports that the frequency of cultivation of these crops has not changed for many years (Jamil Ziyimba, personal communication, 1988).

Outputs

The shift in crops has not only changed the composition of agricultural production in this zone but it has led to an expansion in total production. In addition, the current value of sales of coffee and bananas (and milk, a taste for which also has dramatically increased in the past generation) far outweigh present sales of all cultigens traditionally grown in Bushenyi before colonial rule. This change was completed in the first few years after independence, although the expansion in sales of bananas was a response to the inflation in urban prices for food that occurred a decade later. Thus, the monetary economy introduced during colonial rule produced a new degree of output intensity. In that sense, farmers in this zone have passed through a stage of agricultural intensification during this century for reasons that have little to do with population growth.

Now, for the first time, population pressure is being felt by farmers in the zone, which poses the question of whether they are now going through, or are about to go through, another period of agricultural intensification. With no new cultigens being brought onto the market, output intensity, if it is to be demonstrated as responsive to population growth and land scarcity, must be measured by increases in production over a specified time or area (see Turner and Brush 1987: 6). There are reasons to think that output intensity is probably increasing and is on the verge of changing substantially now that the opportunities for leaving land fallow have diminished sharply. Unfortunately, farmers do not measure their production in standardized units, and data that analyze changes in yields during the past two decades are not available, so a precise judgment cannot be made.[17] However, measures of certain factors influencing yields provide some indication of change.

Since independence there has been a substantial and probably accelerating reduction of land left fallow. In Kyeyune-Ssentongo's 1974 survey (1985: 22), one-quarter of the farms had no fallow areas at all and over one-half had less than 0.4 ha.[18] The expansion of bananas and coffee, both perennial crops with tree lives of several decades, has resulted in much less area devoted to annual food crops. These two perennials covered 77 percent of farm area in the 1974 survey—about 0.91 ha on average (Kyeyune-Ssentongo 1985: 48–49). As dairy production expanded, reclaimed land put to pasture in the past decade has also reduced available fallow. Present practices concerning fallow for other subsistence cultigens are not known. But because each occupies only a small percentage of the area of most farms—generally less than 0.2 ha, except for millet, which is grown relatively infrequently—the amount left fallow to restore soil fertility is low (Kyeyune-Ssentongo 1985: 38). Population pressure and removal of land through leases and fencing ensure that the crop-to-fallow ratio for the vast majority of farmers will continue to rise through the next generation.

Coffee yields are reduced by intercropping and lack of fertilizer or proper maintenance. Trials at government research stations in the 1960s demonstrated that clean weeding could double annual yields per hectare and that adding fertilizer could increase yield one-third more (Butt et al. 1970: 197). Mulching and some intercropping with legumes can also increase yield, but intercropping with bananas will reduce yields by one-half or even two-thirds (Butt et al. 1970: 195, 198). Kyeyune-Ssentongo (1985: 46) found that yields per hectare of coffee interplanted with bananas were only 35 percent of yields from pure stands of coffee.

In 1964, when many farmers in Ankole were introducing robusta coffee, the agricultural census (MAC 1966: 66) reported that it was planted in pure stands on only one-fifth of the hectarage, it was predominant on two-fifths, and not predominant on the remaining two-fifths.[19] A decade later pure stands of coffee in the robusta coffee/banana zone had risen to three-eighths of coffee hectarage, but, because of quota requirements, without significant changes in the total area planted. Kyeyune-Ssentongo (1985: 42) attributes this rise to the maturing of coffee. Farmers could now maintain an economic return to land dedicated to coffee without relying on a second cultigen.

Since then, the problems of the deteriorating economy, particularly the low government price for coffee, the rapidly increasing cost of labor, and the difficulty of acquiring fertilizer and pesticides (for the few who applied them) have caused farmers to put far less effort into coffee. This has led to far lower standards of maintenance, which, in turn, have undoubtedly depressed yields. Thus, one might expect coffee yields in this zone to have increased modestly during the first decade of independence and fallen somewhat since then.

As the increasing hectarage figures presented above indicate, a large proportion of the banana plantations in Bushenyi are young, which probably raises their overall yield. In the 1974 survey (Kyeyune-Ssentongo 1985: 27) the average annual yield of bananas was 9.9 metric ton per hectare. This compares relatively well with the figure of 11.2 metric ton that is considered a "good" yield for southern Ugandan conditions (Mukasa 1970: 140).[20] Kyeyune-Ssentongo (1985: 33) observes that "in general Ankole has the best attended banana plots in Uganda." Unfortunately, I do not know of any more recent measures of banana yields.

Table 2.1 gives the findings of the 1974 survey for hectarage, yields, and number of crops per year for cultigens planted in this zone. The low average crop yield and large variations in yield for most crops— frequently more than 350 kg/ha—suggest the potential for increasing food-crop yields on existing land within this zone (Kyeyune-Ssentongo 1985: 40). The monetary implications of production are discussed in the next section.

The Nature of Changes in the Forces of Production

Throughout the twentieth century there has been a dramatic and universal shift in Bushenyi from reliance primarily on production for subsistence to a far larger proportion of production for sale in the market.

Table 2.1. Average Hectarage, Yields, and Number of Times Planted per Year of Cultivation for Major Cultigens, 1974

Cultigen	Hectarage	Yield (kg/ha)[a]	Number p.a.[b]
Bananas[c]	0.64	9,911.0	—
Clean coffee (mixed with banana)[d]	0.28	349.3	—
Clean coffee (pure stand)[d]	0.17	987.3	—
Sweet potatoes	0.15	21,774.5	2
Millet	0.15	1,393.6	1
Beans	0.08	961.2	2
Peas	0.04	432.4	2
Groundnuts	0.03	1,141.0	2
Sorghum	0.03	2,137.4	1–2

Source: Adapted from Kyeyune-Ssentongo, 1985: 23, 25, 27, 46.

[a]Average yields conceal great variation in actual yields in this zone.

[b]Number of times of planting refers to seasons planted, not to number of times planted per year on the same plot.

[c]Unclear whether this refers to pure and/or mixed stands.

[d]Clean coffee refers to hulled sun-dried cherry (hulling removes about 54% of the weight of the dried cherry).

Except for a few commercial producers, all farmers still grow much of their subsistence requirements—to which they have added new crops for sale. In the late 1960s, Good (1970: 80) found that farmers in this area "prefer to produce the bulk of their subsistence needs themselves. . . . As a consequence, demand for farm produce among rural producers themselves is extremely narrow."

On the other hand, Kyeyune-Ssentongo (1985: 27) found a somewhat greater emphasis on food crops marketed. But, like Good, he felt that the farmer is not entirely driven by commercial criteria, but rather sells whatever surplus remains after subsistence requirements have been met.[21] The only exceptions to this latter economic strategy that were found in the mid-1980s survey of farmers in the same zone were one or two wealthy farmers who bought virtually all of their food requirements from the market. Everyone else grew all or as much of their staple (almost always bananas) as the land to which they had access would yield. However, they also invariably bought some foodstuffs in the market (Kasfir 1984–86). At this time, it is difficult to tell whether farmers are shifting significantly away from a subsistence-first production strategy for all crops and adopting a more complex strategy in which a proportion of some nonstaple crops are grown specifically for sale.

In either case, most farmers in this area fit the classic definition of African peasants who produced much of their own food, but who were inextricably involved in the wider economic system (Saul and Woods 1981; Kasfir 1986). Even those who were wealthy and who, by most criteria, were commercial farmers produced most of their own food. One reason for this appears to be the inefficiency of local rural markets. There was a wide discrepancy despite seasonal variations between farm-gate prices and local-market prices. Kyeyune-Ssentongo (1985: 66) reports that in 1974 local Bushenyi food markets were highly active in livestock and seed crops (beans, groundnuts, and peas) but not in staples like bananas. The open-market prices for foods were never less than 170 percent of the farm-gate price, and for beans it was always more than 250 percent (Kyeyune-Ssentongo 1985: 25–27, 73).

The two most dynamic changes in the income of these farmers over the past decade and a half were the consequences of inflation. First, remittances from family members in wage employment ceased to be important. Second, bananas frequently replaced coffee as the dominant source of farmers' cash income. In the 1960s the mostly likely explanation of variations in income of farmers was the presence of a family member holding a salaried position in the city.[22] Thus, anyone who could get at least his sons into secondary school hoped they would find careers outside farming. By the 1980s the real value of salaries, even of the most highly paid state officials, had fallen to ludicrously low levels. Rich peasants, not just the group of commercial farmers, were likely to earn a higher income than the salary paid to the highest-level civil servants.

In addition, the 1974 survey found that 62 percent of farmer cash income came from coffee, even though a comparison of returns on labor and inputs demonstrated that bananas paid much better (Kyeyune-Ssentongo 1985: 41, 59). The 1984 and 1986 surveys indicated that the proportion of farmer income derived from bananas had grown considerably, in part because the state price for coffee had lagged behind inflation, whereas the open market price for bananas had not (Kasfir 1984–86; Benner 1988). Dairy farming also became increasingly attractive, because the price tended to keep up with inflation.

Neither government nor international agencies play an important positive role in the farming economy. Low coffee prices set by the government, about 20 percent of the world price, and failure to pay farmers quickly go a long way to explain lack of interest in that cultigen. Most of the programs developed in the 1950s and 1960s to supply farmers with subsidized inputs and technical advice have almost disappeared. Local agricultural officials cannot spend much time in their offices, because their salaries will neither feed nor clothe their families. They have no transport to take them into the countryside. Even in the 1960s, extension agents tended to concentrate their attention on a few "progressive farmers." Occasionally in the 1980s agricultural-development schemes were launched, for example in Bushenyi an intensive European Economic Community rehabilitation program intended to improve the quality of coffee. But this program reached few farmers. In the early 1980s, support from international donors enabled the government to distribute subsidized hoes widely, but these amounted to only a drop in the bucket and were frequently diverted to the black market.

Consequences of Changes and Prospects for the Future

To call this area the "robusta coffee/banana zone" is to indicate how thoroughly fundamental changes in farming have occurred during this century, as neither cultigen was widely grown before the colonial period. These changes are only a few of the complex basic choices farmers in this area have made and continue to make. By adopting and selling these cultigens, they have certainly increased output by unit area and by time as measured in cash return. These changes constitute agricultural intensification. This transformation, however, was the direct consequence of the introduction by the colonial government of a monetary economy and not a response to increases in population. Thus far, despite population density far in excess of typical levels in rural Africa, farmers in this zone have not yet found it necessary to adopt new production techniques.

The most important change in choice of food staples has been the shift from finger millet to bananas. This has meant a sharp decrease in labor input per hectare, as millet requires almost twice as much labor as bananas (Kyeyune-Ssentongo 1985: 32, 38). Because the hills in this zone frequently suffer from flooding during rainy seasons, which results in some crop destruction and loss of topsoil, and because well-mulched banana plantations check soil erosion (McMaster 1962: 39), the shift to banana plantations, which tend to be well maintained in Bushenyi, has had an important side benefit.

Sweet potatoes, the third staple in terms of hectarage, require little weeding though much labor in the removal of vines. They are planted on mounds on dry land and on ridges (to avoid waterlogging) in swamps (Kyeyune-Ssentongo 1985: 36–37). The amount of land now devoted to foods other than bananas, millet, and sweet potatoes rarely exceeds one-fifth of a hectare each per household (Kyeyune-Ssentongo 1985: 38). Less than 10 percent of land devoted to foods in 1958 was planted in cassava, though it was on its way toward becoming a staple (McMaster 1962: 66, 67). Only 17 percent of the 1974 sample grew it (Kyeyune-Ssentongo 1985: 38). Since then the amount of cassava grown in this zone appears to have increased considerably, although I know of no reliable measures. The reduced labor cassava requires for food preparation may have been an important reason.

These changes in food crops have important dietary implications. Millet is much higher in protein and carbohydrate content and, therefore, is more nutritious than bananas, its replacement staple (McMaster 1962: 44, 52; Langlands 1974b: 76). Sweet potato and cassava are excellent protection against famine, the former because it can be successfully and quickly grown when weather conditions are poor, and the latter because it can be stored in the ground for a long time. Although both foods can contribute to a balanced diet, as staples they offer relatively little nutrition (McMaster 1962: 71, 74; Langlands 1974b: 76).

The patterns of disease in this area do not indicate that changes in diet have caused serious problems in recent years that might motivate farmers to modify their approach to agriculture. The trends since independence in nutritional diseases suggest a pattern of slow improvement, according to the former Bushenyi Health Officer (Tom Mwebesa, personal communication, 1988). Malnutrition stemming from protein deficiencies and anemia, a moderate problem in the colonial period, are much reduced. Diseases exacerbated by overcrowding show a mixed picture of change. Smallpox has disappeared, whooping cough is much reduced, pneumonia and tuberculosis still carry rates of high morbidity and mortality. Measles has become worse—it is now the most important cause of death among children.

Sexually transmitted diseases also show a mixed record. Yaws, common during the colonial period, has disappeared. The prevalence of syphillis has been greatly reduced, whereas cases of gonorrhea are increasing. Cases of AIDS, an increasingly serious problem in parts of Uganda, are no longer rare in this rural area. The vector of this disease follows the truck route around Lake Victoria, to the east of this agricultural zone (Hooper 1987: 474). Body stature has increased since independence, despite all the political and economic disruptions since 1971. There has been an increase in height and weight, as well as in life expectancy (Tom Mwebesa, personal communication, 1988). In 1985 both crude death and infant mortality rates were only a fraction of what they had been in 1960. Thus far, it is safe to say, neither the epidemiological pattern nor overall changes in health and body size suggest that Bushenyi is now so densely populated that farmers must immediately adopt new techniques to intensify agricultural production in order to remedy deficiencies in food supply.

With regard to cash crops during the past two decades, the general response of farmers in this zone has been to make only small investments toward introducing new cultigens or production techniques. This risk-avoidance behavior is probably closely related to the virtual absence of government technical assistance during this period. Farm studies in Tanzania demonstrate smallholder willingness to adopt new crops and new means of production but—in the absence of external support—only when prices or reductions in cost are especially attractive (Ruthenberg 1968: 343).

The most important change has been the expansion of banana production. Because farmers changed their preference in a staple food to bananas, because the technology needed for successful adoption is cheap and well understood, and because bananas at present generally yield higher returns than coffee, this is a conservative strategy—except in the relatively small number of cases where coffee was uprooted. Farmers with a lot of coffee can maintain their trees with virtually no further investment—at the cost of reduced yields. They switched their attention to bananas without making large investments or taking serious risks. Thus, for the moment, most of them follow a strategy of low investment–low yield.

The main exception to this strategy is dairy farming. Farmers owning purebred imported cattle or crossbreeds must use acaricides on a regular basis, which requires them to maintain access to either spraying equipment or dips. The rapidly rising price of milk, however, has supported these expensive imported inputs. In addition, dairy farmers generally erect at least perimeter fencing. The acaricides and related equipment are essential costs requiring a large capital investment that has produced a return that probably increased faster than the extraordinary rate of inflation over the past decade in Uganda. But it remains a gamble. In 1987 and 1988, for example, when inflation went through the roof, the cost of acaricides far outstripped increases in the market price for milk. In Bushenyi, the dairy industry is a high-risk, high-yield form of production by comparison to either coffee or bananas.

Finally, farmers also consider their other food crops as sources of cash income. Here, as with bananas, most smallholders follow a conservative strategy of limiting sales to surplus production after family subsistence requirements have been met. The difference appears to be that bananas are planted with the intention of selling a portion in the market, while in most cases other food crops are planted in order to satisfy domestic consumption. Here too, the dominant strategy seems to be one of low risk, low yield.

What do these challenges in farming indicate about agricultural intensification? The shift to perennials has reduced the necessity for fallow, thus permitting some additional increase in rural-population density. On the other hand, continued expansion of production beyond domestic consumption will increase the amount of land needed, as commercial exploitation is added to subsistence use. But the dynamic between commerce and subsistence is never simply additive. Helped along by political connections, advantaged by changes in land law, and driven by the pressures of inflation, the alert and the wealthy began to assemble large farms by enclosing public land and buying out small-holders. As they continue to fence and lease large tracts of land, poor farmers are being left with plots too small to provide subsistence. The latter have already begun to borrow land to grow additional food and to seek agricultural employment in growing numbers. The closure of the land frontier in this zone suggests that new forms of agricultural inten-sification specifically in response to population density are probably on the horizon.

Conclusion

The creation in the twentieth century of the robusta coffee/banana zone was a major agricultural transformation. Taking advantage of good climate, adequate water, and reasonably good soils at an appropriate alti-tude, the colonial government encouraged farmers in this area to grow coffee in order to build the state's revenue base. Poll taxes, school fees, new markets, and new consumer goods created a demand for cash that made sales of coffee increasingly attractive to farmers. Once the mistaken policy of encouraging arabica coffee on settler plantations was changed, smallholder adoption of robusta coffee became virtually universal.

The reasons for substituting bananas for millet as the subsistence staple are less clear. Bananas did not become an important cash crop that rivalled coffee until the 1970s. But they did involve less labor and provided the convenience of maturation throughout the year. Change in diet and commodification of the economy resulted in growing new culti-gens with a dramatic increase in production for the market. By indepen-dence this change had clearly resulted in a dramatic intensification of agricultural production, even though the hoe culture remained virtually unchanged, the population-to-land ratio remained low, and public land continued to be freely available.

A further agricultural transformation may now be starting, but characteristic changes in production are not yet in evidence. Thus far, Bushenyi farmers have continued to rely primarily on their own produc-tion for their families' subsistence and have taken few initiatives to shift to neotechnic inputs. The change in balance of cultigens produced for the market from an almost exclusive attention to coffee to greater emphasis on bananas suggests another increase in output intensity, though present high inflation creates too much volatility to know for sure. The more recent interest in dairy production, which has led to conversion of cropped areas and wetlands into pasture, also betokens a new rise in output intensity.

These changes have been made with little assistance from the government or international sources. Indeed, farmers in this area have had to cope with government harassment, with two wars fought near this zone and, above all, with continuing rapid inflation. Not surprisingly, most farmers, with the significant exception of a small group of aggressive commercial farmers, have responded to the highly unpredictable political and economic environment in which they now live by making small capital investments in crop maintenance, particularly coffee, and, in general, by following conservative low-risk strategies. Farmers in the dairy industry provide the main exception, because they must rely on high-cost imported inputs.

Other changes are creating the conditions for passing through a new threshold of agricultural intensification. High and increasing population density in this zone and changes in land tenure have resulted in the disappearance of public land and in rapidly rising land prices. For the first time, large farms have been created and fenced, in part by draining swamps that by custom had been available to all. A sharp reduction in land available for fallow has occurred, but that has been largely masked by the shift to perennial crops over the last three generations. The practice of "borrowing land" to grow food crops, and paying rent in kind and in labor, has become common. The families of some poor and middle peasants often endure a "hungry season." The sons of these peasants will not acquire farms as large as those held by their fathers, nor large enough to provide subsistence for their families. Nevertheless, they are inextricably involved in the monetary economy.

On the other hand, rich farmers have not yet adopted new production technologies, nor found it economic to hire labor on a large scale. Most still produce their subsistence staple with some contribution of family labor and use the same tools as those less well-off. Despite modest technological innovations, these farmers can generally still manage not only to feed their families but often to produce a surplus in food sold in urban centers. Population demands have not reached the point where yields must be increased, even though new land is no longer available. When that time occurs, a new agricultural technology, perhaps the ox-drawn plow, may become a necessary replacement for the hoe for both rich and poor farmers.

Thus, at the moment, the indicators of entry into a new stage of agricultural intensification remain mixed. This zone in Bushenyi does not yet provide a case that helps to settle the question of what happens when a population becomes so dense that the land cannot support its farmers unless they fundamentally change their techniques for food production. But population and agricultural challenges in Bushenyi indicate that a test of that question may not be far off in the future.

Notes

I am grateful for the help I received from Hakim Kasozi and Jamil Ziyimba, my research associates in Bushenyi, from Tom Mwebesa who interrupted his own vacation to gather information in Bushenyi on specific issues raised by this chapter and later provided useful suggestions on an intermediate draft, and from Ceda Ogada and, particularly, Earnest Wotring, my research assistants at Dartmouth College. Helpful suggestions were also made by members of the Workshop on "Population Growth and Agricultural Change in Sub-Saharan Africa." I also wish to thank the National Research Council of Uganda and the Dartmouth College Research Committee for their support of this project. Any errors are my responsibility.

1. For example, the only data that have been published so far from the 1980 census (COMPED 1982) have been provisional population figures for administrative areas, and these have recently been officially questioned (see population discussion below). Annual agricultural reports are still being published, but the department is about ten years behind. Estimates of cropped area and other agricultural statistics continue to be collected, but haphazardly. A new national agricultural census intended to update the data collected in 1963–64 was postponed for several years and finally published after this chapter was completed (MAAIF 1992). Outside researchers frequently encounter suspicious local and national government officials forced to cope with continuing security problems. Nevertheless, officials just as frequently go out of their way to assist researchers.

2. The zone also extends to the East into neighboring Mbarara District.

3. Interviews were recorded with 149 heads of rural households in 1984 and 1986 in 4 parishes in Buhweju, Igara, Ruhinda, and Sheema counties (Kasfir 1984, 1986). The Buhweju interviews concerned smallholder tea production that is part of another zone and will not be considered here. Discussions focused on the extent of production for subsistence and for the market; other

market connections, largely through the purchase and sale of land and live-stock; the consumption of purchased goods, including food; and the payment of taxes and children's school fees. The interviews emphasized the present situation of the farmer but contained a historical dimension through inquiry into the his-tory of land acquired and crops planted and the pattern by which the first generation in the family entered the monetary economy.

4. Urban land was not excluded but is trivial. Land kept idle to meet fal-low requirements was also not excluded. The exclusion of "permanent" swamps raises difficulties as some swamps are arable and many swamps have been drained since Langlands made his calculations. Assuming that they were in-cluded in his figure for permanent swamps, both factors would increase cultiva-ble area. The impact on population density is problematic, however, as it ultimately depends on how many people have access to each drained swamp. It is not possible to determine how many of the swamps have been drained—nor for that matter how much of the forest reserves has been illegally converted to agricultural use. For the specific calculation of the land uses needed to deter-mine cultivable area for each county in Bushenyi District, see Langlands (1971: 171, 175–77, 179).

5. Muwonge (1978: 176) reports much higher population-density figures for Igara and Sheema counties for 1959, 156/km² each and for 1969, 222 and 226/km² respectively. He says he extracted these figures from the *Report on the 1969 Population Census* (SDMPED 1971; SDPO 1976), but does not give an explanation or a page reference.

6. At the county level the density figures for 1980 are also somewhat over-stated because they make no provision for drainage of swamps and reduction of forest land since Langlands made his calculations. Swamps composed 3.4 per-cent and 5.8 percent of the total land areas of Igara and Sheema counties respec-tively in 1971. Forest below 2,000 m amounted to 2.9 percent of Igara. It is impossible to find out how much either swamps or forest have since shrunk in these counties, but, as discussed below for swamps, the amount has been consid-erable. At the same time the fencing of land (including many drained swamps) for commercial purposes, or just as protection against inflation, has increased population density on unfenced land by a far greater amount.

7. The analysis of the error in the *Background to the Budget 1988–1989* (MPED 1988) is presented only at the district level. Taking 4 percent as the er-ror factor for particular counties is a reasonable inference. It assumes that the age structure, at least for infants, is similar throughout the counties of Bushen-yi. Since virtually no infants were reported for the whole district, the error must have occurred in all counties.

8. This figure excludes swamps and open water but not forest reserves, na-tional parks, or urban areas (MAC 1966: 16–17).

9. There was comparatively little fragmentation of plots in Bushenyi in 1964. The agricultural census (MAC 1966: 29) found that on average there were

only 1.5 blocks per holding regardless of the size of the holding—less than in several other districts. Over 71.7 percent of the holdings were not fragmented at all (MAC 1965: 54). A "block" is an area of claimed land that is not interrupted by someone else's holding or unheld land, regardless of how many plots the owner has created on it.

10. It is not clear when bananas became an important subsistence food for Bairu. Good (1970: 178) suggests that it occurred with the arrival of Ganda agents about 1900, but the evidence he provides is not convincing. By 1920 Roscoe (1923: 100–101) regarded bananas as a characteristic, though not primary, food and source for beer for the Bairu, which suggests that bananas may have been adopted earlier.

11. Local farmers say that agricultural officials in Bushenyi never encouraged them to uproot their coffee (Tom Mwebesa, personal communication, 1988). At the same time, though, Uganda's planners called for replacement of some robusta with "tea, vegetables, dairy cattle and cocoa" (Uganda Government 1966: 65).

12. Even larger crossbred dairy herds up to 300 head were reported in Bushenyi for the early and middle 1970s, but these could not be sustained primarily because of problems of insecurity.

13. A small ox-plowing scheme to nose-punch oxen and train farmers in plowing was initiated by Euro Action ACORD in the Oruchinga Valley in neighboring Mbarara District in 1988.

14. This seems too low, particularly since in two of the villages hired laborers accounted for 13 percent and 26 percent of total hours—and less than 4 percent in all six of the others for which he had data. However, these two villages were among the three containing farms over 4 ha, and thus more likely to employ labor more extensively (Kyeyune-Ssentongo 1985: 21, 49). However, another 8 percent of total labor was contributed from outside the family by "friends or visitors." Some of these may have been paid, others may have been relatives.

15. In this sample, however, there was an average of 1.1 wives per husband (Kyeyune-Ssentongo 1985: 51).

16. Roscoe (1923: 97–98) notes some gender specialization in the production of millet in the early years of the colonial period. A generation later, Oberg (1943: 581) reports a sharp division of labor between commercial crops grown by men (though presumably weeded by women) and food crops grown by women.

17. According to the Bushenyi Agricultural Officer, data on yields have not been collected by government officials since the early 1970s (Jamil Ziyimba, personal communication, 1988).

18. The amount of fallow varied widely from one village to another (Kyeyune-Ssentongo 1985: 21, 22).

19. In seven-eighths of the mixed plots, the other cultigen was bananas (MAC 1966: 69).

20. Mukasa (1970: 140) adds that, in general, the management of banana gardens has "seriously declined" with the development of a cash economy and with interplanting of coffee, sweet potatoes, and cassava.

21. He suggests that "commercial" farmers plan to grow this surplus, whereas "subsistence" farmers merely take advantage of good weather. This distinction fails to grapple successfully with the fact that every farmer is involved in the monetary economy. Kyeyune's notion is an attempt to reconcile the older argument that African farmers grow a "normal" surplus in good years because they follow a famine risk-avoidance strategy (Allan 1965: 38) with the evident reliance on a cash income by every Bushenyi farmer. There are obvious difficulties in using the concept of "subsistence" farmers as one side of a dichotomy concerning the presence of commercial intentions when both groups sell on the market.

22. For example, see Hunt's (1979: 263–64) analysis of Mbere, an extremely poor farming community in Kenya. This is a particularly striking confirmation, because her evidence of the overwhelming importance to farmers of urban-wage remittance swamped her application of Chayanov's argument that number and proportion of family laborers would explain peasant income.

References

Allan, William. 1965. *The African Husbandman.* Edinburgh and London: Oliver and Boyd.

BDG (Bushenyi District Government, Republic of Uganda). 1982. Office of the District Commissioner, Files.

Benner, Christopher. 1988. Commodity Production in Bushenyi. Seminar paper, Dartmouth College, Hanover, N.H.

Butt, J.D., B. Butters, J.W. Dancer, and D.N. McNutt. 1970. "Coffee: Local Aspects." In *Agriculture in Uganda*, 2d ed., ed. J.D. Jameson. London: Oxford University Press.

Clay, Jason. 1984. *Expulsion of the Banyarwanda from Uganda.* Boston: Cultural Survival.

COMPED (Census Office, Ministry of Planning and Economic Development, Republic of Uganda). 1982. *Report on the 1980 Population Census, Vol. I, The Provisional Results by Administrative Areas.* Kampala: Government Printer.

DLS (Department of Lands and Surveys, Uganda Government). 1980. *Guidelines to a New Land Policy.* Mimeo. Kampala.

Doornbos, Martin R. 1970. "Kumanyana and Rwenzururu: Two Responses to Ethnic Inequality." In *Protest and Power in Black Africa*, ed. Robert I. Rotberg and Ali A. Mazrui. New York: Oxford University Press.

_____. 1975. "Land Tenure and Political Conflict in Ankole, Uganda." *Journal of Development Studies* 12(1).

_____. 1977. "Ankole." In *Uganda District Government and Politics 1947–1967*. Madison, University of Wisconsin, African Studies Program and Uganda Institute of Public Administration.

Good, Charles M. 1970. *Rural Markets and Trade in East Africa*. Chicago: University of Chicago, Department of Geography.

Harrop, J. F. 1967. "Soils." *Atlas of Uganda*. 2d ed. Kampala: Department of Lands and Surveys.

Hooper, Edward. 1987. "AIDS in Uganda." *African Affairs* 86(345).

Hunt, Diana. 1979. "Chayanov's Model of Peasant Household Resource Allocation." *Journal of Peasant Studies* 6(3).

Ingram, W. R. 1970. "Pests of Bananas." In *Agriculture in Uganda*, 2d ed., ed. J. D. Jameson. London: Oxford University Press.

Kasfir, Nelson. 1984–86. "Farm Surveys in Bushenyi and Mbarara Districts." Unpublished manuscript in possession of author.

_____. 1986. "Are African Peasants Self-Sufficient?" *Development and Change* 17.

_____. 1988. "Land and Peasants in Western Uganda: Bushenyi and Mbarara Districts." In *Uganda Now: Between Decay and Development*, ed. H. B. Hansen and M. Twaddle. London: James Currey.

Kyeyune-Ssentongo, L. L. 1985. *An Economic Study of the Farming System of Central and South Ankole*. Kampala: Makerere Institute of Social Research.

Langlands, B. W. 1971. *The Population Geography of Ankole District*. Occasional Paper No. 42. Kampala: Makerere University, Department of Geography.

_____. 1974a. *Atlas of Population Census 1969 in Uganda*. Occasional Paper No. 48. Kampala: Makerere University, Department of Geography.

_____. 1974b. "Manpower and Nutritional Energy Resources in Uganda." In *Patterns of Food Crop Production and Nutrition in Uganda*, ed. R. J. Hyde and B. W. Langlands. Occasional Paper No. 58. Kampala: Makerere University, Department of Geography.

_____. 1974c. "Soil Productivity Map of Uganda." In *Soil Productivity and Land Availability Studies for Uganda*, ed. B. W. Langlands. Occasional Paper No. 54. Makerere University, Department of Geography.

_____. 1974d. "Cultivable Land: Cultivable Land/Population Ratios 1959 and 1969." In *Soil Productivity and Land Availability Studies for Uganda*, ed. B. W. Langlands. Occasional Paper No. 54. Kampala: Makerere University, Department of Geography.

Langlands, B. W., and S. K. Mbakyenga. 1974. "Soil Classification by Counties." In *Soil Productivity and Land Availability Studies for Uganda*, ed. B. W. Langlands. Occasional Paper No. 54. Kampala: Makerere University, Department of Geography.

Mackintosh, W. L. S. 1938. *Some Notes on the Abahima and the Cattle Industry of Ankole.* Entebbe: Government Printer.

McMaster, D. N. 1962. *A Subsistence Crop Geography of Uganda.* London: Geographical Publications.

MAC (Ministry of Agriculture and Co-operatives, Uganda Government). 1965. *Report on the Uganda Census of Agriculture.* Vol. I. Entebbe: Government Printer.

———. 1966. *Report on the Uganda Census of Agriculture,* Vol. III. Entebbe: Government Printer.

MAAIF (Ministry of Agriculture, Animal Industry and Fisheries, Uganda Government). 1992. *Report on Uganda National Census of Agriculture and Livestock.* Vols. 1-3. Entebbe: MAAIF.

MPED (Ministry of Planning and Economic Development, Republic of Uganda). 1988. *Background to the Budget, 1988-1989.* Kampala:MPED.

Mukasa, S. K. 1970. "Bananas (*Musa* spp.)." In *Agriculture in Uganda,* 2d ed., ed. J. D. Jameson. London: Oxford University Press.

Muwonge, J. W. 1978. "Population Growth and the Enclosure Movement in Ankole, Uganda." *Eastern Africa Journal of Rural Development* 2(1-2).

Nabudere, D. 1980. *Imperialism and Revolution in Uganda.* Dar es Salaam: Tanzania Publishing House.

Ntozi, J., and G. R. Gasana. 1980. The Provisional Results of the Uganda Population Census 1980: An Explanation of the Growth Rates. Paper delivered at the Workshop on Development of an Integrated Statistical System for a Developing Country, location not given.

Oberg, Kalervo. 1943. "A Comparison of Three Systems of Primitive Economic Organization." *American Anthropologist* New Series 45(40).

Pingali, Prabhu, Yves Bigot, and Hans P. Binswanger. 1987. *Agricultural Mechanization and the Evolution of Farming Systems in Sub-Saharan Africa.* Baltimore, Md.: Johns Hopkins University Press.

PUMAFC (Planning Unit of the Ministry of Agriculture, Forestry and Cooperatives, Republic of Uganda). 1972. The Agricultural Zones of Kigezi, Ankole, Bunyoro, and Toro, and Their Potential for Development. Mimeo. Entebbe.

Roscoe, John. 1923. *The Banyankole.* Cambridge: Cambridge University Press.

Ruthenberg, Hans. 1968. "Some Characteristics of Smallholding Farming in Tanzania." In *Smallholder Farming and Smallholder Development in Tanzania,* ed. H. Ruthenberg. Munich: Weltforum Verlag.

Saul, John, and Roger Woods. 1981. "African Peasantries." In *Political Economy of Africa,* ed. Dennis L. Cohen and John Daniel. London: Longman.

SBMEA (Statistics Branch, Ministry of Economic Affairs, Uganda Protectorate). 1961. *Uganda Census 1959: African Population.* Entebbe:SBMEA.

SDMPED (Statistics Division, Ministry of Planning and Economic Development, Republic of Uganda). 1971. *Report on the 1969 Population Census. Vol. I: The Population of Administrative Areas.* Entebbe: Government Printer.

SDPO (Statistics Division, President's Office, Republic of Uganda). 1976. *Report on the 1969 Population Census. Vol. IV: The Analytical Report.* Entebbe: Government Printer.

Taylor, Brian K. 1969. "The Western Lacustrine Bantu (Nyoro, Toro, Nyankore, Kiga, Haya, and Zinaz, with sections on the Amba and Konjo)." In *East Central Africa. Part 13. Ethnographic Survey of Africa*, ed. Daryll Forde. London: International African Institute.

Thomas, D.G. 1970. "Finger Millet (Eleusine coracana [L.] Gaertn.)." In *Agriculture in Uganda*, 2d ed., ed. J.D. Jameson. London: Oxford University Press.

Turner B.L. II, and Stephen B. Brush. 1987. "Purpose, Classification and Organization." In *Comparative Farming Systems*, ed. B.L. Turner II and S.B. Brush. New York: Guildford Press.

————, and William E. Doolittle. 1978. "The Concept and Measure of Agricultural Intensity." *The Professional Geographer* 30(3).

Uchendu, Victor C., and Kenneth R.M. Anthony. 1975. *Agricultural Change in Teso District, Uganda.* Nairobi: East African Literature Bureau.

Uganda Government. 1966. *Work for Progress: Uganda's Second Five-Year Plan, 1966–1971.* Entebbe: Government Printer.

————. 1967. *Report of the Committee of Inquiry into the Coffee Industry*, Entebbe: Government Printer.

Williams, F. Lukyn. 1934. "Blood-brotherhood in Ankole (Omukago)." *Uganda Journal* 2(1).

————. 1936. "Sowing and Harvesting in Ankole." *Uganda Journal* 3(3).

3 / Increasing Variability in Agricultural Production: Meru District, Kenya, in the Twentieth Century

F. E. Bernard

Kenya's current rate of population growth, 3.7 percent per year, is one of Africa's and the world's highest (Population Reference Bureau 1987). At this rate of growth, Kenya's national population of 26.2 million will expand to almost 45 million by the year 2000 (Population Reference Bureau 1992). Although rural-to-urban migration is causing Kenya's towns and cities to grow at twice the rate of natural increase, about 85 percent of its people are still rural (Kenya 1986a). Only 17 percent of rural Kenya is of medium or high agricultural potential.[1] Population densities and population pressure on this small island of good land, primarily in the highlands east and west of the Rift valley, have been building rapidly over the past generation, now reaching several hundred persons per square kilometer—some of the highest rural densities in Africa. Technological and structural innovations and periodic intensification have also characterized agricultural change in this region over the past forty years.

Among the most pressured regions in this island of heavy density are the nine districts of the Eastern and Central Provinces (fig. 3.1) clustered around Mount Kenya. Population-land relationships here are high (table 3.1). Raw densities in the region range from 29 persons/km² in vast and mostly semi-arid Kitui, which has a low capacity to support rain-fed agriculture, to the high-potential Kikuyu districts of Nyeri, Murang'a, Kirinyaga, and Kiambu, all with raw densities of over 200 persons/km². Parts of Kiambu District, which is at Nairobi's doorstep, possess rural densities in the 600 to 1,100 persons/km² range (Kenya 1981).

Physiologic densities, perhaps a more realistic measure, surpass the 200 persons/km² mark, with the exception of Nyandarua, yielding average amounts of land per person significantly below Kenya's estimated

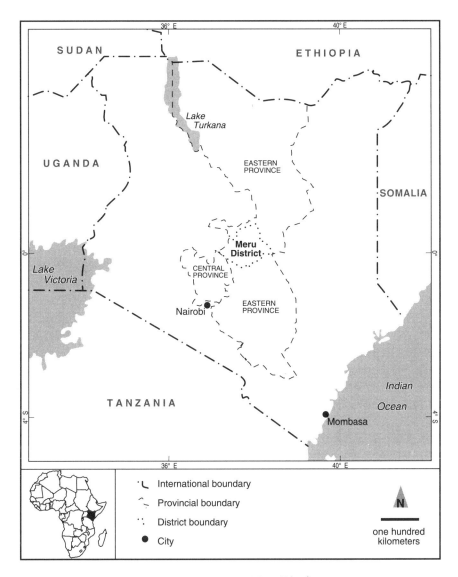

Fig. 3.1. Kenya and Meru District

1988 average of 0.49 ha.[2] With a raw overall density of 188 persons/km[2] and a physiologic density of 428 persons/km[2], Meru District is in the "less-dense" half of the entries in the table. This is a relative position in a densely packed subset. The internal structure and processes of change in Meru have created immense population pressure in medium-and high-

Table 3.1. Population and Land in Eastern and Central Kenya

District	1988 pop. (est.) (000)	Total area (km²)	High and medium potential land (km²)	High and medium potential land (% of total)	Density		High and medium potential per person
					Raw (persons/km²)	Physiologic (persons/km²)	
Kiambu	1,012.4	1,935	1,248	64.5	523	811	0.12
Murang'a	960.1	2,216	1,808	81.6	433	531	0.19
Embu	394.8	2,562	748	29.2	154	528	0.19
Kirinyaga	416.1	1,127	946	83.9	369	440	0.23
Nyeri	685.9	3,284	1,600	48.7	209	429	0.23
Meru	1,214.0	6,446	2,837	44.0	188	428	0.23
Machakos	1,522.5	13,115	3,969	30.3	116	384	0.26
Kitui	670.5	22,803	2,922	12.8	29	230	0.44
Nyandarua	330.1	3,528	2,650	75.1	94	125	0.80

Sources: Kenya, 1985, p. 96; Kenya, 1983, pp. 35, 38, 41, 65, 74, 80, 83, 89, 128; Jaetzold and Schmidt, 1983a, 1983b.

potential regions, and population pressures with accompanying environmental degradation are now also problems in lower-potential, low-lying areas. In spite of these pressures, average agricultural output for the district as a whole does seem not to be steadily declining, although it is perhaps less reliable, more variable.

A unifying characteristic of these central and eastern Kenya districts is a floodtide of rural-to-rural migration. As population densities and pressure build on the relatively small areas of medium- and high-potential land, rural migrants are being forced out of the highlands into marginal arid and semiarid regions to the east and south. Local systems of production in these areas seem unable to cope with this pace of immigration. As migrants from the highlands flow down the ecological and altitudinal gradient, they find their agricultural systems ill adapted to the drylands. Food production often falls below demand. Deforestation, overgrazing, and soil mining also are leading to environmental degradation. As these processes accelerate, land becomes the criterion of wealth. Land shortages in the uplands spur a real estate market. This generates further downslope migration, causing land competition to slide down the gradient. Agricultural change comes slowly to this degrading landscape. The government cannot respond adequately to the needs of either indigenous agropastoralists or recent migrants now caught in a whirlwind of change. As more and more people are drawn into this process of marginalization, both human and environmental problems loom large.

In this paper I attempt to assess the interrelationships between demographic change and agricultural change in Meru District during the period from the 1930s to the 1980s. Meru District has a distinctive story to tell. Yet it is representative of the larger region's experience with population growth and agricultural change. The analysis of Meru, based partly on a synthesis of published materials and partly on unpublished survey data collected in 1986, proceeds along several pathways: (1) a brief description of the quality of the Meru environment and the differences between highlands and lowlands; (2) an examination of traditional interpretations and use of the physical environments; (3) a brief historical and geographical look at colonial interventions in the traditional population-resource system and the role of the colonial agricultural establishment in the introduction of market-based agriculture and other induced agricultural technology and structure; (4) local responses to agricultural change under rising levels of population pressure; and (5) the current population-resource–agricultural change dynamic. Finally, in a concluding section,

I try to reflect upon the primary question of this volume: have the pressures of population in this densely settled area of Kenya led to agricultural intensification, environmental degradation, or agricultural involution?

The Quality of the Physical Environment for Agriculture

Ecologically complex, Meru is a diverse district stretching from the slopes of Mount Kenya and the Nyambeni Range northward to the vast arid "northern frontier" region and southeast to the low Eastern Plateau Forelands (fig. 3.2). Virtually every interior ecological zone in Kenya may be found in Meru, from tropical alpine meadows on Mount Kenya to arid and semiarid ranching zones at the Tana (or Thana) River (Appendix 3.A). The upper-altitude ecological zones for the past fifty years have been heavily settled and affected by agricultural change. They are also the zones of highest agricultural potential. In Meru, as in most parts of central and eastern Kenya, however, it is difficult to exclude completely the low-lying, lower-potential arid and semiarid areas to the east and south, which traditionally have been underdeveloped. These areas are now an important part of the Meru population pressure picture because they have increasingly become the destination for downslope migration from highland areas (Bernard, Campbell, and Thom 1989). As they have filled with people, they have not only become loci of population-resource problems but have also become dependent upon highland agricultural production in times of drought and famine (Bernard 1985; Deitz 1985; Ferguson 1985).

Mount Kenya (5,193 m) and the Nyambeni Range (2,500 m) are the dominant physiographic features of Meru District. They are products of explosive Tertiary volcanism that also extruded a vast thickness of lava eastward over the Basement Complex surface. Ashes and olivine basalts underlie the soils of the mountains and foothills. Soils of variable fertility in the high altitudes give way downslope to deep, fertile, well-drained loams (nitosols, andosols, and cambisols) that are among Kenya's (and indeed Africa's) most fertile and durable (Ominde 1984: 3). These volcanically based loams in turn become sandy clays and sandy clay loams (cambisols, lithosols, and regosols) on the ancient erosional surfaces east of the mountain massifs.

Climatically, Meru receives rainfall in both rainy seasons. Aligned roughly perpendicular to the prevailing easterly winds, the slopes of

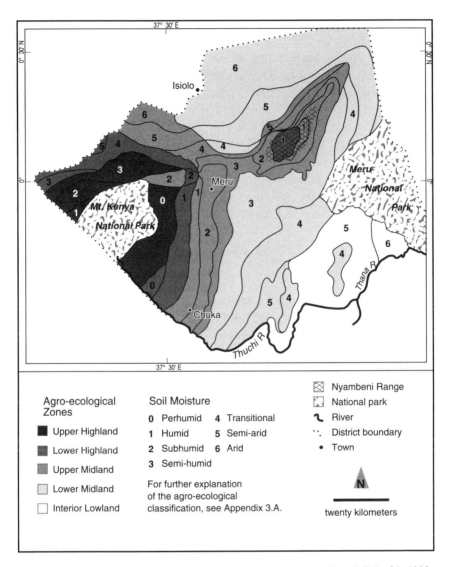

Fig. 3.2. Meru District: agro-ecological zones. Source: Jaetzold and Schmidt 1983.

Mount Kenya and the Nyambeni Range receive enough rainfall for a diverse agricultural economy: Meru Town annually receives an average of 1,403 mm (1,151 mm; 60 percent probability level); Chuka 1,500 mm (1,190 mm); and Muchiimukuru Tea Estate in the Nyambeni Range 2,525 mm (2,046 mm). Most highland and upper-midland ecozones receive slightly more rainfall in the so-called short rains of October to December.

Rainfall in the lower altitudes not only diminishes in amount but also falls less predictably. The lowlands and the Mount Kenya rainshadow area are markedly drier: Tharaka Chief's camp in the eastern lowlands receives only 787 mm (579 mm); Timau Marania, north of Mount Kenya, can expect just 884 mm (741 mm). Agropastoral systems in these zones are at greater risk of crop failure and must depend more upon livestock for subsistence. North of Mount Kenya and northwest of the Nyambeni Range, because of the rainshadow effect, rainfall is sporadic and less than one would expect. Agro-ecological zones sufficient primarily for ranching and livestock activities prevail at high altitudes (1500–2,100 m).

This combination of topography, soils, and climate yields a complex series of ecozones (fig. 3.2). Highland zones (UH and LH—Upper Highland and Lower Highland), once covered by podocarpus and bamboo forests, are now high potential agricultural areas for pyrethrum, wheat, potatoes, vegetables, dairying, and tea cultivation.[3] Upper midland zones (UM), formerly moist montane evergreen forest, possess superb agricultural potential for coffee and tea cultivation, a variety of vegetables and fruits, and livestock activities. In the lower midland zones (LM), an area formerly of mixed deciduous and evergreen forest and savanna, maize, sorghum, millet, and cotton are productively grown. In the lowlands (IL) beyond the mountains, thin soils and low, unreliable amounts of rainfall limit agricultural activities to high-risk cultivation of millet, grams, and cassava and to low-density livestock keeping. This zonal pattern, corresponding closely with altitude, represents the classic ecological gradient of central and eastern Kenya, with narrow ecological zones in the hills and mountains grading eastward toward broad expanses of arid and semiarid plateau forelands (400–1,000 m elevation).

Eastern and southeastern Meru, known today as Tharaka, are part of this foreland region. They comprise dissected erosional plains and massifs of the ancient Precambrian Basement system of rocks. Here soils of moderate to low fertility are highly erosive and subject to rapid deterioration under continuous cultivation and grazing. Soils in the bottomlands have developed on infill from undifferentiated volcanic rocks upslope. Though these areas are limited, they are of much higher fertility. With irrigation, they have moderate to high agricultural potential, potential which today is largely untapped.

Traditional Population-Resource Relationships
and Production Systems

The people known as Meru include a cluster of ethnic subgroups of northern Meru District (Igembe, Tigania, Imenti, Igoji, Mwimbi, Miutuni, and Muthambi), as well as Tharaka and Chuka, who are linguistically and historically distinctive (Kenya 1986b). The northern Meru probably arrived at the foothills of Mount Kenya and the Nyambeni Range by the mid-eighteenth century. The Tharaka and Chuka are likely to have preceded them (Ochieng 1975). The Meru, Tharaka, and Chuka apparently displaced an ancient aboriginal hunting and gathering people, remembered by the Meru as Athi (Kenya 1986b: 50–59). As the upland Meru settled the forested ridges of the mountains, they evolved a permanent agropastoral system capable of sustainably supporting several hundred thousand people by the beginning of the twentieth century.

The Highlands

Meru's mountainous setting became the foundation for an interesting permanent agricultural system. Zonation of soils and vegetation, subtle mountain climates, soil catenas, ridge and valley juxtaposition, and disease ecology were all parts of a complex ecological web. The Meru understood subtleties in their mountain setting. Their system of land use, cropping patterns, livestock activities, and other aspects of natural resource exploitation was based on this understanding. The Mount Kenya Meru seem to have taken advantage of ecological gradients; the Nyambeni Meru probably depended upon a similar though not as clearly zonal system (Bernard 1972: 50–59).

The middle altitudes (about 1,220–1,700 m) were utilized for permanent settlement and cultivation of perennial cultivars. Roots and fruits such as bananas, yams, sweet potatoes, cassava, taro, and sugarcane were important in the traditional food system of highland Meru. Although none of these cultivars occupied vast hectarage, all were commonly cultivated in the highland system to bridge seasonal food shortages, to offset famines, and generally to reduce subsistence risks. In addition to the deep volcanic loams, environmental elements of prime importance here were reliable amounts of rainfall twice per year, fast-flowing streams carrying Mount Kenya rainfall and snowmelt, and the absence of malaria and sleeping sickness. Conditions were ideal for long-term habitation and agriculture.

From the forests, the Meru exploited wild plants for medicines, hunting poisons, food, and ritual. Here they also hunted, kept semi-domesticated bees, and collected firewood and construction timber. They apparently recognized the restorative role of the forest, both ecologically and spiritually (Bernard 1972). Through ritual and traditional law, the Meru protected trees, even in the vicinity of fields and homesteads. All trees were communal property. Permission from a council of elders representing the community was necessary before trees could be cut. This ethic of protection produced a landscape, even in the closely settled zones, covered by a much denser canopy than elsewhere in Kenya (Laughton 1944).

Conservation of forests, soils, and water resources was part of the traditional ethic of permanent occupancy. Conservation seems to have contributed to sustainability in the agricultural system. Stone terraces, trash lines in fields, application of manure on some fields, protection of trees and forests, and small water diversions were observed in early colonial times, though not all in the same place or at the same time. Over the long term, these methods of local resource management, together with large amounts of "empty" land for grazing and bush fallowing off the mountain slopes, enabled rather dense settlement for precolonial Africa. Population of the highlands, excluding Chuka, was estimated to be about 200,000 in 1912 (MDC 1912–13: 23), which would have led to densities in the middle homestead zone of about 130 persons/km^2.

The Meru largely avoided the upper and lower reaches of the mountain slopes for permanent settlement. The zone above about 1,700 m was perceived as being too cold and misty for comfortable living and for cultivation of food crops. The banana, a staple food of traditional Meru, could not survive either the soil or temperature conditions of the upper highlands. But higher ground provided natural pasture for livestock, and the forests yielded products such as honey and timber for families settled below.

Lower zones, below about 1,200 m, were not permanently settled because of unreliable rainfall, higher temperatures, malaria, and sleeping sickness. Wild animals and extensive areas of swampland further impeded permanent habitation. This lower zone, however, was crucially important as a "grain basket" for Meru. Under a system of land-rotation cultivation, annual cultigens such as maize, millet, sorghum, and pulses were grown. When the first European travelers observed these land-scapes, they saw extensive fields of grain in a vast parklike setting—a wooded savanna under bush fallowing (Chanler 1896; Arkell-Hardwick 1903). Both the soils and climate make these areas (LM) productive under a low-intensity system of shifting cultivation (R = 33 or less)[4]— how productive, it is impossible to say, except that in extraordinarily dry years famine was uncommon in Meru (Fadiman 1982). The human role in altering these landscapes was pervasive even though few people were permanent residents in the zone. The essence of life here was not that the region lacked occupants but that it served a special niche in the Meru agro-ecosystem.

Though animal husbandry was an integral part of traditional agri-culture in Meru, products from the field made up the greater part of the diet. Nonetheless, Meru cattle, sheep, and goats were culturally and nu-tritionally significant. Livestock were not raised expressly for meat, but ceremony and ritual occasion provided ample opportunity for meat con-sumption, especially of sheep and goats. Milk was an important part of the diet of mothers and children.

The role of livestock cannot be overestimated in the cultural ecology of Meru. For enhancement of grazing areas, vast regions of the district were burned semi-annually, creating grasslands from savannas. By this process the lava plains in northern Meru were extensively opened. Throughout the highlands small communal pastures and cattle trails linked together the agricultural and livestock systems. In both farming and grazing areas, livestock enclosures were focal points of settlements.

Work in the highland system was shared according to age, sex, and, in some instances, clan (Kenya 1986b: 38). Clearing land and rough cul-tivation were men's jobs, assisted occasionally by uncircumcised boys. Women and young girls sowed seeds, weeded, harvested, and stored the crop. Young uncircumcised boys were responsible for guarding crops from birds and other pests. Stock herding traditionally was the job of young boys, supervised by elderly men. Circumcised young men and warriors were chiefly responsible for taking livestock to distant grazing areas and for the society's security.

The Lowlands

On the plains, at the lower end of the ecological gradient, the Tharaka practiced a markedly different form of agriculture. Barren soils and semiarid and arid climatic conditions precluded many food crops known upslope. No zonal distinctions were made in this area of greater environmental uniformity, but local features of the environment, such as bottomland to interfluve soil variations, were recognized. Mobility in this dry country was a key to survival. Semipermanent settlement near an exotic stream became the focal point for a long fallow system of shifting cultivation (four years of cultivation followed by fifteen or more of fallow; R = about 5) with an overlay of pastoral activities and hunting (Bernard 1972: 65).[5] Drought-resistant sorghum, millet, and cassava were the mainstays of the economy, but crop failure was an ever-present risk. Risk adjustments such as catch cropping, field dispersal, hunting and gathering, trade in foodstuffs and honey, and reliance on sheep and goats all enabled successful existence at low densities in a harsh part of Kenya (Porter 1979).[6] In the early part of the colonial period Tharaka population was estimated to be about 12,000, scattered over the region at a density of less than 10 persons/km².

With the exception of hunting and beekeeping, which were important activities of Tharaka men, labor division in the lowlands was similar to that of highland Meru.

Population, Resources, and Agricultural Change in the Highlands: 1930s–1950s

The colonial period set in motion far-reaching changes in the highland agricultural system and forever altered the relationships between population and land. Initially, the imposition of colonial rule in the early twentieth century in Meru had little or no impact. The British believed the encirclement of Mount Kenya to be politically expedient but then neglected the eastern side of the mountain (Bernard 1979). As the colonial spatial economy took shape, Meru became more and more divorced from emerging nodes of the colony. Poor roads and bridges interrupted communication with Nairobi. White-settler land alienation north of Mount Kenya (Timau and Nanyuki) hindered local development. Meru languished in the shadow of the White Highlands and responded slowly to colonial economic, social, and political impulses. By virtue of its remoteness and position on the "wrong side" of Mount Kenya, compared to the Kikuyu-occupied districts, Meru was initially underdeveloped.

Slowly, political-economic change filtered into Meru. By the 1930s taxation had forced the Meru toward market participation and had encouraged missionaries and agricultural officers to introduce cash-earning opportunities to the highland agricultural system. The colonial policy of dual development led to modest investments in African-occupied areas (Cone and Lipscomb 1972). Families living close to missions, those co-opted by colonial agricultural officers as better farmers, and those who participated in the British system of indirect rule gained special access to land, to education, to new technology for the farm and herd, and ultimately, to wealth. They became the forerunners of a class of advantaged rural people who later led the district as early adopters of new food crops (improved maize, white potatoes, improved beans, vegetables, citrus fruits), cash crops (cotton and coffee), and dairying. Overwhelmingly, they were located in the highlands within a few miles of one of the Christian missions. These people, primarily in the homestead zone, also had greatest access to structural changes gradually brought by both missionaries and the colonial government: education and extension services, an emerging system of roads and bridges, processing and marketing facilities, cooperatives, and, later, credit. People located away from the homestead zone became marginal in both the political-economic and cultural-ecologic senses.

In the 1930s and 1940s, colonial officials began to notice that the highland peoples were becoming more and more densely crowded in the middle altitudes. In the area near Meru Town, a typical farm consisted of six fragments scattered over a distance of six or seven kilometers and consisting of less than one hectare (MDC 1944: 35). The introduction of scientific medicine and health care and the provision of famine relief food contributed to falling death rates (especially among infants and children) and hastened recovery from smallpox and other diseases that had ravaged human populations at the turn of the century (van Zwanenberg and King 1975). Both Protestant and Catholic missionaries contributed to a breakdown in the use of traditional birth control methods (Greeley 1975). By the early 1950s population pressure along the slopes of Mount Kenya and parts of the Nyambeni Range had become a common theme in colonial reports (Bernard 1972). In the colonial lexicon, population pressure meant occasional shortages of food and increasing levels of soil erosion.

The first official census of population took place in 1948. At that time Meru had 315,000 people, of whom about 290,000 were in the highlands distributed at an average density of about 90 persons/km^2 (table 3.2). Concentrations of this magnitude were compounded by a breakdown of the traditional communal system of inheritance and by colonial and traditional barriers to permanent settlement of "empty" areas of the district (Homan 1963). By 1962, Meru had grown to almost half a million (average density of 63 persons/km²), and by 1969, almost 600,000 people lived in Meru District at an overall density of 80 persons/km². The intercensal annual growth rate during the 1950s was about 2.5 percent; during the 1960s population grew at a rate of 3.5 percent per year.

As population grew, more and more families sought productive land. Increasing fragmentation of holdings, in combination with the gradient system of land use, made the agricultural system more and more frustrating and inefficient, especially for women who had to travel miles between ever smaller plots still widely distributed up and down mountain slopes. This required progressively higher inputs of labor per unit of cultivated land and per unit of output and created serious bottlenecks at planting, weeding, and harvest times (Clayton 1964; Sillitoe 1962). As a higher proportion of children attended school, farmwork became more and more the exclusive responsibility of women, creating still further pressures. In several areas around Meru Town, farms were so small that families were unable to subsist (MDC 1949; Homan 1963). Traditional checks on soil depletion were abandoned. Fallow periods in the annual crop fields decreased. Women were forced to cultivate lower-zone fields at least annually. In other words, the frequency of cultivation (R-value) in the first few decades of the century increased from 33 to at least 100.

In this process, trees were cut at unprecedented rates, both for local firewood and construction and for the emerging commercial lumber industry (Reilly 1987). In the 1940s and 1950s, the Meru highland agricultural system was experiencing population pressure leading to land degradation and some degree of involution. The agricultural system could not respond spontaneously, and colonially induced agricultural change had, in some ways, made the situation worse.

The government understood some of these problems and tried to introduce cultigens for famine relief and to promote soil-conservation practices. Several supplementary highland plants were promoted in times of famine. Improved varieties of cassava and sweet potatoes were given especially wide distribution during droughts and locust infestations of the 1930s. As part of a colonywide program in the 1930s and 1940s to combat land degradation in African-occupied areas, the colo-

Table 3.2. Population Growth in Meru, 1948–88

Year	Total population	Percent change	Growth rate	Density (persons/km²) Raw	Physiologic[a]
1948	315,000			43	?
		49.0	2.5(?)		
1962	469,453			63	?
		27.1	3.5		
1969	596,506			80	178
		39.2	3.5		
1979	830,179			111	247
		24.4	3.4		
1988 (est.)	1,032,708			188	428

[a]Medium- and high-potential land as specified in Kenya, 1986c, p. 91.
Other Sources: Ominde, 1968; Kenya, 1970, 1981.

nial administration in Meru attempted to introduce farming practices to maintain soil structure and fertility and to implement techniques to prevent erosion (Clayton 1964: 14–16; Bernard 1979). Most of these measures, such as contour planting, using live wash stops, grazing controls, and reforestation, were failures. Apparently they did not build adequately upon the traditional system. In one instance in Igoji, overt protests against enforced conservation measures forced an abrupt termination of the program (MDC 1949).

Meru's overcrowding at this time was not hopeless. Unlike the Kikuyu-occupied areas, Meru District in 1950 still contained large unsettled areas. One writer claimed that 70 percent of land of arable potential in the Meru highlands was not intensively used (Sillitoe 1962). Much of this land was in the upper and lower tiers of the gradient system. Malaria, sleeping sickness, tsetse infestation, cool temperatures, and inadequate surface water had long been barriers to permanent settlement of these areas. Removal of some of these impediments would open thousands of hectares of good land for Meru families. In the midst of the Mau Mau insurgency, the colonial government proposed that land clearance, new methods of animal husbandry, new crops, structural reform, and water development would make these areas habitable.

A program of resettlement based on freehold tenure and coupled with land adjudication and consolidation of holdings in the middle altitudes would relieve population pressure and create economically viable farms (Kenya 1954; MDAO 1956). From the mid-1950s, resettlement continued to be the solution to involution in the agricultural system and environmental degradation. Resettlement schemes planned and implemented in the 1950s and 1960s enabled some 10,000 families to occupy about 40,000 hectares in various parts of the district. Meanwhile, land consolidation of millions of hectares in the traditionally occupied parts of the highlands began in the early 1960s and continues to the present.

Agricultural Change in the Highlands: 1954–1970s

Resettlement and land consolidation became foundations for a radically different kind of agriculture. With a freehold system of land tenure, no longer was it possible for each family to spread risks over several ecologic zones. Instead each family became fixed to a single plot with a more limited set of potentials. The goal of subsistence plus a modest cash income from the farm, a cornerstone of rural development planning in Kenya since 1954, was not everywhere feasible under these conditions, especially where populations were dense and farms were small. This became the case throughout the highlands of Meru. All farmers cannot grow the food crops they require because different ecologic zones favor different agricultural pursuits. The traditional system was adjusted to this reality, but consolidation and enclosure made use of the entire gradient impossible. Regional exchanges of food, a necessary corollary of land reform in this setting, have not always been possible.

Widespread introduction and diffusion of cash crops has further contributed to a breakdown of the gradient system. Coffee was introduced to Meru in 1935. It was initially limited to a few experimental plots near mission stations because white coffee farmers feared competition from the African reserves (van Zwanenberg and King 1975). After the mid-1950s the agricultural department allowed African farmers to participate more fully in the cash-crop economy. African cultivation of coffee in Meru expanded dramatically in the very regions most densely populated, the former homestead zone of the traditional highland system (Bernard 1972). By 1960, Meru farmers had planted almost 3,700 hectares of coffee trees; by the early 1970s, 12,000 hectares were in coffee. Today, Meru is one of Kenya's leading coffee districts with more than 100,000 growers cultivating 34,500 hectares in coffee. Production in 1986 was about 56,000 tons of cherry, which led to gross payments equivalent to about $5 million.

Tea was introduced to upper midland and highland zones in the

1960s (fig. 3.3). Hectarage has grown from about 1,000 in the mid-1960s to 7,000 in 1986. There are now 18,123 growers producing 28.2 million kilograms of green leaf tea, which earned a gross payout equivalent to about $900,000 in 1986. Cotton, the only other cash crop of significance, is grown in the more sparsely populated lower midland zones. With production peaking in 1984 at almost 4 million kilograms (22,000 ha), cotton production has recently declined. In 1986 there were 8,270 ha in cotton; output was 2.9 million kilograms, which earned gross payouts equivalent to about $41,000.

Cash crops have brought in tax revenues and a substantial flow of capital for infrastructural development and reinvestment in Meru's agricultural economy. In savings and capital formation, Meru is often cited as a success story. However, coffee and other permanent cash crops have also made farmers vulnerable to world market fluctuations as well as union and cooperative inefficiencies and corruption. Coffee farmers in particular have become increasingly reliant on fossil fuel–based technology (especially upon fertilizer and pesticides) and have seen their payouts fluctuate widely with oil prices. Cotton has been subjected to similar market uncertainties and to pesticide and fertilizer dependence. Tea

Fig. 3.3.   Tea production in highland Meru

farming, on the other hand, has generally created less dependency, and tea processing and marketing have been more efficiently managed. Beyond these vulnerabilities, even as early as the 1960s, cash crops had begun to contribute to land pressures in the upper and middle zones of the district by competing for space formerly given to pastures, homesteads, and food crops. The average farm size in the densely populated coffee zone by the late 1960s was just under one hectare (Bernard 1968).

Another agricultural change of importance in the postwar period was broadscale transformation of the staple food economy. Displacement of bulrush millet by maize was the most notable change. Maize increasingly became the primary staple of the highlands. That this happened in Meru is not surprising, for the same process was occurring throughout Kenya (O'Connor 1966; Brown 1968). The popularity of maize, especially in the expanding urban market, undoubtedly stimulated its diffusion throughout highland Meru. As new higher-yielding varieties were introduced by the government in the 1960s, maize became even more dominant (Bernard 1972: 132). By 1976, more than 60 percent of the maize crop was grown from hybrid seeds. In 1982, surveys in the highlands found 75 to 95 percent of the respondents using improved maize seed (Jaetzold and Schmidt 1983b: 124–26). This induced agricultural change, warmly embraced by local farmers, more than any other, enabled Meru District to feed itself in all but the driest years, despite rapidly growing population and ever-increasing densities.

Other changes in the food economy, primarily in postwar times, include adoption of white potatoes and cabbage as staple crops in the upper altitudes and diffusion of haricot beans (again using hybrid or improved seeds) throughout highland Meru as a replacement for traditional pulses (grams, black beans, cowpeas, pigeon peas). Certain minor subsidiary cultigens also became more important elements in the diet. Improved varieties of cassava and sweet potatoes, for example, continued to be distributed by the government during the 1950s and 1960s. Bananas, though losing out to coffee in the middle altitudes, spread to new regions in settlement schemes above and below the midland zones. Sugarcane continued to be important for local brew, and yams maintained their importance in the Nyambeni Range and southern Meru as a starch supplement in highland diets.

Introduced fruits and vegetables have similarly become important to highland Meru diets and in local market activity. Carrots, tomatoes, avocado, eggplant, onions, kale, chili peppers, cabbage, green peas, citrus fruits, guavas, passion fruit, mangoes, papayas, pineapples, and deciduous fruits (especially pears and plums) are all commonly found in local markets. Few of these were grown in Meru fifty years ago. Brought into Meru during the colonial and early independence periods, these crops are now exceedingly important dietary and local commercial horticultural elements. They are perhaps evidence of a trend toward intensification of agriculture, especially when grown in locally irrigated situations and tended carefully by using manure and fertilizers. Yet these and many other agricultural changes described here were not spontaneous, indigenous developments; they were largely programmatic inducements by the government intended to bring rural Meru people into the marketplace to raise revenues for schools, hospitals, and other kinds of development.

As human populations continued to climb through the 1960s and 1970s, and as programs of land tenure took hold, land devoted exclusively to livestock began to shrink. Some pastures were transformed into cash-crop plots; others, out of necessity, were given over to food crops. Some 30,000 livestock were still taken to the northern grazing area (the lava plains northwest of the Nyambeni Range) in the late 1960s, 20,000 in the late 1970s. But in the highlands cattle, sheep, and goats were becoming increasingly peripheral to the agricultural system. Each homestead could keep only one or two heads of livestock. These would be tethered and stall-fed fodder grasses grown on site.

A major exception to de-emphasis of livestock in highland Meru has been introduction of grade dairy cattle, especially to the former upland (UH and LH) zones of the traditional system. About 10,000 dairy cows of various European breeds grazed limited pastures in these zones in 1968. By 1986 the herd of grade dairy cattle had increased to 77,000, of which all but 4,000 were on Mount Kenya (MDAO 1986). These animals depend primarily upon fodder crops (Launonen et al. 1985). Although the number of dairy cattle has increased substantially, the dairy industry is struggling. Price structures, cooperative inefficiencies, and marketing problems have all diminished the economic potential of dairying in the upper zones of Meru (Launonen et al. 1985). Here too, in the livestock economy, there is ample evidence that the pressure of population is forcing intensification of the system through adoption of better-yielding animals and incorporation of a system of stall feeding. The Ministry of Agriculture campaign to promote "zero grazing" is the current expression of this need to intensify.

Population Resources and Agricultural Change in the Lowlands, 1930s–1970s

The least-altered region of Meru over the past five decades has been Tharaka, the vast and sparsely populated eastern lowlands. This area remained at the periphery of the colonial spatial economy of Meru District, which until recently was marginal to Kenya's major nodes of development (Bernard 1979). The British focused inordinate attention on the midland and upland zones in Meru. European missionaries and administrators preferred cool, malaria-free places to conduct their experiments with social and agricultural change. The highland and lowland systems, always substantially different, became more so in colonial times.

The lowlands received little attention in cash-crop or livestock development, no land-tenure reform, and few direct or indirect benefits of the education and health care facilities located mainly in the highlands. The lowlands seem to have been made even more marginal by colonial decision and indecision. The Tharaka, at the foot of the mountains, were also inadvertently the last to experience agricultural change. If Meru District as a whole was comparatively underdeveloped in colonial and early independence times, Tharaka was virtually neglected.

Population, Agriculture, and Resources in the 1980s

Meru District population has soared to over a million rural inhabitants who now occupy the land at an average density of 188 persons/km², with a physiologic density of over 400 persons/km². Growth continues, apparently unabated. The Central Bureau of Statistics estimates an annual growth rate for Meru of 3.91 percent per annum for the decades 1980–2000 (Kenya 1983). This will lead to a population of 1.6–1.7 million by the turn of the century.

The coffee and tea zones have become extremely crowded (table 3.3). Estimated population densities in 1988 for selected highland locations range from 148 persons/km² and 173 persons/km², respectively, in Kiirua and Kibirichia settlement schemes to over 500 persons/km² in the coffee zone location of Upper Abothoguchi (near Meru Town) and in Akithii near the Nyambeni Range. At these densities, the amount of agricultural land per person in almost all highland locations has fallen

Table 3.3. Population Densities of Selected Meru Locations

| | Highlands (all densities persons per square kilometer) | | | | | |
| | | | | 1988 (est.) | | Agricultural |
Location	1962	1969	1979	Raw	Physiologic[a]	land per person
Njia	104	—	—	292	369	0.27
Muthara	57	183	220	303	401	0.25
Kianjai	69	211	205	281	397	0.25
Akithii	74	287	367	501	588	0.17
Upper Abothoguchi	90	289	396	544	649	0.15
Kiirua[b]	26	—	108	148	170	0.59
Kibirichia[b]	21	—	125	173	198	0.50
Nkuene	58	257	303	415	501	0.20
Abogeta	—	171	229	315	378	0.27
Igoji	47	162	257	353	425	0.23
Mwimbi/Chogoria	49	146	390	541	664	0.15
Muthambi	47	173	272	377	449	0.22
Karingani	44	124	215	294	359	0.28
Magumoni	28	139	192	262	316	0.20

| | Lowlands (raw densities in persons per square kilometer) | | | |
Location	1962	1969	1979	1988
S. Tharaka	13	40	46	81
N. Tharaka	5	15	21	33

Sources: Ominde, 1968, pp. 100–101; Kenya, 1970, 1981.
[a]Persons per square kilometer of arable land as defined in Jaetzold and Schmidt, 1983b: 105–6.
[b]Settlement scheme locations.

below the national average of 0.49 ha and is probably below the level of full subsistence, given current agricultural technology (Bernard, Campbell, and Thom 1989).

Land fragmentation has returned to these zones (Kenya 1986b), and, except in Tharaka, settlement schemes are completely filled and are also undergoing some fragmentation. Land use has intensified throughout the highlands (R = at least 130–40 according to Jaetzold and Schmidt [1983b: 114–16]), but there is ample evidence on the landscape that this intensification is somehow connected to land degradation. No comprehensive survey is available.

There is continued removal of trees, particularly to cultivate the remaining valley sides and steep slopes on the mountains (O'Keefe, Raskin, and Bernow 1984: 55; Kamau 1987). As elsewhere in Kenya, there is a fuelwood crisis in Meru. A recent paper on this problem explained that the men have destroyed the once heavily forested district for short-term profit, and now women must desperately search for fuelwood day after day (Kenya 1986b). Heavy commercial timbering, which really has little to do with population density or pressure, does encroach upon forests protecting soils and watersheds upon which people downslope depend. According to staff of the District Agricultural Office in 1986, soil erosion in the midland (UM and LM) zones of both Mount Kenya and the Nyambeni Range is reaching "alarming levels."

At the same time, outflow of highland migrants, together with internal population growth of at least 3 percent per year, is leading to a population-land imbalance in the lowland areas of Tharaka. In several sections land competition between upland migrants and lowland inhabitants has led to armed conflict. Shortening fallow (from R = about 50 to R = about 5), degradation of the vegetative cover of inselbergs and river valleys, and sheetwash and gullying are all problems noted by agricultural officers, particularly in South Tharaka Division. Although densities in Tharaka are sparse (table 3.3), the population-supporting capability of the arid and semiarid environment and barren soils of this region are commensurately low. Famines in 1983–84 and persistent levels of infant and childhood malnutrition suggest that the area is chronically unable to feed itself.

Some of this recent population pressure may be leading to outmigration of Meru workers to other rural districts or to the urban marketplace (table 3.4). However, among eastern and central Kenya districts, in both relative and absolute terms, Meru contributed a relatively minor amount to the out-of-district migrant stream (table 3.4). The pace of outmigration seems to have quickened in the past nine years.

Official statistics of crop production in Meru are woefully inadequate to check the pulse of agricultural intensification. They are based partly on "eyeball" estimates by district agricultural officers and partly on output marketed through various government marketing boards. They provide only the vaguest notion of trends (table 3.5). Though some of the increase in food crops is the outcome of expansion into marginal lands, where maize and beans are being cultivated at the margins of the lower midlands in places where they have perhaps not been previously grown, some of the increase in output must also be the result of a low rainfall year at the beginning of the period (1976) and an excellent crop year at the end (1986). I have statistics for the intervening years, but they show a roller-coaster pattern, dependent largely on rainfall and to a lesser degree upon the political economy of the times. It is folk knowl-

Table 3.4. Eastern and Central Kenya: Net Migration, 1979

District	Inmigrants	Outmigrants	Net migration	Net migration rate[a]
Kiambu	114,599	222,904	−108,305	−157.8
Murang'a	70,128	182,474	−112,346	−173.3
Embu	23,956	23,748	+208	+0.8
Kirinyaga	29,769	29,395	+374	+1.3
Nyeri	46,287	153,011	−106,724	−219.4
Meru	24,275	35,846	−11,571	−13.9
Machakos	44,418	155,008	−110,590	−108.2
Kitui	19,694	71,248	−51,554	−111.0
Nyandarua	93,336	39,213	+54,123	+231.9

Source: Kenya, 1979, p. 57.
[a]Net migration rate shows net effect of immigration and emigration on district population, expressed as increase or decrease per 1,000 population in the census year.

Table 3.5. Crop Production in Meru, 1976 and 1986 (selected cash crops)

Crop		1976	1986	Percent change
Bananas	ha	5,600	16,141	188
	tons	—	132,720	
Beans	ha	18,600	46,707	151
	tons	8,127	67,117	726
Coffee (beans)	ha	16,000	34,500	116
	tons	10,325	13,305	29
Cotton	ha	12,053	8,270	−31
	tons	3,689	2,924	−21
Maize	ha	36,130	66,563	84
	tons	64,130	237,488	270
Millet/sorghum	ha	6,220	7,465	20
	tons	8,678	8,403	−3
Potatoes	ha	7,750	11,625	50
	tons	145,210	107,462	−26
Tea (greenleaf)	ha	5,760	7,003	22
	tons	7,162	28,280	295

Sources: MDAO, 1976, 1986.

edge in Meru that millet and sorghum are declining, but hectarage data do not bear this out. The decline in potato production could perhaps relate to disease; blight is often noted as a problem in the potato-producing areas of the district.

District agricultural officers' summaries of selected crop years will perhaps demonstrate how futile it is to draw other insights from these data: "Very dry and difficult year; many on famine relief" (1976); "Favorable weather. Coffee performed well as did most crops. Maize and Produce Board did not purchase maize this year because their stores were full" (1978); "Generally a hard one due to escalating prices of inputs. Weather favorable but Oct./Nov. rains were excessive, lowering yields of potatoes and beans by 50 and 30 percent, respectively" (1982); "Shortage of inputs, especially seeds" (1984).

Some Recent Field Data

A survey in 1986 of 161 Meru households in twelve sublocations of North and South Imenti, Tigania, and Tharaka (Bernard and Marangu 1991) was one of a number of district-level studies that year of infant and childhood malnutrition. Agriculture was a major focus, particularly food production and the status of the resource base. The year was neither excessively wet nor abnormally dry. According to the District Agriculture Report (MDAO 1986: 26), it was an excellent year for crop production. The rains were timely and well distributed. Inputs were readily available. Record outputs were obtained in subsistence crops.

The survey was equally divided among four ecozones, three in the highlands, one in the lowlands, and focused 75 percent of its efforts in locations with densities greater than 200 persons/km². The information below pertains to these locations. In the absence of final results and more sophisticated analysis, a flow-of-consciousness presentation will reveal the essence of a few population-land-agriculture variables as actually observed in a limited section of Meru. The farms we sampled were all small with a strong subsistence orientation. Fifty-three percent were less than 1.5 ha. The average household supported by this land was seven or eight persons. There were few if any livestock. Our respondents claimed that livestock numbers are diminishing. About 25 percent of the farms had no cattle whatsoever.[7]

The state of the environment as measured by soil erosion, soil fertility, and the frequency of observed marginal land use (especially cultivation of excessively steep slopes, rocky places, and stream sides) is, in a word, "pressured." More than 80 percent of the farms showed some soil erosion; 44 percent had fields with moderate or severe erosion. Soil-fertility decline was suspected in about 80 percent of the cases; marginal land uses were noted in and around 90 percent of the farms and homesteads. On the other hand, at least one soil conservation measure was used by 65 percent of the farmers. Signs of environmental degradation as observed by "outsiders" thus seem to be common. Meru respondents (exclusively mothers of children) themselves also perceived some of the problems associated with rapid rural population growth. Ninety percent judged that the present number of people is greater than their sublocation can comfortably support. A slightly smaller proportion (76 percent) claimed that farm output was declining (especially maize yields).[8]

Compared to some districts in this part of Kenya, the variety of foods given to children is high. A twenty-four-hour recall schedule was used to collect this information. Meru District still produces everything children need for a balanced diet, but not all mothers have access to sources of calcium, protein, and vitamins and minerals from fruits and vegetables. Poverty—insufficient funds to purchase supplementary foods—was most often the explanation why, for example, children are not fed greens, meat, or eggs. Children seemed to have enough caloric intake in the year of the survey. Protein was below standard (only 3 percent of the children had had meat in the previous twenty-four hours). Cow's milk, on the other hand, is widely consumed (48 percent of the children had drunk milk in the previous twenty-four hours; 75 percent of the mothers claimed that children frequently consumed milk).

Food poverty is a problem (Crawford and Thorbecke 1980). Food security seems to be accommodated within the existing kinship system. Sixty percent of the respondents did not have adequate food on hand and about the same percentage noted inadequate food supplies during the dry season. If there are food shortages, the vast majority (over 80 percent) either sell livestock or poultry for cash to purchase food or beg or borrow food or cash from relatives.

If one thinks of infant and childhood malnutrition as being early warnings that a largely subsistence system is failing to keep pace with demand, then the results of the survey are open to interpretation. We used anthropometric measures (weight, height, age) and compared them to standards used by the World Health Organization of the United Nations (WHO 1978). We also looked for overt signs of malnourishment. About 15 percent of the 264 children we weighed, measured, and observed (aged 5 years and under) showed signs of childhood protein-energy malnutrition (CPEM) as measured by low height for age; only 2.5 percent apparently were severely malnourished. However, if one dips slightly below the standard, there is a fairly large proportion of children who would be considered mildly malnourished (an additional 28 percent). This told us that the children in our survey were reasonably well nourished in this average year. But we thought that lurking in these data was the specter of more serious levels of CPEM in a below-average year or in five to ten years when there are many more mouths to feed.

Concluding Remarks

To recapitulate the lessons of Meru's experience, rapid population growth seems to have led in several directions in the relatively brief period of fifty years. To capture a simple trend is difficult. The picture is initially complicated by regional differences. In Meru it is necessary to make distinctions between highlands and lowlands. The highlands have been intrinsically able to absorb greater numbers of people because they have a greater diversity and higher quality of agricultural resources and because they generally possess more resiliency to environmental degradation. Population pressure and involution of the system in mid-colonial times was rapidly dissipated in the 1950s with resettlement schemes, land consolidation, and general intensification of the agricultural system. Open land for new settlement certainly staved off population pressure in the 1960s and 1970s. This expansion, together with the introduction of grade dairy cows and stall feeding, the development of horticultural crops, adoption of hybrid seeds for many food crops, and the use of inputs such as fertilizer enabled Meru District to feed itself in most years. Yet there is ample evidence in the 1980s that a degeneration cycle is again under way. One could conclude perhaps that one of the principal costs of government intervention to "keep up" with population growth has been increased annual variability in agricultural production.

In examining the experience of the highlands one must also remember that they have been the locus of colonial and post-independence structural and technical agricultural investments. Many horticultural and animal husbandry innovations were first implanted in the highlands. These enabled yields to keep pace with population growth and fostered commercialization of agriculture. Intensification was, of course, partly made possible by enhancement of the infrastructure for agricultural change. Highland farmers have long had access to extension agents; farmers' training centers; cooperative, processing, and marketing facilities; credit; and distribution centers for seeds, fertilizers, and pesticides. Recent campaigns to "repair" the environment (soil conservation, agroforestry, and water projects) have also been waged most intensively in the highlands. The political economy of Meru District has thus given the highlands clear advantages in coping with population pressure. By the same token, education, business opportunities, and political influence all have been more accessible in the highlands (particularly in the coffee and tea zones). A middle class of farmers and farmer-businessmen (perhaps 20 percent of the population) have risen above the masses of smallholders—the rural poor who live in less-advantaged zones of Meru (Miller 1984: 72–74).

The lowlands, on the other hand, have had almost none of these advantages. In every sense of the word, they and the farmers and agropastoralists dwelling there are poor. A "saving grace," if one could be so dispassionate, has been that throughout much of the period, population growth has been lower, probably because educational facilities, health care, and improvements in agriculture all were absent. Life was harsher. More infants and children died. Now with internal growth surging upward and the lowlands rapidly filling up, population pressure at comparatively low densities is leading to serious levels of environmental degradation, especially in south Tharaka.

Overall, one gets the impression that rapid population growth of the past several decades in Meru is synchronous with a fair amount of adaptation in the agricultural system and with a broad-scale acceptance of technologic and structural changes brought into the district by the government. Settlement of the remaining empty spaces has been a "release valve" for building pressures on the mountain slopes. However, there remain few unclaimed areas with even modest agricultural potential. Land speculation and conflict center on the small remaining medium potential spaces in north Tharaka and in a few other places.

In the field, one cannot help wonder about involution such as that experienced in the 1950s, followed then by awesome Malthusian forces (perhaps expressed in infant and childhood mortality) and down-spiraling land degradation, reminiscent of the soil erosion crises of the 1930s and 1940s. But to conclude that Meru is headed "down the tubes" in these several ways is far too simplistic a projection. In the last analysis, Meru is a large and diverse agricultural district with a massive rural labor force, more skilled than we think in dealing with adversity and therefore capable of drawing still more output from the rich agricultural resources of this region. Just how long such "mining" of these resources can be sustained is an open question. Latent malnutrition of children, disappearing forests, land disputes and landlessness, deepening gullies, and silted streams all are ominous contemporary signs of serious imbalances between population and resources.

Notes

1. Agricultural potential is defined as the latent capability of land sustainably to support specific agricultural and pastoral activities. For Meru District, agricultural potential is based upon agro-ecological assessment of climate and soils by Jaetzold and Schmidt (1983b). For comparisons among districts a simpler Kenya Ministry of Agriculture system, based simply upon annual rainfall, is used (Kenya 1985: 91).

2. Physiologic density is the number of persons per unit of rain-fed arable land. In Kenya it is the number of persons per unit of land of medium and high potential.

3. A complete list of Meru cultigens may be found in Appendix 3.B.

4. R = Number of harvests per plot per year divided by the number of years in the complete agricultural cycle in years times 100.

5. Exotic here means streams fed by snowmelt and rainfall on the slopes of Mount Kenya and the Nyambeni Range.

6. Catch crop: A crop grown by seizing an opportunity when the ground would otherwise lie fallow between two regular or main crops.

7. These averages for northern Meru farms correspond well with sample surveys taken in the late 1970s and early 1980s by Jaetzold and Schmidt (1983b: 112–25).

8. The fragmentary trend data for yields reported above do not bear out these perceptions. Yet the absence of baseline data makes definitive conclusions impossible.

Appendix 3.A. Meru District Main Agro-Ecological Zones

UH	Upper highland zones Temperature conditions suitable for frost-resistant crops, or for others between the frost periods	2,200/2,400 to 3,000/3,200 m Cool, annual mean temp. 10–15°C; mean nightly min. below 8°C; night frosts occasionally in cold seasons.
UH0	Forest zone Too wet, steep, and important as a catchment area; therefore forest reserve	
UH1	Sheep and dairy zone Too steep, wet, and important as a catchment area; therefore left a forest reserve	
UH2	Pyrethrum-wheat zone Climatic conditions good for pyrethrum and fair for wheat	Cool and subhumid; annual average precipitation 65–80 percent of the potential evaporation (or more to store enough soil moisture for dry seasons affecting pyrethrum)
UH3	Wheat-barley zone Climatic conditions good for wheat and barley, fair to poor for pyrethrum	Cool and semihumid; annual average precipitation 50–60 percent of the potential evaporation and growing periods must have at least 130 days in six out of ten years
LH	Lower highland zones Temperature conditions suitable for high quality tea and cold enough for pyrethrum	1,800/1,900 to 2,200/2,400 m Moderately cool, annual mean temp. 15–18°C; frost rare and limited to basins and valleys
LH0	Forest zone	
LH1	Tea-dairy zone or forest reserve Climatic conditions good for tea, dairy pastures, potatoes, and vegetables, fair for maize	Moderately cool and humid; annual average precipitation at least 80 percent of the potential evaporation or more (to store enough soil moisture for dry seasons affecting tea)
LH2	Wheat/maize-pyrethrum zone 6 Climatic conditions fair to good for pyrethrum and wheat, fair for maize	Moderately cool and humid; annual average precipitation at least 80 percent of the potential evaporation or more (to store enough soil moisture for dry seasons affecting pyrethrum)
LH3	Wheat/(maize)-barley zone 6 Climatic conditions good for wheat and barley, fair to marginal for maize	Moderately cool and semihumid; annual average precipitation 50–65 percent of the potential evaporation; growing periods must be well developed and at least 115 days in 6 out of 10 years
LH4	Cattle-sheep barley zone Climatic conditions fair for barley and wheat; natural pasture for medium-density grazing	Moderately cool and transitional; annual average precipitation 40–50 percent of the potential evaporation; growing periods must be at least 105 days in 6 out of 10 years

(continued)

Appendix 3.A—*Continued*

LH5	Lower highland ranching zone Not suitable for rain-fed agriculture; short grass savanna for low-density grazing; severe erosion damage if overgrazed	2,000m to 2,200m Cool and very dry
UM	Upper midland zones Temperature conditions suitable for Arabica coffee	1,300/1,500 to 1,800/1,900 m Temperate, annual mean temp. 18–21°C; absolutely no frost
UM1	Coffee-tea zone Climatic conditions good to fair for Arabica coffee and tea, the same as maize	Temperate and humid; annual average precipitation at least 80 percent of the potential evaporation or more (to store enough soil moisture for dry seasons affecting tea)
UM2	Main coffee zone Climatic conditions good for Arabica coffee and maize	Temperate and subhumid; annual average precipitation 65–80 percent of the potential evaporation or more (to store enough soil moisture for dry seasons affecting coffee)
UM3	Marginal coffee zone Moisture conditions fair to poor for coffee, then irrigation profitable; fair for maize	Temperate and semihumid; annual average precipitation 50–60 percent of the potential evaporation or more (to store enough soil moisture for survival of coffee in dry seasons)
UM4	Sunflower-maize zone or upper sisal zone With unimodal rainfall good for sunflower and maize, with bimodal rainfall mainly fair; sisal good (large scale)	Temperate and transitional; annual average precipitation 40–50 percent of the potential evaporation
UM5	Livestock-sorghum zone or upper marginal sisal zone Climatic conditions fair for sorghum, poor for maize; natural pasture for low-density grazing; sisal fair to poor	Temperate and semiarid; annual average precipitation 20–40 percent of the potential evaporation; growing periods must be at least 65 days in 6 out of 10 years
UM6	Upper midland ranching zone Only marginally or not suitable for rain-fed crops or dairy; natural pasture for low-to-very-low-density grazing	Temperate and arid; annual average precipitation 15–25 percent of the potential evaporation
LM	Lower midland zones Temperature conditions suitable for cotton (nearly like lowland temperatures)	800 to about 1,300 m Warm, annual mean temperature 21–21°C, mean minimum > 14°C
LM3	Cotton zone Climatic conditions good to fair for cotton, fair for maize	Warm and semihumid; annual average precipitation 50–66 percent of potential evaporation or more (to store enough soil moisture for dry-season affection sugar cane

Appendix 3.A.   Meru District Main Agro-Ecological Zones (*Continued*)

LM4	Marginal cotton zone or middle sisal zone Climatic conditions fair to poor for cotton and maize, fair for pigeon peas, good for sisal	Warm and transitional; annual average precipitation 40–50 percent of potential evaporation or more (in bimodal rainfall areas for survival of cotton in dry seasons)
LM5	Lower midland livestock-millet or marginal middle sisal zone Climatic conditions fair to poor for millets, cowpeas, and grams or sisal; natural pasture for low-density grazing	Warm and semiarid; annual average precipitation 25–40 percent of potential evaporation, or less because growing periods must be at least 45 days in 6 of 10 years
L	Lowland zones Temp. conditions suitable for coconuts and cashew nuts	0–800 m; in Rift Valley, 1,000 m Hot, annual mean temp. more than 24°C
L5	Lowland livestock-millet zone or marginal lower sisal zone Climatic conditions fair to marginal for millets, cowpeas, and grams or sisal; natural pasture for low-density grazing	Hot and semiarid; annual average precipitation 25–40 percent of potential evaporation, or less because growing periods must be at least 40 days in 6 out of 10 years
L6	Lowland ranching zone Not suitable for rain-fed crops; natural pasture for low-to-very-low-density grazing	Hot, semiarid in areas with intermediate rainfall, arid in other areas

Source: Jaetzold and Schmidt 1983a, 1983b.

Appendix 3.B.   Meru Cultigens

Traditional Cultigens	
Food plants	
banana	*Musa sapientum* and *M. paradisiaca*
cassava	*Manihot utilissima*
cowpea	*Vigna uginculata*
gram	black: *Phaseolus mungo*
	green: *Phaseolus aureus*
haricot bean	*Phaseolus vulgaris*
hyacinth bean	*Dolichos lablab*
maize	*Zea mays*
millets	
bulrush	*Pennisetum typhoideum*
finger	*Eleusine coracana*
foxtail (Italian)	*Setaria italica*
pigeon pea	*Cajanus cajun*
pumpkin	*Curcurbita pepo*
sorghum	*Sorghum vulgare*

(*continued*)

Appendix 3.B—*Continued*

sugarcane	*Saccharum officinarum*
sweet potato	*Ipomea batatus*
taro	*Colocasia antiquorum*
Nonfood plants	
castor	*Ricinus communis*
gourd	*Lagenaria vulgaris*
miraa	*Catha edulis*
tobacco	*Nicotiana tobacum*
Introduced Cultigens	
Food plants	
avocado	*Persea americana*
cabbage	*Brassica oleracea capitata*
carrot	*Daucus carota*
chili pepper	*Capsicum* species
eggplant (brinjal)	*Solanum melongena*
grapefruit	*Citrus paradisi*
guava	*Psidium guajava*
kale (sukuma wiki)	*Brassica oleracea acephala*
lemon	*Citrus limon*
mango	*Mangifera indica*
onion	*Allium* species
orange	*Citrus sinensis*
passion fruit	*Passiflora incarnata*
papaya	*Carica papaya*
pea	*Pisum sativum*
pear	*Pyrus* species
pineapple	*Ananas comosus*
plum	*Prunus species*
potato (Irish, white)	*Solanum turberosum*
tomato	*Lycopersicon esculentum*
wheat	*Triticum aestivum*
Nonfood plants	
coffee	*Coffea* species
cotton	*Gossypium* species
tea	*Camellia sinensis*

References

Arkell-Hardwick, A. 1903. *An Ivory Trader in North Kenya*. London: Longman.

Bernard, Frank E. 1968. "Recent Agricultural Change East of Mount Kenya." *Papers in International Studies*. Africa Series, no. 4. Athens: Ohio University.

———. 1972. *East of Mount Kenya: Meru Agriculture in Transition*. New York: Humanities Press. Munich: Weltforum-Verlag.

————. 1979. "Meru District in the Kenyan Spatial Economy: 1800–1950." In *Kenya: A Study of Spatial Economy*, ed. R. Obudho and D. R. F. Taylor, pp. 264–90. Boulder, Colo.: Westview.

————. 1985. "Planning and Environmental Risk in Kenyan Drylands." *Geographical Review* 75(1): 58–74.

Bernard, Frank E., and Leah T. Marangu. 1986. *Childhood Protein-Energy Malnutrition in Meru District, Kenya*. Final Report. Washington: Fulbright-Hays Senior Research Program.

————. 1991. Childhood Malnutrition in Meru. Final Report. Nairobi: Ministry of Health.

Bernard, Frank E., David J. Campbell, and Derrick J. Thom. 1989. "Land and Population Pressure of the Eastern Ecological Gradient of Kenya." *National Geographic Research* 5(4): 399–421.

Chanler, W. A. 1896. *Through Jungle and Desert*. London: Macmillan.

Clayton, Eric S. 1964. *Agrarian Development in Peasant Economies*. New York: Macmillan.

Cone, I. W., and J. F. Lipscomb. 1972. *The History of Kenya Agriculture*. Nairobi: University Press of Africa.

Crawford, Eric, and Erik Thorbecke. 1980. "The Analysis of Food Poverty: An Illustration from Kenya." *The Pakistan Development Review* 19(4): 311–35.

Deitz, Ton. 1985. "Migration to and from Dry Areas in Kenya." *Tijdschrift voor Econ. en Soc. Geografie* 77(1): 18–27.

Fadiman, Jeffrey A. 1982. *An Oral History of Tribal Warfare: The Meru of Mt. Kenya*. Athens: Ohio University Press.

Ferguson, Alan. 1985. *Kibwezi Integrated Survey*. Nairobi: African Medical and Research Foundation.

Greeley, E. H. 1975. *Family Planning in Southern Meru: The Background to Successful Male Acceptance*. Staff Paper. Nairobi: Bureau of Educational Research, University of Nairobi.

Homan, F. D. 1963. "Land Consolidation and Redistribution of Population in the Imenti Sub-tribe of the Meru." In *African Agrarian Systems*, ed. D. Biebuyck, pp. 224–44. London: Oxford University Press.

Jaetzold, Ralph, and Helmut Schmidt. 1983a. *Farm Management Handbook of Kenya. Vol. IIB. Central Kenya*. Nairobi: Ministry of Agriculture.

————. 1983b. *Farm Management Handbook of Kenya. Vol. IIIC. East Kenya*. Nairobi: Ministry of Agriculture.

Kamau, Celia. 1987. "Meru: A Land of Contrast." *Daily Nation*, April 3, p. 11.

Kenya. 1954. *A Plan to Intensify the Development of African Agriculture in Kenya*, comp. R. J. M. Swynnerton. Kenya Colony and Protectorate, Department of Agriculture. Nairobi: Government Printer.

————. 1970. *Kenya Population Census, 1969*. Republic of Kenya, Ministry of Finance and Economic Planning. Nairobi: Government Printer.

————. 1979. *1973 Population Census. Vol. II. Analytical Report*. Republic of

Kenya, Ministry of Finance and Planning. Nairobi: Central Bureau of Statistics.

_____. 1981. *Kenya Population Census, 1979*. Republic of Kenya, Ministry of Economic Planning and Development. Nairobi: Government Printer.

_____. 1983. *Population Projections for Kenya: 1980-2000*. Nairobi: Central Bureau of Statistics and UNICEF.

_____. 1985. *Statistical Abstract 1985*. Nairobi: Government Printer.

_____. 1986a. *Economic Management for Renewed Growth*. Sessional Paper no. 1. Nairobi: Government Printer.

_____. 1986b. *Meru District Sociocultural Profile*. Republic of Kenya, Ministry of Planning and National Development and Institute of African Studies of the University of Nairobi. Nairobi: Government of Kenya.

_____. 1986c. *Statistical Abstract 1986*. Nairobi: Government Printer.

Laughton, W. H. 1944. *The Meru*. Nairobi: The Ndia Kuu Press.

Launonen, R., A. A. Karinpaa, L. Marangu, and S. Minae. 1985. *Rural Dairy Development in Meru*. Helsinki: Institute of Development Studies, University of Helsinki.

MDAO. 1956. *Annual Report*. Meru District Agricultural Officer. Nairobi: Ministry of Agriculture.

_____. 1976. *Annual Report*. Meru District Agricultural Officer. Nairobi: Ministry of Agriculture.

_____. 1986. *Annual Report*. Meru District Agricultural Officer. Nairobi: Ministry of Agriculture.

MDC. 1912-13. *Annual Report*. Meru District Agricultural Officer. Nairobi: Kenya National Archives.

_____. 1944. *Annual Report*. Meru District Agricultural Officer. Nairobi: Kenya National Archives.

_____. 1949. *Annual Report*. Meru District Agricultural Officer. Nairobi: Kenya National Archives.

Miller, N. N. 1984. *Kenya: The Quest for Prosperity*. Boulder, Colo.: Westview.

Mott, F. L., and S. H. Mott. 1980. "Kenya's Record Population Growth: A Dilemma of Development." *Population Bulletin* 35(3).

Ochieng, William R. 1975. *Eastern Kenya and Its Invaders*. Nairobi: East African Literature Bureau.

O'Connor, A. M. 1966. *An Economic Geography of East Africa*. London: G. Bell.

O'Keefe, Phil, P. Raskin, and Steve Bernow, eds. 1984. *Energy and Development in Kenya: Opportunities and Constraints*. Stockholm: The Beijer Institute.

Ominde, Simeon H. 1968. *Land and Population Movements in Kenya*. London: Heinemann.

_____. 1984. *Population and Development in Kenya*. Nairobi: Heinemann Educational Books.

Population Reference Bureau. 1992. *World Population Data Sheet, 1992.* Washington: Population Reference Bureau.

Porter, Philip W. 1979. *Food and Development in the Semi-Arid Zone of East Africa.* Foreign and Comparative Studies, Africa Series XXXII. Syracuse: Maxwell School of Citizenship and Public Affairs, Syracuse University.

Reilly, Mary Jo. 1987. "The Origins of Population/Land Resource Imbalance in Meru District, Kenya." Senior Honors Thesis, Michigan State University.

Sillitoe, K. K. 1962. *Preliminary Notes on the Sociological and Economic Aspects of Land Tenure and Usage in Meru District, Kenya.* Conference Paper No. 5, East African Institute of Social Research, Kampala, Makerere University.

van Zwanenberg, R. M. A., and A. King, 1975. *An Economic History of Kenya and Uganda, 1800–1970.* London: Macmillan.

WHO. World Health Organization. 1978. *A Growth Chart for International Use in Maternal and Child Health Care.* Geneva: WHO of the United Nations.

4 / Defending the Promise of Subsistence: Population Growth and Agriculture in the West Usambara Mountains, 1920–1980

Steven Feierman

The site of this study is the West Usambara Mountains of northern Tanzania. The time frame begins in the mid-1920s, when land was more plentiful than at any other time in the twentieth century, and continues through the late 1970s. Comments will also be made on agriculture in 1890 (as German conquest was beginning). There are by now many local studies on agriculture in the West Usambara Mountains. All describe agricultural production under conditions of extreme land scarcity; all agree that the land is incapable of carrying the number of people who live on it given current technology; and all conclude that the problem gets worse with passing years because of erosion, the impoverishment of the soil, and population growth (Attems 1967, 1968; Heijnen 1974; Egger and Glaeser 1975; Schönmeier 1977; Fleuret 1978; Glaeser 1980, 1984; Sender n.d.).

In the 1950s the British district authorities attacked the agricultural problems head on by requiring that peasants take vigorous measures for erosion control. This provoked intense peasant resistance that made agricultural improvement after that time more difficult, for there was a history of what looked to peasants like oppressive intervention and successful resistance.

The resistance to erosion control aimed at protecting the right of the poorest people to land for subsistence. The erosion-control measures took land that was available rent-free for use by the poor and, through improvements, made it permanently subject to rental. Resistance to erosion control was therefore a battle to retain an existing system of social security. The peasants of Usambara made a collective choice, through intense political struggle, in favor of guaranteed subsistence, even though its long-term effect was to entrench a pattern of shared poverty.

The Environment and Its Social Uses

The West Usambara Mountains are located in Lushoto District, Tanga Region, which is the northeastern corner of Tanzania (fig. 4.1). The mountains are "an uplifted block of metamorphosed, folded and faulted volcanic and sedimentary rocks" (Cliffe et al. 1969), surrounded by plains on the north, west, and south and bordered by the Luengera Valley on the east. The mountains are encircled by very steep escarpments rising from the lowlands. The escarpments' top is about 1,200 m above sea level in most places. The landscape within the mountain block is deeply dissected, with little level area except in occasional basins. The highest peak reaches 2,300 m, and a number of peaks rise above 1,750 m (Heijnen 1974: 34).

Population Patterns

In the precolonial period the people of the western Usambaras were divided into two distinct groups speaking two separate languages. Each group had its own characteristic way of living within the elevations of the western Usambaras. A small minority of the inhabitants of the mountains spoke the Mbugu language, lived in scattered villages at much lower population densities than the rest, and occupied the highland meadows at the center of the mountain block above about 1,500 m. Cattle keeping was a more important part of their economy than it was for the rest of the mountain population. The majority of the population was in the second group. These people spoke the Shambaa language and lived in permanent villages, some of which had existed for hundreds of years. The cultivators walked from these villages to widely scattered farm plots. Cultivation and fallow were alternated in these plots without villagers having to move their residences.

Shambaa-speaking farmers defined (and continue to define) two separate environmental zones. Shambaai was a zone above about 1,000 m. Nyika was located below about 650 m. Mixed shambaai and nyika could be found between 650 and 1,000 m. The zones were identified by

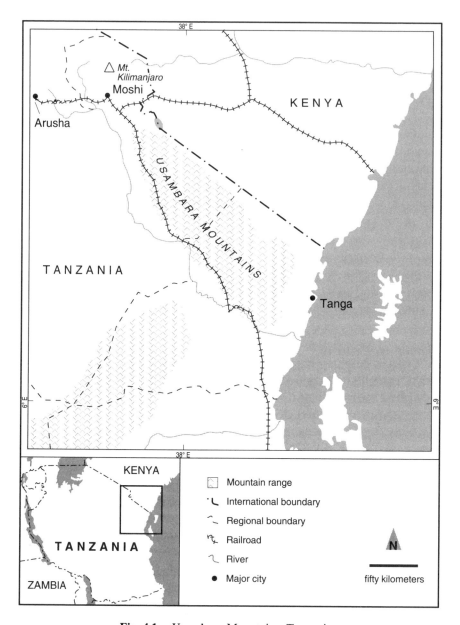

Fig. 4.1. Usambara Mountains, Tanzania

their characteristic varieties of wild vegetation, which were also taken as indicators of the land's potential agricultural use. Bananas were always planted in shambaai; slow-growing maize was planted in shambaai and fast-growing maize in nyika. People identified shambaai as a malaria-free zone and nyika as malarial.

Villages (surrounded by banana groves) were always located in shambaai and always within reach of nyika. For this reason, the greatest concentration of population was around the outer rim of the mountains. Men could get to nyika to hunt wild game, which was scarcer in the mountains, and some people in every village probably had farm plots in nyika. The special crops that grew at warmer temperatures broadened possibilities of hedging the risk of total crop failure, as famine-relief food could not be brought over great distances under precolonial transportation conditions (see Feierman 1972: chap. 1, 1974: chap. 1). By the mid-1920s, the plains around the southern edge of the mountains had been taken up by sisal plantations, which were a market for mountain produce, and left some land (even though it was not level) for peasant food production.

Ancient patterns shaped twentieth-century economy. People continued to live in central villages within reach of nyika, continued to walk to fields instead of moving their houses as soil became exhausted, and continued to balance production in shambaai against production in nyika. As population pressures increased, the plots of a single household tended to become scattered ever more widely. This placed a special burden on women, who walked to their farms more days of the year than men, and who carried the harvest from fields to home. The plots also decreased in size, but the pattern held, although in the 1950s and 1960s Shambaa speakers moved into land formerly occupied by Mbugu-speaking populations.

Rain Patterns

There is enormous variation in the rainfall of the western Usambaras, ranging from nearly 2,000 mm a year in the southeastern part of the mountains, to below 650 mm in the northwest (see table 4.1). The rains fall in three seasons: *ng'waka*, from March to May, *muati* in August, and *vui* from October to December. Ng'waka and muati are both brought by winds off the ocean from the southeast. Rising over the mountains, the air cools and deposits moisture. The southeastern part of the mountains, therefore, receives the largest part of these rains. Vui is brought by winds from the northeast, leaving most of its precipitation along the northern rim. Vui and ng'waka are the two main agricultural seasons, with muati serving as a supplementary season, especially for people living at high altitudes, or when one or the other seasonal harvests has failed. Many households obtain three harvests a year (often with separate plots for each of the seasons), although they get the majority of their calories from the harvest of the primary season of their locality. The north relies more heavily on vui and the south more heavily on ng'waka. Since ng'waka is usually heavier and more reliable than vui, the northern part of the mountains tends to have more frequent droughts than the south, especially the southeast (Attems 1967: 20–22; Cliffe et al. 1969: 8; Feierman 1974: 28; Glaeser 1984: 27). The dry parts of the mountains are places like Malindi that are in the shadow of rain from both directions.

Droughts

Droughts vary in severity according to whether they last for only one of the two main planting seasons (ng'waka and vui) or for two or more successive seasons, and according to how localized they are. Given the local variation in rainfall, in almost every year farmers in the mountains complain about bad rains, either drought, or rains that continue while maize is drying in the fields, or some other problem. When a problem is localized, the shortfall can be made up with purchases of food from neighboring areas. In some famous drought years, however, once every twenty or thirty years, the whole of the mountain area goes without adequate rain all at the same time. These are remembered as periods of great distress.

Two ways of dealing with drought in the nineteenth century were through the use of irrigated plots and through the use of plots in the bottom of wet basins, in which drainage ditches were dug to make adequate farm plots. Irrigation became less common after German conquest, and the wet valley bottoms were increasingly given over to other uses from the 1940s. By the 1930s, food purchases also became a way of dealing with drought. For example, many cultivators worked on sisal estates to earn money for food during the drought of 1932.

Table 4.1. Monthly Average Rainfalls (in mm)

	Bumbuli	Lushoto	Soni	Malindi
January	78	81	79	55
February	71	75	77	43
March	111	137	148	71
April	240	219	176	140
May	160	179	82	60
June	67	53	43	9
July	73	38	37	10
August	75	22	27	7
September	52	16	17	7
October	124	37	17	36
November	128	104	97	79
December	98	107	91	149

Source: Attems 1967: 149.

Types of Soil

Cultivators are aware of the uses of a wide variety of soil types, with fine gradations among them, but no detailed and locally specific reports of soil types have appeared. Milne (as reported in Heijnen 1974) reported five main soil types. (1) Laterized red soils occur especially where rainfall is very high, as in the southeast of the mountains. They have a shallow organic topsoil that quickly deteriorates if the forest cover is removed. (2) Nonlaterized red loams or dark reddish brown clay loams are found widely through the mountains and are fertile and less subject (but not impervious) to erosion. (3) Grey loamy mineral soils, which contain higher concentrations of unleached minerals than the former two types and are more fertile, are relatively uncommon. (4) Grey to black fresh mineral soils are found only in small pockets. These soils are fertile enough to sustain permanent cropping. (5) Valley colluvia vary in color from reddish brown to black (see Cliffe et al. 1969; and Glaeser 1980: 27).

Soil erosion and laterization are serious problems in many parts of the West Usambaras. The forest topsoils are lost quickly through oxidation once the forest is cleared (Milne 1937). Erosion on the hillsides often follows after clearing, depending on the character of the underlying soil and of the cultivation techniques. Shortly after independence, for example, local farmers were given 12,150 ha of forest at Shume, which quickly showed serious soil erosion and declining yields (Matango 1979: 158).

The excess of population over usable land puts great pressure on forests, and so does the need for fuelwood. The Fleurets (1978: 321) have shown that fuelwood replacement for a village of 200 people requires the planting of 1,360 trees each year. In addition to the problems of forest clearing, tilling on steep slopes has led in some places to sheet erosion. In some instances, only subsoils remain (Fleuret 1978: 11). Soils in general are poor in nutrients, especially lacking phosphorus, magnesium, and potash (Attems 1967: 24).

Evolving Population

The difficulty of the mountain terrain and the fact that farmers cultivate steep slopes make it hard to measure population density in relation to arable land with any precision (see table 4.2). One would need measures that distinguish very small bits of usable and unusable land. The parts of the West Usambaras that have usable soils and viable transportation are very densely populated indeed.

In 1978 the district had a population of 286,049 and an area of 3,497 km², which produces a crude population density of 82/km². However, the district's boundaries include the uninhabited Mkomazi game reserve to the north, and also large areas of sparsely populated plains and lowlands. Heijnen (1974: 42) estimates the land actually available to the mountain population as 1,473 km² but explains that even this is a high approximation because he makes no allowance for land suitable only for rough grazing. Nevertheless, using this measure, the population density of the West Usambaras may be as high as 194/km². The estimates of density on table 4.2 are probably low given the high districtwide figures that later emerged in the 1978 census.

Present Population Densities and Road Access

The most densely populated parts of the mountains are considerably denser than 194/km². The particular distribution partly has to do with transportation. Because of the character of the mountains as an uplifted block, it is extremely difficult to build roads linking Lushoto with the rest of Tanga Region. The one all-weather road that achieves this climbs

Table 4.2. Population Density by Division, 1975

Area	1975 density / km²
Soni	295
Vugha	240
Gafe	162
Lushoto	159
Bumbuli	153
Mlalo	139
Mtae	115
Bagabaga	109
Mgwashi	99
Mlola	69
Mbaramo	9
Average	141

Source: TIRDEP 1975–80 as reported in Fleuret 1978.

steeply from Mombo in the plains up to Soni. It was built during the German period by captives taken in the Maji Maji rebellion and whose lives were therefore seen as expendable in difficult road building. Just below Soni, a feeder road branches off to nearby Vugha. At Soni, the main road separates into two, with one branch continuing eastward to Bumbuli, and the other branch continuing westward and then north, first to Gare and Lushoto, and then to Mlalo in the more distant north. The road from Soni to Bumbuli was not an all-weather road before the 1950s, and even now it is very difficult in the rains. The only road that was fully operable through the 1940s was the road from Mombo through Soni to Lushoto, although logging trucks went north from Lushoto and regular trucks carried crops from Mlalo. Today Mlalo has regular bus service that passes through Lushoto to Dar es Salaam or to Tanga. In the 1950s, a partially operable road was built from Mlalo directly down to the northern plains at Kitivo, as a way of opening new farmlands at the bottom for cultivation by peasants living at the top of the escarpment. Population-density figures show that the closer a division is to the main road into the mountains, the higher density population is. The towns listed below Mlalo on table 4.2 are not served by all-weather roads.

The densities are high relative to the carrying capacity of the land, under current technology. In 1971 Moore (reported in Heijnen 1974: 42; Glaeser 1984: 103) calculated carrying capacity, based on assumptions that appear reasonable: that half of all arable land is actually under crops, and that each person requires 2,000 calories a day plus a minimal annual income. Using these assumptions he concluded that Lushoto District could carry a population of 139,000. This was 66 percent of the actual total population in 1967 and would later be 48.6 percent of the population in 1978. Using current technology, the district has too little land and too many people. Egger and Glaeser (1975) raise the possibility that a change in technology, incorporating and adapting the best in nineteenth-century Shambaa agricultural techniques, could increase the carrying capacity, but this has not yet happened.

The Evolution of Population Densities after 1891

In 1890 the population densities were much lower, although there is some debate on just how low they were. Baumann (1891: 13), the German explorer, made a rough census of 180 villages and claimed that the total population was 17,500 and the density 3.8/km².

There are a number of reasons why this estimate is unacceptable. First, Baumann estimated the area of the mountains to be about 4,620 km², which is much larger than it actually was. Second, Baumann had decided that the Usambaras had excellent land for European settlement, and he was making the argument that no population would need to be displaced if settlers came. Events proved that he was wrong. Third, during the time of Baumann's visit local people built their villages in inaccessible areas that could not be seen from the main footpaths, so that invading raiders would not find them, for the 1880s were a time of frequent warfare, unlike the situation half a century earlier. The villages were hidden, surrounded by thickets or banana groves. A number of Europeans who settled in Usambara at the time and got to know it well reported their surprise at finding that areas they had assumed to be completely unpopulated were found, after long acquaintance, to be richly settled (Holst 1893: 113; Karasek 1911–1924: (1) 155; Dupre n.d.: 62).

Fourth, Baumann (1891: 179) estimated that the entire population of the chiefdom of Mlalo was 3,000. LangHeinrich (1913: 7), a missionary with long and intimate acquaintance with the area, estimated that when the war drum was beaten at Mlalo, 3,000 armed men would assemble; some, admittedly, came from neighboring chiefdoms, but other young men would have remained home to guard their villages, and older men did not respond to war drums.

A high estimate of the period's population is given by P. Fleuret (1978) in an excellent dissertation on agriculture in Usambara. On this one detail, however, his conclusion appears unlikely. He reports, without naming the source, that the population of the Mlalo basin in 1905 was 10,000, occupying 83 km^2, with a population density of 120/km^2 (Fleuret 1978: 38–39). This shows, he argues, that the Shambaa were pushing at the limits of their resources as early as the turn of the century. Even if the source is from a careful observer, the conclusion is not firmly grounded. The pattern of agriculture in the late precolonial period was one in which areas around the capitals of major chiefdoms, like Mlalo, were densely settled, with large areas of fallow and forest as one went outward from the center. Even if the core area was densely settled, it did not mean that overall densities were so high.

Fleuret (1978: 37) also cites a German census of 1899 that found the population of Wilhelmstal District to be 86,000. Wilhelmstal included parts of Pare and East Usambara and was therefore much larger than the current Lushoto District. If the census was roughly correct, and if we assume the population of the area comparable to today's Lushoto to be 50,000, then the density would have been 34/km^2. By 1920 the population of Wilhelmstal was listed as 120,000. These were broken down by ethnic group, so that it is possible to come to a closer estimate of the population of the West Usambaras. The total of Shambaa, Mbugu, and Kilindi (the ruling dynasty of the precolonial Shambaa kingdom) was 69,000, with perhaps another 11,000 people listed under other ethnic labels within the borders of what was to become Korogwe District (larger than the current Lushoto District and including it but smaller than Wilhemstal). This means that in the mid-1920s, at the start of our study period, the population density was possibly around 50/km^2. The estimated population of this district in 1929 was 117,690; in 1937 it was 120,000; in 1941 172,770, of whom 136,270 were listed as Shambaa. By 1946 the African population of Korogwe (the district of which Lushoto at that time was a part) was 203,615. Population grew rapidly during the late 1940s and 1950s.[1]

Even though the population density in the mid-1920s was higher than it had been in the late 1890s (assuming that these chancy figures are correct), peasants had some strong advantages in the 1920s. Most of the German planters had left, abandoning their land. Even though the land was placed under the Custodian for Enemy Property and unavailable for cultivation by African peasants, the empty estates were used for grazing. Local peasants were also freed from the heavy labor demands they had been forced to meet during German rule. After 1945, many German farms were sold to new British settlers.

Migration Patterns and Sex Ratios

In the 1920s the people grew crops for themselves and for their children, but they could choose to sell the surplus to sisal plantations, with thousands of workers to feed, in the nearby plains. In 1927 the local cultivators of Tanga and Lushoto Districts produced enough to feed 50,000 workers and to export an additional 758 tons of food. The herds of those years found plentiful grazing land. Young men could choose between caring for cattle, raising food, or working on estates—coffee in the mountains or sisal in the plains. Most kept to their own farms and worked for Europeans only when they were short of cash. The days of Shambaa sisal workers came thirty years later.[2]

Data on sex ratios through the period of rapid population growth (from 1925 to the present) are inadequate. We have a breakdown by sex for 1929 but as given for Usambara District, which included the lowland sisal estates, with their predominantly male work force. The overall figure for 1929 was 101 men for every 100 women. The qualitative reports from the 1920s explained that men from the mountains did not work on the sisal estates and that labor migration from the mountains was not of major importance. This was certainly no longer so by the 1950s. The overall sex ratios for 1967 and 1978 are identical, within the borders of what was by then Lushoto District, without Korogwe (see tables 4.3 and 4.4). At both times it was 87.5 men for every 100 women.[3]

World War II was the period of the most rapid outmigration of men. Under wartime regulations, the government compelled chiefs to account for all their men: the number of "Native Key Men," the number employed on estates, fit for military service, suitable as sisal cutters or for general sisal work, and finally the number to be left at home growing food (the latter group corresponding to about 20 percent of adult men) (Mhando 1977: 109). It was clear from the district reports that sending increasing numbers of men drawn from these categories to their required jobs would put more pressure on women and that labor quotas would be met at the expense of food production.

The male migration from the mountains, which became substantial during the war, continued with intensity after it. By 1952, according to the district commissioner's estimate, one-third of all taxpaying men in Lushoto District worked some part of the year on sisal plantations or for plantation contractors. These were in addition to workers who went to town for employment, to Tanga, Mombasa, or Nairobi. In 1954 recruiters began to send Shambaa families to work at agricultural labor in

Table 4.3. Number of Males for 100 Females in Varying Age Groups, 1978

Age	Number of males
0–4	95.4
5–9	98.9
10–14	99.8
15–24	71.1
25–34	65.6
35–44	81.6
45–54	89.9
55–64	96.3
65+	112.0
Average	90.0

Source: Calculated by the author from *1978 Population Census* (United Republic of Tanzania 1978).

Table 4.4. Percentage of Total Population in Segments of the Population Defined by Age and Sex

Age group	Male	Female
0–4	9.06	9.50
5–9	8.98	9.07
10–14	7.21	7.23
15–24	6.94	9.76
25–34	4.46	6.80
35–44	3.52	4.32
45–54	2.61	2.91
55–64	1.79	1.85
65+	2.11	1.88
Totals	46.68	53.32

Source: Calculated by the author from *1978 Population Census* (United Republic of Tanzania 1978).

the Northern Province, as replacements for Kikuyu laborers, who at that time were seen as politically dangerous.[4]

The age-distributed figures for 1978 are consistent with the fact that many men continued to migrate to work outside the mountains for much of their most productive years.

In 1978, almost 36 percent of the total population was nine years old or under, and more than 50 percent was fourteen or under. Even allowing for some temporary outmigration during the ages over fifteen, these figures point toward the explosive population growth currently under way. The most likely explanation for this is the wide spread of infant inoculations. In the author's survey of a village in 1979–80, the great majority of infants and young children had had most of their inoculations. This can lead to a decline in mortality for the 0–4 age group, even without improvements in standard of living.

The sex ratios vary widely from one small locality to another within West Usambaras. At Mponde, in the south near Vugha, an area rich in smallholder tea farms, there are 100 men for every 100 women. At Mlalo, which had been a land-scarce area for at least four decades in 1978, there were 79.8 men for every 100 women.

Migration, Marriage, and Access to Land

The general figures for sex ratios and population growth hide what are really many different processes, as seen at the village and household level. I documented one pattern of migration in a village survey near Vugha in 1968. This was a coffee-growing area at a time when coffee was still important, a time when non-Christian men used mostly household labor on their coffee farms. I interviewed 62 non-Christian men over the age of forty who, taken all together, had 127 wives (Feierman 1972: 115), for an average 2.05 wives per man. The richest coffee farmers had the most wives. The extra wives, in this polygynous pattern, were potential wives of younger men who remained unmarried (44.5 percent of non-Christian men were aged 20 to 29) and potential wives of younger men who left the West Usambaras altogether and found both wives and farmland elsewhere.

I asked a larger sample of 138 men about the names and life patterns of all their children, including adult sons. Twenty-one percent of married sons (16 out of 77) had permanently settled far from Vugha; none of the married daughters had done this. The pattern left coffee farms concentrated in fewer male hands but kept women in the mountains. It was not a matter of the sons of the poor leaving while the sons of the rich stayed. The pattern was one in which some proportion of most men's sons went off (either permanently or temporarily), allowing the remaining sons to have larger farms than they would otherwise have. The selective permanent outmigration of young men changed in character by the late 1970s when, as a result of Universal Primary Education, the use of family labor declined and polygamy declined very steeply. A new survey of the men in the Vugha sample of 1968 who had been under the age of thirty-nine at that time revealed that they (unlike their predecessors) had not added wives as they became older but (by a preliminary calculation) had only 1.1 wives per man in 1980.

A second pattern was documented at a village near Bumbuli, in a survey carried out in 1979–89. A large proportion of men from the village had cardamom farms near Amani, about thirty miles away, beyond the borders of Lushoto District. In most cases their wives remained near Bumbuli, cultivating food staples. A few wives went along to Amani to cook for and feed groups of adult brothers there. Some brothers stayed home at all times near Bumbuli, to handle male household responsibilities (for example, the care of sick children) for the brothers at Amani.

A third pattern is one much more widely known and expected. Young men, some married, some unmarried, leave the district to work in town. If they are married, they leave wives and children at home in most cases. The most common destination from the West Usambaras is the town of Tanga. If the men are conscientious, they send home remittances to their wives. In any event, women rely on a support network of other wives and, for matters requiring male support, on the fathers and brothers of their husbands.

Yet another pattern, which exists today but was uncommon in the southern part of the mountains in the 1960s, is one in which entire households leave the mountains, either to farm elsewhere or to take up residence in the city. In this case the town might be Dar es Salaam. This happens especially if the husband has stable and well-paid employment. If it is correct, as hypothesized here on the basis of village-level evidence, that more entire families are migrating today than were twenty years ago, then the stability or sex ratios over time may well be concealing substantial increases in migration. It is very likely that this is the case.

In any event the men who leave, even those who leave with wives and children, retain their rights in inherited land, which is seen as being entrusted temporarily to the brother who remains. In this way, many more people retain theoretical rights to land in the West Usambaras than actually live there. The system can be compared to a bank that has lent out a high percentage of the money of its depositors. So long as only a few depositors demand their money on any given day, the bank will not face difficulties. But if all depositors demand their money, the bank must fail. If all those with land rights in the West Usambaras returned home, the situation would be impossible. My rough impression is that a remarkably high percentage of the population of the city of Tanga speak Shambaa, of the variety spoken in the West Usambaras. My informal interviews of Shambaa-speaking men walking in the central shopping area of Tanga—all of them lived in Tanga—reported them having farms in the West Usambaras. None said that they had left the mountains because they had no farm land. All expected to return home to farm their own land at some point.

The general point of this is clear. The West Usambaras are a population fountain, providing emigrants in large numbers to Tanga, to other parts of the country's northeast, and to Dar es Salaam. Yet in most cases those who leave retain theoretical rights to return home.

One of the goals of the survey of 1979–80 was to learn the process by which people were driven off the land altogether. All informants, men and women, comfortable and poor, agreed that the poor would never lack land for cultivating annual crops for their own subsistence. Villagers lend land for subsistence annuals without asking rent. This was substantiated not only by normative statements but also through observation of what happened to people in desperate poverty.

The data presented a paradox. The emigrants living in Tanga claimed they had enough land. The poorest women in the mountains also agreed that they had land for annuals. Yet large numbers of people continue to leave the mountains, which have gone beyond the limits of their carrying capacity, given current technology.

There are, however, cases I observed of people being forced to leave the land. This happened in the case of a very poor widow who had three sons in their late teens. The household did not have land with cash-producing perennials (coffee or tea), and they did not have enough cash to pay for occasional medical treatment or for food during the hungry months of clearing the soil and planting. They therefore worked on other people's land, not because they lacked land but because they had no cash for daily survival. They were unable to cultivate their own subsistence land and were in the process of leaving the village to move from place to place, looking for the highest wages available for casual agricultural labor. It was clear that they were about to lose all contact with their own land, to become proletarianized, even though everyone in their village respected the principle that they had a right to subsistence land. If they lost contact with their village and appeared at one where they were strangers, they would not have the same right to land for subsistence annuals.

Such crises leading to proletarianization were never caused by shortages of subsistence land. They were always the result of cash shortages.

There was a woman, for example, who proved unable to breast-feed her infant. Her husband sold a coffee farm to buy powdered milk. In this case, the sale did not lead to total loss of rights in the mountains, but it pushed the household closer to the margin, without a cash source for tiding over the hard times. The centrality of cash rather than land in the crises leading to outmigration makes the sociology of illness management a core issue for understanding the relationship between farmers' households and their land.

Tenure on Scattered Farm Plots

People live in permanent villages. Each household owns scattered plots to which cultivators walk. In the past a farm plot that a cultivator cleared himself was his property which he could sell. This was true even in the precolonial period. The man allocates farm plots for annuals to each wife for her use and the use of her children. These plots will later become the property of that wife's children. The process of inheritance is in fact one that progresses in stages through the life cycle as the domestic group evolves: the first stage is the allocation of a plot to a wife with young children; later, specific plots are allocated to a son when he is planning to marry; after the father's death, all remaining plots are allocated. The sons of a particular mother (in a polygynous household) usually make sure that their mother has a plot for her use after her husband's death. The whole group of the father's sons is usually seen as holding residual joint rights in inherited land, so that a son would not normally sell an inherited plot without first consulting his brothers, who at the very least have the first right of refusal. Even when land sale has been illegal under Tanzanian government law, people continued to buy and sell land under the guise of selling the standing crops on the land.

Labor

Over the long term, the central problem for labor allocation in the agriculture of the West Usambaras grows out of the fact that villages tend to be permanent. Residents walk out to cultivate widely scattered fields in a variety or settings and use three rainy seasons in addition to drainage agriculture in wet bottomlands. This means that in the month of February, for example, a single household might be harvesting maize from drainage bottom land, weeding maize of the November–December rains, and planting maize of the February–May rains, while at the same time pruning coffee and carrying out a variety of tasks on a number of other crops.

In the mid-1920s, men did the herding and were expected to do most of the clearing and deep cultivation of the soil. Women have always done most of the weeding and harvesting, and these activities might well be going on at the same time as the cultivation of fields to be planted in the next of the three farming seasons or perhaps for the season after that. Near Bumbuli, in more than 150 household economic histories, the men who had been fully grown by the 1920s remembered them as times when cattle keeping was a major enterprise, perhaps the most important one for earning cash, although the archival records for the period show that the district was a major supplier of food grains to the sisal plantations and to drought-prone Handeni District. In the 1940s and 1950s grazing land was rapidly taken out of use, and herding declined in importance as a male activity.

We have already seen that beginning with World War II a large percentage of men in their most vigorous years were absent from the mountains. Their absence led to greater pressure on the labor of those left behind. Young men in their teens help with cultivation. Women do more tasks than they might have done in the 1920s. Men try to schedule their absences so that they can help with cultivation. Many men send home remittances, with the intention of enabling their wives to hire casual labor to help with cultivation. However, in a study of health care payment in Bumbuli in 1979–80, the author found that the remittances are generally seen by the wives as being for their discretionary use. They try to do the cultivation themselves, and they use their husbands' remittances for clothing, children's clothing, kerosene, soap, food supplements, and other necessities. Women, therefore, attempt to take on more of the farm work themselves and to conserve remittances.

There is no question that the whole of the period from 1925 to 1978 was one in which the crisis of women's work time intensified. Colonial government planners expected this to happen during the enforced agricultural march of wartime conditions, but it has continued since with the expansion of men's cultivation and with the increasing scarcity of both land and fuelwood. By the 1960s, some women at Vugha were farming plots at the base of the mountain, and returning every day to homes at about 1,200 m. Walking to scattered farm plots has thus become increasingly time-consuming. This must also somehow be coordinated with child care. Sometimes mothers take along their infants to the farm. Sometimes grandparents, other aged relatives, or young children take care of infants while mothers farm. The permanence of villages and the rising densities have also meant great time expenditures for collecting fuelwood. In the Fleurets' (1978) survey of a single village, a majority of informants spent between six and twelve hours a week collecting fuelwood, in addition to child care, carrying water for household use, walking to distant farm plots, and farming.

There are essentially four techniques for coordinating labor on a wider scale than with units formed of a single wife and her husband. As mentioned above, polygamy was quite important among non-Christian coffee farmers of the 1950s and 1960s. The other alternatives were *ngemo*, or the labor of collective parties, who are then fed and given beer by the host, and casual hired labor, usually paid by the piece (for example, cultivating a particular piece of land for a set amount of money). Alongside these, labor on village projects increased in the 1970s, although the vast majority of agricultural production was not collective. Between the late 1960s and the late 1970s, all kinds of non-governmental labor coordination, except the hiring of casual labor, declined in importance. The main casual laborers are young men, many before marriage age, and women without husbands, either divorced or widowed. Up to the early 1970s, most widows would have been inherited by their husbands' agnatic relatives, but with the declining importance of labor based on large polygynous households, women increasingly found themselves living entirely on their own resources, which for many meant working as casual laborers.

Procedures and Techniques

Erosion Control

The people of the Usambara Mountains practice hoe cultivation to grow annual, biannual, and permanent crops. Each field is deeply cultivated with a hoe before the main planting time once each year. The observers of farming in the West Usambaras disagree with one another on whether erosion-control measures are practiced on the farms. Almost all of these are on slopes for which local farming techniques have been described by British agricultural officers as hopelessly destructive of the soil (University of Dar es Salaam n.d.). Attems (1968: 154) reports that no erosion-control measures are taken, although farmers normally delay weeding, and weeds help hold the soil in place and act as a cover for splash erosion until the crops grow large enough to do this. Egger and Glaeser (1975) argue that avoidance of clean weeding and the use of weeds as mulch are self-conscious and effective techniques for erosion control and for maintaining the quality of the soil.

Crop Rotations

Attems (1968) agrees with Egger and Glaeser (all therefore disagreeing with British agricultural officers) in describing the systematic use of crop rotations. He describes the rotation of cassava and maize, with the length of the rotation determined by a need for a minimum amount of cassava. Larger holdings, he argues, have a larger proportion of maize, and are under maize more of the time. Egger and Glaeser (1975: 79–105) provide valuable case studies. They report that each farmer develops a characteristic strategy that depends on the particularities of soil and rainfall as well as on individual preference. One farmer rotates maize and beans (commonly interplanted) with potatoes and beans. A second interplants maize and beans with a seasonal fallow, so that the weeds that grow during the fallow period can be used as deep mulch. The multiple examples show a range of variation in techniques of interplanting and crop rotation.

Irrigation

Irrigation was practiced in the precolonial period and continues to be used today on a portion of the land. Irrigation requires the cooperation of all who use the irrigation works, and many channels fell into disuse when German settler farmers refused to cooperate with their African neighbors to maintain irrigation channels (Karasek 1911–24).

Fallow Cycles

No systematic data on fallow cycles are available. Banana groves near villages are sometimes interplanted with annuals and sometimes left un-tended through a fallow period, so that wild vegetation grows up among the banana plants. Fields for annuals are often planted in only one rainy season and are left fallow for the remainder of the year. The description by Egger and Glaeser (1975: 79-92) of the use of particular fields between 1973 and 1976 is consistent with this understanding of the general pattern. They describe one field planted with bananas and with clumps of sugarcane and then interplanted with seasonally rotating maize and potatoes. The field had been used this way for seven years, and was scheduled to continue for another year or two before being left fallow for several years. In another field of 2.4 hectares, 0.1 hectare was left fallow. Other fields were planted in beans and maize and were left in seasonal fallow for about half a year each.

The entire history of agriculture in the West Usambaras points to a shortening of fallow cycles since the 1920s, with the process gaining momentum in the most recent period. The 1940s were characterized by protests over the loss of grazing land; the 1950s by the intense pressure of farmers encroaching on European estate land; and the 1960s by farmers moving into forest reserve wherever possible. Between 1978 and 1988 I returned periodically to a single broad valley near Bumbuli, an expansive area of land for annuals. My rough and unsystematic impression was that in 1978 the fields formed a patchwork in the middle of the main rainy season, with most of the land cultivated and some left fallow. By 1988 there seemed to be no fallow left during the main rainy season. All the land for annuals appeared to be under cultivation.

Livestock

Farmers keep small numbers of cattle, sheep, or goats, and almost all keep chickens. In the past, livestock were grazed on valley bottoms held as commonage. Today they graze on the rare fallow fields, on cultivated fields after harvest, or in rough areas alongside roads or in woods.

Introduced Crops

The main commercial crops of the 1920s had been food crops.[5] Coffee was introduced during the German period but was restricted at first to few trees and small numbers of cultivators. It became a major crop in the 1950s. It is normally interplanted with bananas and often also with cocoyams. By the late 1970s, because of low coffee prices and an ineffective marketing structure, most peasants gave up spraying and pruning coffee (which most would have practiced twenty years earlier) as unprofitable. African coffee production in the district grew from 5.6 metric tons of coffee in 1936, to 20.3 tons in 1950, to 142.3 tons in 1956. By 1975 coffee production reached 1,072 metric tons.[6]

European-style vegetables, which spread widely during World War II because of government purchases, are often fertilized with manure. Many farmers build terraces for vegetable plots, even though they refuse to do this on maize plots. Hybrid maize was tried widely in the 1970s but most peasants quickly gave it up. It rotted if rained on near maturity but before harvest. It also proved more difficult to store successfully than local varieties of maize. The district produced 131 metric tons of vegetables in 1932 and 1,118 metric tons in 1948, a level never again to be reached under British rule. By the mid-1970s it appeared that total vegetable production might have been approaching 9,000 metric tons per year (Fleuret 1978: 77–84; Glaeser 1984; 92).

Wattle also spread rapidly in the 1950s, as a tree crop for exhausted land. Bark production increased sevenfold between 1950 and 1955, beginning from about 610 metric tons.[7] Deciduous-fruit production expanded at the same time, reaching about 7,000 metric tons in 1971 (Fleuret 1978: 72). Smallholder tea production began only after independence, but quickly became a major product for the district.

One effect of the expansion of coffee, vegetable, wattle, and fruit production, along with the growth of population, has been the loss of grazing land. In 1927 the large Usambara District (including Korogwe and Pare) had 96,739 head of cattle. In 1982 the district, now without Pare, had 29,137 head. By 1953, the numbers were up to 64,976, and then began to decline rapidly, because of rules that made it difficult to keep them and lack of grazing land. The number in 1956 was 47,000.[8]

Agricultural Equipment

Kocher (1976: 83), who surveyed agricultural equipment ownership at two sites in the West Usambaras in 1973, found that almost all households owned hoes and machetes and over 90 percent owned axes. Between 60 and 70 percent owned coffee-fermenting vats. Just under 25 percent owned coffee pulpers. Over 30 percent owned coffee sieves. Smaller percentages of households owned sprayers and sprinklers, and a few owned carts.

Output

It is difficult to know the overall output of the district. Each village reports its output to agricultural officers, but observation of the reporting process shows that village officers tend to create imaginary numbers to satisfy demands for reporting.

Glaeser (1984: 93-100) estimated yields based on the numbers provided by the Tanga Integrated Regional Development Programme (TIRDEP) in its report of 1975. P. Fleuret (1978: 102), relying mostly on the same source, reports slightly different figures. Attems (1968: 157-58) relies on Agricultural Office yields from the 1960s.

The most substantial disagreement among the sources is about coffee, for which Glaeser (1984: 94-96) reports a very low average yield of 100 kg/ha (at U.S. $0.42/kg) and P. Fleuret (1978: 102) appears to agree, whereas Attems (1968: 157-58) reports yields from three separate areas of 266, 323, and 160 kg/ha. The discrepancy probably has to do with the change in coffee cultivation between the 1960s (when Attems did research) and the 1970s, after prices declined and after peasants had difficulty getting full payment for their coffee production. Glaeser (1984: 95) indicates that intensification of coffee growing would raise yields significantly, but would raise labor productivity only slightly from U.S. $0.80 per day to U.S. $1.12 per day.[9] My own observation is that coffee farmers must pay for fertilizer and pesticides before they know what the size of their harvest will be and also before they know whether they will actually be paid for it. The small gains in productivity are seen by most farmers as not worth the risk.

Glaeser (1984: 95, 98) gives maize yields as 650 kg/ha at U.S. $0.10/kg or U.S. $67.20/ha, and U.S. $0.67/workday. Attems's (1968: 157-58) yield estimates are somewhat lower. According to Glaeser (1984: 93-95) potatoes yield 2,060 kg/ha, which, at U.S. $0.05/kg, yields U.S. $101.8/ha or U.S. $1.54 per workday. Tea (Glaeser 1984: 97) yields 250 to 300 kg/ha, or U.S. $105/ha, which is U.S. $0.98/workday. With intensification, yields could be raised significantly, but they would return only U.S. $1.02/workday. As with coffee, the great fear of farmers is that they will borrow money for inputs, and then bad weather will spoil the crop, making it impossible for them to repay the loan.

The yield for beans as given by Glaeser (1984: 95, 98) is 330 kg/ha, rising to 550 kg for irrigated beans. For unirrigated beans the yield is U.S. $68.60/ha, or U.S. $0.98/workday; for irrigated beans without further improvements in cultivation the yield is U.S. $121.1/ha. My discussions with farmers showed that bean cultivation had high initial outlays for labor if grown as a commercial crop that are beyond the capacity of most farmers. Glaeser (1984: 99) gives a yield of 4 to 6 tons of bananas/ha when intercropped, or U.S. $1.82/workday because of the low labor requirements of bananas. If the bananas are mulched, irrigated, and fertilized, the yield per workday goes down to U.S. $1.58. Glaeser (1984: 100) gives the yield for cassava as 2 metric tons of dried cassava per hectare, for a yield of U.S. $72.8/ha, or $1.40 per workday. Fleuret (1978: 102) gives the yield of tomatoes as U.S. $176.4/ha and that of lettuce as U.S. $117.6/ha.

Government Interventions

Since 1925 the organization of marketing has been inextricably intertwined with government plans for the district and for the whole country. The discussion of change in marketing will therefore be presented together with the narrative of government interventions.

The main thrust of government policy in the 1930s was to require Africans to "grow more crops," using the same technology, land, and labor as before. The emphasis also, until 1948, was on keeping the district (and preferably every household) self-sufficient in food, so that the area would remain self-supporting and unspecialized, but with some selected exports. The increase in population (documented above), together with enforced increases in production, led to problems of soil erosion, recognized in district annual reports by the late 1930s. Some erosion-control measures were required from the 1930s. Immediately after the war, the agriculture department instituted a pilot erosion-control scheme at Mlalo, in the north where sheet erosion had occurred.

A set of erosion-control rules, derived from the Mlalo experiment, was made mandatory for Africans in the West Usambaras in the early 1950s. The Usambara Scheme, as it was called, led to a full-scale farmers' revolt, with a march on the Paramount Chief's capital, planning for an assassination attempt on his life, widespread passive resistance, and periodic local demonstrations.[10] The government abandoned the Usambara Scheme in 1957. The resistance movement ultimately linked up with TANU, the nationalist party that won independence. The farmers, having fought and defeated the Usambara Scheme, would clearly be unwilling to accept other compulsory agricultural improvement schemes that resemble it. The scheme's defeat, therefore, is one of the landmark events for the agriculture of the mountains, closing off options for the future. The reasons for resistance are little understood and touch near the heart of farmers' understanding of collective planning for the future of the West Usambaras.

The scheme was to be introduced in a given number of *jumbeates* (local government units) each year beginning in 1951, so that over the course of several years it would apply to the entire population. In the selected jumbeates, every taxpayer was required, in the first year, to put in a half-acre of tie-ridges (ridges running both across and down hillsides, so as to form squares). The required area was to increase in future years. Scheme rules forbade the burning of plant residues and of weeds that could be used as mulch or cattle fodder. The grazing of stock on plant residues left on cropped land was prohibited, and local people were to be required to plant elephant grass along all water courses, to be done by unpaid communal labor.

The most intense peasant resistance focused on the compulsory building of tie-ridges. One of the central questions for understanding the agriculture of the district is why peasants so fiercely resisted building tie-ridges when they voluntarily terraced vegetable plots and other cash-crop farms. P. Fleuret's answer (1978: 106) is that vegetable prices were higher than staple-food prices, making investment in increased vegetable yields worthwhile even though higher maize yields were not rewarding. This is a valuable contribution but not the whole story.

Much of the intense resistance to erosion-control measures came from women, and it is important to note that women made none of the decisions about vegetable plots, for these were under men's control.[11] Women made many (not all) of the decisions about their own maize plots, on which men shared the work. In general, cultivating a maize plot and preparing it for planting is men's work, and women expected that the men would take charge of the erosion-control measures. However, men in the 1950s had to devote much more of their labor than ever before to cash-earning pursuits, making erosion-control work much more difficult, especially for poorer men. The better-off men usually earned their cash through commercial production at home and were able either to help with erosion control or to pay workers to do the job.

The poorer men earned cash by working outside the mountains. In 1952 about one-third of all Shambaa men worked at sisal-related jobs at some time during the year. Even if these men returned home in the dry season to help with cultivation, additional erosion-control work would have extended the unprofitable home stay significantly. In cases where erosion control fell on the wives, this was a double disaster: men ought to be at home preparing fields, and they were not; and now the work of field preparation was much more difficult. At Mgwashi, the most intense moment of women's revolt against erosion-control work came with complaints from women about their absent husbands.[12]

Erosion-control measures must also have affected the balance of remittances between absent husbands and their farming wives. We have seen that when absent husbands sent money to their wives they did not, in most cases, specify how the money was to be spent. The wife who received a sum of discretionary money could use it to employ a farm laborer to clear her fields, to buy clothes for her children and herself, or to purchase hungry-season food supplements. In many cases, wives chose to do the men's work of preparing fields rather than hire labor: the women then used the money for current consumption. This was especially tempting during the field-preparation season, which was also the hungry season. The probable effect of erosion-control measures was to force women to work even harder at field preparation, and at the same time to spend money (if they could) for added labor. They would have to work harder and eat less, even if their husbands sent cash. Under these circumstances it is no surprise at all that women fought against the erosion-control rules.

In addition, erosion-control directly attacked the system under which landless women gained privileged access to land for growing annual food crops. This system is a last line of defense for the poor against complete proletarianization, or at least against being driven off to farm in the plains—a great fear in the 1950s.

Erosion control was one of a number of changes of the 1950s which threatened women's secure access to land, especially scarce land near villages. Farm plots were rapidly being withdrawn from the cultivation of annual food crops. Coffee, wattle, fruit trees, and terraced vegetable production all spread rapidly. It is not valid to say that this led to the commoditization of land, for land had been bought and sold even in the precolonial period. Nevertheless, an important change in land rights was taking place. The land put into tree or vegetable crops was no longer available for rent-free subsistence use.

Erosion-control measures had the same effect as the conversion of land to commercial perennials—they ended the rent-free use of fallow land for subsistence. Under the regime of compulsory erosion control, land-rich farmers continued to lend out their land as before, but the borrowers were required by the government to build tie-ridges in order to cultivate annuals, such as maize and beans. The owner would take back the newly improved land for his own use the second year. He would offer once again to lend unimproved land to a poor neighbor, but once again the poor person would be forced to construct tie-ridges. If the poor had accepted this system, they would have been able to remain on the land only by accepting the back-breaking work of building permanent erosion-control ridges year after year. Instead, they resisted. Some of the poor farmed on secret hidden farms in the wilderness, some refused to farm altogether, and others cultivated only land too steep for erosion-control measures.

The point of this is clear. Once population began to pass the system's carrying capacity, the land became defined as a source of social security for women, children, and old people who could always earn their basic subsistence on it, however poor that subsistence. We have seen that security is sometimes destroyed by "cashlessness." But in local understanding, access to land is the key, and requiring the improvement of all land would lead directly to a new system of land tenure in which the poorest and most vulnerable members of rural society would be driven off.

What this means, however, is that the highest social value has been placed on keeping land for annual food crops unimproved. Only if it is kept unimproved will the poor retain secure access to subsistence land. Much of recent agricultural planning has, unknowingly, encountered the determination of local people to preserve this system and has therefore failed.

There have been a number of significant initiatives by the Tanzanian government to ease the pressure of land scarcity and to improve agriculture since independence in 1961. First, in 1963 the government opened 12,150 ha of the Shume Forest Reserve to peasant cultivation, as a reward of independence and as a way of taking pressure off the land in the northern part of the mountains. The initial intention was for Shume to be the site of improved agricultural practices, but agriculture there quickly took on the character of the surrounding areas, and soil fertility began to decline.

Second, the government introduced tea as a smallholder crop and provided the basic services for its success. This was a significant advance, because tea is better suited to the soils of Usambara than coffee and had been reserved by the British as a plantation crop. One of the shocking stories of agricultural planning in the 1950s is of the British agricultural officers who encouraged coffee planting and helped develop Native Authority coffee nurseries, even though they knew that coffee would be an unprofitable crop, except at the very high prices that then existed. They encouraged coffee because they wanted to be able to do something popular at a time of farmer resistance and to control erosion.

Third, the Tanzanian government expanded education enormously, with unmeasurable effects on the future of agriculture. One immediate consequence of Universal Primary Education in the late 1970s, as already mentioned, was that children's labor was partially withdrawn from agriculture, and polygyny therefore declined.

Fourth, the policy of villagization had some significant consequences, even though people in the Usambaras had always lived in villages. The villages grew in size. The few people who lived in scattered homesteads moved into villages, intensifying yet further the agricultural consequences of living at central places and farming on distant plots. In addition the villages, as new collective institutions, were able to assemble their own social capital—to construct storehouses and schools, and to coordinate transport for villagers' crops—in addition to serving as an instrument for government education and planning.

Fifth, most important, government control over marketing had a substantial impact on farmers' production. Government-controlled marketing was not new in the independence period. The British had required single-channel marketing for many crops, and the so-called black market was central to the development of stratification in the 1950s. The independence government used African cooperatives as the main channel for purchasing produce. In Usambara this was particularly unfortunate, even though cooperatives had existed since the early 1930s. In 1962, the Usambara Co-operative Union was formed, with nine branches, each of them a primary society (Molloy 1971: 65). Cooperative unions were given loans by a national bank to finance crops, to be repaid from the proceeds of sales. The Usambara Co-operative Union had a record of corrupt and inefficient management. In a 1965 report, Rene Dumont (quoted in Molloy 1971: 71) wrote, "At Lushoto, a ton of maize, bought at Shs. 440/- by the Marketing Board, only brings the producer Shs. 220/-. We have never seen, anywhere in the world, such high deductions reaching half the value of the product." Three-quarters of the farmers did not belong to the primary societies but were required to market their crops through the cooperative anyway.

Agricultural prices paid by the cooperatives were low through the period. One result was the decline in coffee production already noted. Another was the expansion of production of products like vegetables that were not marketed by the cooperative. In 1976 the government, responding to widespread problems, nationalized all the cooperative unions, shifting marketing over to parastatal corporations that, however, were no more successful than the cooperatives at buying farmers' produce at decent prices. Marketing problems have undoubtedly slowed the expansion of commercial-crop production (for which agricultural improvement was acceptable to farmers); at the same time the ethic of subsistence prevented the adoption of erosion-control measures on farms for growing food crops.

Consequences of Change

The people of the West Usambaras made a clear choice when they rejected the erosion-control scheme of the 1940s and 1950s. The mountains serve as a home, a promise of subsistence, to tens of thousands of people who live in other parts of Tanzania and to more people than the land can carry within Usambara, given current agricultural practice. The promise of subsistence will be broken, with real social costs, if farmers begin to adopt permanent improvements on their plots for annual food crops. Since this is unacceptable to most of the population, the land is declining in fertility. Erosion, loss of nutrients, and laterization are proceeding. Land is bought and sold as it has been since the precolonial period, but villagers with no land have a right to land for subsistence crops. Universal primary education led to the decline of polygyny and widow inheritance. This was accompanied by a decline in the use of household labor and by an expansion in the hiring of casual labor. Children in disastrous health circumstances tend to be the children of uninherited widows or of divorcees. These women can meet their needs for land, but not their needs for cash. Since they must work for others, their tie to the land becomes tenuous, and it is possible that an agricultural proletariat will emerge in the coming years.

A significant crack in the system came to light in December 1988.

An official from the area around Mlalo, in north of Usambara, indicated that land for annuals was now being rented at high prices. In the southern part of the mountains subsistence land was still loaned rent-free. If Mlalo's new pattern spreads, then the promise of subsistence will be broken definitively, and the victory won in the fight over erosion control will be seen over the long term as a temporary holding action.

Notes

1. TNA (Tanzania National Archives) Secretariat 1733, District Annual Report, Wilhemstal, 1920. See TNA 11682, p. 177, for 1929; 1937 is from TNA 72/62/6; 1941 is from TNA 72/62/6/II, District Annual Report, Korogwe. TNA 72/62/III Annual Report, Korogwe. District 1946. The estimates are all approximate, but the general trend is clear.

2. On food exports see TNA Secretariat, Annual Report Tanga Province, 1927 and 1929. The district and provincial annual reports through the 1920s and 1930s confirm that not many highland people worked on estates. The judgement on grazing is based on the fact that farmers converted grazing into farms for cash cropping in the 1940s and 1950s. A set of about 150 domestic economic histories the author collected near Bumbuli show that cattle were central to the domestic economy of the area in the 1920s.

3. The figure for 1967 is from Cliffe et al. (1969: 20). The figure for 1973 is calculated from the census figures .

4. TNA 72/62/6/III, 234, Lushoto District Annual Report, 1952; TNA 72/62/6/IV, 12A 1954; TNA 72/62/6/III, 228,1951.

5. TNA Secretariat, Annual Report, Tanga Province, 1927, 1929.

6. 1936 figure from Provincial Commissioners Reports. Fleuret 1978: 63–64; TNA 72/62/6/IV, p. 32A.

7. TNA 72/62/6/III; 304/R3/1.

8. For the herd censuses, see the District Annual Reports. On scarcity of grazing see TNA 72/3/1a/I/24; *Mlalo Basin Rehabilitation Scheme* (University of Dar es Salaam n.d.:12). TNA 72/44/16/2A on farmers' complaints in 1947 about the lack of grazing.

9. Glaeser (1984) gives very interesting data on productivity per workday but does not report his precise definition of a workday.

10. The politics of the Scheme are discussed fully in Feierman 1990.

11. TNA 33049/iv, sheet 411, Usambara Scheme Annual Report, 1951.

12. TNA Usambara Scheme Monthly Report for December 1950, 3 January 1951.

References

Attems, Manfred. 1967. *Bauernbetriebe in tropischen Höhenlagen Ostafrikas,* Afrika Studien, Nr. 25. Munich: IFO Institut für Wirtschaftsforschung.

———. 1968. "Permanent Cropping in the Usambara Mountains," *In Smallholder Farming and Smallholder Development in Tanzania,* ed. Hans Ruthenberg, pp. 138–74. Munich: Weltforum Verlag.

Baumann, Oscar. 1891. *Usambara und seine Nachbargebiete.* Berlin.

Cliffe, Lionel, William L. Luttrell, and John E. Moore. 1969. Socialist Transformation in Rural Tanzania—A Strategy for the Western Usambaras. Rural Development Paper no. 6. University College Dar es Salaam, Rural Development Research Committee.

Dupre, H. n.d . "Land und Volk in Usambara." Manuscript at the Bethel Mission archives, Bethel bei Bielefeld.

Egger, Kurt, and Bernhard Glaeser. 1975. *Politische Ökologie der Usambara-Berge in Tanzania.* Bensheim: Kübel Stiftung.

Feierman, Steven. 1972. "Concepts of Sovereignty among the Shambaa and Their Relation to Political Action." D. Phil. thesis, Oxford University.

———. 1974. *The Shambaa Kingdom.* Madison: University of Wisconsin Press.

———. 1990. *Peasant Intellectuals: Anthropology and History in Tanzania.* Madison: University of Wisconsin Press.

Fleuret, Patrick C. 1978. "Farm and Market: A Study of Society and Agriculture in Tanzania." Ph.D. dissertation, University of California, Santa Barbara.

Fleuret, Patrick C., and Anne K. Fleuret. 1978. "Fuelwood Use in a Peasant Community: A Tanzanian Case Study." *The Journal of Developing Areas* 12: 315–22.

Glaeser, Bernhard, ed. 1980. *Factors Affecting Land Use and Food Production.* Sozialwissenschaftliche Studien zu Internationalen Problemen, Vol. 55. Saarbrücken, Fort Lauderdale: Verlag Breitenbach.

———. 1984. *Ecodevelopment in Tanzania.* Berlin, New York, Amsterdam: Mouton.

Heijnen, J.D. 1974. "National Policy, Foreign Aid and Rural Development: A Case Study of LIDEP's Vegetable Component in Lushoto District (Tanzania)." Bulletin, *Sociale Geografie Ontwikkelingslanden,* ser. ii, no 3.

Holst, Carl. 1893. "Der Landbau der Eingeborenen von Usambara." *Deutsche Kolonialzeitung* 6: 113–14, 128–30.

Karasek, A. 1911–24. "Beiträge zur Kenntnis der Waschambaa." *Baessler-Archiv* 1: 155–222; 3: 69–131; 7: 56–98; 8: 1–53.

Kocher, Hames Edward. 1976. "A Micro-economic Analysis of the Determinants of Human Fertility in Rural Northeastern Tanzania." Ph.D. dissertation, Michigan State University.

LangHeinrich, F. 1913. "Die Entwicklung des Verkehrs in Westusambara." *Nachrichten aus der ostafrikanischen Mission* 27: 7–12.

Matango, Reuben R. 1979. "The Role of Agencies for Rural Development in Tanzania: A Case Study of the Lushoto Integrated Development Project," In *African Socialism in Practice*, ed. Andrew Coulson, pp. 158–72. Nottingham: Spokesman.

Milne, G. 1937. "Soil Type and Soil Management in Relation to Plantation Agriculture in East Usambara." *East African Agricultural Journal* 3(July): 7–20.

Molloy, Judith. 1971. "Political Communication in Lushoto District, Tanzania." Ph.D. dissertation, University of Kent at Canterbury.

Schönmeier, H. W. 1977. *Agriculture in Conflict—The Shambaa Case*. Bensheim: Kübel Stiftung.

Sender, John. n.d. "The Development of Capitalist Agriculture in Tanzania: A Study with Detailed Reference to the West Usambaras." Ph.D. thesis. University of London (School of Oriental and African Studies).

United Republic of Tanzania. 1982. *1978 Population Census*, vol. 4. Dar es Salaam: Bureau of Statistics, Ministry of Planning and Economic Affairs.

University of Dar es Salaam, Department of History. n.d. *Mlalo Basin Rehabilitation Scheme*. Documents of the Pangani Valley Historical Project.

5 / Marginal Coping in Extreme Land Pressures: Ruhengeri, Rwanda

Robert E. Ford

For the foreseeable future, the vast percentage of Africans will continue to make their living directly from the land. Therefore, population-agriculture relationships in rural areas are crucial to the issue of sustainable development. Of particular concern for the future of sub-Saharan Africa is rural population density. Rwanda has the second highest population growth rate in Africa (3.4–3.7 percent/annum) and one of its highest overall population densities (210–350 persons/km²) in Africa (UNICEF 1985: 7–25). Furthermore, 95 percent of its population is considered rural, even though the urban growth rate has increased in recent years.[1] Seven of the ten prefectures or districts in Rwanda have surpassed the 200 persons/km² threshold (Johnson 1986: 20).

A cursory evaluation of the situation suggests that Rwanda has coped remarkably well with land pressures without major deterioration of its agro-ecological resource base (Rossi 1984). This said, positive developments appear to have barely kept the system on a precarious balance between land and people, without really bringing about major improvements in living standards. A critical appraisal forces one to ask: if agricultural production has indeed kept pace with population growth in Rwanda, under what conditions has it achieved this tenuous stability? Even more crucial, are the present coping mechanisms sufficient for the projected demographic challenges of the future?

These and related questions are explored here through a case study of one of Rwanda's most densely populated districts, Ruhengeri. Its experience may serve as a natural experiment for exploring potential scenarios common to many of the high-density tropical montane regions in East and Central Africa (Kates 1987).

Overview of Study Area

Ruhengeri prefecture is located in northwest Rwanda (fig. 5.1). It is subdivided into 16 communes and 177 sectors, covering an area of roughly 1,685 km². In addition to its densely settled population, it has agro-ecological, political, geographical, and socioeconomic characteristics that typify this segment of Central Africa.[2] Some are listed below.

1. A significant increase in tourism to the Volcanoes National Park in the Virunga Mountains is occurring, particularly by those desiring to see the world-famous mountain gorilla. This has heightened national and international awareness for the need of preserving the rare fauna and flora within the rapidly diminishing wild mountain and wetland areas of Rwanda.

2. Major changes in agricultural policy and practice are being stimulated through the aegis of several major research projects located within its boundaries (see PNAP *Projet National de la Pomme de Terre*, the National Potato Project [Zaag 1980; Durr 1983]; GBK *Projet Agro-Sylvo-Pastoral*, a large World Bank-funded dairy/agroforestry project [Rosenblum and Williamson 1987: 99–110]; *SODEPARAL*, a large government tea-plantation cooperative; the USAID-funded ISAR/Farming Systems Research Project in Rwerere). Other projects by the Swiss and German governments as well as NGOs like CARE and ADRA are making useful contributions.

3. Major investment in basic economic infrastructure has been carried out within the region (fig. 5.2). These include: expansion of the hydroelectric power grid from Lake Bulera to many hitherto unserved communities; building and paving a new highway linking Gisenyi through Ruhengeri to Kigali; opening of a new maize oil–extraction plant and associated maize-culture extension activities; expansion of the principal grain-milling operation in Ruhengeri, linked to development of marketing cooperatives to encourage production of wheat; location of a branch campus of the national university near Ruhengeri; building of a new urban market, stadium, and airport in Ruhengeri Town; construction of several secondary-level technical institutes within the region (e.g., in veterinary and agricultural sciences, health/nursing, social work/nutrition). The effects of these and other development aid projects on population-agriculture relationships could become significant (Harroy 1981; Godding 1986).

4. Major spatial realignments and population shifts are occurring,

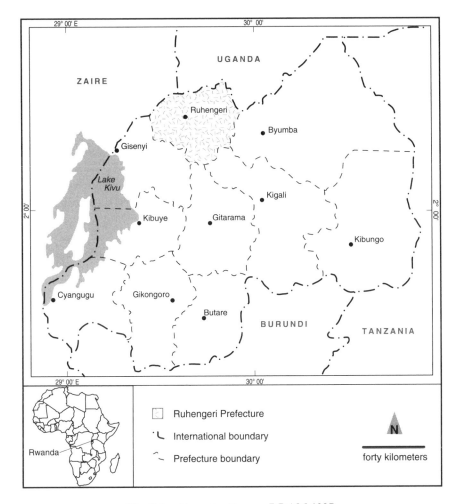

Fig. 5.1. Rwanda. Source: RRAM 1987.

(e.g., settlement pattern and housing-style changes). Causes of these changes include: diffusion of new clay brick- and tile-roofing technology; testing and diffusion of a locally made alternative to Portland cement introduced by a German private voluntary organization; the government policy of encouraging the centralization of public services (e.g., schools, clinics, credit bureaus) at nodal sites in association with new communal administration buildings adjacent to new improved feeder roads; implementation of a new land program (called *paysannats*)

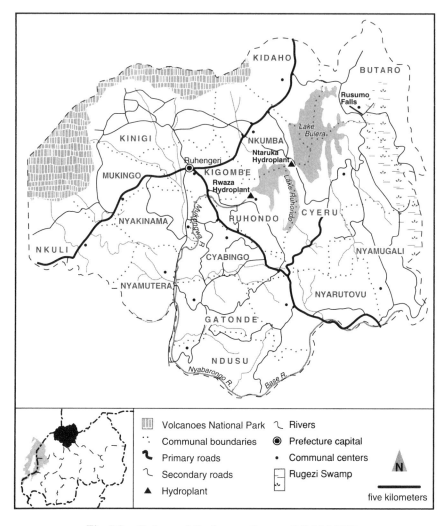

Fig. 5.2. Ruhengeri Prefecture. Source: RRAM 1987.

oriented toward export or commodity agriculture (e.g., pyrethrum, wheat, potatoes, tea, and coffee).

5. The landscape itself is being significantly modified through mass-mobilization reforestation and soil-erosion control campaigns in conjunction with other rural development efforts. Some experimentation with true terrace building has even occurred. Natural vegetation species and formations are being altered significantly or disappearing, except in

the few remaining parks or forest preserves. Even within the latter, an intense humanization of the landscape is rapidly occurring.

6. Changes in the agricultural system are also evident (Heremans et al. 1982; Jones and Egli 1984; RRAM 1987): reduction in fallow cycles; disappearance of traditional pastoralism as a viable lifestyle; farmer pressure on pasture lands (both in the high mountain areas and lowlands); reduction of farm size (Delepierre and Prefol 1973) often below the threshold of economic viability, with concomitant changes in labor patterns, migration, land-tenure patterns (Chrétien 1978; Reintsma 1982; Buschman 1984; Cambrezy 1984; Ruhashyankiki 1985; Feder and Noronha 1987); extensive introduction of new cash crops like tea (Chapuis 1986; Martin 1987); changes in traditional cash crops, for example, competitive pressure on the traditional banana-beer industry by the government monoply brewery (Gotanegre 1983).

The Physical Environment

Relief and Hydrology

Ruhengeri prefecture is characterized by extremely rugged relief ranging from 1,400 m in the south to over 4,500 m on Mt. Karisimbi in the Virunga Mountains (fig. 5.3). This mountainous environment supports a diversity of agro-ecological niches; most are now occupied and exploited for agriculture. The only nonagricultural areas remaining are within the forested Volcanoes National Park (along the border with Zaire and Uganda) and a complex network of lakes and wetlands to the east (Roark and Dickson 1986; RRAM 1987: 7–11, 48; E. Byers 1988).

The stream network in Ruhengeri closely reflects the associated lithology. Except for a few major perennial streams, most water courses are intermittent, subject to brief but destructive flooding caused by violent convective rainstorms, including occasional severe hail (Byers 1988a, 1988c). In the lava zone, surface drainage is constrained due to highly permeable soils. Where lava makes contact with harder bedrock, springlines or even small lakes occur (RRAM 1987: 12).

A RRAM-*Ruhengeri Resources and Management Project* analysis of the water-balance situation for the region's four principal watersheds has identified at least one potentially serious anomaly: "streamflow rates from the Lower Mukungwa have increased considerably over the past

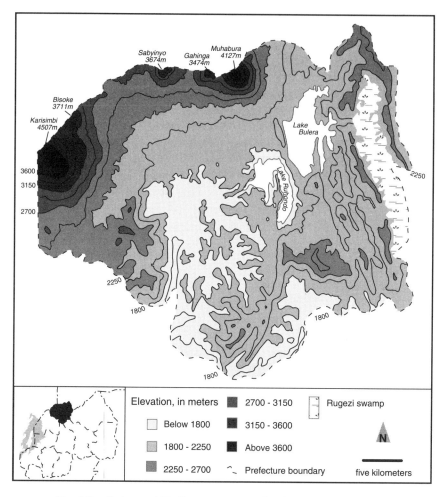

Fig. 5.3. Ruhengeri Prefecture: topography. Source: RRAM 1987.

five years, thus increasing the percentage of runoff assigned to the entire watershed" (RRAM 1987: 47). This anomaly may be explained by inaccurate data-collection techniques, but William Weber, the first RRAM Project Manager, suggests that "the measures reflect increased runoff due to radically changed land-use practices (wetland drainage, deforestation, inadequate soil- and water-conservation practices on farmlands) throughout the watershed" (RRAM 1987: 48). The most recent research on stream hydrology and soil erosion in Ruhengeri (Byers and Nyamulinda 1988; Byers 1988a, 1988b, 1988c; E. Byers 1988; Nyamulinda

1988) has confirmed the actual and potential seriousness of catastrophic rainfall.

Ruhengeri is favored by the presence of extensive wetlands, characterized by permanent standing water and smaller, seasonally flooded bottomlands. These *petits marais* regulate water flow and provide a critical habitat for the water birds of Rwanda. They also have become rich agricultural lands. The primary technique for their exploitation is raised-field horticulture (fig. 5.4). These are highly productive environments, and few bottomlands are now undeveloped.

Nearly 9,000 ha of wetlands and bottomlands cover more than 5 percent of the prefecture with over half of the total area located in the three easternmost provinces. According to RRAM (1987), 56 percent of this area was already developed as of 1980. Within the last six years, an additional 1,000 ha of bottomlands have been converted to agricultural production (fig. 5.4). A major part of this conversion has occurred in Nkuli, where formerly undeveloped bottomland has been put into tea production.

Rugezi Marsh is the largest undeveloped wetland. Only about half of it remains in a more or less natural state. It is located at a 2,000-m elevation and fills an elliptical basin nearly 30 km long, surrounded by quartzite ridges. The Rugezi complex has only one natural outlet, at the Rusumo Falls, where water flows at an average rate of 1.3 m^3/s down to Lakes Bulera and Ruhundo.

The beautiful lava-blocked lakes of northwest Rwanda, many with dramatic ria coastlines, were formed as a result of the Virunga uplifting and subsequent lava flows that deranged the regional drainage systems. The combined lakes cover 4.6 percent of the district. In addition to rainfall and inflow from the Rugezi marsh, they are fed by subterranean infiltration from the Lava zone and runoff from surrounding hills.

Lakes Bulera and Ruhondo are most valued for the production of hydroelectricity, whereas other possible uses are less developed (e.g., tourism, fishing). The combined output from the two hydroelectric stations at Ntaruka and Rwaza presents more than half of Rwanda's annual production of electricity. Water pollution is not a general problem in these lakes except for transported sediment from the Gifurwe Wolfram mine tailings, which contain up to 146 ppm of arsenic, and the endemic contamination of the lake waters by bilharzia (RRAM 1987: 51).

In terms of water supply for domestic use, the major problem is distribution. Distance from a water source is particularly serious in the

Fig. 5.4. Wetland raised fields/mounding and adjacent slope cultivation, Haute Bu-beruka area of Ruhengeri Prefecture. Histosols in valley (*Petite marais*). Note ridged fields/mounds and *uruguro* (homestead) on midslope with surrounding banana grove and scattered woodlots of eucalyptus and linear eucalyptus along road.

Lava Zone where over 16 percent of the population must walk more than two kilometers to obtain water. During the dry season the situation can become even more serious (RRAM 1987: 52–55).

In short, Ruhengeri is fairly well endowed with surface water resources (Roark and Dickson 1986), and expansion of agriculture into its rich wetlands has been a major reason food production has kept pace with population.

Climate

Ruhengeri has a generally cool, humid climate. Temperatures range from an average of 18°C in the lower Mukungwa Valley (1,500 m) to only 12°C at the base of the Virunga volcanoes (2,500 m). Frost and freezing temperatures occur at night in the park above 3,000 m, and occasionally snow covers the summit of Mt. Karisimbi (4,705 m).

Rainfall increases from a low of roughly 1,100 mm/year in the northeastern corner to near 2,000 mm/year in the northwestern mountains. Most agricultural lands receive 1,200–1,600 mm/year, although considerable variability appears as a function of local relief. Rainfall is distributed bimodally, with the primary wet season occurring from March through May and a secondary season from September through December. The principal dry season lasts from two to four months between mid-May and mid-September, whereas the "short dry season" of January to February is more appropriately considered a time of reduced rainfall (RRAM 1987: 8).

Prolonged drought has not posed a serious threat in Ruhengeri during recent times. Analysis of precipitation records since 1928 are ambivalent (RRAM 1987: 8): the period from 1928 to 1960 was characterized by generally lower-than-average rainfall, whereas more humid conditions predominated during the 1960s and 1970s. The first half of the present decade has again been drier, with a particularly bad year for farming in 1984, coincident with the generalized African drought of that year. However, 1986 was wetter than average.

Therefore, the climate of Ruhengeri is adequate to excellent for agriculture, and so are surface water resources; and serious drought, unlike in much of the rest of Africa, is not a serious threat.

The one major climatic hazard of concern is the great potential for catastrophic rainfall accompanied by severe hail and wind, which may lead to severe erosion (Byers 1988a, 1988b, 1988c; Byers and Nyamulinda 1988). Episodes of severe flooding and erosion tend to occur every few years and are generally concentrated in specific high-risk periods such as the transition from wet to dry season or vice versa. The pattern of increasing population density on marginal lands only exacerbates the erosion risk and the potential consequences.

Relief and Soils

The major landscape and soil contrasts in the prefecture are between the newer volcanic areas—from late Tertiary and Quaternary eruptions of the Virunga Volcanoes—and the older surfaces and soils where the schists, micaschist, and quartz formations dominate. A small portion of the district has significant outcroppings of granitic rock along the eastern escarpment of the western Rift Valley (the Zaire-Nile Divide), where they form part of an ancient horst uplifted during the Tertiary.

The four principal soil parent materials are lava, schists, granite, and quartz. Alluvial and colluvial soils resulting from erosion of the source materials and accumulated organic matter are common. The six principal soil types and characteristics are described below (RRAM 1987).

Andepts (soils of volcanic origin) cover roughly 55,000 ha (33 percent of the region) and are concentrated in the northwestern area. Generally these soils have high concentrations of organic matter and are quite fertile; erosion is not a major concern except for a few special areas. On the negative side, there are risks of magnesium deficiencies, low acidity retention, and excessive phosphorus-fixation capacity.

Oxisols of schist origin cover 51,000 ha (29 percent of Ruhengeri) and are located primarily in the eastern half of the region. The oxisols tend to be well drained and acidic with excellent physical properties, but their chemical properties are poor and they are highly susceptible to erosion of the A-horizon, the uppermost soil layer.

Lithic entisols (soils of quartzitic origin) cover nearly 25,000 ha (14 percent of the district) and are concentrated along the north-south ridges of eastern Ruhengeri. These soils have poor texture, a shallow profile, limited agricultural potential, and a high erosion risk.

Oxisols of granitic origin are limited to about 8,000 ha in isolated pockets in southwestern Ruhengeri. Where enriched by volcanic ash deposits and humus development under recent forest cover, these oxisols tend to have good agricultural potential. But the combination of relatively shallow profiles, low saturation levels due to high clay content, and steep slopes mean high erosion risk and declining productivity.

Fluvents (alluvial and colluvial soils) cover thousands of hectares of marshes and bottomlands spread throughout the nonvolcanic parts of the region. They are generally characterized by their high agricultural potential.

Histosols (peat formations of the Rugezi Marsh and smaller bogs) are naturally difficult to manage, have nutrient deficiencies, and are usually waterlogged. They also are subject to problems of subsidence and excessive drying following inappropriate drainage and exploitation practices. In spite of these handicaps they are a major potential resource.

The RRAM (1987: 8–10) study concluded that "the soils of Ruhengeri derive from a variety of sources and have generally good agricultural potential." The principle concern is the following: what are the limits to its potential productivity and how close to those limits is the current situation?

Flora and Ecological Zonation

In Ruhengeri vegetation exhibits a very distinct altitudinal zonation. Unfortunately, less than 10 percent of the district's vegetation remains in its natural state—the lower levels of the Afromontane forest has been almost eliminated. The remaining areas of natural vegetation are: the Volcanoes National Park, which occupies 12,500 ha (7.4 percent of the territory); about 3,000 ha (3 percent) of remnant marshland habitat found in the core of the Rugezi Marsh; and a small portion of the partially deteriorated Gishwati Forest Preserve, where a tree-farm and a dairy complex have been developed by the GBK Project (RRAM 1987: 2–7; Rosenblum and Williamson 1987: 99–110).

The soil-vegetation sequence found on Ruhengeri's hillsides creates an opportunity for a diversity of ecological microniches. At least five major agro-ecological zones can be identified in Ruhengeri out of a total of twelve for the whole country. Land-use patterns in the district can be described in relation to the above-mentioned zones, as well as to slope areas: bottomland, lower (concave) slope, middle slope, upper (convex) slope, and ridgetop. The traditional farming system was adept at matching cultivation practices, cultigens, and settlement patterns to these ecological and slope characteristics (fig. 5.5).

Population Change in Ruhengeri

Density

Ruhengeri has witnessed dramatic changes in population over the last forty years. In 1948 Pierre Gourou (1952) carried out a study of population density in Rwanda (Prioul 1981). Total population for Ruhengeri in that year was 212,961, an average population density of 164 persons/km^2; in 1984 it was 619,070, an average density of 367 persons/km^2 (about a 225 percent increase). Table 5.1 shows the 1984 densities in Ruhengeri by commune, including a corrected density in which only arable land is considered. In the latter case the average density is 447 persons km^2. The map of densities (fig. 5.6) shows that the population in Ruhengeri is not distributed evenly over the landscape (RRAM 1987: 16–18). Many factors appear to be related to this uneven distribution: access to market and other government services, ecology, and culture.

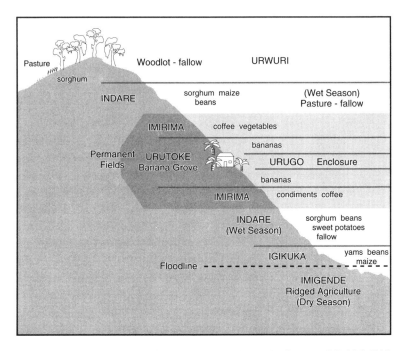

Fig. 5.5. Land-use Catena, Central Plateau, Rwanda. Source: RRAM 1987.

Growth and Migration

Population growth over the last fifty years has seen some significant shifts. From a base of roughly 229,000 in 1936, the population declined drastically due to famine-induced mortality and emigration during the early 1940s (fig. 5.7). One of the major causes of outmigration in this period was the Ruzagayura-Matemane famine that occurred between 1942 and 1944 (Lugan 1976; ONAPO 1982: 91–104). There was also considerable forced and voluntary movement of Rwandese to Kivu and other areas in then Belgian Congo (Chrétien 1978; Cambrezy 1984). By 1950 the numbers had returned to earlier levels, and they then doubled by 1970 to roughly 458,000—a 3.5 percent average annual rate of increase over that twenty-year period. Between 1970 and 1978 Ruhengeri's growth rate was limited to 1.9 percent, but in recent years it has climbed back up to 2.9 percent. The lower rate of the earlier years was due to heavy emigration to lower-density eastern Rwanda (République Rwandaise 1982: 27).

Table 5.1. Population Densities by Commune

Commune	Population, 1984	Total area (/km²)	Population density (/km²)	Corrected area[a]	Corrected density (/km²)
Butaro	46,719	141.6	330	128.4	364
Cyabingo	50,197	86.6	580	86.6	580
Cyeru	51,296	180.9	284	156.6	328
Gatonde	32,108	76.3	421	76.3	421
Kidaho	29,494	89.4	330	73.4	402
Kigombe	42,169	71.3	591	71.3	591
Kinigi	35,077	171.6	204	113.4	309
Mukingo	27,544	106.3	259	62.5	441
Ndusu	37,143	92.2	403	92.2	403
Nkuli	32,209	117.8	273	103.4	312
Nkumba	33,704	101.3	333	83.1	406
Nyakinama	44,117	66.6	662	66.6	662
Nyamugali	39,243	126.6	310	126.6	310
Nyamutera	28,979	56.9	509	56.9	509
Nyarutovu	45,462	125.3	363	125.3	363
Ruhondo	43,609	74.0	589	57.2	762
Total/Average	619,070	1,684.7	403	1,479.8	447

Source: RRAM 1987.
[a]Based on total area minus area in lakes and parks.

Rural-to-urban migration has also increased in recent years; the national urban growth rate was 5 percent between 1970 and 1978. Sirven (1984) feels that urban growth will be the safety valve over the next twenty years. Urban Ruhengeri is also growing: from 12,500 in 1970 to 23,805 in 1986, and by the year 2000 it is projected to attain over 35,000. What effect this may have on the population-resource picture in the rural areas surrounding Ruhengeri is as yet unclear. It could be significant though, particularly because Ruhengeri enjoys a certain political favor in that it is the current president's home district (UNICEF 1985: 9–12).

A survey carried out by RRAM in 1986 found that only 7 percent of the region's population continue to view emigration as a viable solution to land shortage. RRAM estimates that if the actual growth rate returns to near 3.5 percent (the intrinsic growth rate of births minus deaths), this would result in a doubling of the regional population to more than 1.2 million by the year 2006 (RRAM 1987: 16–18).

It appears that the conditions for an accelerated population growth were first achieved during the late colonial period. Major political and socioeconomic improvements in material well-being are generally credited for the growth: vector control and medical service improvements,

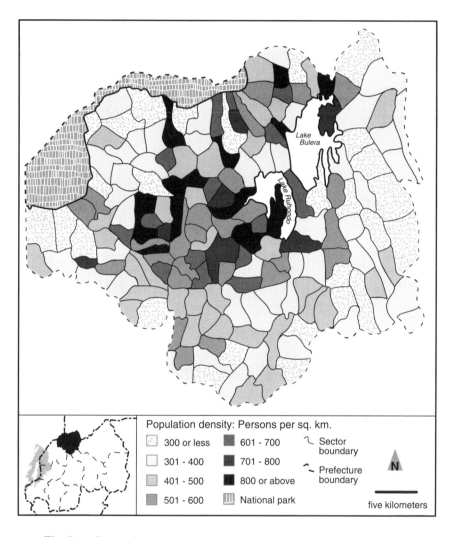

Fig. 5.6. Population density, Ruhengeri Prefecture. Source: RRAM 1987.

education, roads, food reserves, and commerce. Martin (1987) has high-lighted the role of introduced cultigens as a crucial element in population growth. Later, when land pressures appeared, migration was initially chosen as the coping mechanism. But that option is no longer viable; the conditions for a land-people squeeze are thus currently a real threat.

Population in thousands

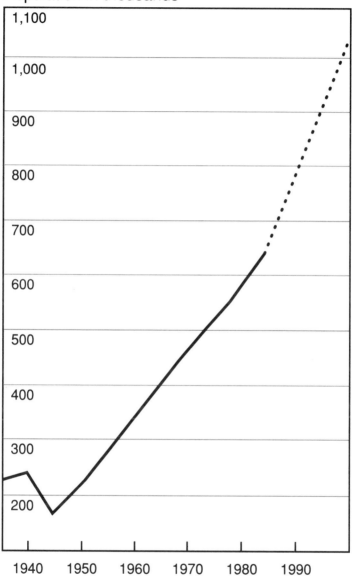

Fig. 5.7. Population growth, Ruhengeri Prefecture. Source: RRAM 1987.

Fertility, Age Structure, and Composition

Unfortunately, the population growth and density situation is not balanced by a favorable age structure or fertility picture. A completed fertility study in Rwanda (ONAPO 1983) gives Ruhengeri an average of 8.9 live births per woman by the end of her reproductive years. Socioeconomic improvements in nutritional and material well-being have reduced mortality, and the total fertility rate may have actually increased. Half of the present population is under twenty, and it is obvious that this large cohort has great potential for population growth, even at remarkably reduced fertility or growth rates (table 5.2).

Furthermore, until very recently, the country has had a pronatalist policy partly emanating from the strong influence of the Catholic church (over 52 percent of the population are Catholic). Only recently, the government has adopted an official anti-natalist policy that encourages birth control as part of an overall maternal and child health and socioeconomic development policy orientation. But its effectiveness so far is largely limited to the elite in the cities (ONAPO 1984).

In short, the government's current strategy is essentially to control population growth over the next quarter of a century and concurrently increase food production through agricultural intensification. Its goal is to stabilize population before agricultural intensification reaches its limit (MINIPLAN 1983). In the interim this strategy also seeks to encourage urban growth and commercial development to siphon off excess population.

Agricultural Land—Natural-Resource Base

General Typology and History of Land Tenure

It was the BaHutu, a Bantu farming people (89 percent of the nation's population), that established long before the fourteenth century the rudiments of the agricultural system seen today (Heremans et al. 1982; Jones and Egli 1984). It appears that they practiced a form of shifting agriculture with extended forest fallow while population densities were low. In the fourteenth to fifteenth centuries the pastoral BaTutsi, a Nilotic people (currently 10 percent of the population) entered Rwanda. They established their core area on the Central Plateau of Rwanda. The earliest known settlers in the region were the BaTwa, a pigmoid people, who practiced forest hunting and gathering. Their impact has been minimal due to their few numbers (1 percent of the population).

Table 5.2. Selected Population Characteristics of the Rural Household in
Ruhengeri Prefecture (Rwanda)

Age of head of household		Sex of the head of household	
	Number		Percent
0–25 years	11,601	Masculine	79.3
25–34 years	41,119	Feminine	20.7
35–44 years	25,351		
45–54 years	18,259		
55–64 years	14,965		
65+ years	13,572		
Total	124,867		

Level of education/head		Sex/age dist. of household	
	Percent		Percent
No education	54.2	Masculine	
Prim. 1–3 years	17.9	0–14 years	51.7
Prim. 4–5 years	11.6	15–64 years	44.2
Prim. 6 years	13.2	65+ years	4.1
Prim. 7+ years	3.1	Feminine	
		0–14 years	50.5
		15–64 years	46.8
		65+ years	2.7

Percent Distribution of Numbers of Persons per Household

Number per household	Percent of households
1	2.4
2	8.3
3	7.8
4	20.5
5	15.3
6	17.0
7	6.4
8	6.3
9	3.2
>9	3.0

Source: MINAGREF/SESA 1984–85: 30–36.

Long before the colonial period, earlier land use and political or tribal conflicts encouraged many BaHutu agriculturists to emigrate into
northwestern Rwanda where independent BaHutu kingdoms were set up
(Mulera, Bugoyi, and Bukiga). Ruhengeri is still part of the cultural
heartland of these early kingdoms and benefits from the current political
dominance of BaHutu leaders in the government (many of which identify Ruhengeri as their home region).

Significant population growth during the nineteenth century led to
modification of the shifting agriculture system to a more permanent

type, except on the forest fringe. By then a land-tenure system called *ubukonde* was firmly in place (Maquet 1967; LeMarchand 1982; Reintsma 1982; Ruhashyankiki 1985); it essentially gave controlling rights to large tracts of land to specific clan chiefs. Land could be subsequently subdivided among male members of the lineages through subdivision, inheritance, or gift. Newer immigrants could obtain land only as tenants or *abagererwa* of the original lineages and their land chiefs. Many current political leaders in Rwanda (including the President) are important traditional land chiefs, as well as modern bureaucrats. That many of these leaders originate from Ruhengeri—and that they are often influential in land issues around the country—has become an important political issue not often considered in the development process (LeMarchand 1982).

With the arrival of the colonial era, the pastoral BaTutsi *ibikingi* (the feudal system emanating from the Mwami or king in southern Rwanda) was extended to Ruhengeri. Some lands, particularly in the higher-elevation areas, came under a European private-ownership system (e.g., plantations of tea, pyrethrum). The independence movement led to civil war, which put the BaHutu in charge, and reinstated elements of the traditional *ubukonde* system; though currently the government is reevaluating the whole legal basis for land tenure.

The final result is yet unclear, though it is interesting that the 1984 Agricultural Survey identified tenancy, gift giving, borrowing, and selling of land as increasing dramatically because of land scarcity (ONAPO 1982).

Field Size, Distribution, and the Arable Land

The land base for agriculture in Ruhengeri was estimated by Delepierre and Prefol (1973) to be a theoretical maximum of 138,946 ha. From this figure were subtracted 20,842 ha considered inappropriate for farming, leaving a "potential arable land base" of 118,104 ha. On this land it was estimated approximately 107,000 families could be supported on a theorized "minimal economically viable" farm size averaging 1.1 ha.

The 1984 Agricultural Survey (Dejaegher 1983; MINAGREF/SESA 1985–1986) identified about 125,000 families in Ruhengeri with total landholdings of 120,616 ha (not quite one hectare per household). In fact, about two-thirds of all families have less than one hectare; and of these, nearly 50 percent have holdings of less than fifty ares (1 are = 0.01 ha).

Another concern is field or plot fragmentation and distance. The typical household in Ruhengeri has its land subdivided into more than six parcels (averaging 15.1 ares per parcel). Some fields can be quite distant from the homestead or *urugo*. In Ruhengeri, about 50 percent of all plots were within five minutes' walk of the homestead or urugo, 32 percent were 5 to 15 minutes, 10 percent were 16 to 30 minutes, and 8 percent were over 30 minutes away from the urugo (MINAGREF/SESA 1985: 79).

The fragmentation has resulted from a diversity of factors: first, dispersion of plots along the catena was and still is an essential strategy of the traditional farming system, where specific soil types, water availability, slope, temperature, and other agro-ecological factors were matched to specific cultigen and cultivar requirements (fig. 5.5; fig.5.8). Those who have a greater diversity of land types available are better able to cope. Second, at the time of marriage access to land to start a new *urugo* was traditionally required; today few heads of households have enough land to subdivide for marriage purposes. Borrowing and buying of additional small, less productive, and usually dispersed plots has become necessary. Those who increasingly can't find land have no alternative other than off-farm employment, land impoverishment, or migration.

But increasing land pressure, including the incipient social differentiation that is currently accelerating, may not be totally deplorable if it stimulates real social and political integration and maturation. Hyden (1983) has suggested that such a process may be a positive and essential step, if it can capture large segments of noninvolved peasants and integrate them into the growing national political and economic structure.

Forest Resources

The forest-resource picture in Ruhengeri is quite complex (Raintree 1983; Balasubramanian and Egli 1986; RRAM 1987, 1988a, 1988b). Several positive and negative trends stand out: on the negative side, native species seem to be losing out to introduced ones for fuelwood and lumber (e.g., eucalyptus, cypress, pines). Furthermore, nationwide since the 1950s, forest cover outside of the preserves and parks has decreased over 40 percent. Official estimates of per capita consumption of wood products is 0.91 m^3 while annual growth is estimated at 0.29 m^3. Official reports further project that one-half of all available land in Ruhengeri by 1996 would have to be forested to produce the necessary wood required under projected population increases (RRAM 1987: 42).

On the other hand, more recent trends in Ruhengeri have been posi-

Fig. 5.8. Contoured bands/ridges on steep slopes in the Haute Buberuka zone, Ruhengeri Prefecture

tive. Between 1980 and 1985 the total area reforested nearly doubled from 5,487 ha to 10,354 ha (table 5.3). Specialized surveys by the RRAM project estimate that small-scale family woodlots continue to be a major source of wood (until recently their production has not figured into official inventories).

Consequently, RRAM estimates that the true forest inventory is closer to 18,000 ha (RRAM 1987: 42). And in recent years the president has given high visibility and priority to reforestation.

Animal Resources/Rangelands

Animal husbandry has long been an integral part of the agricultural system in Ruhengeri, but as population increased, the traditional pasture lands used by transhumant pastoralists rapidly declined. Many bottomlands, once essential pasture areas, are now being converted to intensive raised-field horticulture or tea farms. In addition, there has been widespread upslope movement by farmers to formerly uncultivated high-elevation pastures in the Lava Zone (e.g., *paysannats* for pyrethrum and

Table 5.3. Evolution of Forest Cover in Ruhengeri, 1980–85 (in ha)

Year	Large plantations	Roadside plantations	Small woodlots	Total
1980	3,992	170	1,325	5,487
1981	3,838	170	1,379	5,387
1982	3,991	201	1,458	5,650
1983	3,997	244	2,385	6,626
1984	4,474	356	2,532	7,362
1985	4,358	629	5,367	10,354

Source: Official Statistics of Ruhengeri Prefecture.

potatoes). In addition, many former marginal lands on ridgetops that were kept in woodlots and longfallow also have been brought into permanent cultivation.

Recent statistics tell the story clearly: natural pastures declined from 2,870 ha in 1980 to only 120 ha in 1984. Yet, animal husbandry is not disappearing: according to the Agricultural Survey of 1984, 76 percent of all households still own livestock (RRAM 1987: 20). It appears that maintenance of the animal population is due primarily to extensive use of roadsides, crop residues, forest plots, erosion-control bunds, and the occasional fallow areas not in agriculture.

Furthermore, there is a decided shift from large to small animals, and permanent stabling is rapidly increasing. Sheep and goats increased from 115,864 in 1964 to 279,956 in 1983, whereas cattle increased by only 7,304 during the same period. Estimates in 1986 further suggested that large livestock would decline significantly before the year 2000. Development of an intensified mixed-farming or agroforestry system is foreseen by most experts as the only viable method of coping with increasing land pressure on pastoralism (Gourou 1952: 23, 82; République Rwandaise 1970: 148, MINAGREF/SESA 1985: 55, 57).

In summary, trends in forest and animal resources demonstrate some positive movement, but disturbing negative trends are also evident, particularly in the availability of land.

Environmental Constraints on Agricultural Production

Soil-Erosion Data

Ruhengeri's environmental characteristics make erosion a serious—if not the most serious—threat to its agricultural land-resource base. The erosion risk is clear: the Agricultural Survey noted that approximately 70 percent of all cultivated fields in Ruhengeri are located on the upper and middle slopes of hills, and nearly half of them are on slopes of more than 37 percent. In addition, several of the most popular cultigens are highly correlated with severe erosion (e.g., maize has a C-value of 0.35 and potatoes 0.22, whereas bananas are noted for their high soil-protection qualities, a C-value of 0.04).[3]

Results from an early pilot erosion study (using a Gerlach trap study method) estimated an average soil loss of 13.3 t/ha/year in Ruhengeri (RRAM 1987: 33). Recent work by Byers and Nyamulinda using hydrological and Wischmeier-type runoff plots has shown that soil losses are dramatically higher than originally measured by Lewis (Byers 1988a; E. Byers, 1988; Byers and Nyamulinda 1988; Lewis and Berry 1988; Nyamulinda 1988).

In terms of slope category, the situation in Ruhengeri is quite troubling: 35 percent of all agricultural fields and 58 percent of nonagricultural fields fall into the greater-than-37-percent slope category in which soil losses average 25.7 t/ha/year (RRAM 1987: 30). By ecological zone, the earlier pilot study (MINAGREF/SESA 1986) and the more recent ones by Byers all showed that the Zaire–Nile Divide region has the highest average erosion rates—21.7 t/ha/year as estimated by the earlier Lewis study (RRAM 1987: 30) and over 200 t/ha/year according to the recent RRAM/Byers studies (Byers 1988a,1988b,1988c; Byers and Nyamulinda 1988). The second and third worst rates were found in the Lava and Buberuka zones. In sum, the most serious erosion is concentrated in those regions where marginal soils and slopes are most common.

As serious as the new data appear, it should be stressed that the situation could be much worse. Most expatriates are very impressed with the greenness of the Rwandese landscape and the apparent success peasants have in controlling erosion (fig. 5.9). In my opinion there are several reasons why erosion is (apparently) *not* worse. One reason is due to the year-round effort by traditional farmers to maintain a crop cover on their fields, particularly at those critical times experience has shown them that soils are most susceptible to erosion (e.g., at the transition from the long dry season to the wet season in August/September). Second, many of the traditional cultigen associations have a very low erosion risk (high C-value): beans/bananas, peas, bananas/sorghum, sweet potatoes. Third, because of the patchwork of small dispersed plots, seldom were extensive areas of bare soil exposed to heavy overland flow of water (Rossi 1984; Lewis and Berry 1988; Nyamulinda 1988).

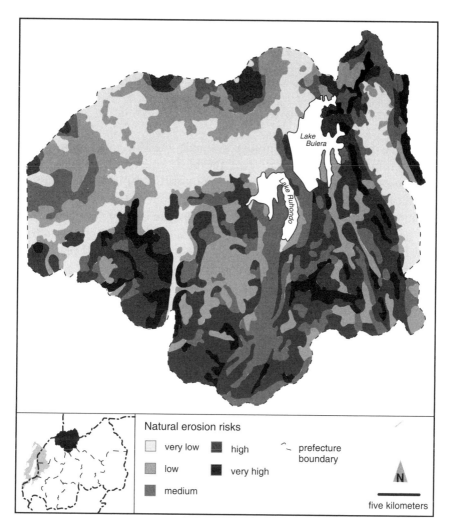

Fig. 5.9. Natural erosion, Ruhengeri Prefecture. Source: RRAM 1987.

In spite of traditional concern for erosion, the government has put great emphasis on supplementing these measures through mass efforts to build erosion-control systems. In 1985, 53 percent of the prefecture (including nonagricultural areas) was estimated to be protected by erosion-control structures, such as infiltration ditches, hedgerows, and terraces. By the end of 1986, the regional average was determined to be 87 percent; this resulted from a major mass-mobilization campaign effort and a redefinition of susceptible areas. In 1988–89 the government continued major efforts to control erosion through its communal organizations. Projects like RRAM were very active as well (Nyamulinda 1988).

Farming-System Productivity and Erosion

In sum, considering the technology available, the Rwandese farming system is remarkably conservative of the basic soil and plant resources. Long occupancy of this highland region in relative isolation and without significant political or economic crises (e.g., slave raids) facilitated the creation of an ecologically stable system. But the current stated policy of the government to *de-emphasize* some of the traditional cultigens that had low erosion risk in favor of newer ones like wheat and maize (because they have higher caloric yield per unit of land) with their associated higher risk may in the long run be counterproductive, particularly if serious erosion increases dramatically.

RRAM's analysis of the perception of agricultural problems, particularly erosion and productivity, is rather enlightening:

> 82% of the population feel that their land has become less productive. . . . The reasons most commonly cited for increased or stable productivity are the use of compost (59%) and improved erosion-control methods (25%). In the Buberuka region, erosion control is rated a more important factor. The principal reasons cited for declining productivity are: reduced fallow periods (56%), erosion (24%), and the perception that the soil is tired (11%). . . . Asked whether signs of erosion were visible on their fields following a heavy rainfall, 82% of those from the Zaire-Nile Divide responded yes. The Plateau and Buberuka regions were next most affected (64% and 62%, respectively), while only 48% of those from the Lava zone perceived erosion problems of this order. (RRAM 1987: 31)

These findings are not surprising given several related facts. First, more than one-third of all Ruhengeri fields have been in cultivation for at least fifty years. Second, only about 14 percent of fields are fallowed each year, and for increasingly shorter periods. Finally, fewer than half of all farmers reported using fertilizer or mulch on any of their fields. Under such conditions, it is not at all surprising that productivity is declining on a majority of farms (RRAM 1987: 28).

RRAM summarized the erosion situation in Ruhengeri by creation of a natural-erosion risk map (fig. 5.9). To this they added the factor of population density to create an additional map of theoretical erosion risk (fig. 5.10). From this activity RRAM concluded that Ruhengeri *does* have a potentially serious erosion problem, though it varies considerably by ecological zone and slope. In addition, Alton Byers, the previous director of RRAM, feels that the Lewis pilot study (MINAGREF/SESA

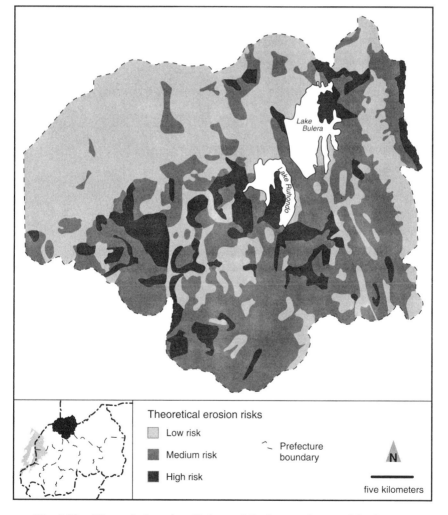

Fig. 5.10. Theoretical erosion, Ruhengeri Prefecture. Source: RRAM 1987.

1986) may have painted a more optimistic picture than is actually the case, and this in turn could have fostered a dangerous complacency.

Therefore, it appears that Ruhengeri is intensifying its agricultural system, but it is achieving this by the mining of its soil-resource base. This trend could be ominous. I would conclude that, although the agricultural system is environmentally stable at present, it may be critically close to instability.

Other Agricultural Constraints.

Besides the limitations of climate and soil, there are other constraints on agriculture in Ruhengeri. These include pests, marketing bottlenecks, low producer prices, poor extension support, an insufficiently cooperative and productive agricultural research service, expensive and insufficient inputs (fertilizers, improved seeds and equipment), and still inadequate crop storage, transport, and distribution systems. Mitigating these and other constraints is one of the principal aims of current bilateral and multilateral agricultural aid efforts in Rwanda (RRAM 1988a, 1988b).

Agricultural Production in Ruhengeri

Agricultural Technology and Frequency of Cultivation

Ruhengeri's farming system is predominantly a form of intensive hoe horticulture. Some variations in cultivation practices are related to soil type, cultigens, and ecological zone. For example, raised-field agriculture dominates in the bottomlands and focuses on growing dry-season sorghum and sweet potatoes. Open-field planting (often monocropping) is more common for wheat and peas and multicropping for rainy-season sorghum and beans. Table 5.4 provides a listing of common single and multiple crop combinations per growing season and the amount of land (in hectares) dedicated to each category.

Perusal of table 5.5 suggests that the farming system has become largely permanent. Note for instance that 77.2 percent of the total average surface area in fields/plots by the average household was under cultivation during the first growing season; during the second season the percentage was 69.2 percent. A related fact is of interest: during the first

Table 5.4. Amount of Land in Hectares in Various Crop
Combinations for Each Growing Season
in Ruhengeri, 1984

Cropping combination	First season	Second season
Single cropping		
Bananas	4,372	11,472
Beans	4,403	9,018
Coffee	1,377	1,195
Maize	5,153	1,307
Manioc	339	149
Peanuts	—	—
Peas	2,899	4,113
Sorghum	4,233	4,427
Soybeans	—	37
Sweet potato	8,052	4,675
Wheat	518	1,936
White potato	7,612	3,822
Other	3,989	3,257
Subtotal	42,947	45,408
Multiple cropping		
Banana/beans	3,985	379
Banana/other	559	621
Beans/maize	4,645	716
Beans/banana	8,095	7,179
Beans/peas	759	—
Beans/sweet potato	768	732
Beans/other	625	2,009
Maize/beans	3,822	—
Maize/other	3,161	3,248
Maize/potato	—	3,817
Manioc/sweet potato	—	93
Manioc/other	188	—
Sorghum/maize	3,456	852
Sorghum/banana	—	833
Sorghum/sweet potato	—	266
Sorghum/manioc	—	—
Sorghum/beans	—	84
Sorghum/other	3,112	1,492
Sweet potato/other	487	1,040
White potato/other	1,230	—
Other crop associations	1,812	3,275
Subtotal	36,704	26,636
Total	79,649	72,044

Source: MINAGREF/SESA 1984–85: 71, 84.

growing season 54.4 percent of the cultivated fields were in monocrop stands, whereas 45.5 percent were in polycrop associations. During the second season the percentages were 62.8 and 37.2 percent respectively (MINAGREF/SESA 1985: 70, 83).

In either case note that more than two-thirds of the household's entire field area was under permanent cultivation. Even fields in fallow are essentially permanently cultivated (the definition of "fallow" in the data cited is for fields that have been left for a rest period of only a few months to two years). Plots rested longer than two years make up less than 10 percent of the entire household's field surface area (MINAGREF/SESA 1985: 70).

Considering these facts it is no wonder then that 82 percent of the population have the perception that the land has become less productive and "tired" (RRAM 1987: 31). The frequency of cultivation, using even the most conservative estimates, is close to 100 and may be as high as 400 for many households.

Under these circumstances, decreasing yields are inevitable, unless effective fertility-maintaining practices are incorporated into the present farming system. Some are already occurring, but much more is needed. The recent Agricultural Survey noted that nearly 40 percent of households manure their fields; this is a strong indication that fertility-maintaining practices are widely known (MINAGREF/SESA 1985: 79).

On moderate-to-steep slopes the practice of contouring (with bands of grasses or shrubs planted on the bunds) has become more common, especially since the massive campaigns of 1985–87 (fig. 5.4). Use of infiltration ditches is also common, though their effectiveness may be suspect under certain conditions (E. Byers 1988; Nyamulinda 1988). Some true terracing experiments by the government are ongoing, but they are minimal. According to the Agricultural Survey of 1984 more than 60 percent of all farms had no protection in their fields against erosion, although it is likely that this figure has changed since the mass-mobilization campaigns of recent years (MINAGREF/SESA 1985: 79).

Animal or machine traction for field preparation, planting, weeding, or harvesting is essentially nonexistent, except on the large export-oriented farm cooperatives producing tea. Use of motor-driven equipment, draught animals, or even human-hauled implements, are simply not used; for example, a recent survey found only 2.9 percent of households have a factory-made wheelbarrow.

In the area of transport, locally made wheelbarrows are used by

Table 5.5. Average Field/Plot Types and Surface Areas (in ares) per Rural Household in Ruhengeri Prefecture, Rwanda, 1984

Field type/usage	Season one	% tot.	Season two	% tot.
Cultivated plots				
Surface area (ares)	63.1	77.2	57.8	69.2
Number of plots	8.3		8.6	
Fallow plots				
Surface area (ares)	9.7	11.8	13.5	16.2
Number of plots	1.2		1.4	
Noncultivated plots (fallowed for over 2 yrs.)				
Surface area (ares)	7.1	8.6	8.4	10.0
Number of plots	1.2		1.4	
Fields of other types				
Surface area (ares)	1.9	2.4	3.9	4.6
Number of Plots	0.3		0.7	
Total surface area/plots				
Surface area (ares)	81.8	100.0	83.6	100.0
Number of plots	11.0		12.1	

Source: MINAGREF/SESA September 1985:70, 83.
Note: Sample survey data from two major growing seasons of 1984.

some for hauling water, crops to market, and firewood. The bicycle is also used, even for some crop transport (but only 5.3 percent of households have them). Shared intermediate-level technology that can service larger groups of consumers or farmers' cooperatives (e.g., grain mills, pyrethrum-processing equipment) is almost totally a government service or in rare cases, a venture of commercial entrepreneurs (MINAGREF/SESA 1985: 49–50).

In summary, the agricultural technology used and the capital invested are rudimentary and require few external inputs. Only recently have exceptions been observed, notably in the increased demand for better seed (for maize, potatoes, and wheat), fungal sprays for potato blight, veterinary supplies, and improved hand tools. But theoretically there is still considerable room for improvement in crop-management practices, provided it is economically feasible and ecologically viable.

Agricultural-Labor Patterns

As in most areas of Africa, division of agricultural labor along gender lines is evident: women do most of the work on subsistence crops (cereals, tubers, legumes), while men work with cash crops (bananas for beer, coffee, pyrethrum). For bananas, land preparation is done 30 percent of the time by males alone and by women 5 percent of the time, whereas for sorghum men prepare the land only 17 percent of the time and women 30 percent. The division is even more marked for weeding and cultivating of sorghum: men perform this function alone 1 percent of the time and women 66 percent of the time. This function is carried out only 22 percent of the time as a male/female team.

In Ruhengeri, where wheat and white potatoes have become important commodity crops, men are heavily involved in their cultivation. There is some sharing of work for the heaviest land-clearing activities (e.g., building the raised fields in the bottomlands for the dry-season cultigens, harvesting of sorghum). But overall, most weeding and crop maintenance, as well as post-harvest activities are done by women alone or with the assistance of children.

A rapidly increasing phenomenon is labor for hire. The agricultural survey noted that for Rwanda as a whole, farm households hired labor at least thirty-two days a year (over half of the time for land clearing and soil preparation and most frequently on beans). Seventy-five percent of the time, payment was in cash (MINAGREF/SESA 1985: 73).

Work outside of the home is on the increase: heads of household worked an average of 31 days a year in agriculture, 11 in crafts, 12 in commercial activities, 30 days in nonagricultural work, and 18 days in nonspecified activities, for a total of 102 days a year (MINAGREF/ SESA 1985: 71). This fact seems to corroborate RRAM's analysis that a depleted land base means that many householders can no longer meet their needs from work on their own land alone.

Cultigens and General Production

As mentioned earlier, climate and hydrology allow Ruhengeri to have two growing seasons, so double and even triple cropping is common. If one includes management of the bottomlands, a wide range of cultigens are available, both of the traditional and introduced types (Jones and Egli 1984; Charley et al. 1986). Martin (1987) has shown that diversification of cultigens was an important strategy for increasing agricultural productivity in colonial Rwanda. In Ruhengeri this strategy has been particularly effective and pronounced.

The predominantly high-altitude areas in the Buberuka, Lava, and Zaire-Nile Divide favor Ruhengeri for production of certain cultigens. For example, it produces 80 percent of the national wheat, 48 percent of the white potatoes, 23 percent of the peas, and 19 percent of the maize. Production of the more traditional cultigens such as bananas, beans, sorghum, and sweet potatoes fall closer to the expected, for a region that represents 6.6 percent of the national territory and that contains 10.6 percent of its population (RRAM 1987: 19).

A 1979 analysis of national yield and production statistics by ONAPO and projected increases for 1986, are quite encouraging. Except for beans, bananas, and sorghum, significant increases in yield (kg/ha) on the order of 10 to 48 percent were predicted for most food crops, including: 48 percent for white potatoes, 27 percent for soybeans, 26 percent for sweet potatoes, and 13 percent for wheat and maize (ONAPO 1982: 186).

Current results have indeed been promising; increases in white-potato yields actually exceeded projections by 1987, as evidenced by a recent glut that occurred in Ruhengeri and Gisenyi markets (the price of potatoes plummeted from 15 francs/kg to 3 francs/kg in three years). The *United Nations* (1986: 536) shows Rwanda as more than doubling potato production between 1974 and 1984, from 143,000 to 330,000 metric tons. The FAO (1986: 10) states that overall agricultural food production indices (1979–81 = 100%) increased from 70.81 percent in 1974 to 104.74 percent in 1985. Indices for cereals over the same period went from 69.7 percent to 114.73 percent, and livestock products from 65.26 percent to 119.5 percent (FAO 1986: 22, 26).

Tables 5.6 and 5.7 provide some selected average 1984 production data per household for major cultigens in Ruhengeri. By value and numbers of households involved, bananas, white potatoes, and beans lead the list. Much of the increased national production in food crops has occurred in Ruhengeri Prefecture. In summary, though individual household data on production are difficult to substantiate, all indications show that total production has improved over the last few years.

Changes in the Forces of Production

Nonfarm Sources of Food, Labor, and Capital

The agricultural household in Ruhengeri is no longer completely self-sufficient in food, labor, or capital, primarily because the per capita land base is so small. This fact has forced a growing number of persons to make up the difference through remittances from children or other relatives, day labor on other farmers' fields, and nonfarm labor in artisanry or commerce. According to the recent national economic survey MINI-PLAN (1986), over 25 percent of Rwandese households now get part of their income from nonagricultural sources.

The sale of agricultural products, (e.g., banana/sorghum beer) is still one of the most important sources of cash to rural households, although nonagricultural sources such as artisanry are growing in importance. For instance, in the North-Central Region, gross household revenues come from the following: 23.7 percent sale of agricultural products, 35.2 percent artisanry, 3.7 percent commerce, 2.2 percent other sales, and 10.4 percent cash remuneration for services (MINIPLAN 1986:83).

The same survey also noted that almost 23 percent of household expenditures were made for food and agricultural needs (e.g., oil, sugar, drinks, meat, as well as some crop inputs and tools); the remaining expenditures for nonagricultural goods and services covered a wide spectrum (e.g., loans, gifts, commerce, taxes, diverse fees and so on).

Role of the Market

A most significant change in recent years has been the phenomenal growth in urban-based demand for food crops—the traditional foods like beans and sorghum, but also new crops like wheat, white potatoes, and maize. Export crops such as coffee, tea, and pyrethrum have generally fallen on hard times in much of Ruhengeri as sources of cash, and tea has become primarily a large cooperative plantation crop. Horowitz and Little (1987) feel that increasingly food crops are the cash crops for the Rwandese peasant farmer. This urban-demand market factor is in my opinion a major development.

Entrepreneurs are finding lucrative markets in other agriculturally related areas as well (e.g., dairying, poultry and eggs, goats and sheep, and market gardening). But the latter affect fewer farmers than the broad demand for basic foodstuffs. The only serious impediment for food crops to become major cash producers in Ruhengeri is government interference in the marketplace through price controls. But Rwanda appears to be sufficiently aware of the dampening effect market controls have on production; at least recent rhetoric by the president and the Ministry of Finance and Planning show some willingness to address this problem.

Table 5.6. Average Production of Selected Crops in Ruhengeri District for all of 1984 (kg/household)

Crop category	All households	Households with crop	Percent[a]
Bananas	1,075.3	1,677.1	64.1
Beans	184.5	190.6	96.9
Coffee	5.5	36.7	15.0
Maize	170.0	179.1	94.9
Manioc	42.8	123.9	34.5
Peanuts	—	—	—
Peas	30.5	55.2	55.3
Sorghum	105.7	139.6	75.7
Soybeans	0.1	9.0	0.7
Sweet potato	544.0	801.6	67.9
Wheat	20.4	77.5	26.3
White potato	977.2	1,982.7	49.3

Source: Calculated from MINAGREF/SESA, 1984–86. Enquête agricole.
[a]Percent of all households in the district.

Table 5.7. Total Production (tons) and Value for Selected Crops in Ruhengeri (U.S. dollars and Rwandese francs, 1984)

Crop category	Metric tons	Francs (100s)	$(1000s)[a]
Bananas	134,270	657,360	6,573.60
Beans	23,045	396,108	3,961.08
Coffee	690	2,646,897	26,468.97
Maize	21,224	39,349	393.49
Manioc	5,345	29,000	290.00
Peanuts	—	—	—
Peas	3,811	78,248	782.48
Sorghum	13,202	154,477	1,544.77
Soybeans	8	—	—
Sweet potato	67,927	335,367	3,353.67
White potato	122,023	832,194	8,321.94

Sources: Calculated from République Rwandaise 1970: 182; MINIPLAN 1983: 56; MINIPLAN 1985: 41–42.
[a]The exchange rate used was 100 Rw.F. to U.S. $1.

International Agencies and Government Role

Ruhengeri has been the focus of extensive bilateral and multilateral aid for both research and applied development work. Not only have many projects in agriculture and natural resources been implemented, but more crucial, their success ratio is quite high for Africa. Most of the projects have been designed to bolster the government's strategic food/

population plan (MINIPLAN, 1983). Some of the key ingredients in the plan are given below.

1. The government wants to widely diffuse Green Revolution technology adapted to the traditional production system, one that will encourage intensification and keep up with the population growth until a projected demographic stabilization sometime after the year 2010 (*Courier* 1984; Buchholz 1984). Biotechnic successes have been significant, as evidenced by the mentioned price drops for white potato producers.

2. The government wants to encourage or even force a change in animal husbandry characterized by a shift to modern dairying and improved traditional herds (using exotic crossbreeds) that will be housed in permanent stables and fed with fodder grown on erosion-control bunds.

3. The development of agroforestry techniques to supply on-farm sources of fuelwood and fodder also is a stated goal of the government (Raintree 1983; Byers 1988c). In Ruhengeri this strategy is being worked on most seriously by the Germans, who first started the acclaimed Nyabisindu Project in south-central Rwanda some ten years ago and who have recently expanded their research to Ruhengeri and Gisenyi Prefectures (Buchholz 1984; Balasubramanian and Egli 1986; Rottach 1986).

4. Organization of cooperatives, marketing boards, and other services to assist farmers in the production of commodity crops such as maize, wheat, and white potatoes is also a high priority. Many agencies both official and nongovernmental are involved in this line of endeavor (e.g., Technoserve, USAID, ADRA, CARE).

Analysis of the agricultural production data, as well as of other social and market trends, suggests that the government's strategy, largely financed by outside donors, is working quite well at the moment. In short, food production appears to be keeping ahead of population growth. Attainment of food self-sufficiency in the near term is a real possibility. That the ecological system is showing some stress, that people must work harder (involution?), and that some nascent social differentiations are causing some disaffection among certain individuals and groups does not, in my opinion, negate the overall positive picture.

Causes and Consequences of Agricultural Production Change

Why and how has Ruhengeri's agricultural system coped with the land-population squeeze? The answer lies as much in the realm of past and recent political and economic history as it does in agricultural technology or ecology. A diversity of factors contributes to Rwanda's relative political and economic stability.

1. Its current president and governing structure have, overall, stimulated reforms that have benefited the majority. But more important, the president has demonstrated a willingness to avoid the extremes of imported ideologies and emphasize pragmatism over dogmatism. The government has been particularly adept at seeking and receiving development aid, and implementation of projects is relatively efficient and effective (Harroy 1981).

2. It has been relatively unified, ethnically and linguistically (assuming the 1990–91 incidents of ethnic/political strife become resolved soon and do not portend an end to ethnic harmony); all three major ethnic groups speak Kinyarwanda, and many of the worst features of feudalism were addressed by its earlier civil war and later reforms after the coup of 1973.

3. The country is extremely well organized politically, down to the family level; this makes resource management, as well as political and social reform, more easily implemented and enforced (e.g., composting, erosion control, family planning).

4. Related to the above is the fact that Rwanda is a compact, minuscule country that has comparatively well-developed transportation and communications infrastructures. Furthermore, local and regional government do a credible job of road maintenance, much of it through *umuganda*—required communal labor by all Rwandese citizens.

5. Economic and fiscal policy has tended to be moderate in philosophy and quite effective, at least through the late 1980s. Neither foreign debt nor inflation is yet as severe as in surrounding countries (though the early 1990s has shown a worsening trend). That Rwanda can exert necessary fiscal control is a sign of growing national maturity and effectiveness.

6. In addition, its somewhat top-down planning functions generally have been efficient and humane, while still allowing for and encouraging considerable free-market entrepreneurship that has greatly increased the availability of consumer goods and services. The latter is a driving force behind the rapid urbanization that is occurring and that many see as Rwanda's population safety valve.

7. The legal and administrative structure is reasonably effective and relatively noncorrupt, compared to neighbors such as Zaire. This means that enforcement of conservation measures, land-tenure laws, farm-

credit systems, and other essential institutional mechanisms, do generally function in a more positive manner and have a strong chance of succeeding (though recently political instability and signs of increased corruption have been noted).

8. The emphasis on applied training and research that is development oriented is very strong at all levels of the educational system. Recent reforms in both primary and higher education appear to be already producing results that could accelerate the efficiency and productivity of the agricultural sector (Bagirameshi et al. 1986; MINISUPRES 1986).

In summary, one of the major reasons Ruhengeri has been able to cope with its land-population pressure is through a diversification of its economy and continued institutionalization of its local governance structures. That room for improvement is yet possible and necessary—as evidenced by some early 1990s political and economic discontent—is quite obvious. Yet overall cautious optimism for the future still seems warranted.

Indicators of Improved Social Well-Being

Analysis of certain measures of nutritional and material well-being over the last twenty years seems to confirm a general improvement in social and material well-being (table 5.8). And it is my opinion that political stability has contributed most significantly to this generally improved socioeconomic situation.

Conclusion and Scenario for the Future

Ruhengeri is presently coping rather effectively with an exploding population on a severely constrained natural-resource base in spite of recent political and economic setbacks. The strategies used to achieve this stability have primarily resulted from the individual efforts of smallholders who have intensified agricultural production on the one hand and society-wide political and socioeconomic changes that have diversified the economy, redistributed the population, and reformed the political system on the other hand.

Whether the *rate* of intensification or political maturation is sufficient for the projected population growth is still problematic, but it is in my opinion, *sufficient* to maintain current living standards into the near future and even improve them slightly without degrading the resource base. Cautious optimism is not unreasonable, all things being equal.

Table 5.8. Indicators of Improvements in Social and Material Well-Being: Conclusion and Scenario for the Future

	1949	1960	1970	1977	1983
Infant mortality rate (<1)	—	150	—	—	130
Infant and child mortality rate (<5)	—	255	—	—	225
General mortality rate	35%(1945)	—	22%	25%(1975)	17%
Life expectancy at birth (years)	35	—	39	46	50
Crude death rate (per 1000 persons)	—	23	—	—	17
Adult literacy rate (male/female)	—	43/21	—	—	51/27
Average index of food production per capita (1974–76 = 100 percent)	—	—	—	—	1981–83 = 114%
GNP per capita	—	U.S. $43(1964)	—	—	U.S. $270
Annual growth rate	—	1965–83 = 2.3%	—	—	1980–83 = 1.6%
Percent of children admitted to nutrition centers malnourished	—	—	1976 = 45%	—	1980 = 38%
Percent population with access to potable water	—	—	1978 = 45%	—	1984 = 64%

Sources: UNICEF 1985: 10–14; UNICEF 1986: 132–42.

Though probably one of the most stressed of Rwanda's high-density regions, Ruhengeri can continue to feed its population for the time that is needed to stabilize it (twenty to thirty years). If population stability *does not* occur, severe economic stagnation will result with concomitant environmental degradation. The latter could foment even more serious political conflict than that which occurred in 1990–92 that could accelerate a trend toward severe environmental deterioration and debilitating involution which at present has been held somewhat in check.

Notes

1. Kigali, the capital, attained a growth rate of 13 percent in 1978, whereas other urban agglomerations in Rwanda grew at an average rate of 5 percent (Nwafor 1981; Sirven 1984: 354).

2. Other reasons for which Ruhengeri was selected are: (1) the published

data on it, from government agencies, academic research reports and other sources, are abundant and recent; (2) I have direct personal field knowledge of its population-resource relationships; (3) I believe the urban effect in Ruhengeri has been less pronounced than elsewhere in Rwanda; (4) of all the high-density districts, I believe it exemplifies much of the diversity of agro-ecosystems affecting agriculture and population in Rwanda; and (5) it illustrates well many other political, spatial-geographical, and socioeconomic developments that have affected the rural areas at large, and in particularly high-density areas. Ford (1990) has discussed many aspects relating to Rwandese population-resource problems as they relate to mountain research.

3. The C-value is a measure used in the erosion equation to show the relative erodibility of certain crop associations.

References

Bagirameshi, J., C. Basihizina, and M. Barnaud. 1986. "Pour une Nouvelle Pratique de la vulgarisation agricole au Rwanda." *Revue Tiers-Monde* 27(106): 419–37.

Balasubramanian, V., and A. Egli. 1986. "The Role of Agroforestry in the Farming Systems in Rwanda with Special Reference to the Bugesera-Gisaka-Migongo Region." *Agroforestry Systems* 4(4): 271–89.

Buchholz, J. 1984. *Green Revolution or Ecological Agriculture: Observations in Bangladesh and Rwanda.* Edited by K. Fliege and L. Ramajho. Saarbrücken: Verlag Breitenbach.

Buschman, U. 1984. *Aspects du droit foncier et le développement rural dans la région du projet.* Etudes et Expériences, Project Agro-Pastoral de Nyabisindu, Rwanda No. 5.

Byers, A.C. 1988a. *Catastrophic Rainfall, Landslides and Flooding in Nyhakinama and Nyamutera Communes, Ruhengeri Prefecture, May 1988.* RRAM Technical Report #2. Kigali, Rwanda: USAID.

————. 1988b. *A Comparative Analysis of Soil Loss in Three Ecological Zones of Ruhengeri Prefecture, Rwanda, 1987–1988.* RRAM Technical Report #3. Kigali, Rwanda: USAID.

————. 1988c. *Geomorphological Effects of Catastrophic Rainfall in the Parc National des Volcans, Ruhengeri Prefecture, Rwanda, May, 1988.* RRAM Technical Report #4. Kigali, Rwanda: USAID.

Byers, A.C. and V. Nyamulinda. 1988. *Soil Loss in Nyarutovu.* RRAM Technical Report #1. Kigali, Rwanda: USAID.

Byers, E. 1988. *Results of the RRAM Hydrological Monitoring Program in Ruhengeri Prefecture, Rwanda, April 1987–September 1988.* RRAM Technical Report #5. Kigali, Rwanda: USAID.

Cambrezy, L. 1984. "Le Surpeuplement en question. Organisation spatiale et écologie des migrations au Rwanda." *Travaux et Documents de l'OR-STOM* 182.

Chapuis, O. 1986. "La Théiculture Rwandaise." *Cahiers d'Outre-Mer* 154: 117–42.

Charlery, B. de M., F. Bart, and O. Barbary. 1986. "La Répartition régionale des cultures vivrières au Rwanda." *Cahiers ORSTOM, Sciences Humaines* 3/4: 453–77.

Chrétien, Jean-Pierre. 1978. "Des Sédentaires devenus migrants: les motifs des départs des Burundais et des Rwandais vers l'Uganda (1920–1960)." *Cultures et Développement* 10(1): 71–101.

Courier. 1984. Food Strategy: New Hope for the Hungry? (Examines Pilot Programs of Mali, Kenya, Zambia, Rwanda, Sahel, and South Africa). March/April: 46–69.

Dejaegher, Y. 1983. "Rwanda Agricultural Survey and Analysis, Project Summary." *Tropicultura* 1: 25–26.

Delepierre, G., and B. Prefol. 1973. *Disponibilité et utilisation des terres au Rwanda, situation actuelle et perspective.* Rubona: Instituts des Sciences Agronomiques du Rwanda.

Durr, G. 1983. Potato Production and Utilization in Rwanda. Working Paper, Social Science Dept. International Potato Center. No. 1.

FAO. 1986. *FAO Monthly Bulletin of Statistics* 9/4 (April).

Feder, Gershon, and Raymond Noronha. 1987. "Land Rights Systems and Agricultural Development in Sub-Saharan Africa." *World Bank Observer* 2(July): 143–69.

Ford, Robert E. 1990. "The Dynamics of Human-Environment Interactions in the Tropical Montane Agrosystems of Rwanda: Implications for Economic Development and Ecologic Stability." *Mountain Research and Development* 10(1).

Godding, J.P. 1986. "External Help as an Obstacle to Development, from the Example of Rural Development Projects in Rwanda (Hilfe von aussen als Hindernis der Entwicklung, am Beispiel von landlichen Entwicklungsprojekten in Rwanda)." In *Ländliche Entwicklung und Gemeinsames Lernen*, ed. H.J. Schurings, pp. 105–25. German Federal Republic, Frankfurt: Verlag für Interkulturelle Kommunikation.

Gotanegre, J.F. 1983. "La Banane au Rwanda." *Cahiers d'Outre-Mer* 36(144): 311–42.

Gourou, Pierre. 1952. *La Densité de la population du Ruanda Burundi.* Brussels: Institut Royal Colonial Belge.

Harroy, J.-P. 1981. "Coopération internationale au développement rural au Rwanda: une forme d'aide nouvelle." *Bulletin des Séances de l'Académie Royale des Sciences d'Outre-Mer* 27(3): 365–86.

Heremans, Roger, Annie Bart, and François Bart. 1982. "Agriculture et paysages Rwandais à travers les sources missionnaires (1900-1950)." *Cultures et Développement* 14(1): 3-39.

Horowitz, Michael M., and Peter D. Little. 1987. "Subsistence Crops *are* Cash Crops: Some Comments with Reference to Eastern Africa." *Human Organization* 46(3): 254-58.

Hyden, Goran. 1983. *No Shortcuts to Progress: African Development in Perspective.* London: Heineman Educational Books, Ltd.

Johnson, Mark. 1986. Report of Densely Settled Districts of Sub-Saharan Africa. Manuscript, Allan Shawn Feinstein World Hunger Program, Brown University, Providence, R.I.

Jones, W.I., and R. Egli. 1984. *Farming Systems in Africa, the Great Lakes Highlands of Zaire, Rwanda, Burundi.* World Bank Technical Paper, No. 27.

Kates, Robert W. 1987. "The Human Environment: The Road Not Taken, the Road Still Beckoning." *Annals of the Association of American Geographers* 77(4): 525-34.

LeMarchand, René. 1982. "The World Bank in Rwanda." African Studies Program, Indiana University.

Lewis, L.A., and Leonard Berry. 1988. *African Environments and Resources.* Unwin/Hyman.

Lugan, Bernard. 1976. "Causes et effets de la famine "Rumanura" au Rwanda, 1916-1918." *Canadian Journal of African Studies* 10(2): 347-56.

Maquet, Jacques. 1967. "La Tenure des terres dans l'état Rwanda traditionnel." *Cahiers d'Etudes Africaines* 7(28): 624-36.

Martin, Susan. 1987. "Boserup Revisited: Population and Technology in African Agriculture, 1900-40." *Journal of Imperial and Commonwealth History* 16(1): 109-23.

MINAGREF/SESA. September, March, May 1985-1986. *Résultats de l'enquète nationale agricole 1984*, Rapport I, II, et III. Kigali: République Rwandaise, Ministère de l'Agriculture, de l'Elevage et des Forêts, Service des Enquètes et des Statistiques Agricoles.

————. 1986. *Document provisoire: pertes de terre dues à l'érosion, Résultats de l'enquète pilote sur l'érosion (année agricole 1984)*, Rapport descriptif (novembre). Kigali: République Rwandaise, Ministère de l'Agriculture, de l'Elevage et des Forêts, Service des Enquètes et des Statistiques Agricoles.

————. 1987. *Description sommaire des principales caractéristiques de l'agriculture au Rwanda*, Rapport 2 (février 1987). Kigali: Ministère de l'Agriculture, de l'Elevage et des Forêts, Service des Enquètes et des Statistiques Agricoles.

MINIPLAN, 1983. *Stratégie alimentaire au Rwanda, objectifs chiffres et programmes d'actions.* Document No. 3. Kigali: République Rwandaise, Ministère du Plan.

_____. 1985. *Bulletin statistique No. 12.* Kigali: République Rwandaise, Direction Générale de la Statistique.

_____. 1986. *Enquète nationale sur le budget et la consommation des ménages. Milieu Rural—(Nov. 1982–Dec. 1983),* Vols. 1, 2, Novembre, 1986. Kigali: République Rwandaise, Direction Générale de la Statistique.

MINISUPRES. 1986. *Projet de réforme de l'enseignement supérieur au Rwanda.* Kigali: Ministère de l'Enseignement Supérieur et de la Recherche Scientifique.

Nwafor, James C. 1981. "Some Aspects of Urban Development in Tropical Africa: The Growth toward Urban Status of Kigali, Capital of Rwanda." *African Urban Studies* 9: 39–56.

Nyamulinda, V. 1988. *Erosion agricole accélérée et techniques biologiques et mécaniques de conservation des sols applicables en Préfecture de Ruhengeri.* RRAM Technical Report. Kigali, Rwanda: USAID.

ONAPO. 1982. Population et environnement. *Actes du Colloque: Famille Population et Développement,* 27 septembre–ler octobre 1982. Kigali: République Rwandaise, Office National de la Population.

_____. 1983. *Rwanda 1983, Enquète nationale sur la fécondité, Vol. 1, Analyse des résultats.* Kigali: République Rwandaise, Office National de la Population.

_____. 1984. *Rapport du séminaire sur la santé familiale,* 16–21 avril. Kigali: République Rwandaise, Office National de la Population.

Prioul, Ch. 1981. "Les Densités de population au Rwanda: leur évolution entre 1948–1978." In *Les Milieux tropicaux d'altitude: recherches sur les hautes terres d'Afrique Centrale (Rwanda, Burundi, Kivu),* pp. 61–80. Talence: Centre d'Etudes de Géographie Tropicale.

Raintree, J. B. 1983. The Agroforestry Approach to Land Development: Potentials and Constraints. *ICRAF,* Nairobi, Kenya.

RRAM. 1987. *Ruhengeri and Its Resources: An Environmental Profile of the Ruhengeri Prefecture, Rwanda.* Kigali, Rwanda: ETMA/USAID.

_____. 1988a. *Agroforestry Activities of the RRAM Project in Ruhengeri Prefecture, Phase II, April 1987–September 1988.* RRAM Technical Report. Kigali, Rwanda: USAID.

_____. 1988b. *Extension Activities of the RRAM Project in Ruhengeri Prefecture, Phase II, April 1987–September 1988.* RRAM Technical Report. Kigali, Rwanda: USAID.

Reintsma, M. 1982. "Land Tenure in Rwanda." *AID Research and Development Abstracts* 10 (314): 56–67.

République Rwandaise, 1970. *Etude de développement, plan intérimaire d'urgence.* Kigali: République Rwandaise.

_____. 1982. *IIIème Plan de développement économique, social et culturel, 1982–1986.* Kigali: République Rwandaise.

Roark, P., and B.H. Dickson. 1986. *Ruhengeri Water Resources Study, Rwanda. WASH Field Report No. 181.* Kigali, Rwanda: USAID.

Rosenblum, Mort, and Doug Williamson. 1987. *Squandering Eden: Africa on the Edge.* Orlando, FL: Harcourt, Brace, Jovanovich.

Rossi, G. 1984. "Evolution des versants et mise en valeur agricole au Rwanda." *Annales de Géographie* 93(515): 23–43.

Rottach, P., ed. 1986. *Ecological Agriculture in the Tropics: Ecofarming in Theory and Practice.* Karlsruhe: Müller.

Ruhashyankiki, N. 1985. "Evolution du droit foncier au Rwanda." *Revue Juridique du Rwanda* 9(3): 243–47.

Sirven, Pierre. 1984. "La Sous-urbanisation et les villes du Rwanda et Burundi." Thèse de Doctorat d'Etat en Géographie, Université de Bordeaux III.

UNICEF, 1985. *Analyse de la situation de l'enfant Rwandais.* Kigali, Rwanda: UNICEF.

———. 1986. *The State of the World's Children.* New York: Oxford University Press.

United Nations. 1986. *UN Statistical Yearbook, 1983–84*, p. 536. New York: United Nations.

Zaag, P. van der. 1980. "Strategy for Developing a National Potato Program for Rwanda." In *Proceedings of the Meeting Root Crops in Eastern Africa*, 23–27 November 1980, Kigali, Rwanda.

6 / Population Growth and Agricultural Change in Kisii District, Kenya: A Sustained Symbiosis?

H. W. O. Okoth-Ogendo and John O. Oucho

Reference to the post–World War II baby boom is applicable beyond the confines of Europe and North America; a similar "boom" in developing countries ushered in an episode of unprecedented population growth, setting the stage for the current demographic momentum in many of them, particularly in sub-Saharan Africa. This region of continental proportions trails all others in both the stage of demographic transition and the level of agricultural production it has reached (see chap. 1). Yet the effects of rapid population growth on agricultural development are difficult to appreciate in a regional or even national framework of great physical and human diversity.

Kenya is a case in point. Its population growth over the last three decades has been the subject of discussion in many fora, although the national perspectives of such discussion conceal disparities at the subnational level. The problem is difficult to understand given Kenya's impressive performance in agricultural development, now being threatened more than ever before by the "demographic quotient," expressed as the proportion of total resources available to the product of population and per capita consumption of resources (Cloud 1971: 9). Meaningful analysis of the relationship between population growth and agricultural change in Kenya must, therefore, be pitched at the district level. This study briefly addresses the population-agricultural relationship for one highland district of dense settlement and intensive cultivation.

The Study Area

Kisii District is situated in Nyanza Province in southwestern Kenya, bordered clockwise by the districts of Kericho, Narok, and South Nyanza, respectively (fig. 6.1). Kisii covers 2,196 km² of this highland area that, from a physical perspective, is classified as one of high agricultural potential. Carved out of South Nyanza District in the early 1960s, Kisii is inhabited by a single ethnic group, the Gusii, who have remained agriculturalists since settling in the area in the nineteenth century (Ochieng 1974). Just previous to their arrival, the area had been occupied by the semipastoral Luo, who, finding it too highly elevated and somewhat too cold, consolidated their settlements at lower elevations toward Lake Victoria. Recognizing that the area was not suitable for pastoralism, the Gusii practiced agriculture from the outset of their entry into Kisii.

Kisii District was selected for this study for several reasons. First, it lies in the heart of Kenya's largest population region, the Lake Victoria Basin cluster (Ominde 1968a). Second, since the colonial period, the district has experienced faster rates of population growth, less outmigration, and higher population densities than its neighboring districts, compounding the effects of this population factor on its agricultural potential. Third, the district's demographic momentum is likely to persist into the first quarter of the twenty-first century, given its current growth rate and low response rate to population-management programs. Finally, the district presents a good laboratory for the analysis of the interplay of agricultural resources, population growth, and state policies within one of the better agricultural zones of eastern Africa.

Environmental Setting

Soils

Out of twenty-one major soil-classification units in Kenya, twelve are represented in Kisii District.[1] The distribution of these units in the district is best explained in the context of the five elevation units of the district, namely hills and minor scarps, plateaus and high-level structural plains, footslopes, piedmont plains, and uplands (Jaetzold and Schmidt 1982: 95–96). The major soil units in the district are upland varieties

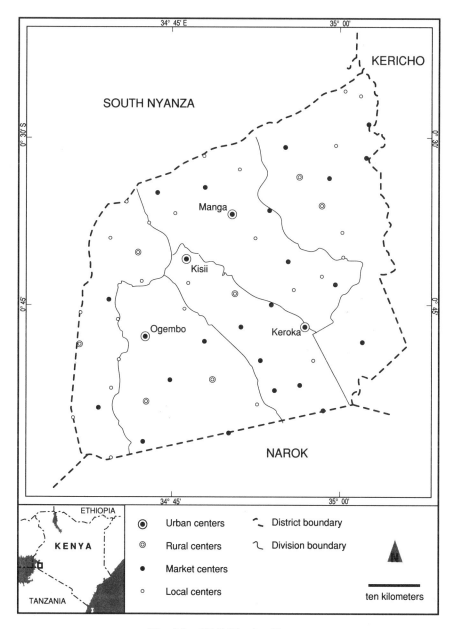

Fig. 6.1. Kisii District, Kenya

with topsoils rich in organic matter; they have moderately high natural fertility and are intensively farmed (fig. 6.2). Soils of very low fertility are found in the eastern and northern parts of the district. In the extreme southern corner of the district are dark cracking soils (which are fertile if well drained) with a deep organic topsoil that have a moderate-to-high natural fertility. The bottomlands are made up of alluvial soils, mainly clays, and subject to flooding (Jaetzold and Schmidt 1982: 95). The predominance of soils with moderate to high fertility in the district helps to explain why it is densely settled and why agriculture is a dependable activity.

Precipitation

Kisii District, like the neighboring Kericho, is one of the few districts in the country that receive rainfall throughout the year. This is because it is situated in the corner of the local convergence of the daily lake winds with the Easterlies during the generally dry seasons in Kenya (Jaetzold and Schmidt 1982: 85). Rainfall has two significant characteristics: mean annual amounts are high (ranging between 1,200 mm and 2,100 mm) and are highly reliable. Drought is not only unknown but also improbable in the district. The highest rainfall is received in the central part of the district; amounts received decrease farther away from the center, particularly on the extreme eastern side. There is a strong positive correlation between rainfall and population distribution as well as density (fig. 6.3).

Although there are no real dry seasons in the district, a distinction can be made between the first rains and other rains. The first rains start around mid-February, the second come around August, and a short third episode sets in by November. This unusual rainfall regime facilitates annual and biannual cultivation, not to mention its contribution to the perennial-tree crops (coffee and tea) that boost the agricultural capacity of the district.

Devegetation Problems

The destruction of vegetation is currently the most alarming form of environmental degradation throughout Kenya. As the watersheds of rivers are deforested, their catchment area diminishes, gully erosion sets in, and the rainfall regime and water supplies change radically. This is true

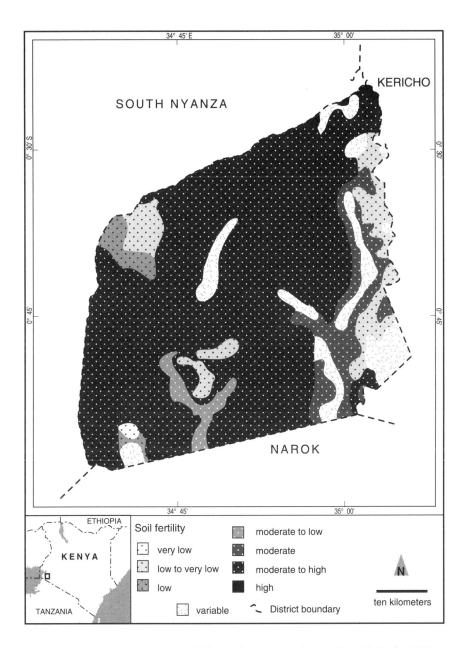

Fig. 6.2. General soil fertility, Kisii District. Source: Jaetzold and Schmidt 1982.

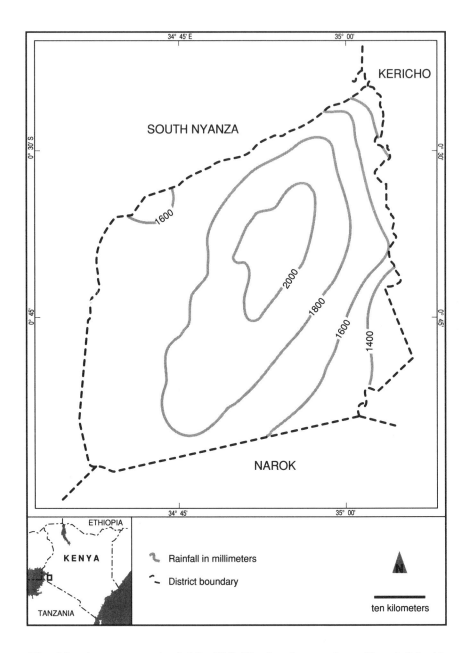

Fig. 6.3. Average annual rainfall, Kisii District. Source: Jaetzold and Schmidt 1982.

for Kisii District, where, apart from Nyangweta Forest, there are no other state-protected forests. The high demand for fuelwood and building poles in the district has led to devegetation of the landscape, which now requires immediate afforestation (Republic of Kenya 1984: 72). Population pressure on existing agricultural areas has led to the encroachment of farms on hilltops (formally forested), thereby creating competition in land use between agriculture and afforestation.

Nature of Population Change

Population Size and Growth

Of the four districts that make up Nyanza Province, Kisii District is the smallest in area but the second largest in terms of population. Table 6.1 reports population growth in the district during the present century, based on informed estimates and population censuses (for the years 1948–79). Between 1948 and 1962, the population of the district more than doubled; it then grew steadily. Currently, the total population of the district is estimated to be above one million. Alongside Kakamega and Machakos, therefore, the district has one of the largest populations in Kenya. Whereas the population growth rate was below 1 percent per annum in the period 1900–38, it rose to a phenomenal rate close to 6 percent during the period 1938–62. Thereafter, a declining trend in the growth rate was recorded, even though the overall population size of the district remains fairly high.

Table 6.1. Population Size and Growth in Kisii District, Kenya, 1900–79

Year	Total population	Annual growth rate (%)
1900[a]	105,000	—
1938[a]	140,000	0.75
1948	255,108	5.99
1962	519,418	5.94
1969	675,041	3.75
1979	869,512	2.55

[a]Estimated.

Changes in Population Density

The district has one of the highest population densities in the country. In 1969, it had an average density of 304 persons/km², a figure that rose to 395 in 1979. This increase of 91 persons/km² in only a decade illustrates the dramatic changes in land pressures that have taken place. Of course, if the population is considered in terms of only the cultivable land, then the "density" figures would probably be much higher.

The average density figure, however, masks the variability in subdistrict densities (fig. 6.4). It is evident that the majority of locations are in the 401-to-600-persons/km² range, although two locations have density figures above 600 (relatively unaffected by urban numbers). These are clearly some of the highest levels of population density in rural sub-Saharan Africa.

Table 6.2 contains a projection of the population size and density in the district during the planning period 1984–88, taking 1979 as the base year. During those nine years (1979–88) the population was expected to increase at a constant rate, about 4.8 percent or the rate of growth in the district in 1979. But given the very high fertility levels in the district and the fact that there is no appreciable contraceptive or family planning to reduce it, this expectation was probably unrealistic. The same can be said for the associated projections of population density.

Population Structure and Migration

As already indicated, the district is dominated by the Gusii, who constitute 98 percent of the population, followed by the Luo as a poor second (0.9 percent). This situation is important given the fact that these cultural-ethnic groups affect both the population and agricultural characteristics of the area.

During the colonial period the Gusii were relatively sedentary. Unlike their neighbors, the Luo of Nyanza and the Luhya of Western Province, the Gusii remained in their homeland, cultivating and apparently indifferent to the attractions of rural-urban migration. They were, however, involved in rural-rural migration as unskilled labor to the Kisii plantation area, for which conscripted labor was procured from the neighborhood (Osoro 1979; Oucho 1981). Recently, and apparently because of the increasing land pressure, the Gusii have become highly migratory, even to urban destinations for wage employment. This is an

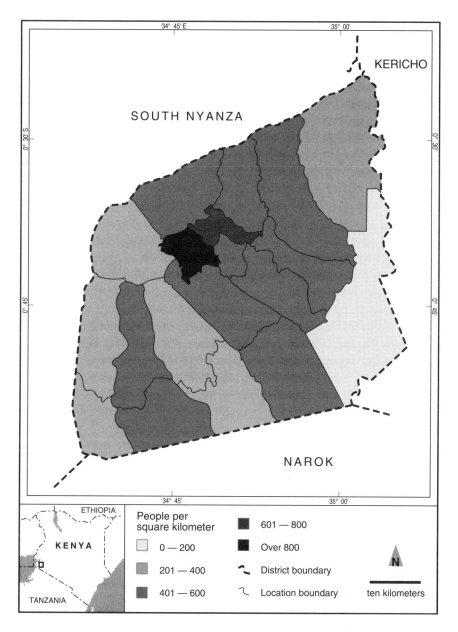

Fig. 6.4. Population density, Kisii District. Source: Republic of Kenya 1981.

Table 6.2.   Census Population and Projections and Population Density Projections for Kisii District by Division, 1979–88

	Population totals				Population density (persons/km²)			
		Census projections			Area in				
Division	1979	1983	1985	1988	sq. km	1979	1983	1985	1988
Manga	214,708	277,082	297,842	332,127	455	472	609	655	730
Nyamira	198,308	255,918	275,092	306,758	640	310	400	430	479
Irianyi	147,419	190,245	204,499	228,039	314	469	606	651	726
Bosongo	118,158	152,484	168,908	182,776	324	365	471	506	564
Ogembo	190,919	246,382	264,842	295,842	461	414	534	574	641

Source: Kisii District Development Plan 1984/88 (Republic of Kenya 1984: table 1.1, p. 2).

important change that has been fueled by the challenges imposed on agriculture by the district's demographic momentum.

Census data provide some insights into migration from and to the district. The 1979 returns indicate that the district recorded a net life-time outmigration of 60,468 people; the net annual migration was 10,780 people (Republic of Kenya 1985: 57–58, 65–66). The district was sur-passed in Nyanza Province only by Siaya (133,717 and 22,381 people respectively), which has become the single most important source of outmigration to the rest of Kenya. Subdistrict data are hard to come by, but locations in Kisii certainly experienced considerable loss of popula-tion due to outmigration. The majority (about 61.3 of outmigrants) were males, a factor that is consistent throughout Kenya.

Two migration surveys carried out in Western Kenya support the contention that outmigration among the Gusii started only recently. A survey of Kisumu Town (the capital of Nyanza Province) found that among the six major migrant ethnic groups, the Gusii ranked fifth; but a survey of the Kericho tea plantation area ranked them second to the highly migratory Luo (Oucho 1984: 130). These interesting results fol-low from the recruitment of unskilled labor by powerful colonial Gusii chiefs and labor-recruitment agents who procured labor for the tea plan-tations to improve their popularity with the colonial government and to obtain commissions.

The sex ratio can be used as a crude measure of net migration in an area. The fact that Kisii District had a sex ratio of 101 in 1969 and 95 in 1979 indicates that in those years it experienced net in-migration and out-migration respectively. Indeed, net out-migration in the district dates back to the early 1970s. Age-specific sex ratios (table 6.3) also pro-

Table 6.3. Age Distribution of Population of Kisii District by Sex and Age-Specific Sex Ratio, 1979 (%)

Age group (years)	Percent distribution of population			Sex ratio (males/females)
	Males (n = 238,042)	Females (n = 244,285)	Total (869,512)	
0–4	21.2	20.2	20.7	100
5–9	17.8	17.1	17.4	99
10–14	15.8	14.6	15.2	103
15–19	12.9	13.5	13.2	91
20–24	8.1	9.0	8.6	85
25–29	5.4	6.2	5.8	84
30–34	4.1	4.3	4.2	87
35–39	2.9	3.5	3.2	93
40–44	2.8	3.0	2.9	97
45–49	2.4	2.5	2.4	105
50–54	1.8	1.7	1.7	97
55–59	1.4	1.3	1.4	125
60–64	1.0	1.0	1.0	100
65–69	0.9	0.7	0.8	125
70–74	0.5	0.5	0.5	100
75+	0.8	0.7	0.8	105
Not stated	0.2	0.2	0.2	95
Total	100.0	100.0	100.0	95

Source: Calculated from Republic of Kenya, 1981: 206.

vide evidence in terms of the least and most susceptible ages of in- or outmigration. The peak ages of migration (20–29 years) reflect a much lower man:woman ratio, implying female dominance in the absence of the more migratory males. This corroborates findings in earlier Kenyan migration (Ominde 1968b; Oucho 1981, 1984).

The Nature of Agricultural Change

The relationship between population growth and agricultural change in Kisii District has been the subject of a number of studies (Mayer and Mayer 1965; Uchendu and Antony 1975; Omare 1981; Jaetzold and Schmidt 1982; KREMU 1983; University of Nairobi 1984). These have been concerned with the impact of the growth rate on the organization of agricultural production and, in particular, on the nature of access to and control of land (i.e., land tenure), the operation of production structures, and the choice of agricultural technology. This section explores those interlinkages and, in particular, the manner in which land pressure affecting changes in land tenure has influenced overall productivity in and employment opportunities outside agriculture.

Population Growth and Land Tenure

In analyzing the effect of population pressure on land tenure, it is important to clarify the manner in which those two variables interact. Generally speaking, tenure systems are expected to accommodate demands arising from constant population increase in an agrarian economy: first, by providing continuous opportunities for access to land either in general or in respect of specific and carefully regulated functions; second, by guaranteeing that access at least in space and sometimes in tempore; and third, by ensuring that mechanisms exist for the redistribution of rights over that land both in the present and in the future (i.e., within and between generations). It has been posited that African tenure systems will continue to perform these functions at varying levels of efficiency as long as the community of producers not only perceive land as the ultimate resource but also continue to act on that perception.

Fundamental changes in tenure arrangements are thus unlikely to occur unless alternative forms of production emerge or, as has happened in many parts of Asia and Latin America, the development of agrarian capitalism begins to marginalize the peasant producer (Okoth-Ogendo 1986a). Until these developments occur, African tenure systems will continue to exhibit a great deal of flexibility and adaptability in the face of mounting pressures. This assumes, of course, that external normative influences, such as were and are still contemplated by Kenya's tenure reform programs, have not been internalized by the producers.

Previous studies of the population and land-tenure interactions in Kisii District suggest a different circumstance from that of Africa in general. According to Uchendu and Antony (1975: 27), for example, this interaction has produced a de jure arrangement approaching the classic freehold system. They cite as evidence of this development the fact that registry records showed a significant number of land sales, borrowing on the security of title, forms of land renting, and enclosures, and the fact that some farmers were even selling their small buildings and buying larger parcels of land in the nearby Sotik Settlement Scheme. They state that the development of enclosures has put a stop to the phenomenon of "general access" by interest holders (Uchendu and Antony 1975: 32).

The implication is that without this development, the very impressive performance of Gusii agriculture, especially with respect to the spread of permanent cash crops, such as tea and coffee, and the introduction of improved cattle, would not have occurred.

Our own observation suggests that no such drastic development in Gusii land tenure has occurred. Indeed, it seems clear that Gusii tenure arrangements have become far more complex than the simple linear progression model that Swynnerton (1954) has suggested and that Uchendu and Antony claim to have observed. What population pressure appears to have done has been to disengage the level of land control in respect of the production function from the lineage and clan structures to the family without drastically altering the access rights of those whose livelihood depends or could conceivably depend upon it. This much was reported by the Mayers (1965: 69) in the early 1960s when they recorded that farms that were being consolidated and litigated by the Gusii remained in every respect "family land." There is further evidence to suggest that even those who were selling so as to purchase larger parcels of land elsewhere were and still are motivated not by the desire for production autonomy but rather by the need to expand the pool of land available for use by present and future family members.

A perusal of the Kisii District land registry conducted in 1974 (Okoth-Ogendo 1986b) indicated, inter alia, that the typical land transaction consisted of a subdivision coupled with a sale, implying that even where land availability per household was generally less than 1.5 hectares (Jaetzold and Schmidt 1982: 99), the so-called "uneconomic holdings" were not being sold; that many of the tenancy arrangements entered by producers in the area had their origins in well-tested customary practices; and that the very high levels of land disputes were evidence of continuous vindication of indigenous tenure rights long after the technical aspect of the government-sponsored tenure reform had been completed in the district.

The migration profile of the district presented would appear to fortify these conclusions. For it also indicates that, until relatively recently, Gusii land-access rules were able to accommodate one of the highest farm-family populations in Kenya, estimated as consisting of 1.6 adults plus 6.5 children per family (Uchendu and Antony 1975: 68), 95 percent of whom were physically resident on the land. By keeping family members on the farm, Gusii tenure arrangements may have resolved an important constraint in smallholder agriculture in Kenya, namely, labor.

Indeed, the very young farm family structure that Uchendu and Antony found in the district (i.e., 54 percent of the families were within the 30–39 age range) implies the availability of relatively productive labor. The fact that the mechanization of resource control has become fairly narrow and more focused also means that greater command of the production function can be achieved.

Population Growth and Agricultural Change

The foregoing adjustments in Gusii land tenure facilitated in no small measure the early introduction by the colonial government of new production technologies in the form mainly of nonindigenous cash crops and superior seeds in the district. Tenure was clearly not an impediment to innovation. Once introduced, however, these innovations (e.g., tea and hybrid maize in the 1930s) in turn became an important factor in the enhancement of the "carrying capacity" of productive land within the district (Garst 1972; Barnes 1976). After the implementation of the Swynnerton Plan in a selected number of districts in the country, Kisii was able to receive the infrastructural and support services—such as roads, credit, marketing and cooperative arrangements, plowing advice, and extension—that have made further diffusion of new technologies and the quantum leap in higher productivity possible. For example, Clayton (1961, 1966) reported that coffee production dramatically increased in African areas in general and Kisii in particular after the plan was put into effect.

By intensifying these support systems after independence—for instance the establishment of a number of agrarian institutions such as the Agricultural Finance Corporation, the Tea Development Authority, the Coffee Development Authority, and the Horticultural Crops Development Authority, all catering to small-scale products—the government made it possible for Kisii District to consolidate the very substantial lead in agricultural production it already enjoyed in the country in general, Nyanza Province in particular. This is clearly evident in a number of respects.

The first is in terms of the nature of the agricultural landscape that has emerged in the district. Everywhere the district is now dotted with small, but neatly divided and hedged, family holdings or individual plots. Because of the need for "ecological equity" among individual cultivators belonging to each family, the holdings and plots typically run in strips up and down the district's undulating slopes. As a consequence, no common grazing land is found in Kisii, and the livestock, of which there are at least 112,000 grade cattle, 336,000 zebu cattle, 110,000 sheep, and 40,000 goats (Gitu 1989), are either on zero grazing or pastured on road reserves.

The second is in relation to the level of intensity of land use that has been achieved in the district. A recent agricultural production survey (Republic of Kenya 1989: table 6.1) reported that nearly 83 percent of the farm families in Kisii have holdings measuring less than 1.7 ha in size. In nearly all cases, the actual plot size (i.e., the area dedicated to a single crop or land-use category) is much smaller. This, according to KREMU (1983), averaged about 0.18 ha, suggesting that each holding may be supporting up to nine land-use categories. It is not surprising, therefore, that virtually every millimeter of land in the district is under continuous cultivation and that fallowing is rarely practiced.

The third is in respect to agricultural production levels in the district. Like other peoples in Kenya, the Gusii devote a considerable proportion of their land to the production of food crops. Of these, finger millet, sorghum, maize, beans, bananas, potatoes, and cassava occupy nearly 70 percent of all holdings in the district (Republic of Kenya 1989: 31–34). There is evidence that considerable surpluses are realized from these crops, especially maize, which is marketed either locally or through the National Cereals and Produce Board (Uchendu and Antony 1975). In addition to food crops, coffee, pyrethrum and dairy production remain an important feature of the district. As early as 1966, the annual value of these in the district stood at K£ 694,800, 643,600, and 654,000, respectively (Uchendu and Antony 1975: 41), representing increases in excess of 300 percent over the 1961 values. Although production during the last decade has not been as dramatic, steady growth continues to be registered in respect to these crops (Republic of Kenya 1984). Current estimates for dairying indicate that at least 39 percent of the milk produced in the district is sold (Republic of Kenya 1989: 38).

It is worth noting that these production patterns are sustained despite very low input intensities. According to a recent production survey (Republic of Kenya 1989: 36), the percentage of farmers using various inputs was manure, 7; fertilizer, 25; herbicides, 4; machinery, 2; hired labor, 12; farm credit, 0; livestock feed, 32; dipping costs, 22. These figures put Kisii among the medium-to-low input use for the country's districts. The explanation may well be that most user inputs are used for coffee, tea, and pyrethrum only, crops that, as indicated, occupy less than 25 percent of the agricultural land in the district. Besides, the size distribution of holdings in the district would clearly inhibit the extensive use of machinery.

Agricultural Change and Employment

The effects of these developments on rural employment can only be inferred as no district-level data are available on rural (i.e., nonformal or nonwage) employment. Some of the implications of a relatively small net outmigration and the relative youth of the Gusii farm family have already been noted. Both of these must be attributed to the fact that agricultural development in the district was a major factor in the generation of productive employment. A smallholder household budget survey undertaken in 1981–82 (Republic of Kenya 1989: 27ff) reported that 31 percent of a household's income in Kisii derived from farm enterprises, placing the district among the medium-to-high performance areas in the country. The fact that cultivation had become more labor intensive, that production of a number of crops such as tea, pyrethrum, and maize has been steadily increasing over the years, and that market behavior (whether regulated or unregulated) for many of those crops remained relatively stable, has had a lot to do with this.

Agricultural production is expected to have further stimulated rural nonfarm enterprises. Uchendu and Antony (1975) noted, for example, that off-farm employment in the district derived from outmigration (among other factors) was high. Within the district itself, there is evidence that as much as 28 percent (or more) of the household income comes from nonfarm enterprises. The rest of the household income (about 41 percent after farm income is taken into account) comes from wages, salaries, and probably remittances (Republic of Kenya 1989). This translates to a considerably high off-farm "rural" employment, about the national average of 43 percent.

Population and Intensification Impacts

This study has shown that population change in Kisii District has led to an extremely high level of intensity in agricultural land use in the area. Although the actual processes through which this has occurred remain complex, it is argued that Gusii land tenure has been remarkably sensitive and adaptable to this population pressure. The fact that land consolidation and legislation were carried out fairly early in the district does not appear to have been particularly cataclysmic precisely because tenure institutions have not been an impediment to agricultural growth; productivity of the Gusii farmers has generally been high.

This level of development has not, however, been achieved without present or prospective costs. Rapid population growth in the face of intensively farmed land can pose a serious threat to environmental quality. In high relief where drainage systems begin and where the top soil is susceptible to erosion, these conditions commonly lead to soil-nutrient depletion. Where fertilizer use is not extensive, as in Kisii, the sustainability of agriculture is questionable. Soil degradation may be accompanied by other forms of environmental damage, especially where deforestation also occurs. The fact that only one protected forest exists in the district and that woodlands occupy less than 8 percent of the land area (KREMU 1983) is cause for great concern.

Further, the heavy dependence on agricultural incomes creates problems for future generations, especially if the rate of population growth remains high or productivity in agriculture declines. There is evidence that insufficient productive employment for some is the cause of a great deal of social instability, evidenced in homicide statistics (Raikes 1989). As no land frontier is present, the situation in Kisii could degenerate unless dramatic increases occur in nonfarm entrepreneurship. This, however, is a developmental problem facing the country as a whole and not just Kisii District. It is one that requires broad national policy options and strategies.

Notes

1. On the hills and minor scarps that dot the Kisii landscape, *cambisols* develop on basic igneous rocks; *rankers, phaeozems,* and *lithosols* develop on quartzites. The plateaus and high-level structural plains have soils developed on two rock types: the *ferralsols* on intermediate igneous rocks and the humic *ferralsols* (with acid humic topsoil) on quartzites. Soils on the footslopes are of three types: gleyic *phaeozems* on colluvium from acid igneous rocks with volcanic-ash admixture; humic *acrisols* on colluvium from quartzite; and luvic *arenosols*. Piedmont plains soils develop on alluvium from undifferentiated basement system rocks; these are haplic *xerosols* and calcarocambic *arenosols*.

Finally, upland soils, which occupy much of the district, consist of different types: luvic *phaeozems* on rhyolites; mollic *nitosols*, chromo-luvic *phaeozems*, nito-rhodic *ferralsols,* nito-luvic *phaeozems,* and humic *acrisols* on granite; *phaeozems* and nito-humic *ferralsols* on biotite/hornblende granites; chronic *luvisols* on acid igneous rocks; eutric *plauasols* and chromic *vertisols* on acid igneous rocks (rhyolites) with volcanic-ash admixture and chromo-luvic *phaeozems.*

References

Barnes, C. 1976. "An Experiment with African Coffee Growing in Kenya: The Gusii 1933–1950." Ph.D. dissertation, Michigan State University.

Clayton, E. S. 1961. "Peasant Coffee Production in Kenya." *World Crops* 13(7): 267–69.

_____. 1966. *Agrarian Development in Peasant Economies.* Oxford: Pergamon Press.

Cloud, P. 1971. "Resources, Population, and Quality of Life." In *Is There an Optimum Level of Population?* ed. S. F. Singer, pp. 8–31. New York: McGraw-Hill.

Garst, R. D. 1972. "The Spatial Diffusion of Agricultural Innovation in Kisii District, Kenya." Ph.D. dissertation, East Lansing, Michigan State University.

Gitu, K. 1989. *Agricultural and Livestock Data Compendium.* Long-Range Planning Unit. Nairobi: Republic of Kenya, Ministry of Planning and National Development.

Jaetzold, R., and H. Schmidt. 1982. *Farm Management Handbook of Kenya: Natural Conditions and Farm Management Information, Vol. II-A, Western Kenya (Nyanza and Western Provinces).* Nairobi: Ministry of Agriculture in cooperation with the German Agricultural Team (GAT) of the German Agency for Technical Cooperation.

KREMU. 1983. *Land Use in Kisii District.* Technical Report No. 97. Nairobi: Republic of Kenya, Ministry of Finance and Planning.

_____. 1984. *Land Use in Kisumu District.* Technical Report No. 104. Nairobi: Republic of Kenya, Ministry of Finance and Planning.

Marris, P., and A. Somerset. 1971. *The African Businessman.* Nairobi: East African Publishing House.

Mayer, P., and I. Mayer. 1965. "Land Law in the Making." In *African Law: Adaptation and Change,* ed. L. Kuper and H. Kuper. Boston: G. K. Hall.

Ochieng', W. R. 1974. *A Pre-Colonial History of the Gusii of Western Kenya from CAD, 1500–1914.* Kampala: East African Literature Bureau.

Okoth-Ogendo, H. W. O. 1976. "African Land Tenure Reform." In *Agricultural*

Development in Kenya: An Economic Assessment, ed. J. Heyer et al. Oxford: Oxford University Press.

———. 1986a. "Some Issues of Theory in the Study of Tenure Relations in African Agriculture." Paper presented at the African Studies Association meeting in Madison, Wisconsin, October 30–November 2.

———. 1986b. "The Perils of Land-Tenure Reform: The Case of Kenya." In *Land Policy and Agriculture in Eastern and Southern Africa*, ed. J. W. Arutzen et al. Tokyo: United Nations University.

Omare, C. N. 1981. "Effect of Population Change on Land-Use in Kisii District, Kenya." M.A. thesis, University of Nairobi.

Ominde, S. H. 1968a. *Land and Population Movements in Kenya*. London: Heinemann.

———. 1968b. "Internal Migration of the Economically Active Age Group in Kenya." In *Ost-Afrikanische Studien (East African Studies)*, ed. H. Berger, pp. 227–40. Erlangen-Nürnberg: Friedrich Alexander Universität Wirtschafts und Sozialgeographisches Institut.

Osoro, J. M. 1979. *African Labourers in Kericho Tea Estates 1920–1970*. M.A. thesis, University of Nairobi.

Oucho, J. O. 1981. "Rural-Rural Migration and Population Change: A Study of the Kericho Tea Estate Complex." Ph.D. thesis, University of Nairobi.

———. 1984. "Rural-Urban Migration Field: The Case Study of Kericho Tea Estate Complex in a Regional Setting." *Geografiska Annaler* 66B(2): 123–34.

Raikes, P. 1989. *Savings and Credit in Kisii, Western Kenya*. Working Paper No. 88.7. London: Centre for Development Research.

Republic of Kenya. 1981. *Kenya Population Census. 1979*, Vol. 1. Nairobi: Central Bureau of Statistics.

———. 1984. *Kisii District Development Plan 1984–88*. Nairobi Ministry of Finance and Planning.

———. 1985. *Kenya Population Census, 1979*, Vol. 2. Nairobi: Central Bureau of Statistics.

———. 1989. *Economic Survey*. Ministry of Planning and National Development.

Swynnerton, R. J. M. 1954. *A Plan to Intensify African Agriculture*. Nairobi: Government Printer.

Uchendu, V. C., and K. R. M. Antony. 1975. *Agricultural Change in Kisii District*. Nairobi: East African Literature Bureau.

University of Nairobi. 1984. *District Socio-Cultural Profiles: Kisii District*. Nairobi: Institute for Development Studies.

7 / Agricultural Expansion, Intensification, and Market Participation among the Kofyar, Jos Plateau, Nigeria

Robert McC. Netting, Glenn Davis Stone, and M. Priscilla Stone

Looking north from the rolling savanna plains of the Benue Valley in the Nigerian Middle Belt, the Jos Plateau escarpment is an abrupt wall rising to elevations of over 1,000 m and pocked with the cones of extinct volcanoes. The cultural ecology of this area is as distinctive as its topography. A large number of small ethnic groups with different languages, social organizations, house types, and costumes traditionally occupied adjoining territories of 300 to 800 km² in the hills and on a narrow band of well-watered oil palm land at the foot of the escarpment (Ames 1934). Some of these groups, such as the Kofyar, lived at densities of 35 to over 200/km², practicing intensive, permanent cultivation on terraced, manured homestead farms. Their dispersed homesteads, each in its own field of grains, tubers, and tree crops with stall-fed livestock, formed hamlets and villages that remained politically autonomous. The folk, whom the British colonialists called "hill pagans," were never incorporated into the Jukun or Moslem Hausa city states that dominated much of the rest of northern Nigeria.

The Kofyar homeland (fig. 7.1) on the southern margin of the Jos Plateau (9° N, 9°15′ E) includes a ridge system fingering south between the Shemankar and the Dep River valleys and also the plains fringe village areas of Doka, Merniang (Kwa and Kwang), Doemak (Dimmuk), and Kwalla (Kwolla). The base of the escarpment is about 300 m (1,000 feet) above sea level. The entire area of approximately 492 km² (190 mi²) had a population of 55,000 in 1952 and 73,000 in 1963 (Netting 1968: 111). Like many of their neighbors such as the Hill Yergam, the Montol, the Tal, the Angas, the Mwahavul (Sura), and the Eggon, the Kofyar

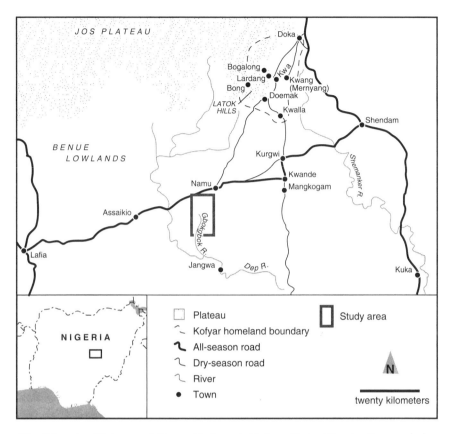

Fig. 7.1. Jos Plateau and Benue Piedmont, Plateau State, Nigeria. By permission of Glenn Davis Stone.

have taken part since the 1940s in a "downhill movement" (Gleave 1966; Udo 1966) onto largely vacant lands in the Benue Valley. Extensive bush tracts south of Namu and Kwande (fig. 7.2), some 30 km south of the Kofyar homeland, have been brought under the hoe. Initial seasonal shifting cultivation of millet, sorghum, and sesame plus the cash crops of yams and rice has been replaced by an intensive sedentary farming system. Though no exact census figures are available, it appears that in the last forty years, between 25,000 and 30,000 Kofyar migrants have permanently settled in this frontier area and decisively entered the market economy as producers of food crops for urban Nigeria.

Relative isolation of the Kofyar in a rugged "refuge area" allowed their traditional system of permanent, intensive homestead farm cultiva-

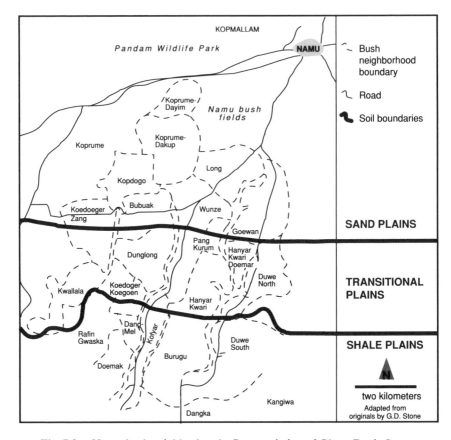

Fig. 7.2. Namu bush neighborhoods. By permission of Glenn Davis Stone.

tion to continue into the present as a viable, self-sufficient system supporting a dense, local population. Recent spontaneous agricultural and economic changes reflect decisions made by the Kofyar to grow cash crops using indigenous, low-energy techniques, and they now sell substantial surpluses of staple foods.[1]

Both the Kofyar homeland and the frontier to which they have migrated are in Qua'an Paan L.G.C. District (formerly Shendam L.G.C.) of Plateau State with its capital in Jos. The area was first conquered by the British in 1909, and further military activity along with forced evacuation of the Latok hills took place as recently as 1930 (Netting 1987). The homeland is connected by a road (that may be impassible in the wet season) to the Jos-Panyam-Shendam all-weather road completed in the

1950s, and Namu has been linked with Shendam and Lafia by an all-weather paved road since 1982 (fig. 7.1). Kofyar had already begun to head-load grain, yams, and palm oil to the tin-mining settlements of the high Plateau in the 1930s, and by the 1950s, lorries began to call regularly during the dry season at Namu, Kwande, and Kurgwi markets. Kofyar farmers could sell their yams and their bags of millet, rice, and sorghum to drivers and merchants who came to the farm gate. The extension of the road network and the increase of motor traffic, fueled by the Nigerian oil boom (Watts 1984), have made possible the efficient marketing of Kofyar primary products and greatly increased access to consumer goods, modern health services, and education.

Environmental Setting

The hill and escarpment terrain of the Kofyar homeland is based on Cambrian to Precambrian granites overlain by weathered basalts from early and late Tertiary volcanism (Morgan 1979). There are deeply incised north-south river valleys and a high stream density with slopes that are farmable although fairly steep (Stone et al. 1984). Settlement of dispersed homesteads is in the wider valleys and along ridges and the summits of flattened hills. The tan or light brown soils resulting from the weathering of granites and quartzites in the Kofyar hills are immature, having a relatively high mineral nutrient status because of the presence of decomposing rock fragments. On the barren slopes outside village settlements, soils may be thin and pebbly, but in moist valleys and where it has been regularly composted on homestead farms, the soil is darker, loamy, and quite fertile. Areas of old lava flows are reddish and oxidized, heavy and gluey when wet and very hard when dry. Such earth of recent volcanic origin on the plains near the escarpment was difficult to farm by traditional methods. Settlement was very dense, however, on the sedimentary deposits and remains of alluvial fans resulting from the erosion of the plateau (Wilshusen and Stone 1990).

South of the Kofyar homeland, which reaches as far as 10 km southeast of the escarpment at Kwalla, the Benue Piedmont physiographic unit (Hill 1979) has thin, irregular soils derived from weathered Basement Complex rocks and large lateritic areas. This undulating plain with occasional bedrock outcroppings and iron pan does not easily support continuous agricultural use. Settlement is sparse on the Benue Piedmont, and the Kofyar, especially those from Kwalla who first moved south into it, often abandoned their farms for better land south of Kwande and Namu (G. Stone 1988). This part of the Benue trough (fig. 7.2) is characterized by the Sand Plains, Transitional Plains, and Shale Plains derived from Cretaceous sandstones and shales. The Sand Plains are dominated by well-drained reddish sands of coarse surface texture with no significant limitations to the production of yams, millet, and sorghum (Stone 1988, citing Hill 1979). The Transitional Plains are edaphically similar, but the finely textured pale clays of the Shale Plains are imperfectly drained and inhibit crop production. Kofyar who have colonized the Shale Plains areas beginning some 9 km south and east of Namu have found that after a few years of cultivation, poor drainage on the clay soils may cause growing yam tubers to rot. In dry years, on the other hand, greater surface runoff also leads to failure of the yam crop. Settlers of the Shale Plains have frequently allowed farms to revert to grassland grazed by nomadic Fulani herds. In some cases the farmers have returned to long-fallowed Sand or Transitional Plains land in an attempt to establish more permanent farms.

Namu at 190 m above sea level is on an east-west watershed forming the northern edge of the sedimentary strata that include the gently undulating Sand and Shale Plains descending gradually to the Gbokgbok and finally the Dep Rivers. That this part of the Benue Valley lacked settlement in the past was not because of the topography or of soils, and the rainfall is relatively good. This is a zone of 1,143 to 1,270 mm (44–55 inches) of annual precipitation. An almost totally dry winter alternates with a rainy season of 200 to 210 days, beginning in mid-April and concluding toward the end of October (Hill 1979). The rains show a bimodal distribution, peaking first in early June and again, following a drier July period, in September (Kowal and Kassam 1978). This was adequate to support a fairly continuous forest of the Guinea savanna type, and the Kofyar claim that their first clearings were threatened by the incursions of wild animals including elephants. Precipitation may be locally even higher due to the orographic effect when moisture-bearing winds from the south encounter the Jos Plateau escarpment.

The presence of oil palms and the growing of maize and cocoyams as staples in Bong village (Netting 1968: 79) testify to an escarpment climate closer to that of the southern Nigerian tropical forest zone than to that of the surrounding savanna. The Kofyar can grow the staple grains, millet and sorghum, and groundnuts as well as yams and cassava, which require more water. Though total crop failure is rare, there is considerable variability in annual rainfall, and a delay in the rains or an early cessation may reduce yields substantially. Severe droughts occurred in 1976 and 1983, and inconsistent early rains forced some Kofyar farmers to replant their 1986 millet twice. When the early rains are adequate, there may be a good harvest of the fast-maturing millet, but later drought may hurt sorghum yields and wipe out many yam crops.

In the past there were periodic food scarcities in the Merniang and Doemak areas at the base of the Plateau. They seemed to be less well watered than the hill communities, drinking water was scarce during the dry season, and a denser population also put pressure on agricultural resources. Communities along and above the escarpment in the Valley, Bong, Hilltop, and Ridge zones (Stone et al. 1984) seem to have had a wider range of crops, more economic trees, more bush land for grazing, and less variable rainfall than their plains-fringe neighbors.

Pests have not traditionally been a major problem on the intensely tilled homestead farms of the Kofyar. The presence of resident households with their dogs in the midst of the fields discouraged predators. Occasional plagues of locusts are remembered, but agricultural operations may have been reduced more by inter-village warfare than by pests, and the human population has been menaced by trypanosomiasis rather than famine (Netting 1973). A rapidly increasing danger to the cash-cropping area is the weed *Striga hermontheca* that parasitizes growing sorghum plants at the root, killing them or reducing yields if they are not removed by a mid-season weeding (Stone et al. 1990). The Kofyar have no modern methods of coping with striga, but they are buying chemical seed dressings to protect their germinating seeds from insects.

Key features of the environment in the past were (1) the location of the Kofyar homeland on and at the base of the Jos Plateau escarpment where a rugged terrain protected the Kofyar from militarily stronger neighbors, and (2) the relatively dependable and adequate orographic rainfall that supported forest crops such as the oil palm in a Southern Guinea Savanna area. These features, along with soils whose productivity could be improved by the addition of organic materials, sustained a dense sedentary farming society. In the recent period of migration into the Benue Valley and the adoption of cash cropping, unoccupied Sand Plains and Transitional Plains soils allowed agricultural colonization. These well-drained sandstone and shale-derived soils with moderate slopes (3.5–4.4 percent) have no limitations for millet, sorghum, and groundnut cultivation, only a minor texture limitation for yams, and severe drainage constraints only for rice (Hill 1979). Only the poorly drained Shale Plains with their finely textured clays present serious problems for all of the important Kofyar crops (Hill 1979), and these areas are being deserted by farmers.

Because of relatively recent conversion of the frontier area from dry forest to first shifting and then permanent cultivation, it is not yet clear whether Kofyar composting and use of chemical fertilizer can maintain the nutrient status of the preferred soils. (In 1992, many farmers were complaining of declining yields.) An even more immediate determinant of agricultural production is the rainfall that is highly seasonal and sufficiently variable to cause unexpected shortfalls and droughts, thus possibly limiting the promise of the Middle Belt to contribute dependably to West African food supplies (Nyerges 1987). The well-spaced precipitation of 1984 as contrasted to the poor rains of 1983 allowed one group of six Kofyar farmers to increase their mean yam production by 91 percent, sorghum by 217 percent, but early millet by only 44 percent. It appears that without irrigation, Kofyar rain-fed agriculture in the Namu area will remain subject to major annual fluctuations. On the other hand, there are no obvious signs that forest clearance and shortened or absent fallows have led to erosion or environmental degradation, nor have the Kofyar migrants been exposed to markedly increased parasitic diseases (cf. Nyerges 1987).

Population Size and Density in the Kofyar Homeland

Although colonial and national population estimates for the Kofyar area have been notably imprecise, both direct and indirect evidence suggests the presence of unusually dense, sedentary farming communities. Extrapolating from the census figures of 25,000 in 1921, 44,000 in 1931, 55,000 in 1952, and 73,000 in 1963 (Netting 1968: 111) would give a possible 1970 population of over 90,000 and, at 3.0 percent annual growth, a 1984 population of 136,000. Lacking hard data on fertility, mortality, or migration, estimates after 1963 are purely speculative, but it is not unlikely that there are well over 130,000 Kofyar in the traditional homeland and in the adjoining areas of the Benue River Valley to which they have migrated.

In 1952 before substantial permanent settlement of the frontier bush lands, population density in the restricted 492/km² homeland territory was 112/km², contrasting sharply with a density of 15/km² in Shendam Division and 19/km² in the Northern Region as a whole (Netting 1968: 110). A district officer (Findlay 1945) had earlier estimated Kofyar density, after eliminating uninhabited and wastelands, at 97/km² in the hills and 463/km² (1200/mi²) on the plains at the foot of the escarpment. Given the varieties of local terrain and natural resources, there were in fact major differences among the population in Kofyar regions. Using my 1960–62 household census figures for sixteen villages and agricultural catchment areas (homesteads and local bush farms) defined by Glenn Stone on 1963 aerial stereo photos, we arrived at hill population densities ranging from 36 to over 92/km² and plains densities of at least 200 and perhaps exceeding 300/km² (Stone et al. 1984: 92).

I have speculated elsewhere that permanent rural population densities of 58/km² (150/mi²) suggest the presence of an appreciable degree of intensive cultivation (Netting 1990). Such unfallowed, annually farmed homestead land may have amounted to about 0.4 to 0.6 ha (1.0–1.5 acres) for each Kofyar household (Netting 1968: 99). If that were the sole source of agricultural support, it would have sustained 167–250 households or 868 to 1,300 people/km², which suggests that even on the plains with large areas of closely packed, contiguous homesteads, substantial areas remained in shifting cultivation or as low-grade pasture and waste lands. Estimated land use under shifting cultivation was from 0.2 to 0.5 ha (0.57–1.31 acres) per household (Netting 1968: 99), making the total household cultivated-land average between 0.6 and 1.1 ha. Maximum densities, ignoring fallow requirements, would thus have been 473 to 868 persons/km², and this practical limit seems to have been approached in only some of the plains communities.

Regional breakdowns of Kofyar population densities showed a regularly patterned *inverse* relationship to production. Plains areas of high population had consistently lower average numbers of grain bundles harvested and livestock owned per household than the more sparsely settled Valley and Bong areas (Stone et al. 1984: 95–96). Because mean household sizes in the hills were also smaller (3.47–5.96) than those on the plains (6.29), per capita differences in cereal supplies and domestic animals were even more pronounced (Stone et al. 1984: 101). Hill villages in the 1960s obviously had larger tracts of surrounding grasslands and, in some cases, forest as well as somewhat less constricted homestead farms. Production indices of the plains suggested real population pressure. There were even indications that there was a higher degree of interhousehold economic inequality in the more crowded plains as opposed to the less dense hill regions (Stone et al. 1984: 100–102).

Migration to the Cash-Cropping Frontier

The most profound change in Kofyar population and society since their incorporation in the British colonial state of Nigeria after 1909 has been the self-propelled movement of substantial numbers of farm families from intensive subsistence homesteads in the homeland at the edge of the Jos Plateau to a larger scale production of food crops for the market on frontier lands in the Benue Valley. The Kofyar made individual household decisions as to when and if to migrate, what to plant, and whether to resettle permanently on the new lands. There have never been government programs for resettlement, agricultural development and extension, credit, or marketing that have affected the Kofyar directly. In fact, they voluntarily began to grow newly adopted yams and rice as well as their traditional millet to sell while maintaining their staple sorghum, millet, and cowpeas for subsistence. They continued to use the familiar technology of hoe cultivation and to organize labor through the household and various means of exchange.

Migration began in the 1920s as the simple expansion of shifting bush cultivation on the southern and western perimeters of the densely settled plains communities of Kwalla, Doemak, and Merniang. People went no farther than a few hours' walk from their homesteads and built only a shelter for occasional overnight stays. The few walled, nucleated communities to the south like Namu (linked ethnically to the Kofyar), Kurgwi with its Hausa traders, and Kwande, a Goemai settlement, maintained a desultory trade in salt with the Plateau and farmed only a small proportion of the surrounding dry forest. In 1951, some thirty Doemak households established farms in Mangkogam south of Kwande, and by 1953, Doedel, the Chief of Kwa, along with the Chief of Lardang and some others, were cultivating about 4 km south of Namu. Kwa in the Merniang home area had a dense population and relatively low per capita crop and livestock production. Doedel encouraged his villagers to grow extra subsistence food for themselves and to produce a surplus for trade and for taxes. The general practice was to visit the bush farm periodically, killing the trees with fire in the dry season, and planting sesame followed by yams, and then the staple sorghum and millet in successive years. By the early 1960s, Kofyar were spending increasing parts of the rainy season on the bush farm, but almost no one had relocated permanently or abandoned the intensively tilled original homesteads. Household members moved back and forth to the Namu bush, according to where their labor was needed.

Migratory bush cultivation increased rapidly in the 1960s, going from 22 percent of 655 households surveyed in 1961 to 46 percent of 677 in 1966 (Stone et al. 1984: 95–96). Where traditional population was heavy as in Kwa, 76 percent of the households had established bush farms by 1966. Even in Bong where there were no migrants in 1961, over a quarter of all households had accepted bush cash cropping by 1966.

With economic success in cash cropping, some families transferred their permanent residences to the new area. By 1984 a survey of home and bush migrant lands showed that 74 percent of 979 households had migrated and 514, over half the sample, had transferred their sole residence to the bush. Deserted huts rapidly disintegrated. Tax lists of this Kofyar officially recognized population in the Namu area alone went from 7,050 (1972–73) to 8,980 (1974–75), 11,061 (1978–79), 12,035 (1980–81), and 12,602 (1984–85). Namu Town was also growing rapidly, and its Kofyar population had reached 1,661 by 1984-85. In the adjoining Kwande District, 11,364 Kofyar were settled by 1984. With new bush areas still being opened up south of Assaikio on the west and in the direction of Ibi on the Benue, it is probable that a minimum of 25,000 to 30,000 Kofyar have taken up cash-crop agriculture in the Benue Valley outside of their original homeland. Tiv from south of the Benue were entering the same area in the 1930s (Rowling 1946), but the Kofyar appear to outnumber both these migrants and the traditional Goemai residents by many thousands.

Density in the bush-farm area southwest of Namu can be more accurately estimated for those neighborhoods or administrative subunits (*ungwa*) where we conducted an intensive household census and mapped homesteads with the aid of aerial photos (Figs. 7.3 and 7.4). The sixteen tabulated ungwa (fig. 7.2) have a total population of 3,590 on 36.22 km², giving a density of 99.12/km² (256.8/mi²) in 1984. These subdistricts, each with an appointed headman (*mengwa*) responsible for tax and other administrative duties to the Native Authority (N.A.) of Namu, average 224 members in 35.25 households. Populations range from 106 to 362, thus approximating those of traditional Kofyar hill villages. Older

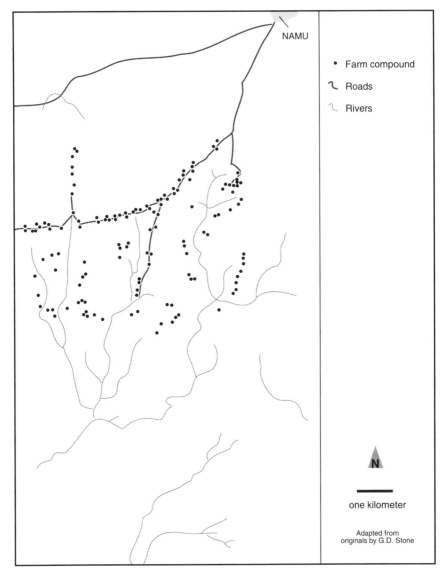

NAMU

- Farm compound
- Roads
- Rivers

N

one kilometer

Adapted from
originals by G.D. Stone

Fig. 7.3. Bush population near Namu, 1963. By permission of Glenn Davis Stone.

neighborhoods like Ungwa Long, Wunze, and Goewan that may have areas of overworked soil, average only 82 to 92 people/km[2], but population in only one neighborhood tops 125/km[2].

Ten measured farms, including both cultivated and fallow land, ranged from 2.79 to 7.95 ha, averaging 5.61 ha.[2] They were occupied by

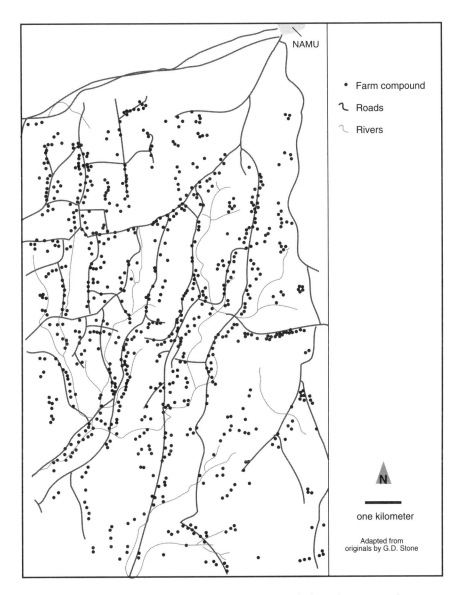

Fig. 7.4. Bush population near Namu, 1977. By permission of Glenn Davis Stone.

households with a mean size of 7.2 persons (slightly higher than the mean of 6.58 for 546 households in the 1984 survey population), and per capita land area for the ten households was 0.56 ha/person. A sample of ten farms measured in 1966 gave cultivated areas (excluding fallow) of 4.33 ha (Netting 1968: 200), suggesting that Namu bush farms may not have changed a great deal in area, though shortened fallow, intercropping, and crop rotation have intensified land use. Some fragmentation among heirs and newcomers is beginning to take place. A land-use survey from aerial photographs covering portions of the Sand, Transitional Plains, and Shale Plains gives cultivated areas of 65.1 percent, 11.3 percent short to long fallow, 1.9 percent roads, 0.9 percent compounds, and 20.8 percent uncultivated or long fallow, of which 15 percent is in stream valleys that are probably uncultivable. This estimation procedure gives average farm size of 5.45 ha.

A 1963 aerial photograph of the study area shows 138 homesteads (Stone 1986, 1991a) in the neighborhoods now occupied by 546 household farming units (fig. 7.3). Using a mean household size of 6.44 based on 320 migrant households surveyed in 1961 and 1966 (Stone et al. 1984: 99), the total estimated population of the area would have been 902, and these would have been temporary residents because all Kofyar at that time maintained homestead farms in their villages of origin. Growth to 3,590 in 1984 meant that Kofyar bush-farming population had increased by 398 percent over twenty-one years. Glenn Stone (1988, 1991a, 1991b) has demonstrated that this substantial continued migration plus natural increase was accommodated by (1) the opening of new farms on the less desirable Shale Plains soils, and (2) the location of homesteads at greater distances from sources of drinking water, thereby increasing daily domestic labor. These strategies of spatial movement and declining cost/benefit ratios accompanied the process of agricultural intensification and land fragmentation among early settlers who remained in place.

It appears that Kofyar population in the bush-farm areas south of Namu increased rapidly from the 1950s to the late 1970s, but growth is now flattening out; none of the farmers we talked to had access to new land within his present neighborhood. As new households are formed, they will have to either take over a parental household, accept a smaller share of land, or move to a frontier 50 km distant or more. By 1992, young men were starting to establish new farms in Taraba State. Existing local population density, combined with a continued active participation in production for the market, suggests that shifting cultivation is now a practical impossibility and that the observed processes of agricultural intensification will continue.

There are already suggestions of the directions that further intensification might take such as the staking of yams, the planting of bananas and citrus orchards, the extension of rice cultivation in swampy areas (already present on smaller-than-average farms), and the use of lower-quality soils for fenced, dry-season cassava gardens. Pump irrigation of vegetable crops from shallow wells is another possibility. Population density is still far below the levels of many Igbo groups and of the Hausa in the Kano Close-Settled Zone (Goldman, Martin, Okafor, and Mortimore, chaps. 8–11 of this volume). To the degree that opportunities for surplus production decline among the Kofyar due to land scarcity, they may be expected to diversify their economic activities, supplementing farming with trade, artisanal work, wage labor, and employment that requires education. This process has already begun among the almost 1,700 Kofyar residents of Namu Town, many of whom continue as part-time farmers.

Population Structure and Household Labor Organization

Demographic evidence for fertility and mortality is notoriously hard to collect in preliterate populations, and our data in these areas are much less reliable than those for migration. Changes in rates must be inferred from aggregate statistics drawn from household censuses with estimated year of birth or age. The material collected on 4,000 individuals in 1966–67 and for 8,728 individuals in 1984–85 indicates a relative increase in the younger age groups of the population. In 1966, 29 percent of the entire population was in the 0–10-year-old bracket and 37.1 percent 0–15, whereas in 1984 the corresponding proportions were 38.7 percent and 47.1 percent. The recent Kofyar population pyramid displays the contours of a broad-based developing-nation population with close to half of its total numbers comprised of dependent children. These cohorts were proportionately less large in 1966. We might speculatively credit this difference to lower infant mortality, to higher fertility, and perhaps to increased fecundity.[3] In any event, it appears that population growth arising from natural increase will remain a significant factor in pressure on land resources, the provision of agricultural labor, and outmigration for the immediate future.

Although population density may correlate with the traditional intensive-farming system of the Kofyar homeland, and although the movement from shifting to intensive exploitation of the frontier parallels demographic growth, it is in the size and composition of household labor groups that the most rapid adaptation to agricultural needs occurs (Netting 1993). The original hypothesis of a regular relationship between small, permanently tilled homestead farms and resident households averaging only 5.3 members (Netting 1965, 1968, 1969) has continued to be supported by reanalysis of data from the 1960s (Stone et al. 1984) and by new evidence. Traditional Kofyar households not only contrasted in size with those of neighboring groups in the same environment who practiced shifting cultivation under conditions of lower population density (Netting 1968: 131), but they also exhibited statistically significant growth to a mean size of 6.44 as they took up swidden cultivation in the land-abundant Namu bush. With no more need to economize on land and a premium on the rapid increase of cash-crop production, Kofyar mobilized labor in part by adding to the number of household workers. Although there is some suggestion that larger households from the crowded plains villages were the first to join the migratory stream (Stone et al. 1984: 98), household size grew rapidly with the number of years spent in the newly opened bush (fig. 7.5). New migrant households in 1966 averaged 5.01 members, whereas those who had spent nine years or more in cash cropping had 8.66 members (Stone et al. 1984: 99). By 1984 mean household size was 8.38, and those households with twenty-six to thirty years have now peaked at over eleven members.

Production of sorghum for subsistence, yams for sale, and cash income rises with household size in our 1984 survey population (figs. 7.6 and 7.7). The social means by which the household is expanded remain polygynous marriage (in 1984, 17 percent of Kofyar homeland households were polygynous, whereas 50 percent of the plains cash-cropping households had plural marriages), which increases the number of adult women workers immediately and the eventual workforce of resident children. The number of multiple-family (two or more married couples) households has also increased from the 5 percent characteristic of traditional family units to 26 percent among those Kofyar who in 1984 maintained both home and Namu bush farms. Household enlargement was only one method of coping with labor needs, and indeed, expenditures on hired agricultural labor rose with household size, so that multiple-family polygynous households of 15.3 members employed almost four times the labor of simple nuclear families with 4.3 members.

With the closure of the frontier and the filling in of bush land by permanent cultivation, local neighborhood populations should stabilize

Average household size (number of members)

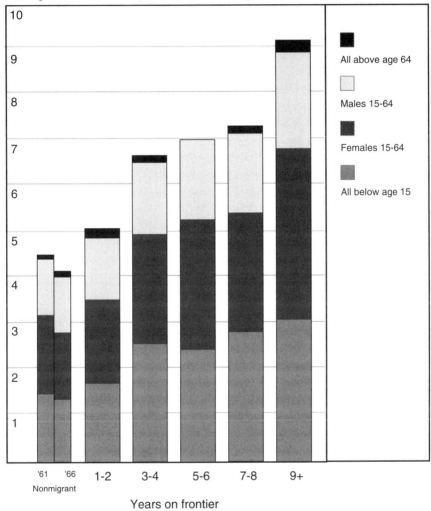

Fig. 7.5. Change in household size with years spent as a migrant cash-crop farmer on the settlement frontier. By permission of Glenn Davis Stone.

and households might be expected to decline in size. There are indications that per capita production does not keep pace with household growth.[4] As fragmentation reduces farm size, the optimum number of resident workers may shrink further. Whereas the economic interests of the household head may be best served by having many wives and sev-

Sorghum Grown in 1983 (average number of bundles per household)

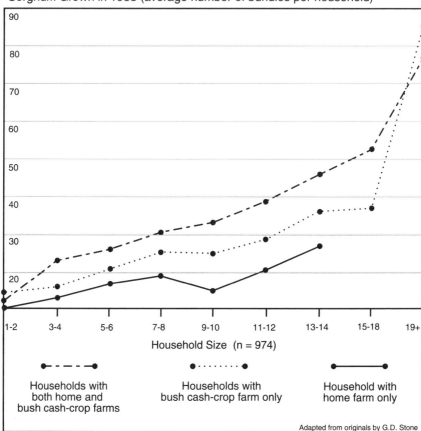

Fig. 7.6. Household size and sorghum production

eral married sons, the junior members who are supplying a major part of the labor supply may see advantages in household independence. We plan to examine cases of household fission for predisposing factors of family size, age, and type of organization, but this analysis has not yet been completed.

Crops and Methods

Kofyar agriculture reflects a series of fundamental changes between the polar types of hill and plains farming, land scarcity and abundance,

Yam heaps planted in 1983 (1000s per household)

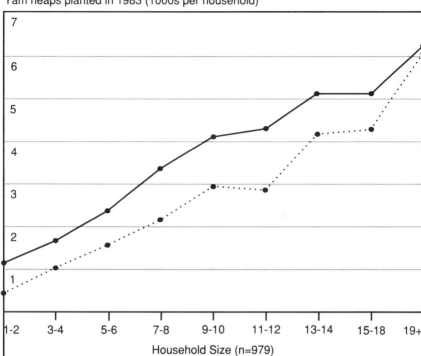

Fig. 7.7. Household size and bush yam production

shifting and intensive cultivation, and subsistence with and without cash cropping. These powerful dynamic processes have been compressed into a span of less than half a century, and they embody the functional evolution of a highly integrated, indigenous farming system. The Kofyar have followed a bimodal Boserup (1965) trajectory from permanent upland cropping (Ruthenberg 1976: 116–22) on terraced, manured, subsistence homesteads to shifting cultivation of uninhabited Benue Plains land for the market production of yams, to a gradual reintensification of farming and permanent settlement of the former bush frontier. Population has gone from dense, sedentary, and isolated in the pre- and early colonial period to migratory and sparse as the new lands were opened and back to dense and permanently settled but now involved in a modern state's network of roads and economic integration. The identification and quantitative analysis of the factors and processes in this complex, kaleidoscopic ecosystem have only begun, but the outlines of systemic change are becoming clear.

Traditional Kofyar intensive agriculture was based on contiguous homestead fields encircling or abutting dispersed, stable residential compounds. These cellular homestead farms clustered in hill valleys or on ridgetops and formed a continuous cultivated landscape on the alluvial fans and sandy plains at the foot of the Jos Plateau escarpment (fig. 7.8). Carefully cultivated, annually manured, and often terraced plots supported intercropped grain and legume staples, vegetables, and fruit trees. The small size of the Kofyar homestead farm and the intensive horticultural techniques of cultivation resemble what have been called compound farms or permanent upland cultivation in Africa and show similarities to European infields and tropical house gardens. Where land is less constricted, Kofyar homesteads may show concentric belts of less intensively tilled cereals and groundnuts at increasing distances from the dwellings (Prothero 1957; Ruthenberg 1976: 122). Monocropped bush fallow fields, often terraced, surrounded village settlements and were used for grazing and the gathering of fodder as well as for periodic swiddening.

The most common homestead crop assemblage was of interplanted early millet, sorghum, and cowpeas with separate small plots of sweet potatoes, cocoyams, yams, groundnuts, and eleusine. Scattered plants of okra, peppers, cucurbits, and cotton would be grown with the grains near the homestead courtyard. Villages with a wetter microclimate used maize and coco yams along with lima beans as the homestead crops. Economically valuable oil palms, locust bean trees, and canarium almonds were protected in the homestead fields, and introduced pawpaw and mango trees were often close to the huts.

The homestead field was cultivated annually in the wet season and never reverted to fallow for more than the few dry months after harvest. The organic content of the plot was maintained by annual applications of composted manure. Each homestead kept goats that were tied by day in a circular stone corral (*bit*) and kept in a mud hut at night. During the March to November or December growing season, grass and leafy branches were cut for the livestock, and water was brought to them for drinking. Some families also had dwarf cattle, ponies, or sheep that were herded during the day and stalled at night. The contents of the

Fig. 7.8. Intensively cultivated homestead farms in the Kofyar Homeland, Kwa Village area.

goat corral, consisting of bedded green material and animal wastes, was distributed onto the homestead field just before the coming of the rains. Slopes that were not too steep and rocky were carefully terraced with contour walls of dry-laid stone. In a further attempt to prevent soil erosion and retain water close to crop roots, both terrace surfaces and level homestead fields were ridged in a rectangular pattern (basin listing) in such a way that there was almost no runoff of rainfall. Typically the millet stalks were buried in these ridges after the July harvest, and the ridges also were banked around the still maturing plants of sorghum. Where swampy conditions or seepage made a field too wet, the Kofyar used mounds separated by ditches to promote drainage.

Shifting cultivation on more marginal fields outside the homestead perimeter relied on less demanding crops such as groundnuts, acha (*Digitaria exilis*), and sesame. Though bush fields were fallowed, they often reverted to grassland rather than tree growth after a period of annual cropping that might be as much as nine years. Groundnuts might be fertilized with household cooking-fire ash that was carefully conserved in a special hut. Bush lands might also be terraced, though with low benches, and there were occasions when the same field was double cropped, first with an early groundnut crop and then with late millet transplanted from a nursery. Whereas the frequency of cultivation of homestead land was 100 (although there were successive harvests of interplanted crops), bush fields might have a use frequency of thirty-seven to as much as sixty-eight. Grasslands were burned annually in the dry season to improve hunting opportunities and to encourage a flush of new growth for grazing. Grass fallows were merely hoed before seeding.

Kofyar tools are as technologically simple as their farming system is complex. The iron-bladed, locally forged Sudanic hoe with a short, hook-shaped wooden handle was and remains the principal implement. It is used to break and turn the soil, to lift it into ridges and heaps, and to uproot competing vegetation. Smaller pointed hoes may be used in weeding. There are also sickles for cutting fodder grass and reaping small grains, knives for cutting larger grains, and axes for harvesting palm fruit and cutting brush and trees. A variety of winnowing trays, wooden mortars and pestles, stone metates, and pottery and metal vessels are used in food processing and preparation. Ramada-like drying racks and mud granaries are present in every farming household. The plow and animal traction have not been adopted.

When the Kofyar began to enter the bush lands to the south of their homeland, they used only the extensive methods of their traditional repertoire and adapted them to production of the new cash crops of yams and, to a lesser extent, rice. They did not cut the forest but merely killed the trees in the dry season by building a fire around each trunk. Sesame might be planted in the first year because it was felt that the previously uncultivated soil was too rich for other crops. Yams planted in the second year in conical heaps were followed in the third year by the early millet-sorghum association, but the traditional cowpeas were omitted because they did not yield well. A bush farmer had to first acquire a stock of yam tubers for planting by working for others or as a gift. Because yams did best in fertile soil, farmers would move the yam field every year to newly opened parts of the farm, often working downslope from the ridge with its road toward the shallow stream valley that separated one neighborhood from another (fig. 7.4). The field was gradually cleared as the standing dead, leafless trees were further burned and finally fell.

Because initially land was plentiful, no efforts were made to fertilize the crops. Farmers did not maintain goats nor did they encourage Fulani cattle herders to corral their stock on the farms, though this practice had already begun as Fulani started to pass through the Kofyar homeland villages in the 1950s (Stenning 1957). Kofyar bush farmers also planted their millet and sorghum in ridges that were relatively low, spaced widely, and without the cross-ridging and basin listing of the homeland. There was little stone for terrace walls, and the gentle slopes could be cultivated without ridging. After perhaps seven years of crops, the farmer would fallow his land for an equal period and use another portion of his farm. Poor soils and overworked land that grew up in imperata sword grass were merely abandoned, and the farmer sought a new field farther in the woodlands. In the Shale Plains, drainage problems became apparent after a few years of cultivation. There was too much water for the maturing yams, and it was difficult to find a dry spot for a compound. Alternately in the dry season, streams dried up, and household water had to be brought from a distance (Stone 1991b).

The general strategy adopted by the Kofyar for maximizing returns from the frontier lands was to bring large areas under the hoe with extensive methods and to accept lower yields per hectare in return for labor-efficient cultivation and increased total farm production. In 1966, a sample of ten migrant bush farms averaged 3.14 ha (7.75 acres) in millet-sorghum and 1.19 ha (2.94 acres) in yams, compared with the 0.62 ha (1.54 acres) in seven sample hill homestead farms (table 7.1). Bush grain production, though only 75 percent of homestead yields, was almost four times the total volume of homestead crops (Netting 1968: 201). Though the Kofyar were not permanently resident in the cash-cropping area, they transferred household labor seasonally for periods of intense work and often left a wife or a younger family member to guard the fields at other times. They also made considerable use of cooperative beer party labor in which groups of thirty to eighty neighbors do a single task like heaping yams on the host's field and are rewarded with large quantities of millet beer (Stone 1992). In addition to this festive labor there was some hiring of migrant workers, often non-Kofyar from the Jos Plateau, who were paid in cash for a contracted job of a few days.

We would expect that as available land was either taken up or found to be inferior and abandoned, the Kofyar would reintensify their land use. The Kofyar were obviously unwilling to accept either a decline in subsistence or a marked fall in cash income as their population on the Benue plains increased and their demand for consumer goods and services rose. The areas of highest fertility south of Namu were occupied first shortly after 1953, and they have never been deserted. Settlement here remains dispersed, but it is now permanent with open farmlands dotted by large compounds, many of which now have rectangular mud-brick houses with galvanized iron roofs. Except along the courses of streams, the only remaining trees like the locust bean and shea butter have economic uses. Clearly demarcated farms bound one another, and each named neighborhood has a neat Roman Catholic chapel. Sixty-nine percent of the households have moved permanently to the cash-cropping zone, abandoning their ancestral farms in the homeland. The rest continue to maintain a traditional homestead, but it is now a distinctly subsidiary residence with limited farming that serves mostly to house elderly parents and children attending school. The old terraced fields are now used for unmanured groundnuts or acha or are grazed by the cattle of the few remaining residents.

Shifting cultivation is no longer a possibility among the sedentary farmers in the Namu bush neighborhoods that have been occupied in some cases for over thirty years. Only about 21 percent of the arable lands are fallowed, and the fallow period has been shortened to one to three years. Intensification is evident in other ways as well. Most Kofyar farmers have begun to keep stall-fed goats again and distribute their composted manure. Pigs, spreading rapidly since their introduction in the early 1960s, are now reared in many households, and cucurbits are

Table 7.1. Comparative Production of Traditional Homestead and Migrant Bush Farms

Type	Number in sample	Average acreage	Production per acre (pounds)				Total production			
			Millet	Sorghum	Cowpeas	Total	Millet	Sorghum	Cowpeas	Total
Traditional homestead (intensive)	7	1.54	400	498	98	996	616	766	151	1,533
Migrant bush farm (shifting)	10	7.75	368	305	74	747	2,855	2,366	572	5,793

Source: Netting 1968:201.

grown especially to feed them. They also consume the malted grain by-product of beer brewing. Within the last decade, chemical fertilizers have been distributed by the government. Most farmers are using several bags a year and seeking more, both of the subsidized supplies and of that purchased on the open market. They are also purchasing small packets of seed dressing and pesticides for use on stored grain. Though Kofyar lack information from extension services on fertilizer dosages and the use of the new inputs, they are experimenting (Richards 1986), and it is apparent that they will invest some of their agricultural profits in commodities that will slow or prevent declines in production. As one farmer told me, either you buy fertilizer or your son must move to another farm.

The combination of ingenuity and disciplined hard work that characterized traditional Kofyar agriculture appears especially in the new system of interplanting, crop rotation, and careful agronomy that has appeared (Stone et al. 1990). More work is expended on dry-season ridging and later hand weeding and thinning of millet, and some sorghum is transplanted to bare areas in the fields. Yams are rotated with the millet-sorghum complex because of the scarcity of long-fallowed fields. After the July–August millet harvest, yam heaps are made in the same field where the sorghum is still growing. This activity helps to both weed and support the sorghum stalks and provides the heaps in which the yams of the following year will be planted. A short-season crop of sesame may be planted on these heaps in the meantime. Vegetatively reproducing yam tubers can be planted during the dry season and covered with a cap of straw and earth so that they are protected from the sun and ready to sprout with the first rains. When, in turn, the yams are harvested during the dry months of January and February, the heaps are broken and reformed into ridges for the cereal succession.

A household millet-sorghum field may also be interplanted with groundnuts or Bambara nuts between the rows, and these are separately owned and cultivated by individual women (fig. 7.9). Many women also cultivate yams for sale on land loaned to them by their husbands (Stone 1988a and b). Along the edges of a field or in the shade of a tree, women may also raise coco yams and native African tubers that do best in a damper, less exposed micro-environment. Both men and women grow rice in swampy plots where grains and yams will not flourish. Because high grass must be uprooted for this crop and harvest also demands considerable labor, rice is not a favored cash crop, but its

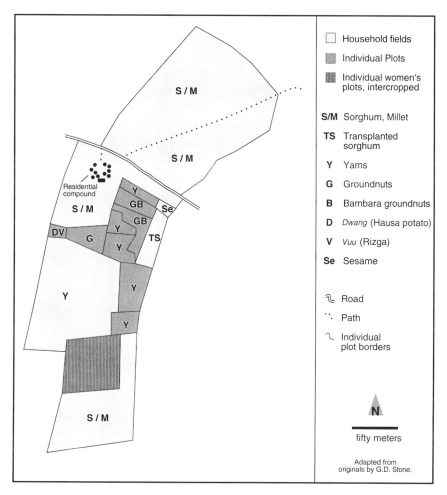

Fig. 7.9. Farm of Shangpan Dakwat, Namu area. Copyright by Glenn Davis Stone.

production allows marginal land to be intensively exploited. Land exhausted by shifting cultivation may also be returned to production by planting cassava, and this is just beginning to appear among Kofyar.

The Nigerian Ministry of Agriculture has a few small projects in the Kofyar area in which tractor plowing and chemical fertilizers are used to produce maize. Mechanization has not made significant inroads among the Kofyar, although contract plowing by a local entrepreneur is sometimes used to break volcanic soil in the homeland that can then be heaped by hand for yams. The capital costs of tractor purchase and maintenance are of course significant, but Kofyar point out that the wide furrows and monocropping associated with plowing are not compatible with their own intercropping and relay cropping (one cultigen immediately succeeding another in the same field) or with the selectivity of repeated hand operations. Even innovative projects like the banana plantation in a stream valley that uses earthen dikes and raised mounds for alternate drainage and irrigation are done entirely with hoes.

It is in transportation that modern machines affect Kofyar agriculture most directly. The export of bulk farm produce like yams, millet, rice, and even bananas is by truck. Individual entrepreneurs and middlemen come on a Kofyar-built network of dry-season roads right to the farmstead gate and purchase crops for cash. Smaller amounts may be taken in pickup trucks, minibuses, and taxis that circulate especially on market days. The Kofyar have purchased some of these vehicles and literally thousands of light motorcycles that, in addition to bicycles, carry people and goods to and from the bush farms, the towns, and the homeland villages (Netting et al. 1989). The availability and cheapness of gasoline, the variety of vehicles for sale and hire, and the roads linking major Nigerian centers of population contribute to the profitability of Kofyar food cropping and prevent the monopolizing of transport services that would raise their cost to rural people. There are some suggestions (Norman et al. 1982: 85) that competitive conditions in internal Nigerian food marketing effectively translate consumer demand and maintain attractive producer prices.

Labor Intensification

With the relative paucity of mechanical technology and new sources of energy in Kofyar agriculture, the change to migrant bush cash cropping and the subsequent intensification to maintain surplus production under conditions of growing population pressure were powered mainly by increased labor application and its effective organization and scheduling (Stone et al. 1990). A central proposition of the original Boserup (1965) model was that problems of scarce land and declining fallow periods could be met by substituting labor for other resources. The familiar tasks of intensification—manuring, livestock stall feeding, terracing, transplanting, crop rotation, more frequent weeding, irrigation—all require extra effort, investment of time for deferred rewards, and a more sustained, less variable labor expenditure than does shifting cultivation. There is now little doubt that intensification demands (1) increased person hours per unit land; and (2) higher annual labor inputs per household and per individual family member (Netting 1993). Controlled comparisons of Hausa savanna communities differing in population density (Norman et al. 1982: 104–7) and of Igbo humid forest villages along a similar population continuum (Lagemann 1977: 90, 93) indicate this labor cost of intensification. The issue is complicated by the difficulty of measuring actual labor time, comparing work across gender, age, and task difficulty spectra, and calculating efficiency, that is, return per unit of labor expended. Theory predicts that efficiency and marginal productivity decline with intensification (Barlett 1976), and labor input in fact generally increases at a faster rate than yield per hectare (Pingali and Binswanger 1984). Without technological change, a decline in labor efficiency may be inevitable.

For intensive Kofyar homestead farming, no consistent figures for labor input were ever collected. The three hoeings of a homestead field of 0.48 ha might require a total of 270 person hours a year (Netting 1968: 133), but the daily chores of bringing grass and water to the goats during the nine-month growing season could easily consume another 270 hours at the minimal rate of an hour a day. Indeed, the proliferation of small tasks such as weeding, harvesting, and processing a variety of cereal, legume, and tuber crops seemed to occupy both men and women for significant parts of almost every day during the growing season. The situation among West African shifting cultivators may involve men working from 530 to 728 hours a year (Cleave 1974), whereas females may spend much less (secluded women among Moslem Hausa) (Norman et al. 1982) or considerably more (females working 954 hours in a Gambian village) (Haswell 1953). One of the few comparative time-allocation studies shows intensive farming systems demanding some 3.5 hours more per day for men and 4 hours more per day for women than does extensive agriculture under conditions of low population pressure (Minge-Klevana 1980).

When the Kofyar embarked on large-scale bush cash cropping, they added to their traditional homestead farm work the additional tasks of the distant Namu swidden. Their time in movement to and from, either on foot or by bicycle increased, and cropping times were staggered with those of the home farm, using later-maturing varieties of sorghum and millet. Though the more rapid and less painstaking farming operations in the bush brought high returns, total labor time per capita had to rise. We do not know the extent of the increase, but the efforts of Kofyar household heads to enlist more hands through polygynous marriage and retention of married sons in the multiple-family household (Stone et al. 1984) suggest the high demand for labor.

We have analyzed time-allocation data for a 1984–85 sample of fifteen households with twenty-six adult males and thirty-six females on which resident enumerators recorded daily each task, its duration, and the labor group involved for each individual (Stone et al. 1990). Our findings are consistent with the descriptive evidence of reintensification by means of elaborate intercropping, crop rotation, and scheduling operations so as to avoid labor bottlenecks. It is apparent that Kofyar may work up to three times as much per year at their agriculture as do shifting cultivators (fig. 7.10). We estimate the average annual labor input at 1,599 hours of fieldwork and food processing for each adult. The mean was 4.4 hours per day in a seven-day week, ranging from a peak of 7.4 hours during March millet planting after the first rains to a low of 2.8 hours daily at the end of January after the dry-season harvest. Heavy grain ridging and yam mounding work absorbed an average of 4.8 to 5 hours daily.

The Kofyar mobilize impressive quantities of labor by (1) achieving balanced equivalent or complementary labor inputs for men and women; (2) using familiar, voluntary, social means of work organization by household and cooperative groups; (3) adding tasks for new crops between the seasonally dictated peak demands of their traditional crops; and (4) extending their labor into dry-season periods of formerly slack labor requirements. Men and women work side by side at most jobs, both as household members and as parts of exchange labor teams and beer party festive labor groups. Few tasks or crops are rigidly assigned to one gender (Stone 1988b). Men do 50 percent of the weeding and transplanting and women do 42 percent of the heavy mounding and ridging. Women's work in brewing subsidizes the large work groups that perform much of the yam mounding. Women put in 53 percent of total work hours in all agricultural activities, but as there are 1.36 women for every adult man in the bush farming communities, women's per capita labor contribution is 42 percent of farm work or an average of 1,473 hours annually. With the addition of brewing, cooking, and other domestic labor (but not of child care), women's per capita labor comes to 53 per-

Mean hours/day/adult

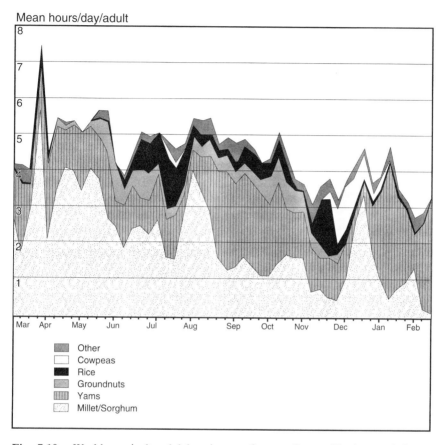

Fig. 7.10. Weekly agricultural labor inputs. Source: Stone, Netting, and Stone 1990.

cent. The remarkable testimony of these figures is that intensive hand cultivation without the plow appears to elicit very equal and quite large amounts of labor from men and women. The Kofyar, in accounting for their relative success in expanding agriculture as compared to Goemai and Hausa (Hill 1972) in similar environments, cite the direct involvement of women in farming as opposed to their seclusion in the compound or their occupation in crafts and marketing.

Though Kofyar agriculture is based on individual muscle power and relatively unspecialized tasks with simple tools that the workers bring to the job, there are a number of conventional ways to organize this labor. The basic unit in both the homeland and the cash-cropping area remains the residential household. The family works together or performs complementary tasks on the fields that belong to the household head and from which all members have the right of subsistence support. Male members have further rights of inheritance in this property and the expectation that the head will provide them with bridewealth from household resources as well as paying their taxes. Sixty-two percent of all agricultural labor is devoted to the household farm.

Both adult junior men and adult women, married and unmarried, may also farm independently, using land allocated by the household head or other land holders. The crops they produce may be sold or used according to their own wishes, and the household head has no claim on the resulting income. Independent production absorbs 15 percent of total Kofyar work hours, but most of this is done by women who work 21 percent of the time on their own crops and a further 10 percent on the individual crops of others. Family and individual labor are particularly well adapted to intensive cultivation because of the high incentives of household members who share in the fruits of their common efforts and the risks of poor production and because supervision costs are minimal (Binswanger and Rosenzweig 1986).

There are occasions in which the household is not large enough to perform a particular task within certain time constraints, but in which careful, disciplined work and a knowledge of Kofyar farming methods is desirable. The obvious choice for labor pooling is to join forces with other individuals or households on a reciprocal basis. Individuals voluntarily form exchange labor groups called *wuk* of five to twenty members. They take turns working on each other's fields, with the explicit obligation to repay all labor received. Households also belong to wuk with their neighbors, sending various household members to each labor event. About 6 percent of all labor is done by exchange groups, and much of this is directed to millet/sorghum ridging and weeding.

When massed labor is required for some of the heaviest tasks of the agricultural year like millet/sorghum ridging, millet storage, and yam heaping, the Kofyar mobilize large *mar muos* neighborhood work groups (Stone 1992). These half-day gatherings employ typically thirty to sixty workers, but they may exceed 100. The host supplies millet beer made from 90 to 180 kg of grain that provides each of the workers about four liters of the nutritious, mildly alcoholic brew. Neighborhood women also exchange labor to grind the malted millet. The festive atmosphere of the work party and the friendly competition among participants who may be urged on by drummers, along with the immediate reward of beer, lessen the drudgery and increase the social attractiveness of group labor. When newly harvested millet must be tied into bundles, lifted to a drying rack, and thatched in the short midsummer trough between rainfall peaks, the cooperative work group that circulates to several households on the same day is well adapted to the task.

It is interesting to see that the high labor demands of yam heaping for the principal cash crop are also met by beer party groups. The work must be done paying attention to the growing sorghum in the same field, and it is also an added task that was not part of the traditional farming system. Kofyar contend that though it creates costs in millet, brewing time, and return labor, beer party work costs less and is more reliable than wage labor. Its cash costs are certainly less, it accomplishes an arduous task much more rapidly than could a household working on its own, and it assembles large numbers of workers dependably with no search, hiring, or supervision expense. Because migrant wage laborers are still scarce and there are almost no landless Kofyar who must work for wages, the traditional beer party institution remains an effective organizational device, and 13 percent of all farm work is performed in this manner.

Farmers wishing to expand their operations beyond the labor resources of the household and cooperative groups can hire small groups of three to five workers who come from the Plateau. They appear in September for yam heaping, and they usually contract for a certain sum at a piece rate (e.g., N-5 equal to $7, per hundred yam heaps).[5] In 1983, 36 percent of our sample cash-cropping households employed wage workers, but the average number of person days was only twelve, constituting an estimated one percent of total agricultural labor input. With the exception of hired labor and the occasional church women's club (*zumunta*) that earns money by working on others' fields, the social organization of Kofyar labor is based entirely on traditional forms. Household members cooperate as part of the mutual dependence of family members for subsistence. Exchange and beer party groups bring together neighbors and often relatives who associate frequently in the local, face-to-face community. The fact that all Kofyar have probably increased their total labor expenditure to produce a surplus for sale has not, up to this point, essentially modified the ways in which the social forces of production are mobilized.

The technical reasons for making next year's yam heaps during the late rainy season in the sorghum fields are further supported by effective labor scheduling (Stone et al. 1990). If only subsistence grains were grown, there would be a trough between the peak labor demands of millet harvest and storage in mid-summer and the sorghum harvest in December and January. This is filled by the yam mounding, and the curve of total labor in the period September–November does not fall significantly (fig. 7.10). Intensive work on rice, which is also a cash crop, is fitted in before the harvests of the two staple cereal grains. The substantial amounts of time that go into millet/sorghum weeding and yam weeding are spread throughout the growing season and reflect the kind of sustained attention that intensively tilled crops demand. Intercropping means that weeding, thinning, and tending several crops at different stages of their growth proceeds simultaneously, and labor use is spread rather than concentrated at seasonal peaks (see Norman et al. 1982: 53–55). Small but nutritionally important crops like groundnuts, cucurbits, sesame, okra, and tuberous vegetables also occupy short periods in women's days.

At an earlier period, the end of the dry season allowed considerable leisure for funeral commemoration ceremonies, hunting, beer drinking, arranging marriages, and warfare. Though Kofyar still take dry-season time for visiting and celebrations, some crop work goes on. Yam harvesting, transporting, and often storing in specially built barns take time in January and February, and yam planting can also be done in the dry season. Fields are cleared for next year's crops, and sometimes hills are made ready for quick grain planting when the rains arrive. Women supplement their agricultural incomes by brewing beer for sale.

The cultivation of cash crops appears to have been voluntarily adopted as an addition to rather than as a substitution for traditional subsistence foods. In fact, millet is grown in larger amounts than previously for both sale in 90-kg bags and brewing the beer that rewards the labor of the big parties of yam heapers. Because the time devoted to yams and rice represents a major allocation and must be integrated with other tasks, it is clear that the Kofyar have consciously chosen to increase their total labor commitments. Yams require intensive treatment. Whereas the average Kofyar household devotes 9 to 25 percent of its cultivated area to yams, 36 percent of the household's agricultural labor time goes into this crop. The addition of rice brings the total cash-crop time to 40 percent and, with further time spent on individual crops of peanuts, Bambara nuts, sesame, and on feeding pigs and chickens for sale, it appears that men and women farmers may devote half of all their work hours to marketed output. One can only conclude that the cash incentive has motivated Kofyar to work more than they did in the past and to choose the labor of intensification over any conflicting preference for leisure. Because they are producing a surplus by these means, it is also evident that population pressure on subsistence is less influential than economic gain in the present intensification of plains production. The market carrot is now performing the former role of the subsistence stick in the homeland communities of the hills. The Kofyar could deintensify and slide back into a less labor-demanding mode of autarchic self-provisioning on the existing land base, but they have obviously opted for continued significant market participation.

Kofyar agricultural intensification demonstrates an elaboration and widening of the primary motivating role of demand affecting the behavior of the farming household. Whereas the original adaptation of permanently tilled and terraced hill homesteads apparently reflected Boserup's (1965) consumption or subsistence demand in response to local population pressure, the recent reintensification on the plains frontier was caused in part by the powerful additional demand for market commodities (Brush and Turner 1987: 31–35). When a shrinking per capita land base no longer permitted extensive means for growing cash crops, the Kofyar accepted the higher labor and capital investments that were required for sustained surplus production. Though we do not have a thorough analysis of commodity prices, transport costs, and opportunity costs of labor, it appears that Kofyar have found the monetary returns on their sales of food crops attractive, and their response to a relatively unconstrained market follows the tenets of neoclassical economics (Brush and Turner 1987: 34–36). Their increases in household labor are not easily accounted for in a Chayanov model that explicitly allows for expansion into unused land, a limited and static role in the market economy, and a refusal of further "drudgery" once the demands of the self-provisioning household are met (Chayanov 1966: 121).

Outputs of Crops and Cash Incomes

It is difficult to relate our data to questions of yield per unit area or total production by dry weight or calories. Although we gathered household- and individual-level information on the crops produced in the last two harvests and the amounts sold and money received, there is no independent verification for these figures. Unlike agricultural economists, we did not use the measured field as the unit of production and labor input, although we measured and mapped a small number of farms. Reported quantities were in several forms: bags of millet (90 kg), headloads of sorghum (approximately 24 kg of grain), yams in 100-tuber lots, enamel basins of smaller tubers, groundnuts, cowpeas, and so on. One of two recent years (1983) was so dry that Kofyar experienced considerable crop losses. Earlier estimates of subsistence grain production in both homestead and swidden fields of two hill villages ranged from a mean of 856 kg for Bogalong to 447 kg for Bong, which relied more heavily on tuber crops (Netting 1968: 91). For seven measured hill farms, estimated annual production averaged 698 kg of homestead sorghum, millet, and cowpeas without including production from bush farms (Netting 1968: 96). For 5.2-person households, grain may approach the rough per capita requirements of 0.45 kg (1 lb.)/day (Hill 1972: 254) or 145 kg/year (Simmons 1976: 16) given for the Hausa, but our data are not sufficient to allow any conclusions.

The 1984–85 survey does provide some tentative findings on subsistence production and income of households in the Namu cash-cropping area. Only quantities of the staple grains, millet and sorghum, are included, and we have not yet analyzed our material on the supplementary food crops of rice, groundnuts, cowpeas, sesame, and tubers. It appears that the bush farm households may have a declared annual production of some 55 bundles of grain, which at 22.7 kg of threshed grain each, would amount to 1,249 kg. This undoubtedly underestimates the actual production, but if it were used for subsistence alone it could support 8.6 people (at 145 kg/person annually). Combined sales of agricultural crops in this sample of 802 households exceeded N800 ($1,120) per household. Another sample of 737 cases gave mean household income from crops as N734 ($1,028), while individuals (usually married women) received an additional N197 ($276), for a total mean annual income of N931 ($1,303).[6]

Our observations suggest that the Kofyar have made substantial changes in residence, farming system, labor inputs, and work organization in order to produce a marketable surplus, but that they have not sacrificed subsistence in food or economic autonomy in pursuit of this goal. Though some town-based craftsmen, traders, or administrators may grow yams, maize, or cassava solely for sale, the rural Kofyar continue to produce the range of traditional staples and livestock that they eat. A year of poor crops may cut sales, but since all the crops grown for exchange can be (and are) consumed in the household, there is little overt evidence of want. The movement into frontier agriculture has been gradual, there is little risk because home farms have been maintained, and the heavy new investments of labor time rather than capital means that Kofyar have not incurred substantial debt. However, land in long-settled areas is no longer free, and a market in land is now developing.

Purchased agricultural inputs are now a necessity as well. In a sample of 136 household heads 56 percent had purchased chemical fertilizer in the last year, 51 percent had hired transport of some kind, and 28 percent had bought grain, either for food or for seed. We suspect that purchases of millet beer and fresh meat are rising, and there is increasing demand for manufactured foodstuffs like bottled beer, Maggi seasoning cubes, and sugar.

The Kofyar are now sufficiently committed to the market that cloth and clothing, bicycles, and carpentered door and window frames are present in almost every household. Iron beds, kerosene lamps, radios, motorcycles, and pan roofs are prevalent. Services are a major item in many family budgets. Post-primary schools often require fees. Free-enterprise medical care in the form of clinics (often run by non-doctors) and medicine stores has spread very rapidly. A survey of 136 Kofyar households indicated that 129 individuals representing 60 percent of the households had sought paid medical care in the last month. The cost to those households with one or more patients was an average of N-32, again for a single month. Women who join savings clubs or invest in livestock may do so for the explicit purpose of accumulating money to be used in case of illness. Agriculture remains the most general source of funds for all of these purposes.

The Larger Economy

Although Kofyar agriculture is firmly imbedded in the market economy while buffered by substantially self-sufficient food production, growing numbers of people are entering nonfarm occupations. Education has given access to employment as teachers, beginning with Catholic mission schools in the 1930s and 1940s. There are now secondary schools at Kwa, Kwalla, and Namu, and some Kofyar teach outside the area, including at the University of Jos. Government officials and businessmen (lorry and taxi owners, yam traders, motorcycle mechanics, saw-mill operators) come from the Kofyar population, whereas those who have converted to Islam have often become very successful as Namu yam or cattle traders, grain-mill owners, truckers, and landlords. It is not apparent how much cash returns to the area as remittances, but the inexpensive transport services mean that people can shuttle back and forth to Shendam or Jos with ease. Professional Kofyar from Jos may come to Kofyar for the weekend, and a number of them have built modern houses there. Their investment in agriculture is apparently still minimal, but growing, and there are no signs of accumulation of land (cf. Reyna 1987). Kofyar do not participate in regular or large-scale labor migration as do other groups in the Nigerian savanna. Unless one can secure professional employment, agriculture may pay better and give a higher level of security than unskilled or informal sector jobs in the city. When government clerks are laid off, they return to their fathers' farms and take up the hoe. Secondary school graduates exhibit a healthy respect for wealthy farmers, and university students spend summer vacations at work in their fathers' fields. Perhaps as a heritage from their own traditional grounding in intensive hill agriculture and as a reflection of current economic achievements, Kofyar do not hold farmers in contempt.

The Consequences of Change

The homeland hill and the cash-crop plains environments have changed in diametrically opposed directions as they switch places on the population/agricultural intensity continuum. The hills have become seriously depopulated, and some smaller villages have practically disappeared. Koepal, a hamlet near Bong, had seventeen homesteads in the 1960s of which two remain. Abandoned houses that are not thatched rapidly disintegrate. Homestead farms may be cropped extensively by the few neighboring families still present, growing unfertilized groundnuts or acha. Some men take advantage of the increased natural grazing possibilities by keeping larger herds of dwarf and Fulani cattle. It is probable that, with disintensification, unrepaired terrace walls are allowing increased erosion, and the scars are visible on the steep hillsides outside of Kofyar villages.

On the other hand, the former frontier lands south of Namu have gone from clearings in a forest with standing dead trees and blackened stumps to an open, carefully tilled landscape that suggests the Kano Close-Settled Zone (Mortimore 1967). Successive lumberings have eliminated the large hardwoods. It is not possible for us to judge the relative decline in the natural fertility of plains soils, but the ubiquity of intercropping, the short fallows, and the rapidly escalating use of fertilizer suggest that farmers are struggling to maintain or increase yields. The best Sand and Transitional Plain lands (fig. 7.2) have remained settled and are used permanently. Some lands near the Namu-Shendam road that were abandoned by shifting cultivators are now being reoccupied, in part by farmers whose recently established Shale Plains plots experienced severe drainage problems. The large shale areas abandoned by hoe cultivators are now pasture for nomadic Fulani herds (Stone 1991b). Individual cases of poor Kofyar yields were generally explained as lacking in timely cultivation or weeding or as receiving inadequate fertilizer. Dramatic soil degradation associated with sheet erosion or gullying is not immediately apparent on Kofyar lands. Whether their system of intensive rain-fed agriculture in a savanna environment is sustainable, and whether it can accommodate higher levels of rural population, is not clear.

Land tenure continues to associate dense, permanent populations and continuing, valuable, heritable rights in resources. Both homestead fields and bush fields were originally held by individual household heads succeeded by their sons. Owners' property rights were recognized, even though a homestead had been occupied for generations by tenants who paid dues in the form of tree produce and occasional beer. Forms of pledge and lease were practiced, and sale was possible though rare (Netting 1968: 164–68). Those bush lands first occupied by means of a token payment to the Chief of Namu and an annual tribute in millet and chickens are now held individually. Whereas no firm claim remained when shifting agriculturalists left exhausted land, intensively tilled fields are now transferred outside the family for a substantial sum in cash. Though such transactions are witnessed by the neighborhood head (*mengwa*), there is as yet no registry of title, and Nigeria treats rural farm lands as belonging ultimately to the state. There is little evidence of land accumulation, in part because the household labor force and the absence of large numbers of paid workers set labor limits on the amount of land effectively cultivated. Though we can document sharp increases in cash income on the frontier, inequality as measured by the

Gini index[7] was not initially growing (Stone et al. 1984: 102). With more families at different stages of the developmental cycle, and with recently founded households having to use more marginal land or a fragment of a former holding, we would expect to find more pronounced economic differences within the Kofyar bush communities now.

When our work is complete, we will be able to provide an accurate profile of Kofyar demography, labor organization, households, production, income, and housing in the cash-cropping area. Some of these indices will be directly comparable with statistics gathered in 1961 and 1966. It is, however, difficult to generalize about the overall welfare of the population. We have not measured nutrition, nor do we have other biological variables for different time periods. We suspect that health care is somewhat better, and access to various versions of Western medicine has, for good or ill, greatly increased. Clothing, transport, house types, and religious observances have changed markedly in the last thirty years. Insofar as migration to the plains and entry into the market economy is concerned, we can only say, as outside observers, that this was what the Kofyar chose to do, and that they are successfully achieving their goals.

Factors in Effective Agricultural Adaptation

Change that takes place without governmental direction or coercive control is worthy of attention. If the Kofyar case of population increase and expansion, agricultural extensification followed by intensification, and significant increase in market production offers salient characteristics that differentiate it from other African situations, they may be as follows.

1. The traditional Kofyar adaptation to dense population in a geographically isolated area was based on intensive homestead agriculture with relatively demanding labor requirements and defined property rights, and this system remained viable through the colonial period into the present. Habits of hard work, individual decision-making, and household economic self-sufficiency continued to be economically rewarding.

2. Indigenous methods of cultivation, technology, and labor organization could be applied effectively to food crops for which there was an economic demand.

3. Adjacent areas of fertile, unused land provided a frontier that could be exploited initially without permanent departure from the homeland, high risk, or large capital investment. Subsistence grains maintained household self-sufficiency in food.

4. Kofyar change emerged from individual trial-and-error experimentation, considerable communication and cooperation among neighbors of the same ethnic group, and freely chosen economic incentives of the market. Individual farmers had various options for settlement, farming system, and labor mobilization.

5. The newly adopted cash crops were also foodstuffs sold within Nigeria. Unlike commodity crops such as cocoa and cotton, they were edible and could be consumed in years of partial crop failure. Purchasing power was never monopolized by a marketing board, and producer prices have continued to be attractive.

6. Governmental and international agency direction (misdirection?) and control of this process were absent. Expensive technology and purchased inputs were not mandatory, and innovations had to be cost-effective. Bureaucratic demands for tax, tribute, or *dash*, were generally minimal, because the process of agricultural production and distribution took place outside of official awareness.

7. Reintensification and accompanying increased labor arising in a gradual, evolutionary manner from the pressures of internal population (inmigration and natural increase) on resources whose potential is understood and from well-articulated desires for the goods and services of a cash economy are seen by Kofyar to be reasonable and profitable rather than coercive and exploitative. *The Kofyar are "making it" in part because no one made them do it.*

8. The potential for continued intensification of Kofyar agriculture using chemical fertilizers, tree crops, rice, and possibly irrigation exists, and Kofyar individuals may be expected to diversify their nonfarm economic activities.

Notes

1. The Kofyar data are derived from three periods of field research, by Netting in 1960–62 and 1966–67 and by M. Priscilla Stone and Glenn D. Stone in collaboration with Netting in 1984–85. The most recent work was supported by the National Science Foundation (BNS-8318569 and BNS-8308323) and by the

Wenner-Gren Foundation for Anthropological Research. The computer analysis of quantitative material was directed by Glenn Stone and aided by additional funding from the University of Arizona Social and Behavioral Sciences Research Institute and the Department of Anthropology. Studies in the 1960s were made possible by fellowships from the Ford Foundation Foreign Area Studies Program and the Social Science Research Council. The collection of time-allocation data was organized and supervised in the field by Priscilla Stone, and the maps and graphics in this chapter were produced by Glenn Stone.

2. We estimate that average 1984 Kofyar farm size in the surveyed area south of Namu is 5.4 to 5.7 ha and that 79 percent or 4.3 to 4.5 ha are under cultivation, whereas 21 percent are fallow.

3. Mortality declines might be linked to the opening of several busy commercial clinics in Namu Town and to the proliferation of medicine shops selling antimalarial and antibiotic drugs. Roads and motor vehicles make hospitals in Shendam and Jos accessible to the Kofyar. Female fertility may be rising with a decline in post-partum sex prohibitions that appears to be reducing birth spacing from three years to two. There may even be a higher fecundity rate with fewer women suffering from secondary sterility due to venereal disease.

4. For instance the 173 percent increase in the number of adult workers in the multiple monogamous household as opposed to the simple family produces only a 78 percent increase in sorghum production, 64 percent more yam heaps, and an 89 percent growth in average cash income.

5. The official exchange rate in 1984 for Nigerian currency, the *naira*, was ₦1 = $1.40. An unofficial or parallel market rate was closer to ₦1 = $0.40.

6. A limited sample of eleven households covering the year 1984 when rainfall was adequate gave average income from household crop sales at ₦1,844 ($2,582) plus independent production of women at ₦1,297 ($1,816) per household or ₦679 ($951) each. Total income from the sale of crops alone, excluding proceeds from livestock sales, beer brewing, or wage labor, was therefore ₦4,141 ($5,797) or more than four times the 1983 amount.

7. The Gini index of inequality is derived from a Lorenz curve that plots the cumulative percentage of household income against the cumulative percentage of households. A straight line with a slope of 1 represents perfect equality and the Gini index measures the degree of departure from this state of equality.

References

Ames, C. G. 1934. *Gazeteer of Plateau Province*. Jos: Jos Native Authority.

Barlett, Peggy F. 1976. "Labor Efficiency and the Mechanism of Agricultural Evolution." *Journal of Anthropological Research* 32: 124–40.

Binswanger, Hans P., and Mark R. Rosenzweig. 1986. "Behavioural and Material Determinants of Production Relations in Agriculture." *Journal of Development Studies* 22: 503–39.

Boserup, Ester. 1965. *The Conditions of Agricultural Growth.* Chicago: Aldine.

Brush, S. B., and B. L. Turner II. 1987. "The Nature of Farming Systems." In *Comparative Farming Systems* ed. B. L. Turner II and S. B. Brush, pp. 11–54. New York: Guilford Press.

Chayanov, A. V. 1966. *The Theory of Peasant Economy.* Homewood, Ill.: Richard D. Irwin.

Cleave, J. H. 1974. *African Farmers: Labor Use in the Development of Smallholder Agriculture.* New York: Praeger.

Findlay, R. L. 1945. "The Dimmuk and Their Neighbors." *Farm and Forest* 6: 138–42.

Gleave, M. B. 1966. "Hill Settlements and Their Abandonment in Tropical Africa." *Transactions of the British Institute of Geographers* 40: 39–49.

Haswell, M. R. 1953. "Economics of Agriculture in a Savannah Village." *Colonial Research Studies* 8. London: HMSO.

Hill, I. D., ed. 1979. *Land Resources of Central Nigeria: Agricultural Development Possibilities, Vol. 4B, the Benue Valley.* Surbiton, England: Land Resources Development Centre, Ministry of Overseas Development.

Hill, Polly. 1972. *Rural Hausa: A Village and a Setting.* Cambridge: Cambridge University Press.

Kowal, J. M., and A. W. Kassam. 1978. *Agricultural Ecology of Savanna: A Study of West Africa.* Oxford: Clarendon Press.

Lagemann, Johannes. 1977. *Traditional Farming Systems in Eastern Nigeria: An Analysis of Reaction to Population Pressure.* Munich: Weltforum Verlag.

Minge-Klevana, Wanda. 1980. "Does Labor Time Increase with Industrialization? A Survey of Time-Allocation Studies." *Current Anthropology* 21: 279–98.

Morgan, W. T. W. 1979. *The Jos Plateau: A Survey of Environmental and Land Use.* Occasional Publications (New Series) No. 14, Dept. of Geography. Durham, N.C.: University of Durham.

Mortimore, M. J. 1967. "Land and Population Pressure in the Kano Close-Settled Zone, Northern Nigeria." *The Advancement of Science* 23: 677–86.

Netting, Robert McC. 1965. "Household Organization and Intensive Agriculture: The Kofyar Case." *Africa* 35: 422–29.

_____. 1968. *Hill Farmers of Nigeria: Cultural Ecology of the Kofyar of the Jos Plateau.* Seattle: University of Washington Press.

_____. 1969. "Ecosystems in Process." In *Ecological Essays*, ed. David Damas, National Museum of Canada Bulletin No. 230. Ottawa: National Museum of Canada.

_____. 1973. "Fighting, Forest, and the Fly: Some Demographic Regulators among the Kofyar." *Journal of Anthropological Research* 29: 164–79.

——. 1987. "Clashing Cultures, Clashing Symbols: Histories and Meanings of the Latok War." *Ethnohistory* 34: 352–80.

——. 1990. "Population, Permanent Agriculture, and Polities: Unpacking the Evolutionary Portmanteau." In *Evolution of Political Systems*, ed. Steadman Upham, pp. 21–61. Cambridge: Cambridge University Press.

——. 1993. *Smallholders, Householders: Farm Families and the Ecology of Intensive, Sustainable Agriculture*. Stanford: Stanford University Press.

Netting, Robert McC., M. Priscilla Stone, and Glenn D. Stone. 1989. "Kofyar Cash-Cropping: Choice and Change in Indigenous Agricultural Development." *Human Ecology* 17: 299–319.

Norman, David W., E. B. Simmons, and H. M. Hays. 1982. *Farming Systems in the Nigerian Savanna*. Boulder, Colo.: Westview Press.

Nyerges, A. Endre. 1987. "The Development Potential of the Guinea Savanna: Social and Ecological Constraints in the West African 'Middle Belt.' " In *Lands at Risk in the Third World: Local Level Perspectives*, ed. P. D. Little and M. M. Horowitz, pp. 316, 336. Boulder, Colo. : Westview Press.

Pingali, Prabhu L., and Hans P. Binswanger. 1984. *Population Density and Agricultural Intensification: A Study of the Evolution of Technologies in Tropical Agriculture*. Research Unit Report ARU 22. Washington, D.C.: World Bank, Agriculture and Rural Development Section.

Prothero, R. M. 1957. "Land Use at Soba, Zaria Province, Northern Nigeria." *Economic Geography* 33: 72–86.

Reyna, S. P. 1987. "The Emergence of Land Concentration in the West African Savanna." *American Ethnologist* 14: 523–41.

Richards, Paul. 1986. *Coping with Hunger: Hazard and Experiment in an African Rice-Farming System*. London: Allen and Unwin.

Rowling, C. W. 1946. *Report on Land Tenure in Plateau Province*. National Archives. Kaduna: Jos Provincial Files 2/27 3324.

Ruthenberg, Hans. 1976. *Farming Systems in the Tropics*, 2d ed. Oxford: Clarendon Press.

Simmons, Emmy B. 1976. *Calorie and Protein Intakes in Three Villages of Zaria Province, May 1970–July 1971*. Samaru Miscellaneous Paper 55. Zaria: Ahmadu Bello University Institute for Agricultural Research.

Stenning, Derrick J. 1957. "Transhumance, Migratory Drift, Migration: Patterns of Pastoral Fulani Nomadism." *Journal of the Royal Anthropological Institute* 87: 57–73.

Stone, Glenn D. 1986. The Cultural Ecology of Frontier Settlement. Paper presented at the meetings of the Society of American Archaeology, April.

——. 1988. "Agrarian Ecology and Settlement Patterns: An Ethnoarchaeological Case Study." Ph.D. dissertation, University of Arizona.

——. 1991a. "Settlement Ethnoarchaeology: Changing Patterns among the Kofyar of Nigeria." *Expedition* 33: 16–23.

————. 1991b. "Agricultural Territories in a Dispersed Settlement System." *Current Anthropology* 32: 343–53.

————. 1992. "Social Distance, Spatial Relations, and Agricultural Production among the Kofyar of Namu District, Plateau State, Nigeria." *Journal of Anthropological Archaeology* 11: 152–72.

Stone, Glenn D., M.P. Johnson-Stone, and R. McC. Netting. 1984. "Household Variability and Inequality in Kofyar Subsistence and Cash-Cropping Economies." *Journal of Anthropological Research* 40: 90–108.

Stone, Glenn D., Robert McC. Netting, and M. Priscilla Stone. 1990. "Seasonality, Labor Scheduling, and Agricultural Intensification in the West African Savanna." *American Anthropologist* 92: 7–23.

Stone, M. Priscilla. 1988a. "Women Doing Well: A Restudy of the Nigerian Kofyar." *Research in Economic Anthropology* 10: 287–306.

————. 1988b. "Women, Work, and Marriage: A Restudy of the Nigerian Kofyar." Ph.D. dissertation, University of Arizona.

Udo, Reuben K. 1966. "Transformation of Rural Settlement in British Tropical Africa." *Nigerian Geographical Journal* 9: 129–44.

Watts, Michael. 1984. "State, Oil, and Accumulation: From Boom to Crisis." *Environment and Planning* D: *Society and Space* 2: 403–28.

Wilshusen, Richard H., and Glenn D. Stone. 1990. "An Ethnoarchaeological Perspective on Soils." *World Archaeology* 22: 104–14.

8 / Population Growth and Agricultural Change in Imo State, Southeastern Nigeria

Abe Goldman

This paper examines aspects of the agricultural and related resource-management systems found in an area of southeastern Nigeria that contains some of the highest rural population densities in sub-Saharan Africa. The original data come from a series of village-level surveys carried out in Imo State in the southern portion of Igboland. The surveys were conducted under the auspices of the International Institute of Tropical Agriculture (IITA) in Ibadan, Nigeria, with the objective of providing baseline data and analysis for the implementation of improved resource-management systems for this kind of area. Earlier studies and surveys are also examined to supplement and compare with the recent field data. The first of the three main sections briefly examines environmental and demographic conditions in the major agroecological region in Imo State, which is where the highest population densities are found. The second section deals with the elements of agricultural change in the survey regions and the variations among areas of differing population density. The third section then examines the range of ways in which farming and resource systems have adapted to the combination of high land-use pressures and major environmental constraints on production. The conclusion discusses the nature and extent of change in the survey areas and some of the implications of the experience of this region.

Population, Environment, and Agriculture in Imo State

The Natural Resource Base: Potentials and Constraints

Imo State is located in the humid forest zone of southeastern Nigeria, an area characterized by high rainfall, highly weathered acidic sandy soils, and generally flat relief. Total annual rainfall ranges from around 2000 to 2500 mm per year, distributed over eight humid months (March to October, with a slight decline in August in some areas). Although highly modified, vegetation is profuse in most places. This includes some secondary forest, extensive stands of oil palm (some with high densities), woody and herbaceous bush regrowth on fallow fields, and crop stands, including compound gardens. Because of the importance of oil palm to the local economy, the area has often been designated the "oil palm belt" of southeastern Nigeria (Udo 1970).

Acidic soils originating from sandy deposits cover over 60 percent of the land area of the state (fig. 8.1), comprising part of a region often known as the coastal plain sands (Obihara 1961). These ultisols are aged and heavily leached, have high acidity, low natural fertility, low levels of organic matter and humus, and generally exhibit rapid loss of mineral nutrients and organic matter during cropping (Vine 1954; Obihara 1961; Jungerius 1964; Lekwa 1979). They are, however, easily worked for cultivation, in contrast to some of the heavier clay soils in other nearby regions. Although there are somewhat different geological and geomorphological areas in the north and northeast of Imo State (Jungerius 1964; Ofomata 1975), this case study is confined to the coastal plain area in order to focus on the impact of population variation in a region of relative environmental uniformity.

As in much of the humid zone of West and Central Africa, soil productivity in this area declines rapidly after one or two years of cultivation, following which the land must be left fallow for a number of years before it can again be cropped. This is a common condition because most of the nutrients of these systems reside in the vegetation and associated biological elements rather than in the highly leached acidic soils (Nye and Greenland 1960). In the sandy ultisol region of Imo State, fields are generally planted for only one season and then left fallow (with cassava allowed to remain for six months or more after the other crops have been harvested). At the existing low levels of inputs, acceptable R-values (the percentage of years of cultivation in the full cultivation/fallow cycle) for these ultisols are said to be in the range of 15 to 20—that is, fields should be planted only one year in six, or at most one year in five (Young and Wright 1980). Even at intermediate input levels, the acceptable R-value for these soils rises only to 35.[1] It is also frequently said that past fallow periods in these kinds of areas were seven years or more and that this is the minimum required for stable yields

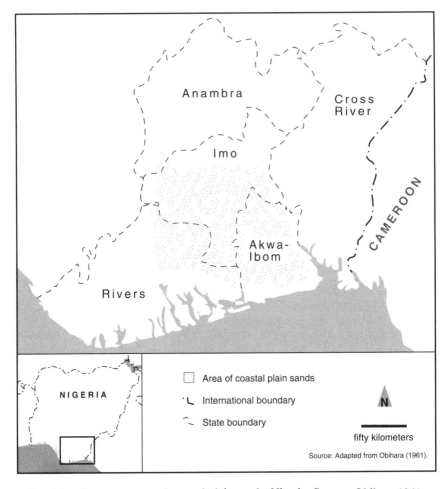

Fig. 8.1. Eastern states and coastal plain sands, Nigeria. Source: Obihara 1961.

(Nye and Greenland 1960; Obi and Tuley 1973); one cropping year followed by a seven-year fallow gives an R-value of 12.5.[2] These constraints on soil productivity, caused by the combination of high rainfall and the nature of the soil parent material, probably comprise the main limiting factor to increased production in this environment.

The negative elements of the region's resource endowment are at least partly balanced by the important positive element of the rich and varied vegetation. This vegetation and its byproducts are essential components of the soil/crop system. Numerous studies have established the key role played by the fallow vegetation in the process of regenerating soil productivity and protecting the soil from erosion and nutrient degradation (Nye and Greenland 1960; Moss 1969a, 1969b). Moreover, the fallow vegetation and the remaining stands of secondary forest also provide a range of noncrop outputs that are important to the people in the region, touching most aspects of farmers' lives (Walker and Latzke-Begemann 1985). The need for stakes in the production of yams, for example, resulted some time ago in the development of an indigenous fallow-management system that was designed to provide them. More generally, the significance of the resource role of the vegetation means that the implications of demographic, agricultural, and technological change need to be considered in relation to not only crop production but also the outputs and functions of this important resource.

Population

Although accurate figures are not available, the total population of Imo State may be around six million (table 8.1).[3] With a statewide population density probably between 430 and 520 per km[2], it is, after Lagos, the most densely populated of Nigeria's twenty-one states. Moreover, there are areas in the state falling within the ultra-high density belt of the Igbo heartland (fig. 8.2), which may reach densities of over 1,400 persons per km[2], and are probably the most densely populated rural areas in sub-Saharan Africa. Even the least densely populated Local Government Areas (LGA, the administrative unit just below the state) in Imo State are in the range of 150 to 200 per km[2] (table 8.1, fig. 8.2), which is still very high by the standards of sub-Saharan Africa as a whole.[4]

The historical reasons for the high concentration of population in this region and for the ultra-high centers are undoubtedly complex and not fully understood. The question is intriguing because, unlike many of the high-density areas of eastern and southern Africa, this is not in general a region of favorable agricultural potential. Most historical discussions have focused on various ecological, agricultural, and socioeconomic factors that have made some portions of the area relatively more attractive than others. These are insufficient causal explanations for the high density of the region as a whole (see Morgan 1959; Udo 1963; Grossman 1975; Shaw 1976). A full depiction of the demographic history of the region may be beyond the scope of the available evidence.

Udo (1963) suggests that soil quality in the whole region may have

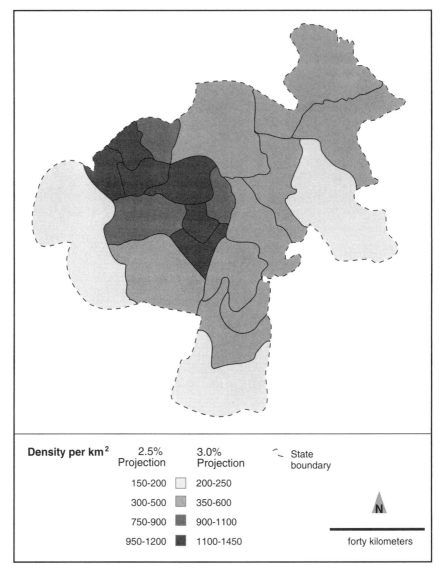

Density per km^2

	2.5% Projection	3.0% Projection
	150-200	200-250
	300-500	350-600
	750-900	900-1100
	950-1200	1100-1450

State boundary

N

forty kilometers

Fig. 8.2. Imo State, local government areas: population density. Source: Nigeria 1953 Census.

been considerably higher in the past than at present because of the effects of the original forest cover and the longer fallow periods that used to prevail. Other writers have pointed to the comparative ease with which many of the soils can be cultivated as a positive quality (Gross-

Table 8.1. Population and Densities of Survey Regions and Projections to 1988

Region	Area (km²)	1953 pop.	1953 density	1988 pop. (@ 2.5%)	1988 density	1988 pop. (@ 3%)	1988 density
Ahiazu-Mbaise LGA	107	53,645	501	127,311	1,190	150,950	1,411
Etiti LGA	207	72,048	348	170,985	826	202,733	979
Ihitte	51	17,002	333	40,349	791	47,841	938
Uboma	179	20,257	233	48,074	553	57,000	655
Ikwuano	681	36,082	144	85,630	341	101,530	405
Ukwa	925	66,320	72	157,391	170	186,615	202
Total Imo State	12,689	2,324,687	183	5,516,955	435	6,541,347	516

Source: Derived from Nigerian 1953 Census figures.

man 1975). Whether in relation to past or present conditions, however, even the higher levels of soil quality in this region are good only in relative terms. None of the soils in southeastern Nigeria compares in quality with the volcanic soils in most areas of high population concentration in eastern and southern Africa, or with the fertile alluvial soils often associated with dense populations in many other parts of the world. Southeastern Nigeria may still be anomalous in an African or a world context, having so many people concentrated in an area with such limited productive capacity.

Unfortunately, beyond saying that population density in southeastern Nigeria is extremely high, it is difficult to know just how high it is. Although it is by far the most populated country in Africa, containing up to one-fifth of the total population of sub-Saharan Africa (World Bank 1986), until 1991 there had been no official census in Nigeria since 1963. (Data from the 1991 census were not available at the time of this book's publication.) Moreover, the 1963 census was regarded as highly inaccurate in many areas (Yesufu 1968). Close examination of those figures for this region, especially at the LGA level or lower, shows some gross inconsistencies with the data from the previous census in 1952–53.[5] The dubious quality of the 1963 data leaves the 1952–53 census (the first house-to-house census in Nigeria) as the last one whose accuracy is defendable and in many cases the only basis for a current projection of population. But the last thirty-five years have seen massive demographic changes, with rapid growth of urban areas, extensive local and long-distance migration, and in this area in particular, significant effects of the Civil War of 1967–70. Consequently, projections from the 1953 data can at best give only an indication of the possible order of magnitude of current population. This may be still useful for ordinal categorization at the LGA level, under the assumption—difficult to test in practice—that intraregional changes in density have not been so great as to overturn the relative rankings of the LGAs.

One final demographic comment: the sex ratio (the ratio of males to females, multiplied by 100) is often taken as an indicator of outmigration, if there is reason to believe that a disproportionate number of migrants from a region are males of working age. The 1953 census data show that the sex ratio for the area now comprising Imo State was 100.2 for the 0–14 age group, but fell to 79.1 for ages 15–49, indicating a large surplus of females over males in this prime working-age category. This suggests a high outmigration rate even thirty-five years ago. Although one of the effects of the Civil War was to push Igbo migrants in other parts of the country back to their home areas, and current levels of outmigration may still not equal those of the past (R. Cohen, personal communication), it is clear that outmigration has been an important feature of the demography of the region for a long time.

Agriculture and Agricultural Systems

The region is characterized by a root crop- and oil palm–based cropping system. A variety of other vegetable crops (mainly for use in the sauces eaten with the main dish of cassava or yam), some grains (mainly maize and, in a few regions, rice), and various legumes are also planted. A wide range of tree crops, both domesticated and semi-wild, are also used for food (Okere 1983; Walker and Latzke-Begemann 1985). Most crops are grown for both domestic consumption and sale.

Of the root crops, the various species of yam (*Dioscorea* spp.) have historically been the most important, and many traditions are associated with their cultivation, preparation, and use (Coursey 1966; Coursey and Coursey 1971). Yams are still a major part of the cropping systems in the region, but yam production is costly in terms of labor, planting material, and staking requirements, and good yams need fairly fertile soil. Partly because of these costs, yams have largely been displaced by cassava as the main staple crop and also as the main income-earning crop throughout the region.

Cassava (*Manihot esculenta*) has become the most important food crop in the region, and is cited as such in all of the villages surveyed. In addition, it is said to be the main income-earning crop (exceeding both oil palm and yam) in about 70 percent of the surveyed villages. It has several advantages over yams, as well as numerous other crops, in being tolerant of poor soil conditions, having relatively low labor requirements for production (though processing requires considerable labor), being propagated from stems rather than roots (thereby having much lower planting material costs), and having very flexible harvest timing (as it is capable of storage in the ground for long periods, sometimes two years or more). The variety of food products that can be prepared from cassava (including the processed cassava meal, *garri*, which is well suited to transport and sale in urban areas) is also cited by farmers as a factor contributing to its growth in popularity.

Cassava began to become an important crop in this area by the 1920s or earlier, although it was first introduced into Nigeria several hundred years ago, probably by the Portuguese (Forde and Scott 1946; Morgan 1955; Agboola 1968; Martin 1984). In some areas, the displacement of yam by cassava as the major staple seems to have occurred as long as forty to fifty years ago. Green (1941), in her village study in what is now Imo State, remarked that cassava and cocoyam had already become more important in daily diets than yam, and Jones (1945) found that cassava had become the main staple in many densely populated areas. In the detailed Uboma study, undertaken in the early 1960s (Oluwasanmi et al. 1966), cassava was found to represent over 75 percent by weight of total root-crop output on the average farm (although because of the difference in market prices, the value of this output was only slightly higher than that of yam). A number of writers have remarked on the linkage between the scarcity of land in the area and the relative growth of cassava production (Forde and Jones 1950; Morgan 1955; Uzozie 1971), a linkage further explored in the third section of this paper.

Until recently, cocoyam (including the two species, *Colocasia esculenta* and *Xanthosoma sagittifolium*, both of which are referred to as cocoyam in West Africa) was also one of the major annual crops in the area, often exceeding yams in importance in both the amount and value of production (Lagemann 1977; Upton 1966). Tolerance of shade and moist conditions are among the factors making it well suited to this environment. However, farmers say that planting of cocoyam over the last decade has been sharply reduced, mainly because of severe yield declines, particularly for the *Xanthosoma* species. From farmers' descriptions of symptoms, this is probably caused by the "cocoyam-root rot blight complex," a soilborne disease that has been spreading through southern Cameroon and Nigeria and that may, it is feared, become the major limiting factor to cocoyam production in the tropics (Théberge 1985; Caveness et al. 1987; Nnoke et al. 1987). A substantial reduction in planting of cocoyam was mentioned in almost all of the villages in our survey. Cassava appears to have become the main replacement for cocoyam in diets and production patterns. (Women are the main producers of both cocoyam and cassava.) This substitution has been another factor in the growing importance of cassava in the area.

Palm oil has been an important export cash crop in this area for over a century and has been a major part of the local diet for far longer than that. Numerous studies have investigated its role and importance in the economy of the area (Forde and Scott 1946; Kilby 1967; Martin 1984, 1988), which has expanded and receded at various times with the fortunes of the world palm oil market. In addition to its purely economic role, oil palm (*Elaeis guineensis*), which is virtually ubiquitous throughout this region, has important effects on agronomic conditions and practices, and it generates numerous other outputs of importance (the fronds are used for fuel, animal feed, staking, and other uses; palm wine is made from both oil and raffia [*Raphia* spp.] palms, etc.). Crop shading may be an important negative impact, especially at the high densities at which oil palm is found in some cultivated fields. There may also be both positive and negative impacts on soil conditions, although the aggregate effect under farm conditions has apparently not been determined.

In addition, maize, telfairia (*Telfairia occidentalis*, fluted pumpkin, the leaves of which are an important green vegetable in soups), and egusi melon (*Citrullus colocynthis*, the seeds of which are also used in soups) are important crops in virtually all of the villages surveyed and are all consumed domestically as well as locally marketed. Wetland rice was introduced in one of our survey regions, Uboma, in the mid-1960s mainly through the Uboma Project (Oluwasanmi et al. 1966; Anthonio and Ijere 1973). It is now considered a major crop in about half of the villages surveyed in the Uboma region but is rarely found in the other survey regions (although there is some upland rice in some parts of Ukwa). Most of this rice is produced for local sale.

In our survey, farmers were asked about crops that had declined or disappeared within the last twenty years and those that had been newly introduced or expanded significantly during this period. On the whole, the incidence of declines seems to be more striking than that of new introductions or expansions. In addition to cocoyam, declines were cited for groundnuts (*Arachis hypogaea*), lima beans (*Phaseolus lunatus*), yam beans (*Sphenostylis stenocarpa*), velvet bean (*Mucuna sloanei*), coconut (*Cocos nucifera*), aerial yam (*Dioscorea bulbifera*), and three-leaved yam (*Dioscorea dumetorum*). With the exception of aerial and three-leaved yams, which have declined mainly because of taste preferences in favor of other foods, the main factor in the crop declines seems to have been the incidence of new or increasingly virulent diseases and pests which farmers say have sharply reduced yields. In addition, plantains (*Musa paradisiaca*), an important food and cash crop in many areas, are now seriously threatened by the appearance of black Sigatoka disease (caused by the fungus *Mycospaerella fijiensis*) in West Africa (IITA 1988).

There have been only a few introductions of new crops in the region to balance these declines and losses. Some new varieties of cassava, maize, and cocoyam (including a resistant cocoyam variety known as "Coco-India" that has expanded in two of the survey regions, Ihitte and Uboma) were mentioned by farmers in a few areas. In addition to rice, the rice areas of Uboma have promoted production of vegetables and other cultigens through intensive use of the wetland areas in the dry season. Otherwise, there were a few instances cited of the introduction of pineapple, cowpeas, and several other minor species.

The extent to which food crops are marketed seems to have increased in some areas and decreased in others over the past twenty years. Survey responses on this appear to be related partly to the degree of land-use pressure and partly to the state of roads and market access. In the two highest-density regions, almost all villages reported that market sales of food crops had declined, mainly, according to farmers, because of population increase and yield declines. In the three lower-density regions, about 60 percent of the villages reported increased marketing over the past two decades. In these cases, farmers generally said that greater market demand for foodstuffs (both in urban and in other rural areas) and the increased accessibility of markets and transport overcame the effect of declining yield levels.

Survey Sites and Methods

The surveys reported here were conducted between November 1987 and July 1988 in five regions in Imo State. Differences in population density (taken from the 1953 data) served as the primary basis for selecting and stratifying the survey regions, the location of which is shown in figure 8.3.[6] The sample includes both the highest- and lowest-density LGAs in the state in 1953 (Ahiazu-Mbaise[7] and Ukwa respectively). Table 8.1 shows the areas, 1953 census figures, and population densities of the five

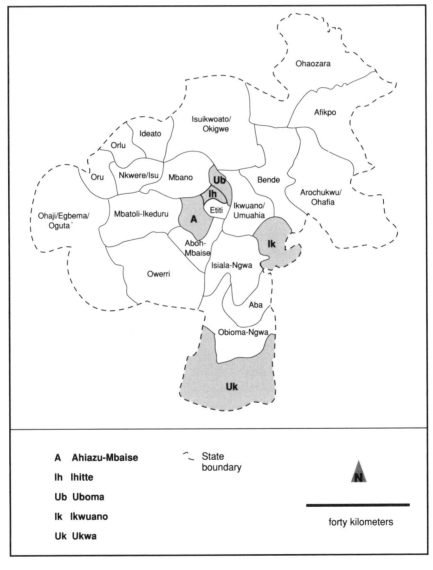

Fig. 8.3. Location of survey areas in Imo State

survey regions. Projections of 1988 population at annual growth rates of 2.5 and 3 percent are included to give a sense of what population might be under these assumptions. There is approximately a sevenfold range in density between the least and most densely populated regions.

The survey unit has been the village, with questionnaire interviews conducted with groups of farmers who were asked to characterize conditions and practices in their village. Ten or more villages in each survey region are included, giving a total of fifty-eight villages.[8] This village-level approach has various strengths and weaknesses compared to survey techniques that focus on individual households or farmers, either in a single village or sometimes in a small number of villages meant to represent varying conditions (e.g., high, medium, and low population density). The major disadvantage is that most of the quantitative data are fuzzy and at best represent modal or mean values with little indication of the distribution of values within the village. The same holds for much of the qualitative information on the prevalence of various practices. The corresponding advantage of the approach, however, is that it can describe the range and distribution of differences among villages (or other appropriate social units), which a single-village or even a three-village study usually cannot do (Dvorak, 1988).[9]

Agricultural Change and Variation in the Survey Regions

Fallow Periods and Rotations

It is a common conception that throughout this crowded area, traditional shifting cultivation has been transformed into a bush fallow system with ever-declining fallow lengths and, as a result, declining yields (see Lagemann 1977; Okigbo 1984). Although fallow periods are a key element, little direct research has been done on the rates at which they are changing, the extent to which they vary over the region, and the context of decision making on fallow rotations. Some fragmentary information is available in past studies of farming systems in the area. In addition to general information about fallow lengths, previous studies have noted the existence of group-based rotation systems in parts of Igboland (as well as other areas in Africa) in which the village as a whole, or a kindred subgroup rather than individual farmers, is responsible for making decisions on fallow rotations (Forde and Scott 1946; Mbagwu 1970; Francis 1987).

In our village interviews, farmers were asked about the main forms of land tenure in the village and whether the rotation pattern is determined on a group or individual basis. They were also asked to assess the length of time most fields in the village are currently left fallow (on outer fields but not on compound gardens), the minimum and maximum fallow periods used in the village, and the usual fallow period(s) used twenty years ago (i.e., just before the civil war).

Group Rotation Systems and Land Tenure

In a number of villages in the sample, a group rotation system exists in which all farmers in the village (or in the kindred group) move their cultivated fields each year from one portion of village land to another.[10] Our survey data indicate that, although it does still exist, this group rotation system is now common in only one of the survey regions and is found in less than one-third of the sample villages overall. As shown in table 8.2, the system is concentrated in the lowest-density areas, Ukwa and Ikwuano, and does not appear at all in the high-density areas of Mbaise and Ihitte. There is also a partial linkage with communal land tenure, as suggested in the table.

The apparent inverse relationship between population density and the prevalence of group rotation makes it tempting to conclude that this illustrates an evolutionary progression in which the group rotation system breaks down with increasing population. However, the situation may not be so clear, because, for one thing, farmers indicate that group rotation practices were by no means universal in the past. Group rotation is said not to have been practiced during the lives of the respondents in most villages in the three higher-density areas. Moreover, the fact that all the villages in Ukwa still have a kindred-based rotation system despite a very rapid decline in fallow periods there (see below), whereas in Ikwuano and Uboma, villages with similar or longer fallow periods have individual rotation systems, suggests that there may be a strong cultural dimension to this practice. Therefore, insofar as there has been a progression from group-based rotation (and land tenure) to individual systems, such a change seems to have taken place a fairly long time ago in some places, whereas it still has not occurred in others that are experiencing high land-use pressures.

In addition, the data suggest that this group rotation system may or may not coincide with communal land tenure. Whereas all of the vil-

Table 8.2. Group Fallow Rotation and Communal Land Tenure

	Mbaise (N = 14)	Ihitte (N = 10)	Uboma (N = 13)	Ikwuano (N = 11)	Ukwa (N = 10)	Total (N = 58)
% villages with group rotation	0	0	15	45	100	29
% villages with communal land	0	0	8	0	100	19

lages in Ukwa both have communally owned land and practice group rotation, the linkage is much less regular outside of this area. Most villages with group rotation outside Ukwa have individually owned land. This suggests that if land is communally owned, a group rotation pattern is likely to prevail, but the reverse is not necessarily true.

Lengths of Fallow Periods

Many of the previous farming-system studies in the area comprising Imo State commented on fallow-period lengths and their connection with population density. Table 8.3 summarizes these reports on fallow lengths, together with estimates of population density from those sources (derived from census or other data).

This compilation illustrates that even forty to fifty years ago, there were places in Imo State in which the usual fallow period had already been drastically shortened—to two years in the case of Umueke (in Mbano LGA), studied by Green (1941) in the late 1930s. This is roughly equivalent to the lowest levels cited even today for highly crowded regions and would be considered unsustainable in this environment by most soil scientists (Young and Wright 1980). It is intriguing to consider what has occurred in such areas as a result of the population growth over the past two to five decades, a period during which, under even the most conservative assumptions, population increased at least two- to threefold.

Second, for at least the last fifty years, there has been considerable variation in fallow periods in the region. In most cases, researchers ascribed the variation to differences in population densities and associated land-use pressures.[11] Moreover, sharp variations were often found in close proximity. Even in a relatively compact area such as Uboma (about 80 km^2), common fallow periods were reported in the mid-1960s to range between one and seven years—a range that may duplicate that

Table 8.3. Fallow Periods Reported in Previous Studies in Imo State

Author/date	Area/category	Fallow length	Est. pop. density
Harris (1942)	Ozuitem Clan (Bende LGA)	3+ yrs	100
Green (1941)	Umueke village (Mbano LGA)	2 yrs	>235
Chubb (1961 [1947])	"Overfarmed areas" (incl. Mbaise, Ihitte)	"Almost disappeared"	250–420[a]
	"Heavily farmed areas" (incl. Uboma, Ikwuano)	3–5 yrs	100–180[a]
	"Underfarmed areas"	(no data)	30–80[a]
Morgan (1955)	Ukwa (Asa and Ndoki Clans)	7 yrs	60–120
	Ngwa	3–5 yrs	170–360
Upton (1966),	Southwest Uboma	1–2 yrs	"high density"
Uboma study	Northeast Uboma	6–7 yrs	"low density"
Mbagwu (1970)	Northern Ngwa	2–3 yrs	?
	Southern and northeast Ngwa	3–5 yrs	?
Lagemann (1977)	High-density village	1.4 yrs (mean)	750–1000[b]
	Medium-density village	3.9 yrs (mean)	350–500
	Low-density village[c]	5.3 yrs (mean)	100–200

[a]Based on mid-1940s data considered to have been underestimated.
[b]Based on projections from 1963 census (believed to be overestimated in many cases but may be underestimated for the low-density village).
[c]Lagemann's low-density village, Okwe, is included in our sample in Ikwuano.

of the Imo State survey region as a whole. As discussed below, this wide range of variation and the proximity of areas with sharply differing fallow lengths has had a number of important impacts on the farming systems in the area.

Our survey attempted to obtain information on current and past fallow periods in the regions studied. Table 8.4 summarizes the mean values reported by villages in each survey region for the usual current fallow length in the village as well as the usual fallow length twenty years ago and the amount and percentage by which these have changed.[12] Figure 8.4 is a diagram of the mean values by survey region for reported past and current fallow periods by the 1953 population density for the region.

Over the total sample, common fallow periods at present range from zero to six years, with a mean value of 2.7 years. The lower half of this range may be a source of concern for the continuing resource productivity of the region. Only about 30 percent of the sample currently maintains fallow periods of four years or more, which might be considered a

Table 8.4. Current and Past Fallow Periods in the Survey Regions (number of years)

	Past[a] (usual fallow)	Present[a] (usual fallow)	Change	Change (%)	% cases zero change
Total sample (N = 50[b])					
Mean	4.5	2.7	1.8	40.6%	17%
Range	(1−9)	(0−6)	(0−7)	(0−100)	
Ahiazu Mbaise (N = 14)					
Mean	2.3	0.9	1.4	60.0%	7%
Range	(0−5)	(0−2)	(0−3)	(0−100)	
Ihitte (N = 10)					
Mean	3.5	2.2	1.3	36.1%	22%
Range	(2−5)	(1−3)	(0−2)	(0−57)	
		(N = 9)	(N = 9)	(N = 9)	
Uboma (N = 13)					
Mean	4.3	3.3	1.0	19.8%	42%
Range	(2−7)	(2−6)	(0−4)	(0−67)	
		(N = 12)	(N = 12)	(N = 12)	
Ikwuano (N = 11)					
Mean	5.5	4.6	0.9	15.0%	45%
Range	(5−7)	(4−6)	(0−3)	(0−43)	
Ukwa (N = 10)					
Mean	6.7	2.9	3.8	54.3%	0
Range	(5−9)	(2−4)	(2−7)	(33−78)	0

[a]Farmers were asked what the most common fallow period was in the village twenty years ago and what it is at present.

[b]A balanced sample of fifty villages, ten from each region, is used for the "total sample" figures in order not to bias the results. In the figures for each region, sample sizes vary as indicated.

reasonably stable fallow length for this environment (giving an R-value of 20). In about 25 percent of the sample villages, common fallow periods are reported to be under two years, which is often considered to result in degradation of soil productivity (Nye and Greenland 1960).

About twenty years ago, there was a wider total range of fallow periods—one to nine years—and the mean for the sample was considerably higher, 4.5 years.[13] Seventy percent of the villages had fallow periods of four years or more, whereas there were only two villages (4 percent) with fallow periods of under two years. Overall, common fallow periods have declined by an average of 40 percent over the period. Fallow periods are reported to have been reduced in all of the survey regions—though not in all villages—but the rate of change has not been uniform across the regions.

Fallow length (in years)

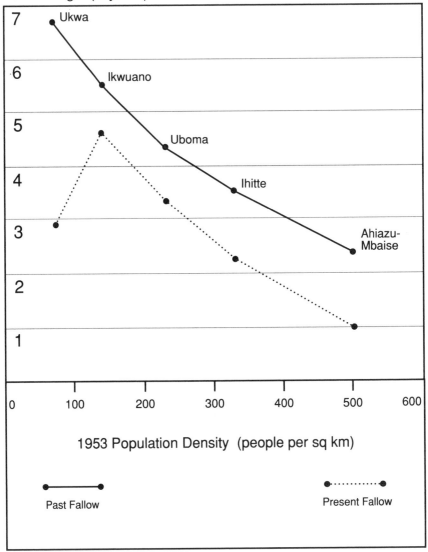

Fig. 8.4. Reported past and present fallow lengths

Figure 8.4 suggests that there may have been a linear relationship between population density and the mean reported usual fallow periods for all five of the regions in the past and for four of the five regions at present. The 1953 population-density values are given on the horizontal axis because these are the only ones known with any assurance. Consequently, the linearity of the relationship is dependent on the degree to which population-growth rates have been uniform across these areas: if the five regions experienced fairly uniform growth rates between 1953 and about 1968 (for the reported past fallow periods) and to the present, then there is a likelihood that fallow periods and population densities in this area may have been linearly related. If there have been very different growth rates, then the relationship has probably not been linear. Reliable current census data are necessary to settle the question.

The survey data also suggest that there has been at least one significant anomaly among the survey regions. Ukwa, the least densely populated area in the past, has apparently had a far more rapid rate of decline in fallow periods than any of the other regions. The villages there report a percentage decline in fallow periods second only to that in Mbaise, the most densely populated region (table 8.4). In absolute terms, common fallow periods in Ukwa have been reduced by an average of 3.8 years, which is two to four times as high as any of the other regions. The differences are also reflected in the proportion of villages in which no decline in fallow periods were reported. In Uboma and Ikwuano, the other two lower-density areas, over 40 percent of the sample villages reported no fallow reduction, but every one of the villages in Ukwa reported that fallow periods have declined substantially. The discrepancy between the experience of the last twenty years in Ukwa and Ikwuano, the areas with the lowest densities in the past, is especially striking. Although there were only moderate increases in land-use pressure in the latter, judging by the reduction in fallow periods, the former apparently experienced an intense growth in land-use pressures and a very rapid decline in fallow periods.

One of the possible explanatory factors for this is that there has been a large difference in the natural rate of population increase between Ukwa and the other regions, but the rates of in- or outmigration might have varied. There was no evidence of any major event that might have altered land availability in all the survey villages in Ukwa (such as a regionwide land expropriation). Any inherent physical difference in the resource base in Ukwa also is unlikely to have caused such a large discrepancy. There is, as noted above, a difference in the prevalence of communal land tenure and group rotation in Ukwa, though its relation to the growth of land-use pressure is unclear. There may also have been differences in the pattern of farmers' responses to population increase in Ukwa, as discussed below. Unfortunately, there are only suggestive indications but no definitive data to confirm the importance of any of these factors. Nonetheless, both the evidence of the fallow periods and some of the other data on fallow resources discussed below suggest that the experience in Ukwa has been distinctive from that in the other survey regions.

Crop-Yield Declines

Farmers in our survey generally ascribe sharp declines in crop yields to these fallow-period reductions. Although it is difficult to quantify the extent of these yield declines, we tried to obtain rough estimates by asking the number of stands of cassava currently needed to fill a basket compared to the number that would have been needed twenty years ago for the same size basket.[14] Resulting estimates of yield decline were extremely high: even in the moderate cases, farmers estimate past yields to have been around twice those obtained at present, whereas in severe cases, past yields are said to have been ten to thirty times the present levels. There also seems to be a rough correspondence with density and fallow-period levels. The highest estimates of yield decline were given by the farmers in Mbaise (an average ratio of past-to-present yields of 13) and the lowest estimates in Ikwuano (average ratio of 4). Changes in agronomic practices, such as cassava-harvest timing, which can affect yields, have also occurred in some places.

Despite the suggested correspondence with reported fallow lengths, significant yield declines were reported even in cases where there was said to have been little or no reduction of fallow periods (see many of the villages in Ikwuano). A possible cause for this, sometimes mentioned explicitly by farmers, may be increased losses to pests and diseases. The most commonly mentioned or observed examples on cassava are cassava mosaic virus, which may have increased in incidence and severity, as well as cassava mealybug (*Phenacoccus manihoti*) and possibly cassava green mites (*Mononychellus progresivus* and *M. tanajoa*), both new and virulent pests in the region.[15] Some recent research suggests that increased pest losses may be linked to low soil fertility.[16]

Fallow-Vegetation Resource Use

Aside from crop-yield declines, the impacts of declining fallow periods also appear in other aspects of farming and land-use systems. One of the most direct links is in the use of fallow-vegetation resources. Despite the fact that primary and even most secondary forest has been eliminated throughout most of the survey region, there remains a varied range of bush vegetation that regrows rapidly once fields are left uncultivated. This fallow vegetation is the key to the regeneration of soil productivity after the cultivation period, which is why the reduction of fallow periods is so critical a factor in reducing yields. Beyond its ecological function in regenerating soil productivity, the fallow vegetation provides a range of resource products that are important to the livelihoods of people in the area. These include firewood, stakes for yams and other crops, wild foods, construction materials, and medicinal raw materials.

As fallow periods have shortened, the amount and quality of these resource products have diminished, and farmers now frequently use inferior species for many of these functions or have to purchase products that were previously common-property resources (or of which they owned sufficient quantities themselves). Shortages are not equally severe in all areas, but shortages in some areas help to induce a commodification of resource products and restriction of access rights in areas where there is no internal shortage *per se*. Our survey focused mainly on the use of fallow vegetation for yam stakes and fuelwood and on the existence and degree of commodification and access restriction for these resource products.[17]

Various patterns of change are evident in the use of these resource products in the survey regions. Among these, there seem to be five good indicators of the extent of resource pressure: (1) whether or not staking material is purchased from sources outside the village; (2) whether or not fuelwood is purchased from sources outside the village; (3) whether bamboo is one of the main species used for yam stakes; (4) whether palm fronds are one of the main species used for fuelwood; and (5) whether and to what extent access is restricted to these raw materials in fallow fields. In addition, sales of the main wood products, principally for stakes and fuelwood, are generally an indication of both surplus supply and market access (the markets being either in other rural areas or in towns and cities).

Table 8.5 summarizes the percentage of villages in each of the survey regions in which these conditions are said to exist. The first four columns are aspects of the commodification of woody products from fallow vegetation. Especially in a humid forest environment such as this, staking and fuelwood purchases from outside the village generally indicate resource scarcities within the village. The survey data show that purchase of yam stakes from outside the village occurs in almost all the villages in Mbaise and Ihitte, the two most dense regions but is less frequent in Uboma and rare in Ikwuano. The proportion increases again in Ukwa, paralleling the pattern of the fallow periods. Fuelwood purchases from outside the village are less common than purchases of stakes. None of the villages in Uboma or Ikwuano say that they purchase fuelwood, but about two-thirds of those in Ihitte and 30 percent of those in Mbaise and Ukwa do.

Sale of fuelwood (and construction materials) to urban areas, and sale of stakes to other rural areas become common features once transport infrastructure makes it possible to express market demand in rural areas. Sales are highest in areas such as Uboma which have surpluses and also border on areas with scarcities. A number of the villages in Ikwuano are remote from urban or dense rural areas and are served only by poor-quality roads. This accounts for the low sales in those villages despite adequate supply.

Almost no sales occur in the Ihitte villages because of the scarcities there, but they are common in most of the other survey regions, including Mbaise because of the planted *Acioa* fallow system there (see below). Species distinctions, especially for yam stakes, also help to generate market demand for fallow products. Stems of the bush *Acioa barteri* are universally said to make the best staking material because of their strength and termite resistance. *Acioa* is available in most areas (partly because it was planted for this purpose in the past), but with very short fallow periods, it does not have the opportunity to regrow sufficiently to produce good stakes. Use of bamboo for yam stakes has begun only recently in most places. Bamboo stakes do not last as long as those from *Acioa*, and they often must be purchased because bamboo grows in only certain locations. Use of bamboo is high in Ihitte and Mbaise but quite low in Ikwuano. In Ukwa, four of the survey villages say that bamboo use started recently, but various other species are used in the other villages.

Palm fronds make poor fuel compared to wood, but they are generally freely available; their widespread use for fuel probably indicates serious shortages of other fuelwood species. It is only in Mbaise and Ihitte that they were mentioned as one of the main fuel species.

Access rights and restrictions tend to be variable and complex, but

Table 8.5. Indicators of Resource Pressure on Fallow Vegetation (% positive responses)

Survey region	Staking purchases[a]	Fuelwood purchases[b]	Bamboo as stakes[c]	Palm fronds as fuelwood[d]	Access restrictions	
					Stakes	Fuelwood
Mbaise (n = 14)	92% (13)[e]	29%	93%	85% (13)	100%	36%
Ihitte (n = 10)	90% (9)	67%	100%	44% (9)	86% (7)	0 (8)
Uboma (n = 13)	22% (11)	0	69%	0	62%	22% (9)
Ikwuano (n = 11)	9%	0	9%	0	9%	0
Ukwa (n = 10)	30%	30%	40%	0	5%	10%

[a]Purchasing of poles for yam stakes from sources outside the village.
[b]Purchasing of fuelwood from sources outside the village.
[c]Bamboo as the first or second most used species for yam stakes in the village.
[d]Palm fronds as the first or second most used species for fuelwood in the village.
[e]Figures in parentheses indicate smaller sample sizes.

there are a few generalizations that can be made from the survey findings: (1) access restrictions for staking material are usually more stringent than for firewood; (2) there is a gradation of access restrictions, ranging from full privatization of fallow materials, to special restrictions (applying only to preferred species or only to people outside the village or community), to virtually no restrictions (both full and partial restrictions are included in table 8.5); and (3) even when there are said to be no formal restrictions, there are certain generally accepted standards of behavior that apply (e.g., one does not take materials from land that has just been cleared for planting without explicit permission).

The access restrictions reflect the degree to which these resources have become privatized rather than remaining common-property resources. Such privatization has proceeded furthest in Mbaise and Ihitte and is least evident in Ikwuano. As with most other indicators, restrictions in Ukwa are higher than would be expected from its 1953 density. The restrictions there are of a special kind, relating to communal land tenure: access is limited to anyone belonging to the land-owning kindred group.

The fallow-resource data indicate that the greatest scarcities are found in Ihitte and Mbaise, the two highest-density areas. In Mbaise, however, the scarcity of woody products is mitigated by the widespread planting of the preferred staking species, *Acioa barteri*, which is also used for fuelwood. The lowest degree of scarcity appears to be in

Ikwuano, the area that also has the longest overall fallow periods. Relative to its (1953) population density, Ukwa seems to have unusually high levels of scarcity, paralleling the rapid decline there of fallow periods.

The cross-sectional sequence suggests that as population density increases: (1) fallow-vegetation resources increasingly become commodities, with greater purchasing in areas of scarcity and increased sales in areas of surplus; (2) there are changes in the species used as those preferred become more scarce and costly; and (3) access to resources that were formerly common properties becomes increasingly restricted. These processes are related to changes in fallow-period lengths that play an important role in determining the quantity and quality of fallow vegetation. As with fallow periods themselves, the extent and rate of change is not uniform in all areas nor is it entirely predictable from population density alone. Factors such as market access and the purposive management of fallow vegetation, as well as a range of other responses to resource scarcities are also instrumental in determining the rates and degrees of change.

Adaptations to Land-Use Pressure

Farming-System Adaptations

There are numerous ways in which tropical farming systems are considered to have adapted to the pressure of population growth on available land resources (e.g., Floyd 1969; Gleave and White 1969; Ruthenberg 1980). Table 8.6 lists some of the main adaptations that characterize the agricultural systems of this region, as derived both from our survey and from secondary sources. These are grouped into four nonexclusive categories: (1) changes in the land-use system; (2) changes in agronomic practices; (3) changes in systems for producing noncrop outputs; and (4) methods of expanding system boundaries.

Several general observations about these categories of adaptations are useful. First, many of them involve various aspects of the agricultural "intensification" process, a term that has been used to refer to a variety of changes in agricultural systems and practices (Grigg 1976). However, they are not necessarily synonymous with intensification.

Second, although these features of the farming systems are examined mainly in terms of their roles as adaptations to increasing land-use

Table 8.6. Farming-System Adaptations to Land-Use Pressure

Land-use system
    (Extension of cultivation to previously unused land)
    Shortening of fallow periods
    Field differentiation and creation of high-intensity production niches
        Compound farms
        Wetland rice areas
        Short-fallow fields ("cassava fields")
    Land-use transfers
Agronomic practices and Systems
    Crop-species changes
    Soil-management changes
        Use of composts, manure, etc. (enhanced recycling of soil nutrients)
        Fertilizer use (import of soil nutrients)
    Crop-management changes
        Crop-density increase
        Pest-management increase
        Change in cassava harvest timing
Noncrop output systems
    Fallow-vegetation system changes
        Planting and management of fallow vegetation
        Commodification/privatization of resources from fallow lands
    Livestock-system changes
Expansion of system boundaries
    Land-use transfers/expansion of cultivation to unused land
    Food imports from other areas
    Nonfarm activities for income generation
    Outmigration from area; seasonal or permanent

pressure, their functions are not necessarily limited to this, nor was this necessarily the major reason for their origin. Indeed, most have been long-standing features of the farming systems in this area, and many are found even in lower-density areas elsewhere in Africa. They do, however, play a role in helping farmers of this region adapt to the problems of restricted land availability.

Third, these categories can be viewed as indicators as well as adaptations insofar as differences in land-use pressure give rise to variations in their prevalence or character in different areas. However, they may be adaptations without being good indicators of variations in land-use pressure if they occur more or less to the same extent throughout the area.

Finally, many of these adaptations are interrelated in their effects, and some may be substitutable for one another. It is useful to keep in mind that these measures are intended to fill a variety of needs at the household level, including food supply for domestic consumption (involving the desired types and combinations of foodstuffs at various times of the year); generating cash income for household needs; providing land-based resources such as wood stakes, fuelwood, and construction materials for agriculture and general consumption; and maintaining and enhancing the productivity of the resource base. Many of the adaptations are designed primarily to address one or another of these objectives, though they may also affect others. Some have significant effects on most or all of the objectives.

Land-Use System Changes

Changes in the land-use system probably comprise the most important category of adaptations to land-use pressure. These generally involve attempts to increase (or prevent a decrease in) the amount of land cultivated in any one period. Such efforts assume a particular importance in this agro-ecozone because of the rapid decline in soil fertility under cultivation and the critical importance of an extended fallow period to restoration of productivity. In effect, all of these adaptations involve a shortening of fallow periods within one or another system boundary.

The adaptations in Table 8.6 are listed mainly from the point of view of the individual farmer or farm household. From this vantage, shortening of fallow periods and differentiation of fields involve plots of land that are usually under the control of the individual farmer or household, whereas land-use transfers and sometimes expansion of cultivation involve plots outside the individual household's ownership or control. Thus, the former result in an increasing intensity of cultivation on the individual farm (sometimes also for the kinship group or village, when land ownership is based on these), whereas the latter results in a diffusion of land-use pressures over a larger area (i.e., a trade-off of a lesser degree of intensification in a location that is generally already intensively managed but an increase in land-use intensity elsewhere).

Expansion of Cultivation

The expansion of the existing boundaries of cultivation is frequently considered to be the main means by which output in sub-Saharan Africa as a whole has increased in recent years to meet growing needs (FAO 1986). Because there is relatively little unused land in this densely populated area, this is usually not a major option for farmers in Imo State while they remain within the boundaries of the region. A few elements of this process of extension of cultivation do exist, however. Three main examples can be mentioned, each of which overlaps with one of the other types of adaptation: (1) migration to lower-density areas, usually outside Imo State, to bring into cultivation land that is unused or not intensively used; (2) use of small pockets of land within Imo State that are still under relatively long fallow cycles; and (3) drainage and planting of unused swampland or other special types of land not currently planted (e.g., sacred forest groves).[18]

Shortening Fallow Periods

The degree to which fallow periods are being reduced throughout the area was discussed in the previous section as a major symptom of land-use pressure and as the source of various negative outcomes. However, shorter fallows have both costs and advantages. The costs include reduced soil productivity, lower annual yields, and associated effects on weed growth and pest and disease incidence. There is also degradation in the quality and quantity of the fallow vegetation, which can result in tangible costs to the farmers as the resource products derived from fallow vegetation become marketed commodities.

The advantages stem mainly from the increased output produced over time from a given parcel of land, even though this may be at the expense of lower yields in any one cropping period.[19] The timing and sequence of output is also significant, as a minimum amount needs to be produced every year for household consumption and income generation.[20] The net returns depend on a number of physical and socioeconomic parameters, including the soil-regeneration function (relating fallow periods and yield levels); the economic value of output (with appropriate discounting for future output); the decay function for stored output; and the extent and timing of household needs and demands. This suggests a multistage process in which shortening the fallow period is among the initial adjustments to conditions of decreasing land availability; its negative effects may then elicit a further set of responses.

Field Differentiation and High-Intensity Production Niches

This category includes special fields, or production "niches," that are managed more intensively than other fields, often with no fallow period or very brief fallows and usually, but not always, with the addition of various inputs to maintain fertility levels. Three major examples in the survey regions include compound gardens, wetland rice areas, and short-fallow cassava fields, although there may also be other examples and variants. The first two of these are highly productive and are maintained with considerable nutrient input and recycling, whereas the latter often has low productivity but is a specialized high-intensity site with an abbreviated fallow cycle.

COMPOUND FARMS AND NUTRIENT RECYCLING. Various techniques to enhance nutrient recycling are practiced throughout southeastern Nigeria, but they are largely confined to the compound gardens. These are small farms or gardens surrounding the household compound in which vegetables, fruits, tree crops, and some staples are planted, usually continuously without any intervening fallow period. Continuous planting is made possible by the constant addition of organic matter and other nutrients in the form of animal manure (mainly from goats, sheep, and poultry), food by-products and household wastes, ashes, and leaves and other plant materials. Such organic material additions are extremely important to stabilizing soil productivity and preventing yield declines in these kinds of soils (Vine 1954; Nye and Greenland 1960). In addition, the trees and crops in such gardens create a multistoried farming ecology capable of mobilizing nutrients, water, and sunlight from different levels of the soil and atmosphere (Niñez 1987).

Compound farms have been important components of the farming systems in this region for a long time (Green 1941; Harris 1942).[21] They are largely, although not exclusively, maintained by women to provide foodstuffs for domestic consumption (Walker 1985). The main benefits of these gardens cited by farmers and by other writers include providing food at times of the year when other foods are not available (especially the "hungry season" before the harvest of the main staples [Okere 1983; Walker 1985]); serving as production sites for various fruits, vegetables, and other foods that are not planted elsewhere; providing a secure and convenient source of food close to the home, including the extra security desired for valuable items such as yams that may be threatened by animal pests or theft; and serving as sites for experimentation with new crops (Richards 1985). It also appears that the compound gardens are helping to preserve, at least to a limited extent, some of the species that have been declining in the farming systems in general (e.g., cocoyams and yam beans). This wide range of benefits apparently justifies the almost exclusive concentration of recycled nutrients (manure and compost) and the associated labor, both of which are in limited supply, in the compound-garden areas. There is said to be little extension of this type of activity to most outer fields.

Some writers (see Lagemann 1977) have suggested that further intensification in the already intensively managed compound-garden subsystem has been one of the main means of offsetting output and yield declines in the outer fields. Unfortunately, there is little direct information on changes over time in compound gardens at any one location. However, there have been some cross-sectional studies of compound farms in villages with differing densities, and most conclusions about the growth in importance of compound farms is based on these.

Lagemann (1977) discussed differences in attributes and outputs of compound farms in his study of three Imo State villages with differing population densities. Among his main findings were that the compound farms in the high-density village were larger, had greater crop density, lower yields, and accounted for a greater proportion of total farm output than those in the medium-density village. He found no compound farms as such in the low-density village.[22] Similarly, Snelder (1987) carried out a study of species composition on compound farms in three villages with varying densities in Rivers State, just south of Imo. She did not find a correlation between density and the size of compound farms, but she did observe that annual food crops such as cassava were becoming more important on compound farms in the high-density village and that there were fewer tree crops and less species diversity than on those in the lower-density villages.

Our survey found some differences in the management of compound farms among the regions. These appeared most clearly in the contrast between Mbaise and Ukwa, the highest- and lowest-density regions (in 1953). In Mbaise, it was generally said that all households maintained compound farms; the full compound is planted every year; manure and compost additions are spread through the entire compound; some farmers now use fertilizers in the compound farms, which have begun to blend with the near fields. In Ukwa, by contrast, the intensity of management of the compound farms seems to be much lower. Not all households have a compound field; among those that do maintain one, the entire compound area is not necessarily planted each year, so that there is often a rotating fallow period on the compound plot; the manure and compost additions are not spread through the entire field but are generally just placed in one spot; the outer fields are more distant from the compounds, with no blending as in Mbaise; and there is no fertilizer use (either on the compounds or, in most cases, on outer fields).

Thus, it appears that intensification of nutrient recycling on the compound farms (and perhaps an increase in their size) may have been one of the important ways of coping with land shortages and yield declines. There are, however, severe limits to the further expansion of this avenue of intensification. In addition to constraints on land available for compound-farm expansion, farmers regularly cite constraints on available compost and manure supplies (especially given the absence of cattle in the area), and on available labor to supply the nutrient materials, particularly to more distant fields. These are said to be the main reasons why these recycling procedures are confined to the compound gardens and not extended to the outer fields.

WETLAND RICE DEVELOPMENT. Rice is grown to a significant extent in only one of our survey regions. It was introduced as part of the Shell Uboma Project in the mid-1960s (Oluwasanmi et al. 1966). By 1972, seven years after its introduction, the area under rice in Uboma was estimated at about 430 ha (Anthonio and Ijere 1973). Substantial capital and technical assistance were provided by the project and the Ministry of Agriculture for dam construction and swamp and paddy development, as well as initial training and seed supply. In the Uboma villages, where rice is currently grown (7 of 13 survey villages), farmers now consider it one of the top four or five food crops (much of it being grown for sale); in some cases, rice is now rated second only to cassava.

Perhaps even more important, this has resulted in the creation of an entirely new, intensively managed production niche. In most cases, rice is planted every year in the wet season, and a variety of vegetables and other crops (including cocoyam and some maize and cassava) are planted as dry-season crops. Not only do many households have small individual plots in the rice areas, but farmers from neighboring villages who want to plant rice will rent portions of land from the owners. Moreover, fertilizer use is said to be widespread in these areas, even when it is not used elsewhere, and mulching and other soil- and water-management techniques are common.

Of course, many villages do not have areas suitable for rice or have not been able to develop the areas that might be suitable. Indeed, the demonstration effect of wetland rice development in the villages in which it has occurred has not gone so far as to stimulate similar development in the other Uboma villages, although people do rent rice plots on an individual basis. Neither within nor outside of Uboma did we encounter a case of a village or group of villages organizing on their own and investing the capital and labor needed for rice-land development. This suggests either that the returns to such investment may not be adequate to justify the costs involved without some subsidy, or that the level of organization required may be too great an obstacle. This experience demonstrates, however, the potential for creation of a major new niche for intensive production.

SHORT-FALLOW FIELDS. In some cases, farmers seem to be differentiating outer fields in response to declining soil fertility. The main example is a distinction between "yam fields" and "cassava fields." Although yam and cassava are often still planted in the same plot, some outer fields are managed on a very short fallow cycle (two or fewer years) and are no longer considered suitable for yams. They then become "cassava fields," with mainly cassava planted there. Although yields are low, farmers may be compelled to take this course in order to obtain regular output. Unlike the other two examples, this is an instance of intensification at a low productivity level (though total output over a period of years may be higher than if longer fallow periods were maintained).[23]

Land-Use Transfers

Numerous writers have commented on the extensive movement of farmers within Imo State (and Igboland in general) to obtain land for farming, which was a common practice even fifty or more years ago (Green 1941; Forde and Scott 1946; Chubb 1961 [1947]; Mbagwu 1978). These transfers of land-use rights are generally on a short-term basis, either as gifts or for rent, or they are pledges in which money is loaned in return for use of the land until repayment. In general, it seems that the system is supported by strong social norms, and farmers feel it is appropriate to supply land to those who need it, especially if any relationship of kinship or friendship is involved. Taken as a whole, this amounts to a regionwide system of land-use interchange in which shortages in some areas or by individual households are mitigated by the use of land in other areas in which supply is more plentiful.

All the surveyed villages participate in one way or another in this system of land interchange (table 8.7). Some are primarily "exporters" of land (i.e., outsiders come there, but most villagers do not go elsewhere to obtain land); others are primarily "importers" (village members mostly go out, but few come in for land). There are also cases in which both export and import of land use occurs.

It seems that both the availability of land in the village and the proximity to an area with a differing level of land availability help to determine the extent of interchange in any one place. The differences across the regions seem roughly parallel to (past) density levels, with the exception of Ukwa, in which the extent to which people go out for land seems higher than expected. It is also interesting that even in some of the most densely populated areas farmers say that outsiders come to obtain parcels of land, although in these areas, this mostly occurs among people with some kind of close link and is basically on a gift basis; in the less-crowded areas, land is more commonly rented, although gifting also occurs. It is clear that this practice is now and has for a long time been an important social means of diffusing land-use pressures over wider areas. While slowing the increase in land-use intensity in more crowded areas, it presumably increases the intensity of land use in other areas with lower levels of population pressure.

Agronomic Practices and Systems

This category of adaptations includes changes in cropping and management practices that may have been partly or largely induced by increasing land scarcity, shortened fallows, and declining yield levels. Much of the agricultural research at national and international research centers and related extension effort is directed at inducing changes that would fall into this category. In addition, much of the technological change associated with Boserup's (1965) theory of the stimulatory effect of population pressure on innovation would also be in this class. Nevertheless this category does not seem to have been the main locus of change or adaptation to land-use pressure in this area over the last several decades. The main types of these adaptations reviewed include changes in the species grown, in soil-management practices, and in crop-management practices. Particularly for the latter, those discussed here are likely to be only a partial list; more detailed field-level studies would probably reveal other changes in agronomic practices that have occurred as a result of land-use pressures.

Table 8.7. Reported Prevalence of Land-Use Transfers (% positive responses)

	Mbaise (N = 14)	Ihitte (N = 10)	Uboma (N = 10)	Ikwuano (N = 11)	Ukwa (N = 10)	Total (N = 55)
Villagers go out for land	100	100	50	55	90	80
Outsiders come to village for land	36	50	100	100	90	73
Rent[a]	20	60	80	100	100	80
Gift only[a]	80	40	20	0	0	20

[a]Percentages of main form of land transfer for those villages responding that outsiders come into to obtain land.

Crop-Species Changes

The major changes in crop species were discussed earlier. The growth in importance of cassava production has occurred throughout the region, in both high- and low-density areas and, as noted, was probably motivated partly by soil-fertility decline but also by numerous other factors. All of the survey regions experienced this major increase of cassava, and there were no population density–related differences that could be determined, though it is possible that a more detailed farm-level study might find differences in the proportion of cassava grown in various areas. Changes in cassava varieties were alluded to by farmers but were not examined in detail. As mentioned, the other major changes in staple-food crops have been the decline in cocoyam, which was apparently caused mainly by disease incidence, and the introduction of rice in the Uboma area. The latter was not mainly motivated by land-use pressures, but it has had some impact on total land productivity and land-use intensity in those areas.

Soil-Management Changes

Soil-amendment practices can be divided into two types: enhanced recycling or concentration of nutrients that are already present in the system and importation of nutrients from outside the system. The former include the composting, manuring, mulching, and other procedures that farmers say are mostly confined to the compound-garden areas.[24] In addition, the burning of cleared fallow vegetation and subsequent incorporation of ashes into the soil is a recycling technique that is almost universally practiced. It is thought to have both positive and negative effects, but especially on acidic forest soils, the balance is probably positive (Nye and Greenland 1960). The extent to which burning practices or their impacts may have changed in response to high populations was not explored in our survey. Shorter fallows alter the composition of the vegetation that is burned and result in more frequent burns, but the effects these changes may have on soil conditions would require further specialized study.

Fertilizer use is the main form of nutrient import. Although it has been promoted for some time by extension agents and the state Agricultural Development Project, and positive fertilizer responses have been found at the National Root Crops Research Institute (NRCRI) located at Umudike in the Ikwuano region, it appears that adoption is still not very widespread.[25] For at least the last several years, fertilizers have been fairly widely available in Imo State through the Imo State Agricultural Development Project (ISADAP) distribution centers at subsidized prices.[26] The use of fertilizers is widely promoted by local extension agents and demonstrated on numerous small "corner plots" located on farmers' fields throughout the state.

Nonetheless, the data suggest that in most areas, fertilizer use remains low. The reasons farmers state for this poor rate of adoption include insufficient knowledge (which fertilizers to use, how to apply them), limited cash availability and high costs, and a widespread belief that fertilizers reduce the storability of yams. The latter may be the main obstacle since it is so pervasive, even among farmers who have not themselves tried fertilizers. Experiments at NRCRI are said not to show any direct evidence of this, although scientists there suggest that the increased water content of fertilized tubers may make them bruise more easily when harvested and thereby more susceptible to rot (E. Nnodu, personal communication). The approximate extent of fertilizer adoption in villages in the survey regions is detailed in table 8.8.

It seems from this information that the only region in which fertilizer use is widespread is Mbaise, the highest-density area. This is in sharp contrast, however, to the other high-density area, Ihitte, in which adoption was said to be extremely uncommon. There are also differences among the medium- and lower-density areas, with cases of both high and low adoption levels in Ikwuano and Uboma, whereas adoption is said to be low or nonexistent in almost all villages in Ukwa.[27] On the whole, with the exception of Mbaise, fertilizer adoption throughout the region seems lower than would be expected given the various factors

Table 8.8. Reported Fertilizer Adoption (% of villages)

	Percentage of farmers in village using fertilizers	
	≥40%	<40%
Mbaise (n = 14)	93	7
Ihitte (n = 10)	0	100
Uboma (n = 13)	31	69
Ikwuano (n = 11)	18	82
Ukwa (n = 10)	10	90
Total sample (n = 58)	32	68

that should encourage its use: widespread concern by farmers about reduced soil fertility; probable yield-increasing response to fertilizers; relatively low subsidized price; wide availability; and extensive promotion. More study would be useful to determine the reasons for this low rate of adoption.

Crop-Management Changes

A number of examples of crop-management changes seem, in part, to be responses to land-use pressure. Farmers in Mbaise and Ukwa mentioned changes in the length of time before most cassava harvesting was done, which they ascribed mainly to the impact of lower yields.

In a few other cases, farmers alluded to changes in planting density (especially of cassava) that were related to lower yields, although we did not have the opportunity to examine this in detail. In addition, increased pest and disease losses were cited by farmers to be responsible for much of the yield decline they had experienced. There is some pesticide use, which is probably a relatively new practice, but this has recently been inhibited because of rising input prices and unavailability of the main chemicals. The incidence of diseases, such as cassava mosaic virus, and pests, such as cassava mealybug (*Phenacoccus manihoti*), is very high, and the losses these cause may be enhanced by the low soil-fertility conditions found in the area. An increase in pest-control measures (including cultural controls and resistant varieties, as well as appropriate chemicals in some cases) could help to increase yields and thereby relieve land-use pressures.

In sum, in most areas it does not seem that changes in agronomic and related practices have been a major locus of adaptation and of response to increased population and land-use pressures over the last two decades. Various preexisting trends have continued, including the growing importance of cassava in the crop system, possibly a continuing increase in the role of the intensively managed compound farms, and a number of crop-management practices that seem to have been intensified. Possibly the only major new elements are the growth of fertilizer use, which has, however, occurred on a substantial scale in only one of the five survey regions, and the introduction of wetland rice with its associated intensive management techniques, which has also been of very limited extent.

To the extent that it is valid, this conclusion raises at least two sets of questions. (1) Why it is that the agricultural research and extension effort that have been directed at altering the very practices that fall into this category (including the use of improved cultivars) has seemingly had such minimal impact; has the apparent shortfall in results been due to some shortcoming in the nature and extent of the effort itself, or is it mainly due to the character of the region? Although this is an issue of great importance, it would require an analysis of the research, extension, and related work that is beyond the scope of this paper. (2) If the major changes and adaptations of the last two or three decades are not to be found in this category, then where have they occurred, and what are the implications of this?

Noncrop Output Systems

Agricultural land and other resources are, of course, also used for noncrop outputs. Among these, the outputs derived from fallow vegetation and, to a lesser extent, the livestock systems were examined. In both cases, a number of changes and variations across regions were found, and some practices had changed in response to increases in land-use pressures.

Changes in Fallow-Vegetation System

Many of the differences among regions in relation to fallow-vegetation systems were discussed. One set of responses has related to the increasing commodification and privatization of fallow vegetation and its resource products, which by custom were previously often available to the community at large. As discussed, there are now sharp differences among the regions in the degree of access restriction and privatization for many of the products, particularly yam staking material and to a lesser extent, firewood. The highest degree of privatization seems to prevail in Mbaise, and the general trend among the other regions accords with the gradient of (past) density, although Ukwa has a higher-than-expected level of restriction. In a number of cases, farmers mentioned that changes in customary rules of access were recent occurrences or were likely soon to be installed because of the high level of demand and pressure on these resources.

Purposive management of the species composition of fallow vegetation has also been a feature of many of the survey regions. In over 80 percent of the villages surveyed, farmers report that *Acioa barteri*, the fallow species considered to produce the best yam stakes, was planted in the past. This practice is said to date back at least eighty years, as even the oldest informants said that *Acioa* had already been planted when they were children. The only region where such planting did not occur was in Ukwa. Currently, much of the *Acioa* is present as old stumps with extensive root systems from which bushes regenerate rapidly after the crops are removed from the field. Some farmers have special fields in which *Acioa* has been planted and maintained in rows, but in most areas, the *Acioa* stumps seem just to be scattered through a field at lower densities. Some current planting is said to be occurring in about one-third of the total sample, though this is often said just to be at a low level.

In Mbaise, however, there exists a widespread, intensively managed, planted *Acioa* fallow system that is a significant element in the farming system. In almost all of the villages in our Mbaise sample, farmers report that current planting is continuing, and many farmers maintain managed "*Acioa* fields," with high densities of *Acioa*, often arranged in rows with filling in of gaps. The regrowth rapidly forms a canopy that shades weeds and other woody species, creating a virtual monocrop. Such fields are often on a different fallow cycle, since three years is said to be the minimum time needed to produce adequate yam stakes. (As noted, farmers in Mbaise report that the most common fallow length averages 2.3 years, and many fields are fallowed for only one year, or have no fallow period.) Only a proportion of total cropped land in this area is managed in this manner as *Acioa* fields. As might be expected, the *Acioa* produced is unambiguously considered to be private property, and there is much buying and selling.

By contrast, no such system was reported in Ihitte, the other high-density area, although all the villages reported that *Acioa* had been planted there in the past. Ihitte, in fact, appears to be the area with the greatest shortage of *Acioa* and other fallow products. It has the lowest proportion of villages selling staking material and of villages using *Acioa* as the main staking species, as well as the highest proportion of villages reporting that firewood is bought from other villages. It is not clear why an intensive fallow-management system similar to that in Mbaise has not taken hold in Ihitte, or is not more common in other areas. In Ihitte, it seems rather that the major method of coping with shortages is by importing materials from other areas and (possibly) by outmigration and general movement of economic activity out of agriculture. This suggests that high pressure on land use and on fallow resources does not necessarily induce the adoption of intensive resource-management systems.

Livestock-System Changes

Most households in the area have some poultry, goats, and sheep. The main interactions between the livestock, cropping, and fallow-vegetation systems are in the manure supplied for fertilization (used mainly in the compound gardens), the consumption of crop residues and fallow vegetation for animal feed, and the fact that the animals can act as crop pests. They are also, of course, a source of income, meat and eggs, for the household.

In most cases, farmers report that the numbers of their livestock have been declining over the past twenty years. In Mbaise, Ukwa, and Ikwuano, 88 percent of the villages reported declines in the numbers of goats kept, 85 percent in the numbers of sheep, and 68 percent in the numbers of poultry. The most commonly cited reason for the declines, especially of goats and sheep, was the additional labor needed to gather feed as stall feeding has replaced free grazing and browsing.[28] This was said to have been made necessary by the increase in the intensity of land use, particularly the more frequent and intensive use of compound gardens, in which goats and sheep had previously been allowed to graze during periods when no annual crops were present. Therefore, land-use pressures have helped to induce a contraction of the livestock system. This, in turn, reduces the manure available for use in the compound gardens and elsewhere just when that nutrient source has become increasingly valuable. There was no example encountered in these three regions of any major attempts by farmers to reverse the declining trend in the livestock system.[29]

Expansion of System Boundaries

There are a number of ways in which farmers and other rural inhabitants try to circumvent the limitations of the local agricultural and land-use system, which can be classed as attempts to expand the system boundaries. In some cases, renting or otherwise obtaining land in other areas are examples of system expansion, as discussed above. Other non-agricultural examples include importing food from other areas, outmigration from the local area, and undertaking nonfarm activities for income. It was possible to explore these in only a cursory way in our surveys. It was not feasible to obtain information about the extent and nature of nonagricultural economic activities, but these are said to have been extremely important for some time and have probably grown in recent years with the great increase in urbanization. It seems reasonable to assume that this has been one of the major adaptations to the agricultural-land shortages in most of the region.

Some survey information was obtained about food imports and outmigration. In all of the villages in Mbaise and Ukwa, respondents say that purchasing of staple foods (cassava, yam, and maize) has increased over the past twenty years. In most of these cases, this was said to have been almost unknown in the past, but it has now become a common practice. By contrast in Ikwuano, only 36 percent of the villages responded that such purchasing had increased; in the remaining villages people say they still generally do not purchase staple foods.

To gauge the extent of outmigration from the villages, farmers were asked to estimate the proportion of young people from the village currently living elsewhere. In almost half of the villages, a rate of over 50 percent of outmigration was reported among this group (table 8.9). Farmers also often said that the proportion had been even higher until recently, when employment opportunities in the cities began to decline. Ukwa, however, was a notable exception to this pattern, with none of the villages reporting over 50 percent outmigration, and almost 40 percent reporting outmigration of 20 percent or less. Moreover, the Ukwa respondents generally said that outmigration of young people had begun only recently.

Despite the crude nature of these estimates, there is such a striking divergence between the responses in Ukwa and those in the other regions that this itself suggests a partial explanation for the much more rapid growth in land-use pressure there than in the other areas. Particularly striking is the contrast between the estimates given in Ukwa and those in Ikwuano, which might account for the sharp differences in the two regions' experiences over the last few decades.[30] If the safety valve of outmigration has not been operating in Ukwa until quite recently, then the population increase over this period might have put greater pressure on agricultural resources there than elsewhere and so given rise to the unexpectedly high indications of shortages and rapid change in resource availability in recent years.

It seems, in sum, that there are a number of respects in which this category of nonagricultural activities represents a set of responses that has been extremely important in this region, although it was possible to collect only sparse data on these topics.

Conclusion

The Experience of Change

It seems that the last two decades have not, on the whole, been a period of great change in the farming systems of the area, despite the substantial population increase that has occurred during this time. The main changes that have taken place include the reduction of fallow periods; the growth in importance of cassava and the decline of cocoyam; changes in the usage patterns and availability of fallow-vegetation resources; the introduction of fertilizer; and the development of wetland rice cultivation. The first three occurred in almost all of the survey regions, though not necessarily to the same extent everywhere, whereas the latter two are found only in some regions and villages. It is likely that there have also been other changes related to increased land-use pressure—including changes in the size and management of compound farms, an increasing differentiation of outer fields, and an increase in the frequency of land-use transfers—but these were not investigated in sufficient detail to draw definitive conclusions about them.

Three general points about the experience of agricultural change in the area bear further discussion:

1. Most of the changes found represent continuations of previously

Table 8.9. Estimates of Outmigration (% of villages)

Estimated outmigration[a]	Mbaise (N = 10)	Ihitte (N =4)	Uboma (N = 7)	Ikwuano (N = 8)	Ukwa (N = 8)	Total sample (N = 37)
<20%	40	0	0	0	38	19
20–50%	20	25	29	25	62	32
>50%	40	75	71	75	0	49

[a]Estimates of the proportion of young people from the village currently living elsewhere.

existing trends. Only fertilizer use and the introduction of wetland rice are new elements, and the latter is the only example of major transformation of the production systems of the area. It is, however, very limited in geographic scope and has not spread beyond the area of its initial project-based introduction. The former also seems not to have been widely adopted in most areas. A major issue of concern is how and to what extent the future course of change in the area will depart from present trends and involve discontinuous, transformational change, and what, if any, outside interventions could facilitate such a departure.

2. The changes and innovations in agronomic practices have, on the whole, been less extensive than might have been expected. These are, however, those toward which most agricultural research and extension effort has been directed and also among those that Boserup (1965) and others postulate will be stimulated by population growth. It is only in the highest-density survey region and in the wetland rice subsystem that these kinds of innovations seem to have been widely adopted. It is possible that, in these kinds of humid forest systems, innovations in agronomic practices are more likely to be adopted in the context of highly productive new subsystems (often with multiple outputs) rather than as individual components. An alternate possibility may be that the low degree of innovation has resulted from the low returns to agriculture during this historical period. The pattern and pace of innovation might alter significantly under different macroeconomic conditions.

3. Although a substantial shortening of fallow periods has been the general experience, almost 20 percent of the survey villages in the total sample and 40 percent or more of the villages in two of the survey regions reported no reduction of fallow lengths. However, other changes have occurred in these villages, including increased fertilizer use, the increase in the importance of cassava, and some changes in fallow-product usage. This suggests that the direction of causation may not run simply

from a compelled reduction in fallow length to technological change, but that in some cases technological changes may be adopted as a means to help forestall a reduction in fallow periods.

Variations among Regions

Synchronic variation among areas of differing population density and land availability is often used as the basis for conclusions about how farming systems evolve with population increase. This case study was designed to examine differences in system characteristics and in experiences of change among areas that are similar in environmental and cultural conditions but vary in population density. Such variation has been a long-standing feature of this area, noted in many past studies. Various differences were found in both current farming-system conditions and the rates at which they have changed over the past two decades or so. Many, but not all, of these differences correspond with the population gradient.

There seem to be three main patterns of variation among the survey regions with respect to the farming-system conditions investigated. In the first, there is a gradation consistent with (past) density levels but with Ukwa, the area with the lowest density in the past, having higher-than-expected indications of resource pressure. Among the characteristics that follow this pattern are the current reported fallow length and the percentage by which it has changed; the scarcity of products derived from fallow vegetation, as revealed by various indicators; the extent to which farmers go outside their village to obtain additional farming land ("land-use imports"); and the extent of outmigration. These characteristics are apparently related to population-density levels, and may change with increasing density. The exception in Ukwa implies a much higher rate of change in land availability there than in the other survey regions over this period. There have probably been a number of reasons for this, but the survey responses suggest that one important factor may be that the rate of outmigration there has, until recently, been lower than in the other areas. In addition, the intensity of soil-management practices, both nutrient recycling in the compound gardens and fertilizer use, seems to have been lower in Ukwa than in the other areas. Finally, it is possible that the persistence of communal land tenure and group rotation in Ukwa has had some inhibiting effect on innovation, though there was no direct evidence for this.

There is also a second pattern of variation that has a density-related gradient but without Ukwa as an exception (although sometimes one of the other regions may be exceptional). This includes the reported fallow lengths in the past; a number of farm-management characteristics (including group-based rotation, the intensity of compound-farm use, and fertilizer adoption); a low intensity of fallow-vegetation management; and the extent to which outsiders come to the area for farm land ("land-use exports"). In all of these, conditions in Ukwa seem consistent with those in the other lower-density areas or indicate a low level of intensification, despite the apparently rapid change in land availability in this area. This suggests possible lags in adjustment of some of these features during periods of rapid change. Such changes as a breakdown in the group rotation system, an increased intensity of compound-farm use, and the introduction of fertilizer use may appear in an area experiencing rapid change only after a lag period during which the effects of decreased land availability become manifest.

Finally, there is a category of singular cases, in which a certain feature appears in only one of the regions. The two main examples are the wetland rice system in Uboma and the intensive *Acioa*-management system in Mbaise. Both of these are complex subsystems, and the fact that they have remained exceptional despite the increases in land-use pressures in many regions suggests that the diffusion of such complex systems may not readily occur. Therefore, it is unclear whether these can be taken to indicate likely directions of change in other areas.

Finally, it is important to note that the variation in land and resource availability is itself an important feature of the area and has stimulated interactions among regions with differing levels of resource pressure. The main interactions have been in land-use transfers, in the commodification of resource products, and in food sales and purchases. All of these have helped farmers cope with the increasing resource scarcities that have appeared over the last few decades. Some, notably the land-use transfers, have been important characteristics of the system for a long time.

Prospects for Future Change

Other than the fact that the system has not collapsed, the experience of the last two decades does not seem to hold much cause for optimism about future changes in the agricultural systems of this area. Both the constraints of the resource base and the large number of people trying to make use of it limit the expectations for agricultural transformation.

There are, however, at least two factors that may make the coming decade differ from the preceding two. One is that Nigeria, together with other countries of West Africa, is experiencing an altered set of macro-economic conditions, including currency devaluation, restrictions on food imports, more active government promotion of agricultural production, and the end of the oil boom. In addition, the high degree of urbanization in this area and, especially in Nigeria, the well-developed state of transport infrastructure help to stimulate the growth of effective market demand for agricultural output. Not all signs are positive, though, and such factors as the increased cost of imported materials due to devaluation (including fertilizers and many agricultural tools and equipment) may be serious impediments. Nevertheless, there is at least some hope of new stimulus to the agricultural economy—although it is unlikely to occur equally in all parts of the country—or indeed of this area.

At a more local level, there may be greater impetus for changes in agricultural practices as the land-use transfer system comes under increasing strain and as fallow-vegetation resources also become increasingly scarce. Improving productivity in areas already under short-fallow regimes will become a more necessary and valuable goal with the constriction of the "internal-land frontier." The scarcity of fallow products and their increasing market value may also stimulate the adoption of more intensive fallow-management systems (perhaps resembling the *Acioa*-based system in Mbaise) that both enhance soil productivity and provide valuable outputs. At the same time, the availability of new disease-resistant varieties of cassava and other staple crops of the area may help reduce some of the important pest and disease losses that have contributed to yield declines in recent years.

This expected outcome of impending changes in resource conditions is not, of course, inevitable. Resource-degrading techniques may instead be adopted in attempts to realize short-term goals at the expense of the resource base. The task of agricultural research and extension efforts will be to develop and make available to farmers a range of appropriate technological innovations that will match their needs and circumstances and will be suited to the range of conditions characteristic of this area. Flexibility for local adaptation as well as the ability to serve both short-term output and long-term resource goals will need to be among the important characteristics of these new technologies.

Notes

This paper is based on survey research undertaken on behalf of the Resource and Crop Management Program of the International Institute of Tropical Agriculture (IITA) in Ibadan, Nigeria, where the author worked as a Rockefeller Foundation Social Science Fellow between 1986 and 1989. The survey was conceived, designed, and carried out as a collaborative effort among Dr. Karen Dvorak, Ir. Joost Foppes, Jonas Chianu, and the author, all of IITA, with the strong support of the Imo State Agricultural Development Project (ISADAP). The author is grateful to Dr. O. Nduaka, project manager, and Dr. E. Okoro, chief research officer of ISADAP, whose assistance and interest helped make the project possible and to the numerous extension agents and supervisors working with ISADAP who helped organize the village interviews. Mr. A.N. Merengini of the Michael Okpara College of Agriculture also provided valuable advice during the course of the project. At IITA, Drs. Karen Dvorak, Joyotee Smith, I.O. Akobundu, B.T. Kang, Ted Lawson, Felix Nweke, Mwenja Gichuru, and Dunstan Spencer all made valuable comments and contributions to the project and to earlier written drafts. The skills of Jonas Chianu as an interpreter have been of key importance. The financial support of the Rockefeller Foundation and of IITA are gratefully acknowledged. Finally, the author and all of the collaborators are grateful to the many Imo State farmers who tolerated the long interviews and provided information about their lives, work, and problems.

1. In contrast, acceptable R-values for the nonacidic alfisols found in many of the savanna areas of West Africa might be 30 to 40 with low input levels and 50 to 60 with an intermediate input level (Young and Wright 1980).

2. Some researchers, however, dispute the view that fallow periods have already fallen below the level required to maintain stability, noting that stable yield levels have been found in cropping rotations of much shorter duration in the area (Vine 1954).

3. With this population, Imo State would have more people than seven other countries in West Africa: Gambia (0.7 million), Guinea Bissau (0.9 mil.), Mauritania (1.7 mil.), Liberia (2.2 mil.), Togo (3 mil.), Sierra Leone (3.7 mil.), and Benin (4 mil.)—and a total similar to that of Guinea (6.1 mil.), Niger (6.5 mil.), and Senegal (6.6 mil.) (1985 population estimates from World Bank [1986]).

4. Overall population density in sub-Saharan Africa is estimated to have been around 16 persons/km² in 1980 (FAO 1986). The highest density category in the FAO map of African population density (based on 1980 figures) is 190+ persons/km².

5. The annual growth rates implied by the comparison between the 1953 and 1963 data on a local level vary so widely and range from such high to such

low values that they are not credible. The implied annual growth rates for the survey areas range from 0.5 percent to 14.5 percent.

6. One LGA was initially chosen from each of the four density categories shown in figure 8.3: in descending order, these are Ahiazu-Mbaise (listed as "Mbaise" in the following tables and discussions), Etiti (including both the Ihitte and Uboma regions), Ikwuano-Umuahia, and Ukwa. Three of these were also selected because previous studies had been conducted there (Morgan [1955] in Ukwa; Oluwasanmi et al. [1966] in Uboma; Lagemann [1977] in Ikwuano). Ahiazu Mbaise was chosen because it was the most densely populated LGA in the state in 1953 and is the site of an intensive local agroforestry system (A. N. Merengini, personal communication). In two cases, the survey regions are currently LGAs (Ahiazu-Mbaise and Ukwa), whereas in the others, the LGA was subdivided, and areas that were "clan regions" or county councils under former local government administration were used.

7. The territory of the Mbaise clan was administratively divided into Ahiazu-Mbaise and Aboh-Mbaise in the 1970s. Our survey research was conducted only in Ahiazu-Mbaise. For the sake of simplicity, this is referred to only as Mbaise in the following pages.

8. This represents 27 percent of the total number of villages in the five regions (ISADAP n.d.).

9. Although the findings of a three-village study such as Lagemann's (1977), or sometimes a single-village study, are also often used for this, the degree to which such results can be extrapolated depends on the extent of intervillage variation within a region and within strata, which is rarely tested formally.

10. In a six-year cycle, for example, there will be six defined portions of village land, each often having its own name. Every household will own (or may be allotted in the case of communally owned land) plots of land in each of the areas. If a household does not have enough land in one of those areas, it may borrow or rent land from another village household or it may try to obtain land in another village.

11. Harris (1942), however, also linked land-use pressure to declining world prices for palm oil. He said this tended to drive people back to food production for income, thereby increasing land-use demand. In contrast, during the earlier periods when world palm oil prices were high, there was more concern with nonfarm activities partly because general prosperity caused increasing demand for consumer goods of various kinds.

12. In the prevailing cropping system in the region, fields are planted only for one year, and cassava is left in outer fields for up to two years after planting. It was decided to define the fallow period as the time between the final yam harvest (usually November or December of the year in which it was planted) and the next time yam would be planted in that field. Thus, cassava remaining more than one year was defined as part of the fallow period. The fallow period

estimate was sometimes expressed as a range (e.g., 2–3 years) in which case a mean value of 2.5 years was used for analysis. The current minimum and maximum fallow lengths in the village were also collected but are not included in the table. (The sample sizes refer to the number of villages in each region.)

13. Although the accuracy of responses about fallow periods in the past is always subject to question, one positive indication is that the 2–7-year range of fallow periods said by our respondents to have prevailed in Uboma twenty years ago is consistent with the values reported in the Uboma study carried out at that time (Upton 1966).

14. Note that this results in relative estimates of yield per plant, not necessarily yield per unit area. This actually seems more consistent with the way in which farmers conceive of crop yields, especially in a comparative sense. However, the translation between yield per plant and yield per area is not necessarily straightforward, as it is affected not only by stand density, but, especially for cassava, by the length of time for which the crop is allowed to remain in the ground before harvest.

15. Upton (1966) reported that mosaic virus was almost universally present in Uboma at the time of his study. In our survey, farmers in many areas, including villages in Ikwuano where there was little fallow reduction, said that the extent of symptoms caused by or resembling mosaic virus was quite a new phenomenon. Green mites can cause symptoms very similar to those of cassava mosaic disease (Théberge 1985). Mealybug infestation is distinctive and was said to be a recent occurrence.

16. Recent surveys of the cassava mealybug in southeastern Nigeria by the Africa-Wide Biological Control Program at IITA suggest that both the incidence and severity of damage are greater in areas with shorter fallow periods, especially on the low-nutrient soils of this region (P. Neuenschwander, personal communication). However, further analysis is needed to confirm this preliminary finding.

17. Yam vines have to be staked in this environment to receive adequate sunshine, and farmers may need several hundred to several thousand yam stakes per season. Depending on the method used, the type of yam grown, and the desired tuber size, stakes can range from moderate-sized tree branches or split bamboo poles, to large limbs or heavy poles that may be three meters or more high.

18. Migrant Igbo farmers can be found in many of the lower-density areas in the surrounding states of Bendel, Cross River, and Rivers. Longer-distance migration also occurs, but its current extent is uncertain, and there are important political and cultural limiting factors. Within Imo State, there are pockets of unused swampland or other types of land that have been opened for production in recent years. The total amounts of such land may not be large, but as discussed below, initiation of wetland rice cultivation in wetland areas may have

important ramifications for the farming system. Finally, a recent survey by Cantor (1986) suggests that farmers have been encroaching on sacred groves in parts of Iboland in order to increase cultivated land.

19. It is essential to include a temporal dimension in any assessment of the returns to fallow-period changes and related soil-management practices. For example, a parcel of land cropped once every three years (i.e., a two-year fallow period) may give 100 units of output, while if cropped every five years (four-year fallow) would yield 150 units of output. Over fifteen years, however, the total output of the shorter fallow cycle would be 500 units, whereas the total output of the longer fallow cycle would be 450 units.

20. The fragmentation of plots and land holdings found throughout this agro-ecological zone is also in part an outgrowth of these conditions and requirements. If, for example, each plot is planted only once every five years but production is required every year, at least five plots are necessary, each capable of producing the minimum required output. Of course, other factors are also involved in fragmentation of holdings, including inheritance patterns and micro-level ecological differences.

21. It is likely that they originated as a cultural response to household food-supply needs rather than as an adaptation to land-use pressures. Among the evidence suggesting this is the fact that compound farms are present in both lower- and higher-density areas in southeastern Nigeria, whereas they are rarely found in either low- or high-density areas in the southwest of Nigeria (Okafor and Fernandes 1987).

22. The low-density village in Lagemann's study was Okwe, in the Ikwuano area, and he reported that there were no compound farms there. However, this village was in our Ikwuano sample, and our survey showed that compounds do exist there, with the use of manure and household wastes and continuous planting of a range of crops.

23. This principle of differentiating fields by lengths of fallow and cropping patterns may also have been used in the past. In 1954, Vine reported that near Umuahia, fields that had been under short-fallow regimes for a long time were planted only with yellow yam (*Dioscorea cayenensis*), which is more tolerant of poor soil conditions than other yam species. The preferred white yams (*D. rotundata*) were usually planted on better land or received more manure. The differentiation of lower-fertility cassava fields may be a successor to this practice.

24. Although, when asked, farmers rarely mentioned use of mulching and other techniques in the outer fields, except to control soil temperature on yam mounds, some mulching with leaves and crop residues was observed (e.g., in the area around iroko trees [*Chlorophora excelsa*], which drop large amounts of leaf litter, and which farmers consider to be an extremely good tree for enhancing soil fertility, although it is now relatively rare).

25. Fertilizer trials at NRCRI (formerly known as the Federal Agricultural Research and Training Station) at Umudike (located in our survey region in Ikwuano) have consistently shown positive responses of cassava yields to the addition of nitrogen, phosphorus, and potassium as well as somewhat lower responses to calcium and magnesium (Federal Agricultural Research and Training Station 1975, 1976). However, it is also true that organic matter additions are often necessary in these soils in addition to fertilizer, partly to help combat the acidification that can be caused by nitrogenous fertilizers (Kang and Juo 1983).

26. The official fertilizer price has, however, risen in the last few years from N2-3 to N10 (about $2.50 at the exchange rate at the time of the survey) per 50-kg bag of the compound fertilizer 15:15:15.

27. Much of the fertilizer use in Uboma is said to be concentrated in the intensively farmed rice areas, which are generally planted every year.

28. In many areas, there are local government ordinances requiring that goats and sheep be kept tethered. Offenders can be, and often are, fined by local authorities.

29. In Ikwuano, however, the International Livestock Center for Africa (ILCA) is conducting on-farm investigation of the feasibility and acceptability of "intensive feed gardens," usually as part of the compound farms and as an adaptation of the alley-farming concept. Much of this work is still in its early stages (Attah-Krah and Francis 1986).

30. Differential proximity of the two regions to urban areas is not an adequate explanation, as most of Ukwa, which is located between the major cities of Aba and Port Harcourt, is more accessible than is much of Ikwuano, which has poor roads and many villages that are not very accessible to the city of Umuahia. One would have expected that the rapid growth of Aba and Port Harcourt over the last two decades would have exerted a strong urban pull in Ukwa for some time. Instead, it seems to have been a recent phenomenon.

References

Agboola, S. A. 1968. "The Introduction and Spread of Cassava in Western Nigeria." *Nigerian Journal of Economic and Social Studies* 10(3): 369–85.

Anthonio, Q. B. O., and M. O. Ijere. 1973. *Uboma Development Project, 1964–1972*. London: Shell International.

Attah-Krah, A. N., and P. A. Francis. 1986. On-Farm Trials and the Evaluation of Alley Farming. Paper presented at the International Workshop on Alley Farming for Humid and Subhumid Regions of Tropical Agriculture, 10–14 March, 1986, Ibadan, Nigeria.

Boserup, E. 1965. *The Conditions of Agricultural Growth*. Chicago: Aldine.

298 / A. Goldman

Cantor, Jill Ann. 1986. "Land Tenure and Agroforestry in Southeastern Nigeria." M.Sc. thesis, Madison, University of Wisconsin.

Caveness, F.E., S.K. Hahn, M.N. Alvarez, and Y. Ng. 1987. "The Cocoyam Improvement Program at IITA, 1973 to 1987." In *Cocoyams in Nigeria: Production, Storage, Processing and Utilization*, ed. O.B. Arene et al., pp. 52–57. Umudike, Nigeria: National Root Crops Research Institute.

Chubb. L.T. 1961 [1947]. *Ibo Land Tenure*, 2d ed. Ibadan: Ibadan University Press.

Coursey, D.G. 1966. "The Cultivation and Use of Yams in West Africa." *Ghana Notes and Queries* 9: 45–54.

Coursey, D.G., and Cecilia K. Coursey. 1971. "The New Yam Festivals of West Africa." *Anthropos* 66: 444–84.

Dvorak, K.A. 1988. Resource Management in the Humid Tropics: Working Paper on Defining Research Domains. Unpublished, IITA.

FAO. 1986. *Atlas of African Agriculture. African Agriculture: The Next 25 Years*. Rome: FAO.

Federal Agricultural Research and Training Station. 1975, 1976. *Annual Reports*. Umudike, Nigeria: Federal Agricultural Research and Training Station.

Fernandes, E.C.M., A. Oktingati, and J.A. Maghembe. 1984. "The Chagga Home Gardens: A Multi-Storeyed Agro-Forestry Cropping System on Mt. Kilimanjaro, Northern Tanzania." *Agroforestry Systems* 2: 73–86.

Floyd, Barry. 1969. *Eastern Nigeria: A Geographical Review*. London: Macmillan.

Forde, Daryll, and G.I. Jones. 1950. *The Ibo and Ibibio-Speaking Peoples of South-Eastern Nigeria*. Ethnographic Survey of Africa. Western Africa, Part III. London: Oxford University Press, for the International African Institute.

Forde, Daryll, and Richenda Scott. 1946. *The Native Economies of Nigeria*. London: Faber and Faber.

Francis, Paul. 1987. "Land Tenure Systems and Agricultural Innovation: The Case of Alley Farming in Nigeria." *Land Use Policy* 4: 305–18.

Gleave, M.B., and H.P. White. 1969. "Population Density and Agricultural Systems in West Africa." In *Environment and Land Use in Africa*, ed. M.F. Thomas and G.W. Whittington, pp. 273–300. London: Methuen.

Green, M.M. 1941. *Land Tenure in an Ibo Village in South-Eastern Nigeria*. Monographs on Social Anthropology, No. 6. London: Percy Lund, Humphries, for The London School of Economics and Political Science.

Grigg, D.B. 1976. "Population Pressure and Agricultural Change." *Progress in Geography* 8: 135–76.

Grossman, David. 1975. "Iboland's Population Distribution: A Geographical-

Historical Approach to an Explanation and Application." *Journal of Developing Areas* 9: 253–70.

Grove, A. T. 1951. "Soil Erosion and Population Problems in South-East Nigeria." *Geographical Journal* 117: 291–306.

Harris, Jack. 1942. "Human Relationships to the Land in Southern Nigeria." *Rural Sociology* 7: 89–92.

Idachaba, F. S., et al. 1985. *Rural Infrastructures in Nigeria*, 2d ed. Ibadan: Ibadan University Press.

IITA. 1988. *IITA Annual Report and Research Highlights, 1987–88*. Ibadan, Nigeria: IITA.

ISADAP. n.d. *Village Listing*. Owerri, Nigeria: ISADAP.

Jones, G. C. I. 1945. "Agriculture and Ibo Village Planning." *Farm and Forest* 6: 9–15.

Jungerius, P. D. 1964. "The Soils of Eastern Nigeria." *Publication Service Géologique du Luxembourg* 14: 185–98. (*Publicaties van het Fysisch-Geografisch Laboratorium van de Universiteit van Amsterdam* 4.)

Kang, B. T., and A. S. R. Juo. 1983. "Management of Low-Activity Clay Soils in Tropical Africa for Food-Crop Production." *Proceedings of the Fourth International Soil Classification Workshop, Rwanda, 2–12 June, 1981*. Brussels: ABOS, AGCD.

Kilby, P. 1967. "The Nigerian Palm Oil Industry." *Food Research Institute Studies* 7: 189–94.

Lagemann, Johannes. 1977. *Traditional African Farming Systems in Eastern Nigeria: An Analysis of Reaction to Increasing Population Pressure*. Munich: Weltforum Verlag.

Lekwa, Godwill. 1979. "The Characteristics and Classification of Genetic Sequences of Soils in the Coastal Plain Sands of Eastern Nigeria." Ph.D dissertation, Michigan State University.

Martin, Susan. 1984. "Gender and Innovation: Farming, Cooking, and Palm Processing in the Ngwa Region, Southeastern Nigeria, 1900–1930." *Journal of African History* 25: 411–27.

———. 1988. *Palm Oil and Protest: An Economic History of the Ngwa Region, South-Eastern Nigeria, 1800–1980*. Cambridge: Cambridge University Press.

Mbagwu, T. C. 1970. "The Oil Palm Economy in Ngwaland (Eastern Nigeria)." Ph.D. dissertation, University of Ibadan, Nigeria.

———. 1978. "Land Concentration around a Few Individuals in Igbo-Land of Eastern Nigeria." *Africa* 48: 101–15.

Morgan, W. B. 1955. "Farming Practice, Settlement Pattern, and Population Density in Southeastern Nigeria." *Geographical Journal* 121: 322–33.

———. 1959. "Agriculture in Southern Nigeria (Excluding The Cameroons)." *Economic Geography* 35: 138–50.

Moss, R.P. 1969a. "The Ecological Background to Land-use Studies in Tropical Africa, with Special Reference to the West." In *Environment and Land Use in Africa*, ed. M.F. Thomas and G.W. Whittington, pp. 193–238. London: Methuen.

———. 1969b. "An Ecological Approach to the Study of Soils and Land Use in the Forest Zone of Nigeria." In *Environment and Land Use in Africa*, ed. M.F. Thomas and G.W. Whittington, pp. 385–407. London: Methuen.

Niñez, V. 1987. "Household Gardens: Theoretical and Policy Considerations." *Agricultural Systems* 23: 167–86.

Nnoke, F.N., O.B. Arene, and A.C. Ohiri. 1987. "Effect of N.P.K. Fertilizer on Cocoyam Declining Disease Control and Yield in *Xanthosoma sagittifolium*." In *Cocoyams in Nigeria: Production, Storage, Processing and Utilization*, ed. O.B. Arene et al., pp. 222–26. Umudike, Nigeria: National Root Crops Research Institute.

Nye, P.H., and D.J. Greenland. 1960. *The Soil under Shifting Cultivation*. Technical Communication No. 51. Harpenden: Commonwealth Bureau of Soils.

Obi, J.K., and P. Tuley. 1973. *The Bush Fallow and Ley Farming in the Oil Palm Belt of Southeastern Nigeria*. Misc. Report 161. London: Ministry of Overseas Development (ODM), Land Resources Division.

Obihara, C.H. 1961. "The Acid Sands of Eastern Nigeria." *Nigerian Scientist* 1: 57–64.

Ofomata, G.E.K., ed. 1975. *Nigeria in Maps: Eastern States*. Benin City: Ethiopia Publishing House.

Okafor, J.C., and E.C.M. Fernandes. 1987. Compound Farms of Southeastern Nigeria. *Agroforestry Systems* 5: 153–68.

Okere, L.C. 1983. *The Anthropology of Food in Rural Igboland*. Lanham, Md.: University Presses of America.

Okigbo, Bede. 1984. "Improved Permanent Production Systems as an Alternative to Shifting Intermittent Cultivation." *Improved Production Systems as an Alternative to Shifting Cultivation*, FAO Soils Bulletin 53. Rome: FAO.

Oluwasanmi, H.A., et al. 1966. *Uboma: A Socio-Economic and Nutritional Survey of a Rural Community in Eastern Nigeria*. World Land-Use Survey, Occasional Papers, No. 6. Bude, England: Geographical Publications Limited.

Richards, Paul. 1985. *Indigenous Agricultural Revolution: Ecology and Food Production in West Africa*. Boulder, Colo.: Westview Press.

Ruthenberg, Hans. 1980. *Farming Systems in the Tropics*, 3d ed. Oxford: Clarendon Press.

Shaw, Thurstan. 1976. "Early Crops in Africa: A Review of the Evidence." In *Origins of African Plant Domestication*, ed. J.R. Harlan, J.M.J. de Wet, and A. Stemler, pp. 108–53. The Hague: Mouton.

Snelder, D. 1987. *A Case Study on Compound Farms in Southeastern Nigeria.* RCMP Project Report. Ibadan, Nigeria: IITA.

Théberge, Robert L., ed. 1985. *Common African Pests and Diseases of Cassava, Yam, Sweet Potato and Cocoyam.* Ibadan, Nigeria: IITA.

Udo, R. K. 1963. Patterns of Population Distribution and Settlement in Eastern Nigeria. *Nigerian Geographical Journal* 6: 73–88.

———. 1970. *Geographical Regions of Nigeria.* London: Heinemann.

Upton, M . 1966. "Agriculture in Uboma." In *Uboma: A Socio-Economic and Nutritional Survey of a Rural Community in Eastern Nigeria,* ed. H. A. Oluwasanmi et al., pp. 83–104. World Land-Use Survey, Occasional Papers, No. 6. Bude, Cornwall, England: Geographical Publications Limited.

Uzozie, L. C. 1971. "Patterns of Crop Combination in the Three Eastern States of Nigeria." *Journal of Tropical Geography* 33: 62–72.

Vine, H. 1954. "Is the Lack of Fertility of Tropical African Soils Exaggerated?" In *Proceedings of the 2nd Inter-African Soils Conference,* pp. 389-412, Leopoldville.

———. 1956. "Studies of Soil Profiles at the WAIFOR Main Station and at Some Other Sites of Oil Palm Experiments." *Journal of the West African Institute for Oil Palm Research* 1(4): 8–59.

Walker, Judith. 1985. Interim Report: Compound Farming Systems of Southeastern Nigeria. Unpublished. Ibadan, Nigeria: IITA.

Walker, Judith, and Ute Latzke-Begemann. 1985. List of Plant Species and Their Uses in Southeastern Nigeria. Unpublished. Ibadan, Nigeria: IITA.

World Bank. 1986. *World Development Report, 1985.* New York: Oxford University Press.

Yesufu, T. M. 1968. "The Politics and Economics of Nigeria's Population Census." In *The Population of Tropical Africa,* ed. J. C. Caldwell and C. Okonjo, pp. 106–16. London: Longmans.

Young, A., and A. C. S. Wright. 1980. *Rest Period Requirements of Tropical and Subtropical Soils under Annual Crops.* Report on the Second FAO/UNFPA Consultation on Land Resources for Populations of the Future. Rome: FAO.

9 / From Agricultural Growth to Stagnation: The Case of the Ngwa, Nigeria, 1900–1980

Susan Martin

This chapter establishes three major long-term trends in the relationship between population growth and agricultural change in the Ngwa-Igbo region of eastern Nigeria.

The first, characteristic of the first thirty years of this century, is a trend of agricultural diversification and commercialization. The adoption of cassava, the latest in a long series of New World species, and the expansion of oil palm export production enabled the Ngwa farming system to support a dense population (by African standards) at a rising standard of living. Thus, this trend may be described as a form of agricultural intensification—that is, as a set of changes that increased returns to the land and labor resources in Ngwa agriculture.

The main motive for these changes was probably to improve the local standard of living rather than to support a growing population. Colonial census data indicate that the local population was growing slowly, if at all, during this period. Thus, the relationship between agricultural growth and population pressure may have worked in a way exactly opposite from that envisaged by Boserup (1965). Improvements in the standard of living may eventually have stimulated increases in population density by improving children's nutritional status and life expectancy. Certainly, throughout this century Ngwa women have spent much of their income on dietary inputs that had been scarce in their region, especially meat, fish, or salt. However, as Goldman notes in chapter 8 of this volume, the causes for the historically high population densities of the Igbo region as a whole remain obscure, and the causes of accelerated growth since 1930 are equally hard to ascertain. Detailed historical research on changes in the nutritional and health status of the Ngwa and other Igbo peoples is urgently needed to resolve this point.

The second trend established in this paper was dominant from the late 1920s to the 1950s. It involves high rates of population growth, accompanied by continuing efforts to sustain per capita food crop production and cash incomes from agriculture. In the latter case, such efforts were repeatedly frustrated by falling produce prices. One result of this was that the reduced amount of cash available for investment by Ngwa men was typically devoted to financing trade, urban businesses, or the education of their sons, all of which could be expected to yield higher cash returns than the purchase of agricultural inputs.

The budget studies made of a neighboring and very similar village economy by Harris (1943) indicate that it could take a long time to build up the capital to make such investments. Efforts to increase agricultural production thus remained essential to keep up household consumption levels in the short run. In the prevailing context of capital and land scarcity such efforts necessarily placed heavy demands on labor. Up to the 1950s the continuing spread of cassava and its increasing use as a substitute for yams in the local diet, helped to increase yields per acre without threatening soil fertility. But the new crop demanded heavy female labor inputs for processing at a time when the volume of oil palm exports was continuing to increase, again placing heavy demands on female as well as male labor resources. In the export sector, at least, the statistics analyzed in this paper indicate that farmers were experiencing diminishing cash returns to these increasing labor inputs. Thus the second trend is at best one of thwarted intensification—running to stand still—and at worst one of involution, defined by Geertz (1968) and Chrétien (1983: 20–21) as the elaboration of inputs such that agricultural production keeps pace with demand but at the cost of decreasing returns to inputs (especially labor).

An obvious response to the involutionary trap is to search for off-farm occupations. From the 1950s this search gathered strength among the Ngwa, and it is the hallmark of the third trend established in this paper. In a period of increasingly rapid population growth, the withdrawal of much male labor from agriculture was not accompanied by any relaxation of the demands placed by food farmers on local land resources. Oil palm export production gradually declined but was replaced by increased cultivation of cassava, which was sold in urban markets as well as being eaten by full-time farmers as their staple food. Since the oil palm grew in natural symbiosis with long-fallow food farming and (unlike yams and cassava) was not cultivated in separate fields, the net result of the switch to cassava as a staple cash earner has been to increase demands on Ngwa land resources. As Goldman has shown in chapter 8, Igbo farmers in general have continued to experiment with new ways of increasing land productivity. Yet with limited supplies of labor and capital, and with no new cultivars to play the same kind of role as cassava did when it initially replaced yams earlier in the century, they have found this an almost impossible task. At best the situation can only be described as one of stagnation, in which existing techniques are being exploited to the full without radical innovation. At worst, as in some of the most densely populated Igbo villages studied by Lagemann (1977: 50–62), "soil mining"—a spiral of decreasing yields and increasing soil degradation—could set in.

Although Lagemann (1977) and Geertz (1968) associated the processes of involution and soil mining with population growth, in the Ngwa case the commercial changes that went on at the same time were equally important. A root cause of stagnation in agricultural techniques was capital scarcity, and this was closely related to declining world market prices and later to heavy government taxation of the main agricultural source of cash income, oil palm produce. These external forces also encouraged the withdrawal of labor from agriculture and the switch from oil palm to cassava as a cash crop, both of which have increased the risks of soil mining. At the same time, especially during the mineral oil boom of the 1970s, it became possible for some Ngwa households to improve their living standards and accumulate wealth through urban employment and "informal-sector" enterprises.

Given the Nigerian government's current policy of improving agricultural producer prices, there is every reason to hope that the new Ngwa rich will establish a fourth trend by starting to invest in agriculture. It could even happen, though this seems less likely, that the less successful young urban men will begin returning to work in the rural areas. In this case, the challenges posed by increasing population densities and depleted soils might begin to be met by renewed, effective innovation.

The Ngwa-Igbo Region: Location and Environment

The Ngwa region (fig. 9.1) lies at the heart of eastern Nigeria's oil palm belt, which has a long rainy season lasting from March to November,

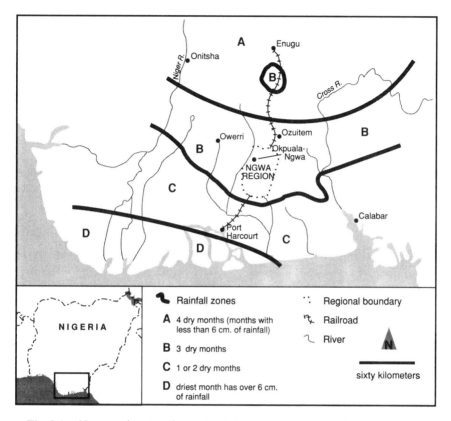

Fig. 9.1. Ngwa region: location and rainfall. Sources: Udo 1970; Ofomata 1975.

and an annual rainfall of between 2,030 and 2,540 mm. Local temperatures reach 28°C during the heavy rains of July and 34°C at the height of the dry season. The warmth and humidity of the Igbo region as a whole provide opportunities for growing a wide range of crops during a long growing season and are thus important environmental keys that, in association with local farmers' successful track record of experimenting with exotic cultivars, may help to explain its high population density.

Initially the Ngwa region was covered with dense rainforest, but by the beginning of the twentieth century it was fully settled by farmers practicing hoe-based long-fallow yam cultivation. Some Igbo and Ibibio farmers practice a mixture of upland and river-valley cultivation, but patterns of land use in the Ngwa region are more uniform because the local terrain is unusually flat, with few rivers or streams apart from the main Imo River itself (Mbagwu 1970: 25). The flat terrain also means that soil erosion is not a major problem by contrast with regions like Okigwi and Orlu to the north (Grove 1951).

Soil Degradation

The soils are deep, ferralitic, porous, and sandy. Udo (1970) also describes them as being leached and infertile, and this is an important environmental key to the problems facing farmers today. Several studies made of agriculture in the Ngwa and neighboring regions at intervals since 1930 indicate that the present degraded state of the local soils is the product of change over time. Evidence was collected in the late 1930s by J. S. Harris (1943), in 1954 by W. B. Morgan (1955), and in 1959–64 by T. C. Mbagwu (1970) and L. C. Uzozie (1971). All these studies provide valuable impressionistic data, although it must be emphasized at the outset that they cannot compare with more recent studies, for example Lagemann (1977), in statistical precision. Also the earlier authors were not consciously seeking to document changes in soil fertility over time. They were mainly interested in interregional comparisons, for example, of the effect on farmers' prosperity of variations in soil quality and marketing facilities and in comparing the cropping patterns used on different fields. A final limitation on the usefulness of the early studies is that they provide snapshots of just a few villages within the region rather than a comprehensive soil survey showing the full range of soil types and fallow periods within the farming systems of southeastern Nigeria. A major reason for this limitation was the tenuous and indirect nature of colonial rule in the region (Martin 1988: chaps. 3 and 9). The colonial Agricultural Department lacked both the power and the resources to make detailed estimates of soil fertility, except on its own experimental farms.

Fallow Cycles

Thus, the best evidence on the causes of soil mining comes from the cross-section survey conducted by Lagemann in 1974–75. Lagemann (1977: 9–11, 50–54, 64–68) confirmed the view held by colonial officials that the fertility of southeastern Nigerian soils could only be fully replenished by a fallow period of six years or more. He found that cassava yields varied proportionately with the fallow period in three Igbo villages with fallows of 1 to 3 years, 4 years, and 6 years, respectively. This suggests one way in which historical analysis could help establish the point at which soil mining began to occur in any one part of southeastern Nigeria: first find the date at which the fallow period fell below six years and then examine whether this fall was compensated for by any change in farming techniques designed to maintain the fertility of the more frequently cropped fields.

In the case of the Ngwa region, evidence from colonial records indicates that the fallow period was about seven years in 1917 but fell during the following decades to between four and six years (CSO 1917, 1927; Gardner 1929). Fallows were shortest in the more densely populated northern Ngwa region and longest to the south of Aba (fig. 9.2). This range of fallows was still prevalent when Morgan made his survey in 1954, but by the time of Mbagwu's 1960s survey, the fallows had fallen again to between two and five years. In 1980-81, when I did field work in the northern Ngwa region near Okpuala-Ngwa, fallows had fallen as low as one year on many farms, and the low yields gained for yams and cassava were a common topic of conversation.

This evidence indicates that land resources have been under pressure in the Ngwa region throughout the twentieth century and that the danger of soil mining has become especially acute over the past thirty years. The remaining sections of this chapter will explain the commercial as well as the demographic causes of this pressure on Ngwa land resources, and will describe the various land-use strategies that Ngwa farmers have developed in response.

Trade, Population, and Agricultural Growth in the Ngwa Region, 1900-1930

The Impact of Colonial Rule

On the eve of colonial rule, which was imposed over eastern Nigeria between 1901 and 1909, the Ngwa were actively engaged in expanding their agricultural production by both more intensive use of local oil palm resources and extending the area of land under cultivation. For several centuries they had been extending their settlements through the thinly populated areas to the north, south, and east of their original base at Okpuala-Ngwa (Oriji 1977: 50-87, 130-36).

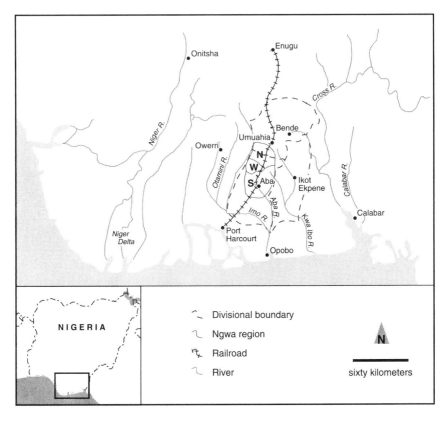

Fig. 9.2. Ngwa region: divisional boundaries, 1920s–1930s. Sources: Abacom 1930; CSO 1933–34.

British colonial officials effectively put a stop to this expansion, as their German counterparts did in neighboring Cameroon (Guyer 1984a: 11; Martin 1988: 22). They froze the boundaries of the Ngwa region at the limits reached by 1900 and spent much of their time during the 1910s and 1920s suppressing armed land disputes between the Ngwa and their southeastern Asa and Ibibio neighbors. The frequency of such disputes indicates that the Ngwa may well have been forced to abandon their strategy of expansion around 1900 even if colonial rule had not intervened, because they had already reached the limits of the thinly settled forest.

After 1900 the Ngwa turned their energies from colonizing new areas of virgin forest, toward the increased production of food crops and of palm oil and kernels for export, using the land surrounding their existing settlements. The main motive for these changes was probably to increase their standard of living rather than to respond to population pressure, because during the first twenty years of the century their population was growing slowly, if at all. In the southern Ngwa region (Aba Division) the 1921 census estimate of $67/km^2$ was actually lower than that of 1911 (table 9.1). Developments during the 1920s are harder to assess, because head taxes were introduced to eastern Nigeria in 1927, leading to an undercounting of men and to an even stronger resistance to the counting of women and children. The women's protest culminated in the Aba Riots or Igbo Women's War of 1929 (remembered by Ngwa women as the Women Riot). For this reason S.M. Jacob, the compiler of the 1931 Nigerian census, recommended that his figures for the Eastern Province should be scaled up by some 20 percent (Census 1931: 6, 23). Even if this is done (as in table 9.1), there remains little sign of rapid population growth during the 1920s. The estimated population density of Aba District in 1931 was above the 1921 estimate, having risen to $83/km^2$; but the density of Bende District (which included the northern Ngwa region and was not recorded in Talbot 1926) was estimated in 1931 at $107/km^2$, well below the 1911 census figure of $129/km^2$.

Table 9.1. Population Densities (per km^2), Eastern Nigeria, 1911–63

	1911	1921	1931	1953	1963
Northern Ngwa			133		
Western Ngwa			105		
Southern Ngwa			78		
Ngwa (average)			105		237
Divisions					
Aba	74	67	83	160	—
Bende	129	—	107	150	186
Ikot Ekpene	169	169	192	247	369

Sources: Census 1911: 634; Talbot 1926: Table 4; Census 1931: 97–99; Census 1953a: 3; Census 1953b: 2; Census 1963a: 1; Census 1963b: 3; Ngwa people: CSO 1933–34.

Note: These figures refer to the divisional boundaries established in 1921 (map 2). The only major change between then and 1963 was the establishment of a separate division for the Ngwa, which included most of the old Aba Division and part of the old Bende Division. The towns of Aba and Umuahia were excluded from the new Ngwa and Bende Divisions in the 1963 census figures. The old Aba Division had an area of 2,142 km^2 and a population of 178,000 in 1931; the old Bende Division had an area of 2,500 km^2 and a population of 267,000 then. The Ngwa inhabited an area of 1,228 km^2 in 1931, enlarged to 1,329 when the new Ngwa Division was formed.

The Introduction of New Crops

During the early twentieth century, Ngwa farmers were encouraged to pursue a higher standard of living by improvements in transport facilities and export prices that stimulated the expansion of palm oil and kernel production, and also by the availability of a new cultivar, cassava. Both the expansion of commercial palm production and the introduction of cassava fitted in well with the established patterns of innovation and intensification within Ngwa agriculture whereby farmers had taken advantage of international trading contacts to add to their range of cultivated crops and to gain access to foodstuffs, as well as manufactured goods, that could not be produced locally.

Such patterns of innovation may well help to explain one of the great paradoxes of African demographic history: the fact that eastern Nigeria that was severely affected by the Atlantic slave trade, emerged from it with one of the highest population densities in tropical Africa. During the period of the Atlantic slave trade a wide range of American food crops had been introduced to the Ngwa farming system (Harlan et al. 1976: 329–33), including not only starchy staples like maize, cocoyams, and plantains but also delicious fruits and vegetables like pineapples, peppers, and cherry tomatoes. These new cultivars made the forest diet varied and interesting. Cocoyams were especially important in helping to fill the "hungry season gap" that existed within the annual cycle of yam cultivation. Yams were harvested from July to December and could be stored above ground for several months if tied in latticework stacks that kept each tuber separate from the rest. However, these stocks rarely lasted until July. The cocoyam was harvested between January and June, providing an ideal supplementary staple food (Forde 1937; Harris 1938–39; interview with A. Chigbundu, Dec. 1980).[1]

The introduction of these cultivars helped to encourage migration into and within the wetter forest regions of eastern Nigeria, where the long growing season provided ideal conditions for their incorporation into the indigenous yam-farming systems. The wider availability of imported iron for use in making matchets (axes) facilitated population movement into areas of virgin forest by providing effective tools for land clearance. In this way, the imports associated with the Atlantic slave trade counteracted its direct demographic impact (Morgan 1959; Northrup 1978: 208–19). Later, during the nineteenth century, the switch from slave to palm produce exports was accompanied by a growing trade in

Dutch gin and Manchester salt, supplementing the established imports of cloth, iron, and guns (Latham 1973: 73-75). Dried Norwegian stockfish was added to this list of imports in the mid-twentieth century, supplementing the meager supplies of protein available in a region where diseases like sleeping sickness constrained the range of domestic animals that could be kept and where dense populations of spare-time hunters had virtually eliminated wild game (Basden 1966a: 30, 1966b: 306-8).

Meanwhile, agricultural intensification was also occurring within the Ngwa food-farming system through the incorporation of a new cultivar: cassava. This crop was brought to the Ngwa region by the middlemen and Christian pastors who moved inland along the newly cleared river trade routes after 1907. During and after World War I, more farmers saw cassava, learned how to process it in order to remove the poisonous prussic acid, discovered its value as a staple that could be harvested all year round, and planted it in the slack period within the cultivating season from May to September. As with other New World crops such as the cocoyam, it was women who were the first to experiment with cassava, which they could plant on the edges of yam fields or on land just entering into fallow, thus reducing the need to call on male cooperation for land clearing. Men generally adopted a scornful attitude to the new plant, and women spent a long time preparing it in a way that made it look as much like pounded yam as possible. Thus, although the new crop saved time on farming operations and increased output per hectare of land, it absorbed extra time in cooking. During the early years of cassava cultivation, when it was used as a supplement to yam cultivation rather than as a substitute for it, this innovation probably increased output per head while also increasing women's workloads. It therefore forms part of the same trend of intensification as the growth of oil palm export production (CSO 1917; Rivprof 1928; interviews of O. Kanu, A. Njoku, and A. Nwogu Feb. 1981; Guyer 1984b).[2]

The Oil Palm Export Trade

The long-established trading links between the Ngwa and the outside world were greatly strengthened in the early twentieth century by colonial efforts at river clearance, and by the opening of Nigeria's Eastern Railway in 1916 (fig. 9.2). The Imo River was navigable for six-ton trade canoes from 1907 to 1914 and again from 1927 onward, as clearing parties mounted an annual campaign against fallen trees and screw pine growth. Larger steel canoes could travel as far as Aba from 1907 onward. African traders from Opobo took immediate advantage of these transport improvements, establishing trading posts along the Aba and Imo Rivers as far as the northern Ngwa region, and often becoming the local agents of the European firms who came to dominate the railway trade (Martin 1988: 43–50). In turn, Ngwa farmers responded with enthusiasm to the arrival of the middlemen, especially as this came at a time when real export prices were soaring after a long late-nineteenth-century depression, reaching levels in 1910–14 that have never since been surpassed (tables 9.2 and 9.3).

The oil palm export industry was an ideal source of income for farmers in a densely populated region with little spare land, because the oil palm grows in natural symbiosis with long-fallow, root-crop cultivation. The export industry was essentially a processing industry that, by the early twentieth century, involved the labor of both men and women at various stages in a complex operation. Men climbed and harvested the palms; women separated the fruit from its bunches, and boiled it in preparation for some energetic pounding, which was performed by men. Women then undertook the more painstaking task of separating out the nuts and fibers of the fruit, squeezing the fibers to obtain oil and drying and cracking the nuts to obtain palm kernels. In regions with sparser population but a better water supply, in particular the Niger Delta, a less time-consuming method was used in which the fruit was not boiled, but was left to soften in a creek-side canoe and then washed and trodden to free the oil. The Ngwa method produced a higher-quality oil that could be used locally for cooking as well as be exported. Indeed, the Ngwas' Ibibio neighbors had already developed a thriving local trade exchanging oil for yams along the Cross River (Latham 1973: 5–7; Martin 1988: 32–34).

Over the period 1900–1930, exports of palm oil and palm kernels from the Ngwa, Ibibio, and neighboring regions more than doubled (table 9.2). The palm fruit used in producing these exports was harvested from the existing palms that had grown up in groves on the sites of abandoned compounds, or in ones and twos scattered around the fallowed yam fields. Following the British Colonial Office's decision to keep Nigerian land in African hands under communal systems of ownership, rather than alienating it to European planters, the oil palm industry continued to develop in a way that increased farmers' economic yield from their land without transforming local patterns of land use. In its early

Table 9.2. Palm-Produce Exports from Calabar, Opobo, and Port Harcourt, 1906–48 (thousand tons per annum: five-year averages)

	Palm kernels	Palm oil
1906–09[a]	31	26
1910–14	39	32
1915–19	Figures incomplete	
1920–24	52	45
1925–29	68	59
1930–34	81	65
1935–39	95	80
1940–44	125	77
1945–48[a]	122	71

Source: Archives listed in Martin 1988: 150–53.

[a]Four-year average.

Table 9.3. Total Palm-Produce Exports from Nigeria, 1906–64 (thousand tons per annum, five-year averages) and Barter Terms of Trade, 1910–48 (index: 1910–14 = 100)

	Palm kernels		Palm oil	
	Exports	Barter terms	Exports	Barter terms
1906–09[a]	136	—	68	—
1910–14	174	100	78	100
1915–19	185	44	80	50
1920–24	203	27	90	32
1925–29	255	34	123	38
1930–34	275	24	122	21
1935–39	330	28	136	25
1940–44	321	12	134	11
1945–49	318	18	130	18
1950–54	401	—	180	—
1955–59	432	—	174	—
1960–64	397	—	145	—
1964–66[b]	409	—	145	—
1970–72[b]	213	—	10	—
1976–78[b]	172	—	2	—

Source: Helleiner 1966: Table IV-A-B; Kirk-Green and Rimmer 1981: 74; and on barter terms of trade: Martin 1988: 146–47.

[a]Four-year average.

[b]Three-year average.

stages, the expansion of the industry also increased local incomes per head because the processing activities described above were carried out in the spare time left between busy farming days, which in turn were fairly evenly spread throughout the year. During the 1920s, as production continued to expand and the first strains on labor supplies were beginning to appear, Ngwa farmers began to experiment with the labor-saving Niger Delta style of oil processing, indicating a willingness to innovate in order to continue the trend of agricultural intensification that the initial expansion of the industry had begun (Martin 1988: 50–55, 100–102).

Intensification Thwarted, 1930–1950

Before World War I, rising export volumes were accompanied by rising incomes. However, during the war, the terms of trade began to turn against the Ngwa and other African commodity producers (table 9.3). From the 1920s onward, further increases in export production were no longer a means by which farmers increased their standard of living but rather a means by which they struggled to restore their incomes to the levels enjoyed before the war. Their struggle was ultimately unsuccessful: between 1925–29 and 1945–49 the income terms of trade (that is, the real purchasing power of exports produced) fell by 41 percent for palm oil producers, and 5 percent for palm kernel producers, despite increases of 20 percent and 79 percent in their respective volumes of output (tables 9.2 and 9.4).

In theory this struggle could have stimulated a search for labor-saving innovation, continuing the trend of intensification. But in practice such innovations were slow to appear for three main reasons. First, the labor-saving Niger Delta method of oil processing, mentioned above, was of limited use because it produced a lower grade of oil: European buying firms were becoming more quality-conscious at this time, reinforcing the long-held preferences of Nigerian consumers. Second, labor-saving oil processing machinery was still at the experimental stage and was extremely expensive, although 362 Duscher hand presses had been bought from the Agricultural Department by eastern Nigerian farmers by 1936. Perhaps the most important reason was the third: that the people within Ngwa society who controlled most of the income from palm oil production—senior men—were finding it increasingly difficult to control the people who did most of the work in export production—women and junior men.

Table 9.4. Income Terms of Trade for Palm-
Produce Exports from Calabar, Opobo, and Port
Harcourt (1910-14 = 100)

	Palm kernels	Palm oil
1910-14	100	100
1915-19	Figures incomplete	
1920-24	36	45
1925-29	59	70
1930-34	50	42
1935-39	67	63
1940-44	40	26
1945-49	56	41

Sources: Same as for tables 9.2 and 9.3.

Within Igbo society in general, senior men, the holders of each patrilineage's ceremonial staff or *ofo* controlled access to lineage land and were entitled to a share of the yams and palm oil produced by junior lineage members (CSO 1933-34; Meek 1950: 106-9). However, during the 1920s and 1930s these rights began to be challenged by several groups of young men, and others began to turn to off-farm work in their spare time as a means of earning cash that lineage heads would have no established rights over. Meanwhile, senior men were spending a large part of their income on bridewealth payments and on loans made to secure the loyalty, and often the labor, of clients. They were also becoming increasingly skilled in the use of the new Native Court machinery to reinforce their control over the natural resources used in yam and palm oil production. Ultimately these tactics secured their control over the dwindling income from palm oil export production, but litigation was as expensive as marriage and patronage, and all three tactics left them with little spare cash to invest in machinery (Martin 1988: chaps. 5, 7, and 8).

In the absence of labor-saving innovation, and in the colonial framework of fixed village boundaries, growth in output could only be achieved by applying more labor to the local land resources. Ngwa efforts to expand palm oil and kernel production were assisted by the growth of the local population, which rose by 100 percent and 50 percent in the Aba and Bende Divisions respectively between 1931 and 1953 (table 9.1). In turn this population growth required an increase in food production. In both areas, the burden of increased labor inputs was borne to a disproportionate extent by women. Although men continued to be involved in palm oil processing and in farm cultivation as before, the center of gravity of Ngwa commercial agriculture was shifting away from these activities, toward those that women controlled. This is partly a reflection of women's own willingness to shoulder extra workloads in order to maintain household consumption levels. The volume of palm kernel exports rose by 80 percent, markedly faster than the region's population between 1925–29 and 1945–48; and cassava emerged as an increasingly important cash crop for local urban consumption, processed into the fine grainy form of *garri* (Nwabughuogu 1981: 214–17, 258–59). Ngwa women interviewed in the early 1980s (Kanu, Nwannunu, and Nwosu)[3] recalled that they spent most of the money thus earned on food, for example stockfish, and clothing for their children.

Although Ngwa women did their best to maintain their family incomes by increased production during this period, falling produce prices meant that their attempts were doomed to failure. Meanwhile, it proved impossible to minimize the time spent in kernel-cracking by innovation: early colonial experiments proved that this is an exceptionally difficult activity to mechanize (Boyle 1915). In the area of garri production, women obtained some relief when young men began to help them with grating the raw cassava root, but at the same time they were experiencing increased labor burdens overall as cassava began to replace yams within the Ngwa farming system.

By 1954 cassava was no longer being planted just along the fringes of yam fields but was being interplanted along the rows of well-established yams in the middle of their growing season, during July and August. The planting and harvesting of cassava, as well as most of the processing, continued to be women's work so that the gradual displacement of yams by cassava involved a switch from male to female labor in staple-crop planting and harvesting. Since cassava tolerates poorer soils than yams, this switch enabled farmers to keep up the nutrient yields from fields that had been on relatively short (four to six years) fallow cycles since the late 1920s and may even have delayed the further reduction in fallow periods that eventually began in the 1950s by enabling more food to be produced on existing fields than had been possible when yams were the dominant crop (Morgan 1955: 331).

While women shouldered a greater share of household labor burdens, junior men turned their ambitions, and eventually their energies, elsewhere. The movement of junior men off the farm had its origins partly in the social conflicts and in the reinforcement of the *ofo*-holders' power outlined earlier and partly in the coming of colonial rule and Christianity. For the lucky few, tremendous opportunities for emancipation were offered by the growth of colonial towns, with their distinctive job opportunities in domestic service, building, dock, and clerical work. Conversion to Christianity also had an emancipating effect because the new church hierarchies were quite different from those of ordinary village society, and because education opened the door to many of the better-paid urban jobs. Finally, the low real-price levels of palm produce during the 1920s and 1930s encouraged the belief that the best way to make a fortune was to work for the middlemen or the Europeans, or even to invest in a bicycle and set up as an independent trader.

In 1980–81 I was able to interview a number of men who, having held this belief in youth between the 1920s and the 1940s, had later used their savings to redeem pledged family land or to marry, and returned to agriculture. But it was noticeable that many of them retained sideline activities like herbalism or builder's contracting and had heavily invested in education for their sons (and, more recently, daughters) who were now pursuing lucrative urban careers. Their life stories underpin the general observation that temporary rural-urban migration was giving way to a more permanent change in careers by the 1960s, leading to an acute shortage of young male family labor in rural Ngwa households even before the Nigerian Civil War and the oil boom of the 1970s (Mbagwu 1970: chap. 5; Berry 1985; Martin 1988: chaps. 6–8). This withdrawal of male labor from the land, combined with a continuing shortage of local investment and the withdrawal of government credit schemes for mechanization after 1950, helped to push the Ngwa agricultural system still further away from the path of intensification. After 1950, while off-farm incomes grew, the women who remained on the farm with their children faced an increasingly difficult struggle to feed their household without further impoverishing their soils.

Taxation, Population Growth, and Agricultural Stagnation, 1950–1980

The tendency of young Ngwa men to move away from agriculture was reinforced after the mid-1950s by colonial economic policies, which in turn set the tone for the policies pursued by Nigeria's independent governments toward the agricultural sector. During and after World War II Nigerian palm kernels were in high demand on the world markets, but real producer prices continued to fall (by 42 percent between 1952 and 1964) because the Marketing Boards were following a policy of accumulating sterling reserves (Helleiner 1966: 160–62). They were also raising funds to pay for development projects, but none of these were oriented toward the palm kernel industry. Most of the development money spent on the palm oil industry was used to establish large-scale Pioneer oil mills that were outside the farmers' control. In 1950 a popular loan scheme to enable farmers to buy Duscher hand presses was terminated and since then the only credit schemes available have been associated with schemes to encourage the planting of improved varieties of oil palm (Kilby 1967: 189–94; Usoro 1974: 88–110). Although admirable in themselves, especially because the new palms were shorter and thus removed the need for dangerous and time-consuming tree climbing by harvesters, these schemes could not solve the key problem of low producer prices for palm produce. During my stay in the Ngwa region in 1980–81, I found that even where farmers had planted the new palms they often preferred later to invest in urban housing or poultry farms, rather than in the paid male labor needed to fertilize and harvest the trees.

In the wake of the Marketing Boards' final blow to agricultural incomes, young Ngwa men turned more firmly toward the urban economy whose growth was soaring, not the least because of growing employment opportunities in tax-funded government offices. The population of Aba grew from 58,000 to over 130,000 between 1953 and 1963, while that of Port Harcourt grew from 72,000 to almost 200,000, and that of Umuahia from under 20,000 to 155,000. Meanwhile, as the population density of the rural Ngwa region itself soared, more than doubling from 100/km^2 to 237/km^2 between 1931 and 1963 (table 9.1), cassava rose to dominance as the staple Ngwa foodstuff. In 1964 Mbagwu (1970: 56–78, 229–45) found that in the northern Ngwa area, where densities were well above the Ngwa average, the fallow period had shrunk to two years and cassava was cultivated in full fields, not just between the rows of yams as in the previous intercropping system. Elsewhere in the Ngwa region cassava was being grown as a cash crop and processed into garri for urban sale. This practice absorbed time formerly taken up with palm oil production and allowed female farmers to keep up their incomes in the wake of the collapse of palm produce prices. By the time I lived in the northern Ngwa area in 1980–81, cassava had replaced palm produce as the main cash crop there too, although some palm oil was still being produced for sale on the domestic market, which now absorbs all of Nigeria's production (table 9.3).

Through their expansion of cassava production Ngwa women have coped with the withdrawal of male labor and the collapse of the oil palm export economy. But this achievement has been won at great cost to local land resources. Although cassava is not a land-hungry crop by comparison with the yam, it makes much greater demands on local soils than the oil palm that typically grows up as part of the secondary forest on fallow land, or in dense groves on the sites of abandoned compounds (Hartley 1977: 4–7). Before the introduction of the 1950s planting schemes, cultivation of the oil palm in the Ngwa region typically meant avoiding cutting it down when clearing land for farming; the tree thrives alongside yams, cassava, grain, and vegetables in the local intercropping system. By contrast, cassava is not a fallow crop; it can be planted on a field about to go into fallow after yam cultivation, but it does not form part of the secondary forest fallow vegetation that restores land fertility. Furthermore, although it can tolerate shorter fallows than the yam, it cannot tolerate the fallows of one to three years that are common in the Ngwa region today (Morgan 1955; Uzozie 1971). By the 1970s, the process of soil mining identified by Lagemann for the Igbo village of Umuokile had begun in the Ngwa region, too. The people I lived with in the early 1980s dated this profound transition to the period of the Nigerian Civil War. For the Ngwa region, in the heart of Biafra, the war had brought intense suffering that marked the watershed between a time of ample yam supplies and income and the present time when "life is hard in the Nigeria" (Martin 1988: chap. 10).

Despite the general decline of agricultural incomes and land yields evident over the past thirty years, two encouraging developments have occurred that show that the search for means of successful agricultural intensification has not altogether ceased. First, as Morgan noted in 1955, ideal conditions for the growth of manured compound farming were created by the rise of permanent settlement during the early colonial period following the freezing of village boundaries. As population pressure grew after 1930, increasingly creative use was made of compound land, for example, by planting plantain trees on the site of old latrines. Mbagwu emphasized the importance of compound farms as a source of yams and vegetables during the 1960s; Lagemann noted the increased attention being paid to compound farms in the more densely populated villages of his 1970s survey. Some farmers were even applying chemical fertilizer to their compound pineapples during my stay in the northern Ngwa region in the early 1980s. It remains unclear whether such refinements of the compound farming system have done more than simply compensate for the impact of declining yields on the cassava fields, so that, although the process of soil mining may have been arrested, successful intensification has not been achieved. Yet this development remains a positive sign of farmers' desire to maintain and take advantage of more fertile soils wherever possible; a sign that suggests that they would be likely to take up new methods of restoring the outlying fields' fertility if viable methods were made available and supported by credit provision.

The second encouraging development within Ngwa agriculture has been the adoption of cassava-grating machinery, which Mbagwu (1970: 211–35) recorded in the southern Ngwa region in 1964–65. In the village of Obegu there were twenty-four machines hired out to cassava growers to grind up the raw root. At that time there were no such machines in the northern Ngwa region, but by 1981 they were widely used there, too. Typically they were owned by a wealthier older man who would make a small charge each time a woman brought her cassava to his compound for grating. The adoption of these machines has cut out one of the most labor-intensive stages of garri production, and indicated the continuing willingness of at least some senior Ngwa men to finance agricultural intensification when the activity concerned is profitable. Given the recent Nigerian government's decision to increase agricultural producer prices, further developments of this kind may well occur, even without the intervention of agricultural extension workers.

Conclusion

The agricultural changes that have occurred in the Ngwa region over the past eighty years include elements of three main patterns: successful intensification; thwarted intensification, verging on involution; and stagnation, with a growing risk of soil mining. The period of rapid population growth since 1930 has also been the period when the greatest risks of involution, and later soil mining, have emerged. Yet there is no inevitable link between population pressure and such negative forms of agricultural change. Population growth in itself can stimulate any number of different patterns of agricultural change, including the extension of cultivation into fresh areas as well as the three patterns of change identified above. Furthermore, agricultural stagnation need not imply overall economic stagnation and declining standards of living if, as in the Ngwa case, it is accompanied by a rapid growth in off-farm activities and incomes.

The Ngwa were halted in their process of territorial expansion in the early twentieth century by Ibibio opposition and by the imposition of colonial rule. Since then they have never stopped exploring the alternative options for increased production and improved standards of living. In the pivotal period of the 1930s to 1950s, commercial forces and government taxation tipped the balance between successful and fruitless agricultural intensification and so helped to stimulate investment outside agriculture. Since the 1950s this outside investment has been accompanied by growing occupational diversification. As Nigeria's mineral oil boom comes to an end, the diversification process is becoming more difficult to sustain, and the pursuit of successful agricultural intensification is once more being seen by officials as essential, not least to provide food for a growing population. The historical evidence in the Ngwa case suggests that by giving appropriate technical assistance and favorable economic incentives to small farmers, such a pursuit could well be successful. Ngwa farmers still have the energy and innovative flair to support a renewed trend of agricultural growth if they perceive this as being worth their while.

Notes

1. Mr. A. A. Chigbundu, aged c. 60, of Ahiaba-Okpuala, 19 Dec. 1980.
2. Mrs. Onyema Sabina Kanu, aged c. 100, of Umuala, 24, 28 Dec. 1980; Achonna Njoku, aged c. 80, of Umuacha, 13 Feb. 1981; Augustine Amaeze Nwogu, aged c. 75, of Amiri, 6 and 8 Feb. 1981.
3. Mrs. Onyema Sabina Kanu, 13 Feb. 1981; Mrs. Jemima Nwakwa Nwannunu, aged c. 75, of Umuacha, 21 Dec. 1980; Mrs. Selina Danne Nwosu, aged c. 65, of Ahiaba-Okpuala, 15 Dec. 1980 and 21 Feb. 1981.

References

Abacom. 1930. *Report of the Commission of Inquiry [Aba Commission] Appointed to Inquire into the Disturbances in the Calabar and Owerri Provinces, December 1929.* United Kingdom Public Record Office (U.K.P.R.O.) file C.O. 583/176/1002/1930.
Basden, G. T. 1966a [1921]. *Among the Ibos of Nigeria.* London: Frank Cass.
_____. 1966b [1938]. *Niger Ibos.* London: Frank Cass.

Berry, S.S. 1985. *Fathers Work for Their Sons*. Berkeley: University of California Press.

Boserup, E. 1965. *The Conditions of Agricultural Growth*. Chicago: Aldine.

Boyle. 1915. Letter from Boyle to Bonar Law, 12 Aug. 1915. U.K.P.R.O. file C.O. 554/24

Census. 1911. *Report on the Southern Nigeria Census, 1911*, U.K.P.R.O. file C.O. 592/9.

_____. 1927. Assessment Reports, Aba Division, 1927. Ibadan Archives file CSO 26/20610.

_____. 1931. *Census of Nigeria, 1931, Vol. I, Nigeria*. Lagos: Government Printer, 1933.

_____. 1933-34. Supplementary Intelligence Reports on the Ngwa, by J.G.C. Allen, Nos. I-III. Ibadan Archives file CSO 26/29033.

_____. 1953a. *Population Census of Nigeria, 1952-53*, Nigeria, Department of Statistics. Lagos: Government Printer, n.d.

_____. 1953b. *Statistical Digest, 1966*, 4th ed. (Eastern Nigeria). Enugu: Government Printer, 1967.

_____. 1963a. *Statistical Digest, 1968-B70* (South-Eastern State of Nigeria). Calabar: Government Printer, 1971.

_____. 1963b. *Statistical Digest, 1971* (Eastern-Central State of Nigeria). Enugu: Government Printer, 1974.

Chrétien, J.P., ed. 1983. *Histoire Rurale de l'Afrique des Grands Lacs: Guide de Recherche*. Paris: Karthala.

CSO. 1917. Extract of a Report by the Director of Agriculture, 10 Aug. 1917. Ibadan Archives file CSO 19/5, N 2037/1917.

Forde, C.D. 1937. "Land and Labour in a Cross River Village, Southern Nigeria." *Geographical Journal* 90: 24-51.

Gardner. 1929. Letter from Gardner to Resident, Owerri Province, 29 May 1929, Enugu Archives file Abadist 1/1/12, C4/1929.

Geertz, C. 1968. *Agricultural Involution: The Process of Ecological Change in Indonesia*. Berkeley: University of California Press.

Grove, A.T. 1951. "Soil Erosion and Population Problems in South-Eastern Nigeria." *Geographical Journal* 117: 291-306.

Guyer, J.I. 1984a. *Family and Farm in Southern Cameroon*. African Research Studies No. 15. Boston: Boston University African Studies Center.

_____. 1984b. "Naturalism in Models of African Production." *Man* N.S. 19: 371-88.

Harlan, J.R., J.M.J. de Wet, and A. Stemler, eds. 1976. *Origins of African Plant Domestication*. Paris and the Hague: Mouton.

Harris, J.S. 1938-39. Ibo Papers, 1938-9. 2: Ozuitem Food Crops. Manuscript. African Manuscripts 1505 (8), Rhodes House, Oxford.

_____. 1943. "Papers on the Economic Aspect of Life among the Ozuitem Ibo." *Africa* 14: 19-23.

Hartley, C. W. S. 1977 [1967]. *The Oil Palm (Elaeis Guineensis Jacq.)*. London: Longman.

Helleiner, G. K. 1966. *Peasant Agriculture, Government and Economic Growth in Nigeria*. Homewood, Ill.: Richard D. Irwin.

Kilby, P. 1967. "The Nigerian Palm Oil Industry." *Food Research Institute Studies* 7(2): 189–94.

Kirk-Greene, A., and D. Rimmer. 1981. *Nigeria Since 1970*. London: Hodder and Stoughton.

Lagemann, J. 1977. *Traditional African Farming Systems in Eastern Nigeria: An Analysis of Reaction to Increasing Population Pressure*. Munich: Weltforum Verlag.

Latham, A. J. H. 1973. *Old Calabar, 1600–1891*. Oxford: Clarendon Press.

Martin, S. M. 1988. *Palm Oil and Protest: An Economic History of the Ngwa Region, South-Eastern Nigeria, 1800–1980*. Cambridge: Cambridge University Press.

Mbagwu, T. C. 1970. "The Oil Palm Economy in Ngwaland (Eastern Nigeria)." Ph.D. dissertation, University of Ibadan.

Meek, C. K. 1950 [1937]. *Law and Authority in a Nigerian Tribe*. London: Oxford University Press.

Morgan, W. B. 1955. "Farming Practice, Settlement Pattern and Population Density in South-Eastern Nigeria." *Geographical Journal* 121: 320–33.

———. 1959. "The Influence of European Contact on the Landscape of Southern Nigeria." *Geographical Journal* 125: 48–64.

Northrup, D. 1978. *Trade without Rulers*. Oxford: Clarendon Press.

Nwabughuogu, A. I. 1981. "Political Change, Social Response and Economic Development: The Dynamics of Change in Eastern Nigeria, 1930–1950." Ph.D. diss., Dalhousie University.

Ofomata, G. E. K., ed. 1975. *Nigeria in Maps: Eastern States*. Benin City: Ethiope Publishing House.

Oriji, J. N. 1977. "A History of the Ngwa People: Social and Economic Developments in an Igbo Clan from the Thirteenth to the Twentieth Centuries." Ph.D. dissertation, The State University of New Jersey, New Brunswick.

Rivprof. 1928. D.Os., Aba and Bende, to Resident, Owerri Province, 11 and 21 June 1928, Enugu Archives file Rivprof 8/15/390, O W 482/27.

Talbot, P. A. 1926. *The Peoples of Southern Nigeria, Vol. IV, Linguistics and Statistics*. London: Oxford University Press.

Udo, R. K. 1970. *Geographical Regions of Nigeria*. London: Heinemann.

Usoro, E. J. 1974. *The Nigerian Oil Palm Industry: Government Policy and Export Production, 1906–65*. Ibadan: Ibadan University Press.

Uzozie, L. C. 1971. "Patterns of Crop Combination in the Three Eastern States of Nigeria." *Journal of Tropical Geography*, 33: 62–72.

10 / Agricultural Stagnation and Economic Diversification: Awka-Nnewi Region, Nigeria, 1930–1980

Francis C. Okafor

Where the quantity and quality of land are wanting in agrarian societies, the physiological requirements of the populace may not be met, and environmental and economic disequilibria of varying dimensions may occur as demand for agricultural products increases. In wealthy communities, this disequilibrium can be countered by the use of a wide array of technologies that counteract environmental degradation. In poor communities such as exist throughout most of sub-Saharan Africa, farmers must make adjustments with far fewer technological options, particularly those that require capital outlay, and, therefore, may reach beyond the agricultural sector for livelihood options.

The agricultural situation throughout most of southeastern Nigeria exemplifies the latter case. Growing populations have given rise to very high population densities of farmers who attempt to meet their needs within a relatively poor physical environment for intensive agriculture. Their agricultural adjustments in this situation heavily rely on traditional technologies and procedures that have intensified cultivation on decreasing land holdings and on diversification of income from nonfarm activities.

Despite the knowledge that concentrated populations supported by comparatively intensive cultivation have had a long history in southeastern Nigeria, few records exist with which to detail the dynamics of population-agriculture relationships. This study focuses on the Awka-Nnewi region for the time period 1930 to 1980. The primary source of data is a detailed field survey of thirty-six villages in eight Local Government Areas (LGAs) carried out initially in 1976–77 and updated in 1982. Questionnaires were administered to a sample of heads of farming households in order to obtain information on land and labor activities. Additional information was gathered by means of informal discussions with farmers; they supplied information on cultivation methods, crop mixes, and soil-fertility maintenance. Analysis of this information is enhanced by comparisons to locales in the study area that are, comparatively, more sparsely settled and have more fertile soils.

Awka-Nnewi Region

Southeastern Nigeria, comprising the present Akwa-Ibom, Anambra, Cross-River, Imo, and Rivers states of Nigeria, stands out prominently on maps of sub-Saharan Africa that show population distribution and crude densities (fig. 10.1). The Awka-Nnewi region (fig. 10.2) is the core of this population concentration. Land in this area remains a scarce resource on which various adjustments in agricultural practices, settlement structures, and land-tenure systems have been made to accommodate the needs of the increasing number of people. The Awka-Nnewi region, for the purposes of this study, refers to eight out of the twenty-three LGAs in the Anambra State of Nigeria. The eight LGAs—Anambra, Aguata, Awka, Idemili, Ihiala, Njikoka, Nnewi, and Onitsha—constitute a contiguous area situated in the southeastern section of Nigeria and forming part of the eastern portion of the lower Niger plains. The eight LGAs cover an area of 4,416 km² that represents one-third of the Anambra state's total area. The region extends from 5°43′ N to 6°45′ N and from 6°55′ E to 8°16′ E (fig. 10.1).

The eight LGAs constitute the core area of one of the most densely settled zones of Nigeria (indeed, of Africa) and are generally acknowledged to have relatively poor conditions, at least soilwise, for agriculture, with the exception of a few narrow riverine strips. The Igbo inhabit the region, sharing a common culture and responding similarly to the land's intensive pressures by way of rural-to-rural migration, rural-to-urban migration, and engaging in nonfarm activities.

Finally, the Awka-Nnewi region possesses some locational attributes that provide the opportunity for studying the rural economy as it relates to both the region and the surrounding area. This region constitutes the most immediate rural hinterland of Onitsha (fig. 10.2), a river port on the left bank of the River Niger, and the site of one of the leading urban markets in West Africa. Daily and periodic markets generate vigorous

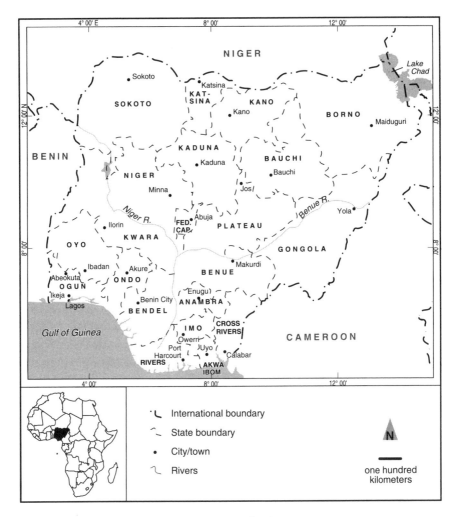

Fig. 10.1. Nigeria

regional trade for foodstuffs. Enugu-Ukwa, the capital city of Anambra State, is located about sixty kilometers northeast of the Awka-Nnewi region (fig. 10.2), and it exerts an areal influence. Throughout the Awka-Nnewi region there is a fast-developing transport network serving many hitherto isolated rural communities, and there is also a growing cash and exchange economy brought about by urban-rural interrelationships and by rural economic growth.

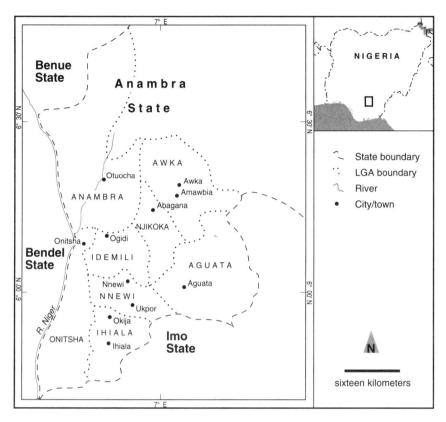

Fig. 10.2. Awka-Nnewi region. Source: Ofomata 1975.

Environmental Setting

Agricultural change is in part a function of the inherent or natural qualities of the area farmed. The constituents of relief, soil quality, precipitation, and drainage contribute to an areal differentiation in productivity of any agricultural region. The Awka-Nnewi region does not have sharp contrasts in physical makeup, but microvariations accentuate the variance in the pattern of agricultural change. The river floodplains in the western section of the region, and the hills, valley bottoms, and rough terrains in different parts of the region possess different composites of fertility and the soil's water-holding capacity.

Climatically, the Awka-Nnewi region is uniform, falling within that part of southeastern Nigeria that has a well-defined rainy season of six to seven months (April to October) and a pronounced dry season of five to six months (November to March). Reliable weather records are not available for the survey villages and towns, but the mean annual rainfall in the region is in the order of 2,300 mm, with peaks in July and September and a break in August. Applying Mohr's (1944) definition of a dry month as one with less than 60 mm of rainfall, the Awka-Nnewi region has three dry months in the year (December to February). This drought constrains crop growth from late November to about early March, and it is only in the riverine plains that year-round cultivation is possible. The latitudinal location of the Awka-Nnewi region exposes it to abundant and constant insolation. The mean daily maximum temperature is usually above 27° C all through the year. It is highest in February and April, but does not exceed 35° C.

It must be emphasized that these climatic characteristics are averages. Local and annual fluctuations, particularly in rainfall, characterize the region, and are of great agricultural importance. Rainfall strongly affects yields and timing of farming activities. Furthermore, the general intensity of the rainfall and the local variations caused by differences in topography are significant in terms of their impact on soil fertility, soil erosion, and leaching.

If the vegetal cover in the Awka-Nnewi region were to bear a close relationship to the climate, the region would carry a dense tropical rainforest, only slightly modified by the geological and topographical diversity of the area. With the exception of the Niger-Anambra floodplains dominated by fresh-water mangrove and raffia palms, however, the primary forest cover has been reduced by human activity to a secondary plant cover, so much so that large parts of the area may be termed an oil palm bush, from the ubiquitousness of oil palms in protected reserves and in crop farms. Generally, only a few trees of economic value have escaped clearance through firing and other human activities. In some areas, forest has given way to a "derived" savanna and farmland mosaic. High forest remains only along the main rivers and around sacred shrines.

The immediate result of forest degradation, apart from the scarcity of firewood and wood for house construction, yam stakes and fencing poles, is the widespread incidence of soil erosion. Soil erosion dominates the landscape and is threatening the very existence of a large section of the community. Soil deterioration and degradation, in terms of the progressive loss of nutrients and breakdown of soil structure, occur almost universally over the region. Ofomata (1976) has estimated that about 47 percent of southeastern Nigeria is affected by one form of soil erosion or another. Fluvial and sheet types of erosion are more widespread and affect the entire upland section of the region.

More notorious and devastating is the gully erosion in the Aguata around Agulu, Oko, Awgbu, Nanka, Ekwulobia, Aguluezechukwu, and Nkpologwu in Aguata LGA, and Nnobi, Alor, Ojoto, Obosi, and Nkpor in Idemili LGA. Soil erosion in these two areas is mainly due to physical factors of the environment, although the human components are not entirely absent. The high rainfall intensity of the region accelerates the action of some tributary streams that initiate and advance headward erosion into their source region, which is an escarpment underlain by friable sandstone. Thus, this form of lithology susceptible to quick erosion, coupled with concentrated runoff resulting from heavy downpours, has contributed immensely to the development of spectacular gullies and "badland" topography aptly described by Floyd: "The resultant landscape today is catastrophic in its dimensions. Facing the observer on the scarp edge are the cliffed walls of a large erosion amphitheater or complex of gullies. In the foreground, a gasping chasm fully a quarter of a mile wide and 350 feet deep has exposed highly colored layers of soil, sands and clays—deep red, yellow, white, pink, even violet in hue. Against these colors is set the dark green foliage of relict patches of rainforest which have slumped into the ravines, elsewhere, the disintegrating soil has left vivid red smears down the gully walls" (1969: 69).

In the other parts of the escarpment not yet seriously affected, insufficient fallowing of farmland, overcropping, deforestation by tree cutting and forest fires, and indiscriminate creation of pathways have helped to promote gully erosion.

In spite of wide-scale occurrence of devastation by erosion, soil-conservation measures are still undertaken without coordination. Although the federal government has intensified erosion checking in this region, the menace of soil erosion still stares the local farmers in the face, forcing them individually to adopt several curative and preventive measures. Some of these measures observed during the field work include: (1) construction of contour "bunds" and "dwarf" walls to prevent excessive runoff and overgrazing by stray domestic animals; (2) planting of earth-holding trees such as cashews, Indian bamboo, and bahama grass; (3) construction of side drains, "soak-away" pits, and earthen dams; (4) dumping of refuse at gully heads to hold the soil and prevent it from slumping; and (5) use of "wave-bedding" planting techniques and of terracing as soil-protection devices.

There is, however, very little evidence to indicate that these measures achieve much success. As the pressure of population mounts, the incidence and hazards of soil erosion are escalating, leading to further loss of scarce land and deterioration of soil fertility. More ominous is the fact that the highland areas most susceptible to erosion hold the concentrations of population and settlement, whereas the plains are relatively sparsely populated.

Soils are a resource of major agricultural importance in the Awka-Nnewi region, and the inherent fertility of the soils has become a critical factor in the agricultural potential. The soil types reflect both the climatic uniformity and the geological-topographical diversity of the region. The entire area overlies rocks of the Tertiary and Cretaceous ages. The rocks show great variation in grain size and in mineral composition, ranging from very coarse-grained sandstones to shales and clays.

A generalized subdivision of the soils on the basis of productivity can be made based on the FAO genetic classification system. The first group are the hydromorphic soils derived from recently deposited materials. These soils include the pale brown loamy alluvial soils of the Niger-Anambra Plains and the Mamu River floodplains (fig. 10.3). These soils are perennially moist and replenished by annual floods. Potentials exist for the use of these soils for swamp rice and other crops, if drainage can be controlled. The moist soil conditions even in the dry season make it possible to raise "early" crops, in particular vegetables for the neighboring urban centers.

More widespread are the ferrallitic soils—unconsolidated sands and sandstones rich in free iron but low in mineral reserve—that lose fertility very rapidly under cultivation. This soil group occurs in all other parts of the Awka-Nnewi region except the floodplains. A prominent characteristic of this group is a wide occurrence of the red earths or the acid sands (Grove 1951). The soils are acidic, with a pH of 5.0–5.5 on the surface, and, consequently, most of the cultigens must be tolerant to acidity. The profile is poorly developed, and excessive leaching occurs. But under a forest cover, there is a well-developed horizon below the litter, consisting of red-brown loamy sand with roots and plant residues (Obihara 1961). The acidity increases with depth as a result of the natural removal of bases from the depths and their subsequent deposition on the surface through root action on leaf fall from forest trees and high

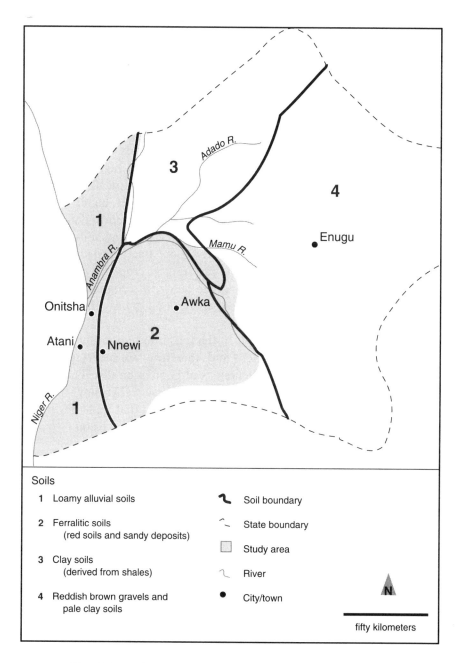

Fig. 10.3. Soil types, Awka-Nnewi region. Source: Floyd 1969.

bush. Under cultivation, these soils become more acidic through loss of organic matter but because they are easy to work, they are intensively farmed under the traditional rotational bush fallow. These soils are perhaps capable of being raised to high fertility by the actions of long fallow or through intensive application of manure or chemical fertilizer.

In the absence of soil-capability data at a local scale, some qualitative statements can be made about soil-fertility differentials in the Awka-Nnewi region. In the Niger-Anambra lowlands with the young hydromorphic soils, the loam and clay soils possess high amounts of available nitrogen that encourages abundant production of food crops for the surrounding soil-deficient region. On the other hand, the acid sands and the lateritic soils of the uplands are frequently deficient in most basic nutrients. Although it takes less time for sand soils to reach field capacity after the onset of rains, the more finely structured loam soils retain more water and, therefore, can support crops for longer periods after the rains end. Local farmers are quick to recognize the different soil types and their fertility characteristics and modify their farming methods accordingly.

On the whole, most of the soils in the region have poor nutrient status and low organic matter content and, therefore, are a very poor medium for plant growth. In the discussions of population distribution and land use that follow, it will be useful to recall these soil groups and their characteristics because it is the poor soil condition that underlies much of the population-pressure problems of the Awka-Nnewi region.

Population and Its Change

The primary problem faced by any researcher dealing with population studies in Nigeria is the all-pervading deficiency of data. Both political and logistical factors have militated against an accurate census in the country (Aluko 1965: 371). Official population counts in Nigeria began as early as 1866 (Olusanya 1975: 254), with decennial censuses taken in 1911, 1921, 1931, and 1952–53. The year 1941 was omitted because of World War II. However, the first population census with fairly detailed statistics was not taken until 1952–53. Regrettably, the 1963 census figures, though accepted in official quarters, are generally regarded as substantially inflated, considering the phenomenal increase recorded for the 1952–53 to 1963 intercensal period. An attempt was made in 1973 to obtain a correct count, but the figures presented were regarded as flagrant overcounts, leading to its official rejection. Under the present circumstances, the 1963 (Federal Office of Statistics 1952–53, 1963) census figure is the officially accepted population in Nigeria, and the present populations are computed by extrapolating the 1963 figures assuming a growth rate of 2.5 percent per annum, a figure compatible with the growth rate in other developing countries with similar socioeconomic conditions.

Thus, no precise figures on population size for the period before 1953 are available for the Awka-Nnewi region. The 1950–80 population growth and change estimates discussed in this study are based partly on extrapolation and partly on government estimates. It must then be noted that the reliability of population statistics gathered through these methods has to be seriously questioned.

It is probable that the population growth in the Awka-Nnewi region before 1952 was quite high. According to Dike (1956), the forebears of the present Igbo were already living in this area at the dawn of human history. It is asserted by Jeffreys (1931) and Forde and Jones (1950) that part of Igboland was an important culture area with old-established iron-making centers. It is also believed that the dense forest provided opportunity for extensive cultivation, thereby encouraging the Igbo to remain in situ for a long time and to build up large populations. The high densities of population are also associated with a perennial plant whose product was a major item of export—the oil palm. It is believed that the present poor soil is a result of overuse by the resident population. This concentration of population was increased by waves of migration into the territory. The earliest one occurred in prehistoric times and is associated with the development of the north-south trade with the Igala kingdom in the north. This trade antedated the Portuguese Atlantic coast trade of 1450–1550. The next migratory wave came from the east near the Cameroon Mountains and Central Africa. Lastly, movements linked with the activities of Benin warriors occurred eastward, resulting in the occupation of such locations as Onitsha and some riverine settlements east of the river. This historical résumé is pertinent in showing that population size and growth in the Awka-Nnewi region are rooted in antiquity and have developed over centuries of slow but continuous growth.

Compared with other parts of Nigeria, the most important features of population in the Awka-Nnewi region are its size, density, and rate of growth. Although Nigeria recorded an annual population increase of 5.7

percent between 1953 and 1963, the region, made up then of Awka and Onitsha Divisions, had an annual increase of 8.8 percent (table 10.1).

There have been frequent revisions of administrative boundaries and by early 1976 the Awka-Nnewi region was split into eight LGAs with a projected population of about two million (Anambra State Ministry or Finance and Economic Development 1977). The 1977 estimate discounts migration, especially the mass-population movements during the political disturbances in Nigeria and the consequent civil war of 1967–70. It is suspected that the population in the Awka-Nnewi region must have swollen due to large-scale withdrawal of Igbo migrants from other parts of the country. Some undocumented local accounts in some of the towns and villages during the civil war showed phenomenal increases in population. Because the economic implications of a high man-land ratio got worse during and immediately after the civil war, most of the old migrants and many new ones again dispersed to other parts of the country. But there has been no significant change in the critical people-land ratio. If there is a general increase in the population, as seems likely, the relevant conclusions drawn from this study stand reinforced.

The most handy descriptive tool of people-land ratios is the crude arithmetic density, expressed in number of persons per area unit. Table 10.2 shows the range of population density in the LGAs. There are considerable variations in density among the eight LGAs against the region's average density of 591 people/km². The highest concentration of population is in Ihiala, Njikoka, and Nnewi LGAs. Microstudies have revealed very high densities in some locations. For example, a village study conducted in Enugu-Ukwu (Njikoka LGA) in 1966 recorded a population density of about 1,900 persons/km² (Grossman 1968). Also, survey data in Nnewi Town (Nnewi LGA) have shown population densities of over 2,000 per km² (Okafor 1986). This information seems to be more realistic and indicates that the present densities are above the 1977 figures. Even on the basis of the 1977 projection, it is noticeable (table 10.3) that the pressure of population is critical in a number of LGAs. For example, whereas Njikoka contains more than 17 percent of the region's total population but with only 7.8 percent of the total land area, Anambra LGA has about 30 percent of the land and less than 14 percent of the population. The index of dissimilarity between the distribution of population and area implies that 19 percent of the population would have to be redistributed in order to achieve an evenness among the LGAs.

The axis of high population concentration runs diagonally from northeast to southwest through the middle of the region and contains

Table 10.1. Internal Population Change in the Awka-Nnewi Region, 1953–63

Division	Population 1953	Population 1963	Absolute change	Percentage change	Annual growth rate
Awka	295,048	694,196	399,148	135	13.5
Onitsha[a]	466,193	710,674	244,481	52	5.2
Awka-Nnewi region[b]	761,241	1,404,870	643,629	85	8.5

Source: Computed from Census of Nigeria (Federal Office of Statistics 1952–53, 1963).
[a]The population of Onitsha Division excludes that of Onitsha town. For the purpose of this study, the Awka-Nnewi region excludes this major urban center.
[b]Awka and Onitsha Divisions as of 1952 cover the present LGAs in Anambra State covered in this study.

Table 10.2. Population Density in the Awka-Nnewi Region

Local govt. area	Area in km²	Population 1977[a]	Population density per km²
Aguata	789.8	353,257	447.3
Anambra	1,295.0	280,908	217.0
Awka	590.0	248,880	421.8
Idemili	295.3	154,144	522.0
Ihiala	321.2	193,544	602.6
Njikoka	340.0	355,304	1,045.0
Nnewi	272.7	256,965	942.3
Onitsha	429.1	227,227	529.5
Awka-Nnewi region	4,333.0	2,070,229	482.4

Source: Computed from Anambra State Population Projection of 1977 (Anambra State Ministry of Finance and Economic Development).
[a]Compound growth rate of 2.5% is assumed over the years.

Table 10.3. Comparison of Spatial Distribution of Population by Region (projected 1977 population)

Local govt. area	Percentage Population (1)	Percentage Distribution area (2)
Aguata	17.1	18.2
Anambra	13.6	29.9
Awka	12.0	13.6
Idemili	7.4	6.8
Ihiala	9.3	7.4
Njikoka	17.2	7.8
Nnewi	12.4	6.3
Onitsha	11.0	9.9
Total	100.0	99.9[a]

Source: Computed from Anambra State Population Projection of 1977 (Anambra State Ministry of Finance and Economic Development).
[a]The rounding of figures accounts for the loss of 0.1%.

such rapidly urbanizing towns as Awka, Nnewi, Ihiala, Okija, Ogidi, Ukpor, and Umunze. Apart from these, there are over twenty-five towns whose populations number up to 30,000 each.

The population concentrates on the sandy uplands of marginal fertility and with frequent water shortages rather than on the well-watered alluvial soils of the river valleys. The reasons for this apparent anomaly require clarification, because they are pertinent in understanding the population adjustment to land hunger in the Awka-Nnewi region. Explanations have intrigued many researchers (Trewartha and Zelinsky 1954; Harrison-Church 1974; Udo 1975). For example, Harrison-Church (1974) concludes that "Population distribution is not as in Europe, the result of long trial and error over many centuries by advanced people; in each type of environment, tradition is stronger in West Africa than in most temperate regions. Attachment to the soil, even in poor areas and dislike of nearby but non-traditional areas, are important factors."

Reaching a similar conclusion, Buchanan and Pugh (1955: 97) have referred to the pattern of population distribution as "immature" because "the close adjustment of densities to environmental conditions which is typical of long settled areas is here lacking." Such interpretations may be debatable, particularly if viewed as the only reason for population concentrations. For example, archaeological and historical evidence shows that Awka-Nnewi has been occupied for about five to six thousand years (Shaw 1970).

No matter what the explanation for the population concentration in this region, it contains areas of extremely high population density in close proximity to relatively sparsely populated areas, and there is a high correlation between poor soils and high population density. This relationship appears to be a microcosm for many areas in West Africa, although the reasons for it are poorly understood.

In this study region, where prima facie evidence of population pressure has been established, the most important demographic response has been rural-rural and rural-urban migration. Dense population, resulting in increasingly fragmented and uneconomic farm holdings, is the basic push factor of rural outmigration to towns and less densely settled rural areas. The urban centers all over Nigeria provide a haven for most of the uprooted villagers, whereas the rest move to rural "immigration cells" that absorb migrant labor and tenant farmers. Broadly speaking, rural-rural migratory movements from the Awka-Nnewi region stretch over long distances and have an intricate pattern. Both Udo (1975) and

Grossman (1968) have identified two major destinations that attract a sizeable number of rural-rural migrants. These are the Nike Plains of northern Igboland, and the Asaba-Issele-Uku fertile lowlands in Bendel State west of the river Niger. In addition, within the Awka-Nnewi region itself, a few favored spots such as the Mamu and the Niger-Anambra lowlands attract rural-rural migrants who want to take advantage of the relatively low population density and less critical people-land ratio. Consequently, the migrants attempt to make adjustments to maximize resources spatially. Also, the emphasis on trading activities in recent years as a result of integration into the market economy has opened up some rural centers within the Awka-Nnewi region to migrants who prefer to locate as close as possible to their natal homes in order to minimize the travel time needed to visit their homes.

Agriculture and Its Change

The harsh soil conditions of the Awka-Nnewi region greatly influence the major characteristics of land and labor use in agricultural production. The typology of agriculture that has emerged is a product of the combined action of ecological and socioeconomic factors, whereas the form of labor is a response to the stress of increasing population pressure and the opportunities offered by the development of a modern market economy. The pattern of response has led to the dynamics of change that include land redistribution and tenure, crop composition and combination, and labor apportionment and use. Therefore, it is necessary to examine the prevailing farming system in order to follow the trajectory of change through time.

The Farming System

The various types of agriculture identified in the Awka-Nnewi region are common to African peasant agricultural systems. The farming system basically consists of subsistence holdings in two locations. These are the compound land and the distant or rather outer farm; the number of holdings per farming household ranges from two to six, comprising both the compound and the outer farmland. The compound land lies in the immediate surroundings of the house and benefits from farmyard manure, which is rarely extended to the outer farm. Because a relatively high level of fertility is maintained, more demand is made on the compound land. It carries the major economic trees such as oil palm, coconut palm, kola, citrus and breadfruit, in addition to the major staples such as cocoyams, cassava, and vegetables. Also, farming enterprises that require very close attention are performed on the compound farmland. The outer farmland is usually located a few kilometers from the compound and is generally larger in size than the compound, but population pressure is consistently reducing the size of outer farmland. In fact, in some localities, no outer farmland exists at present. For example, about 90 percent of the farming households interviewed in Aguata, Nnewi, Njikoka, and Ihiala had no outer farmland.

The existence of the two farmlands in any section of the region is the result of the interplay of four principal factors: the extent of fertile land, the distance of farmland from the village location, the extent of population pressure, and the tenurial system.

Outer farmland has long been held in bush fallow. This rotation system, which worked successfully in the past, is based on the interplanting of food staples (yams, cassava, and maize) in one section of the outer farmland with another section in fallow. Ideally, the fallow section is not cultivated until it regains fertility. In reality, the duration of the fallow essentially depends on the population pressure, demand for farmland, and the rate at which the fallow vegetation returns. In the Awka-Nnewi region the crop-fallow ratio ranges from 200 (double cropping) in the compound farmland to 66 (one of the years in fallow) in the outer farmland.

On comparing the two types of farmland on the basis of their productivity it was found that the compound lands were more productive in terms of yields (measured in output/ha). The problems of lower fertility, movement of inputs, menace of domestic and wild animals, and adequate maintenance reduce yields on outer farmland.

The dynamics of the farming system cannot be fully understood without considering land tenure. Although land tenure in the Awka-Nnewi region defies neat categorizations because of local variations, communal and individual tenurial patterns are apparent. In the communal form of tenure, residents of a village community have rights to the use of some portion of the land, but in no way is the land to be alienated from the community (Chubb 1961). Under the customary communal tenure system, land belongs to the dead, living, and future generations. In this context, none of the members of the community actually "owns" the land. Rather, each head of a family is entitled to an allocation or some portion of land for the cultivation of annual and seasonal crops. Because he has only usufruct rights, he is not allowed to sell his portion of land or to borrow money by using it as a collateral.

Over the years, the communal system of land tenure has been undergoing radical modifications as a result of population pressure. Communal holdings have been fragmented by family units and individuals. Although an individual may have a possessory title to his own share of the land, there may still exist some community ties that restrict the disposal of land. It is this individually owned land that is often inherited through patrilineal lines. Under the traditional system, each son is entitled to a portion of his father's land. Land has also been transferred by pledge, lease or sale, and permanent demarcation of holdings has become necessary.

Population pressure has heightened individual ownership of land; the surviving community lands in the Awka-Nnewi region are few and far between. The bulk of the community-owned land remains in Anambra LGA, where there is a relative abundance of land available to the farming population (table 10.4). In other LGAs, land tenure has been individualized so much that many landless adult males are emerging. Already, the majority of the farmers have little room for land expansion and thus resort to various intensification practices to cope with the critical people-land ratio.

The problems of population pressures have led to altered rotational patterns—a modified bush-fallow system involving cropping sequences on a fixed area of farmland. This system of bush fallowing, although more demanding on soil because of more frequent cropping, is not as land extensive as shifting cultivation or the pure rotational bush fallow. Rather, it demands a greater skill in decision making with regard to assessment of soil-fertility potentials, assignment of cultigens to different soil types, and the frequency of rotation. These decisions are aimed at achieving higher agricultural production while maintaining soil fertility (Lagemann 1977). It is only in a few localities that the rotational bush-fallow system still survives. In others, the system is fast breaking down as the farmed fields are no longer allowed an adequate time for rest and regeneration.

A survey of the distribution of the farmlands in the Awka-Nnewi region shows that the majority of the farmers are now confined to compound farms, particularly in the LGAs with a more critical people-land ratio. About 64 percent of the farming households surveyed own only compound farmlands against 36 percent that still retain some outer farmland but more of compound land (table 10.5). In order to keep the compound land productive, the surveyed farmers adopt the following methods of soil rebuilding: (1) mulching—all kinds of small branches, twigs, and leaves from trees and shrubs are used in mulching the soil; (2) application of animal waste—dung from goats and chickens is applied to the soil; (3) composting of grasses from the fallow areas and household refuse in pits.

The declining significance of outer farmland has been ongoing for a long time. By 1951, for instance, Grove (1951) estimated that about 35 percent of the farmland in Oko village (Aguata LGA) was classified compound land. Based on our data from the same village, the compound land is estimated at 63 percent. Whereas the outer fields are cropped in a bush-fallow system through which soil fertility is partially replenished, the compound land has been subjected to permanent and continuous cultivation. At best, a portion of the compound land is occupied by the old cassava stands for one year, but it is usual for each fragment of the compound land to be cultivated annually in a quasi-rotational form. To maintain this system when rotational bush fallow has been eliminated, several cultural practices are introduced to improve productivity and maintain soil fertility. Some of these land-use intensity practices commonly adopted in the Awka-Nnewi region are discussed below.

Land-Use Intensity

With continuing population growth, many households aim at intensive cultivation of the available space. To do this involves deeper cultivation of the top soil to prevent cultigens from wilting and a more careful adaptation of cultivation techniques to the needs of each species. In the very high population-density zones of Nnewi, Aguata, and Njikoka LGAs, yams, particularly the prestige types, are no longer cultivated on mounds. Instead, deep trenches are dug and manured, and the yams are planted in them. The trenches are dug months before the planting period and are filled with leaves and house refuse that are later covered to accelerate decay before the yam is planted. The result has been demonstrably better yields for similar crops planted on compound plots rather than in the outfields and generally higher calorific production and income per hectare.

Table 10.4. Landownership Pattern among Farmers in the
Awka-Nnewi Region, 1977

Local govt. area	Population density per km²	Number of respondents	Communally owned land (%)	Individual land (%)
Aguata	447.0	38	2.75	97.25
Anambra	217.0	30	16.10	83.90
Awka	422.0	33	5.37	94.63
Idemili	552.0	40	6.74	93.26
Ihiala	603.0	45	3.48	96.52
Njikoka	1,045.0	40	4.48	95.52
Nnewi	942.0	34	1.35	98.65
Onitsha	530.0	30	9.36	90.64
Awka-Nnewi region	591.0	290	6.20	93.80

Source: Computed from survey data.

Table 10.5. Distribution of Farming Households According to the Ownership
of Farmland Types, 1977

Local govt. area	Population density per km²	% owning outer and compound farmland	% owning compound land only
Aguata	447.0	43.6	56.4
Anambra	217.0	65.8	34.2
Awka	422.0	36.3	63.7
Idemili	522.0	45.9	54.1
Ihiala	603.0	53.8	46.2
Njikoka	1,045.0	16.6	83.3
Nnewi	942.0	12.5	87.5
Onitsha	530.0	15.8	84.2
Awka-Nnewi region	591.0	36.3	63.7

Source: Computed from survey data.

In the erosion-prone areas of Idemili, Njikoka, and Aguata LGAs, farmers have devised a unique practice of terrace farming on hillsides. Contour ridges are made across the dip of the hillsides and in some places dead tree trunks are used to support the ridges. The contour and the ridges are staggered in a manner that will allow enough but not excessive runoff across the plot. Lower down the hillslopes, most individual plots are surrounded by low walls about one meter high or are enclosed by fences. They are usually built to minimize fluvial and sheet erosion, by encouraging rain water to soak into the soils, and to ward off domestic animals from farm plots.

In some regions of Africa, the alternative to poor returns in food crop production has been a resort to cash cropping (Ruthenberg 1968). In the Awka-Nnewi area such an emphasis has not been encouraged because of the relatively low labor demand in the production of oil palm, which is the only cash crop of importance. The production of oil and kernels from the wild palm requires only the little labor used in gathering the fruit, pressing out the oil, and breaking open the nut to extract the kernel (Martin 1988: 119–36).

All through the region emphasis has been placed on higher-yielding food crops, with cassava dominating in almost all the LGAs. Table 10.6 is a summary of the estimated monetary value of the sampled farmers' total annual output of food, cash crops, and livestock. The estimate includes yields from both the compound and the outer farms. The preoccupation of the farmers with the production of food crops stems from the fact that the Awka-Nnewi region is generally a food-deficit area, and farmers strive to meet their food needs before producing crops for export (Udo 1971). However, the farmers in Onitsha LGA take advantage of the nearness of Onitsha Town to grow such crops as oranges and bananas for sale in the city, hence the contribution of up to 25 percent from cash crops there.

From the yield estimates of individual staples, it was observed that on compounds, cassava (manioc) gave an average yield of about 9,500 kg/ha, whereas the yam plot had a yield of 5,300 kg/ha. Our estimates of the yields from the outer fields showed lower yields. Because cassava has low fertility requirements and is less vulnerable to the vagaries of climate and disease (Jones 1959), it is a particularly valuable staple in the Awka-Nnewi region, considering the region's poor soils. Cassava was initially introduced to supplement yams, a staple of comparatively high protein content; but cassava has recently superseded yams as the main food staple.

Therefore, in crop choice factors such as cost of transport, market demand, and cash income from sale of produce are less important than the food needs of the farm family. The factor of food need goes beyond intensive multicropping. The cultigens chosen also reflect the desire of the farmers to expend minimum inputs in terms of money and work days, while they expect maximum outputs per unit area.

The minimal supplement from livestock is not unexpected. Livestock rearing, though an integral part of the farming system in this part of Nigeria, does not constitute a reliable source of animal protein or

Table 10.6. Estimated Monetary Value of Farmers' Annual Agricultural Income in the Awka-Nnewi Region, 1977

Local govt. area	Landholding per capita (ha)	Percentage contribution			
		Cash crops	Food crops	Livestock	Total
Aguata	0.73	16.9	81.4	1.7	100
Anambra	1.37	23.1	68.4	8.5	100
Awka	0.39	19.6	69.0	11.4	100
Idemili	0.41	13.8	78.9	7.3	100
Ihiala	0.84	14.6	81.2	4.2	100
Njikoka	0.26	11.4	85.1	3.5	100
Nnewi	0.14	9.3	88.3	2.4	100
Onitsha	0.41	25.4	61.0	13.6	100
Awka-Nnewi region	0.57	16.8	76.0	6.6	100

Source: Computed from survey data 1977.

cash income. Because of the prevalence of tsetse flies and the vectors of trypanosomiasis, only resistant species of livestock can be kept in southern Nigeria. Thus, in the Awka-Nnewi region, livestock form only a minor part of the agricultural economy. In general, households in the land-hungry areas tend to keep what livestock they have as a result of tradition perpetuated by their difficult crop-raising environment. A survey in 1982 showed the existence of a few commercial livestock and poultry farms that supply meat and eggs to urban markets and educational institutions. Again, it is impossible to divorce these trends from the general prospects of agricultural production in the Awka-Nnewi region. As much as possible farming households, especially in the land-hungry zones, are attempting to diversify their economic activities in order to earn money to pay for the extra food needs of the family.

Perhaps the most important aspect of agricultural intensification is the development of multicropping and intercropping. Whereas the former means taking more than one harvest from the same field during the same agricultural year, the latter involves cultivating more than one variety of species in the same plot at the same time. To get the most out of the land, farmers embark on simultaneous operations as well as sequential use of their farmlands. Farmers grow crops in mixture by relay cropping or through various spatial arrangements involving row, strip, or "random" patches of different cultigens in the same plot at a time. This practice of farming, according to Igbozurike (1971), has given sustenance to tropical agriculture in the absence of modern technological inputs that have sustained production in advanced countries. To a great extent, the intensity of intercropping is observed to be positively related to the degree of population pressure and land scarcity. In Anambra LGA, characterized by relatively low population density and little evidence of pressure on land, most of the farm plots have a two to three crop mixture of yams, cassava, maize, and sometimes cocoyams but with many cases of yam in pure stands. In the other LGAs curious combinations of food and tree crops occur on diminutive plots. Farmers try to insure good soil coverage. Crops are interplanted to provide a regular and varied supply of food, reduce weed competition, and minimize leaching of nutrients and soil erosion. Shade-tolerant cultivars, such as cocoyam and pepper, are planted near banana and plantain stands.

An attempt at categorizing the land use in the study region in terms of agricultural practice and intensification requires delimitation of the area into three agro-ecological zones. Two villages grouped per agro-ecological zone were studied in detail in 1982. Table 10.7 shows the observed relationships among different sizes of farmland and the associated crop combinations. The number of crops in a mixture was established by taking a total count of the number of species in a farm in one growing season. Each farmer tries to grow as many seasonal and perennial crops as possible for both food and cash but varying the combination to suit local socioeconomic and environmental conditions.

When the farms were compared on the basis of their location, cropping pattern, and productivity per unit area, it was found that those under intensive intercropping and located in zones of acute shortage of land were more productive in terms of gross values per hectare. For example, the gross value of crops from a typical intercropped farm in Agulu was found to be about ₦1,830 (U.S. $457) per hectare compared with the value of ₦980 (U.S. $245) per hectare from a farm in Otuocha containing five combinations or crops (U.S. $1 = ₦4 in 1986). This finding is supported by comparisons among mixed and monocropping in terms of harvested tonnage and value of output per unit of land (Norman 1974; Abalu 1976). Besides the advantages in terms of yield, the farmers also view their system of intercropping as effectively serving their self-provisioning requirements of mature staples and vegetables at different periods of the cropping season. On a typical intercropping farm, one is likely to find many cultigens at different stages of growth and maturity. In the Awka-Nnewi region, this pattern of intensive inter-

Table 10.7. Relationship between Farm Type and Crop Combination Value

Agro-ecological zones	1980 population density of representative village group (per km²)	Average size per farmer (ha)	No. of crop combinations in a growing season
Underfarmed (Anambra LGA)			
Aguleri	164	0.38	7
Otuocha	379	0.94	9
Heavily farmed (Ihiala LGA)			
Uli	1,213	0.27	13
Achalla	1,634	0.16	12
Overfarmed (Njikoka LGA)			
Agulu	2,036	0.13	15
Anugu-Ukwu	2,378	0.09	17

Note: The population densities were calculated from a 1980 projected population figure for the study area while the average farm size was calculated from a sample of farmers from the village groups.

cropping helps to alleviate the problem of perennial food scarcity, as one or two mature cultigens may be available for harvest at any time to supplement the foodstuffs purchased from the market.

The livelihood responses to intensive land pressures have not all dealt with agriculture, and those that have cannot all be attributed solely to the output-intensification motive of Boserup (1965) or of other demand models. For example, the switch to certain cultigens such as cassava has as much to do with its low labor requirements as it does with its productive qualities. Also, as will be detailed, outmigration for nonfarm employment has become a significant factor. Indeed, income derived from nonfarm sources now exceeds farm income for most farmers throughout the region.

Nature of Changes in the Forces of Production

In many other areas facing population pressure, the most prevalent solution to the demands imposed by population growth has been the adoption of more intensive labor techniques. But there is a minimum farm size below which it is impossible for a farm unit to subsist and pay for social services. When this limit is reached, extra local factors are introduced. An emerging trend in the Awka-Nnewi region is an increasing involvement in nonfarm activities by adults and children alike. About 40 percent of the total labor input is devoted to nonfarm activities that vary according to the opportunities available, the location of the village or town, and the skills and expectations of the members of the household. There is a readiness to drop agriculture entirely or to look elsewhere to supplement income from agriculture.

Because obtaining full employment in agriculture under the circumstances of land scarcity is difficult, the "surplus" labor created by this situation is forced into dependent relationships with outside persons or organizations to meet some of their household requirements. This has been accomplished by villagers seeking alternative employment in the towns or participating in petty trading and small-scale industries. Thus, in the Awka-Nnewi region, the burden of subsistence is shared by men, women, and children working in both farm and nonfarm activities in the villages. Table 10.8 shows the amount of labor devoted to farm and nonfarm operations in a sample of survey villages. There is a high incidence of nonfarm activities in the villages with scanty agricultural potentials. By the sheer volume of nonfarm economic activities going on in these villages it could be proper to designate their economy as periurban and partial farming, but the people still regard the environment as an agrarian setting in which nonfarm activities are expected only to render support. Agricultural activities are seen to dominate the scene, but because of low yield expectations, greater labor attention is usually given to nonfarm activities. In many households, the strategy for gaining a livelihood involves placing members in different activities that hold promise rather than having many of them in only one nonfarm activity. Because of the manner in which some of these activities are carried out, their minute scale, and their locational ubiquity, they do not lend themselves directly to enumeration. Moreover, except for major construction work and such jobs as palmwine tapping (from which, traditionally, women are excluded), women and children are actively engaged in various occupational combinations. Because of the level of commitment of those members of the household engaged in nonfarm activities, it is difficult to engage extra hands in farm work during the peak season for agricultural labor (Okafor 1979a).

The most diverse range of nonfarm activities is found among the households in which a minimum of household labor is devoted to agriculture. To meet basic needs, each household's income is based not only on the diversity of activities but also on the greater proportion of time that each member must now spend on nonfarm activities. The result, in terms of the length of the average working day, is that there is little choice but to work long hours for several days a week. This develop-

Table 10.8. Population Density and Division of Labor in Farm and
Nonfarm Activities in the Awka-Nnewi Region

| Local govt. area | 1977 population density per km² | Households in sample | Labor input | |
			% farm	% nonfarm
Aguata	447.0	38	23.6	76.4
Anambra	217.0	30	63.8	36.2
Awka	422.0	33	36.4	63.6
Ihiala	603.0	45	40.8	59.2
Idemili	522.0	40	38.6	61.4
Njikoka	1,045.0	40	20.8	79.2
Nnewi	942.0	34	16.8	83.2
Onitsha	530.0	30	18.8	81.2
Awka-Nnewi region	591.0	290	32.5	67.5

Source: Compiled from field survey 1977.

ment has contributed to as much as 67 percent of all labor being directed to off-farm activities (table 10.8). Furthermore, the level of involvement in these activities does not seem to be subject to seasonal fluctuations, quite unlike in agriculture. The people do not usually allow their nonfarm activities to be sacrificed to the agricultural calendar.

The continuing increase in the intensity of nonfarm activities in the Awka-Nnewi region raises the question of whether agricultural development is actually receiving its due attention. It is difficult to determine the extent to which nonfarm employment is a genuine reflection of the existence of "surplus" labor that cannot be absorbed into permanent agricultural employment. The Awka-Nnewi region still has the characteristics of a rural agrarian economy but needs strong support from the government in the form of technical assistance and inputs. This study shows that in some areas there is a tendency for farm production to decline as off-farm employment grows in importance. In many instances, the income from nonfarm sources is not invested in agriculture as a result of the uncertainty of agricultural returns. In the long run, there is a possibility that under conditions of low agricultural production, the economic advantages of occupational diversification involving many types of nonfarm activities may eliminate under- and unemployment within the rural communities.

Role of Government

Given the low level of technology and lack of scientific information possessed by the farmers in the Awka-Nnewi region, the problem of successfully introducing modern methods of agricultural production has been one of the most intractable setbacks facing various attempts by the government to raise agriculture in the region above the level of peasant production (Okafor 1979b). Programs aimed at transforming the traditional systems have sometimes resulted in total failure. The record of achievement has on the whole been discouraging.

In the present study, a survey of fertilizer use among the farming households shows that only 20 percent of them use fertilizers (table 10.9), compared with those that still adopt various other methods of soil conservation, such as regeneration using natural fallow and the application of farmyard manure. Also, 7 percent of these farmers apply chemicals such as Aldrin Dust and Gamalin 20 to yams in order to kill the yam beetle and pest. The survey also showed that 53 percent of the farmers interviewed have not tried fertilizer and are not prepared to do so in the near future. Rather, the farmers indicated that they would be ready to apply pesticides and insecticides, which cost much more than fertilizers. This suggests that cost considerations are not the major prohibitive factor to fertilizer adoption. Many farmers have had disappointing results from the application of fertilizers without pretest of soils to find out the deficient nutrients. Others got poor results because the fertilizers were applied at the wrong time. It is, however, important to note that the readiness to apply fertilizer is greater in areas of high population pressure. The correlation is not surprising, but the government has not seriously exploited this readiness because of logistic and administrative problems. For example, the field staff in the fertilizer-promotion program possess few soil-testing kits used for calorimetric testing, and only a few farmers have had their soils tested and have been advised on the type of fertilizer to use. Because the farmers protect capital expenditures, they are extremely reluctant to invest what little capital they have in what would appear to them as an unknown and, therefore, risky venture.

Another problem that has hindered the spread of fertilizer is the multicropping and intercropping systems adopted by the farmers; these do not lend themselves to the application of the right type of fertilizer for all the crop combinations. The fertilizer required for one species may be toxic or harmful to the growth of another. Furthermore, there is a growing fear that cultigens, particularly yams, produced by the application of fertilizers do not keep long in the barn and are more susceptible to disease. This fear has jeopardized the spread of fertilizer use. The

Table 10.9. Fertilizer Use in the Sample Households of Awka-Nnewi Region, 1982

Local govt. area	Population density per km²	Number of respondents	Users	Nonusers	% of users
Aguata	447.0	55	8	47	14.5
Anambra	217.0	30	3	27	10.0
Awka	422.0	41	7	34	17.1
Ihiala	603.0	42	8	34	19.0
Idemili	522.0	51	11	40	21.6
Njikoka	1,045.0	61	13	48	21.3
Nnewi	942.0	58	18	40	31.0
Onitsha	530.0	44	9	35	20.5
Awka-Nnewi region	591.0	382	77	305	20.2

Source: Compiled from 1982 field data.

challenge facing the government to increase the adoption rate of fertilizer includes not only adequate supply of fertilizers and the removal of the institutional and infrastructural bottlenecks in the distribution system but also mounting a wide-scale campaign of educating the local farmers on the need and correct application of fertilizers.

Another area in which the government is trying to effect changes in the forces of production is through extension services. The extension workers constitute the contact point between the agricultural extension services and the farm population, and they are supposed to guide the farmers from awareness to sustained adoption of improved farm practices. Although it is difficult to quantify the effectiveness of the extension worker/farmer contact, the small number of extension workers in the Awka-Nnewi region compared with the number of farmers they are supposed to serve shows that there is a lack of extension staff. Table 10.10 shows that the extension workers have been able to reach between 3.8 and 7.3 percent of the farmers. Besides, it is generally the so-called progressive farmers with influence and larger, economically more important holdings that receive regular assistance and guidance from the extension service. In effect, the majority of the farmers are not influenced by the activities of the extension services. Considering the ratio of one extension worker to about 603 farming households, of one for every 42 km², experts are in agreement that this ratio is out of tune with meaningful extension work.

Other incentives provided by the government include the spread of agricultural information through the press, radio, television, and public enlightenment programs. Although it is difficult to evaluate the overall success of these programs in the Awka-Nnewi region, it is noteworthy that the low level of literacy in the region mitigates against wide dissemination of agricultural information, even when it is produced in the local language. The acquisition level of modern agricultural information remains very low and informal. Farmers prefer to seek information from friends and neighbors than to get advice from a demonstration station or an extension staff. Therefore, traditional farming knowledge learned from parents and guardians and passed down through succeeding generations is still the most influential source of farming knowledge. On the whole, there are gaps within the agricultural information network system: between farmers and extension workers and between extension workers and research institutions.

Role of International Agencies

Successive governments in Anambra State have explored external help in solving the problems of declining agricultural productivity. In addition to the state farms managed by the State's Agricultural Development Corporation (ADC), there are a number of World Bank agricultural projects that have been established at Ogboji, Ufuma, Nawfija, and Do-Anambra river plains. The projects involve swamp and irrigated rice production. The World Bank rice projects in the Awka-Nnewi region are built around small, existing schemes and make use of local labor as much as possible. Selected farmers are allocated farm plots of about 15 ha of swamp and 25 ha of irrigated land. Credits are also made available. At harvest the paddy is bought from the farmers, processed, and sold to the public.

In spite of these efforts, the Awka-Nnewi region remains a food-deficit area. A lot of food is imported from Bendel State (*garri* and yams) and from some northern states (beans, dried fish, meat, onions, and cattle). The government has not succeeded in introducing any meaningful agricultural technology that involves the application of modern farm practices. Therefore, the following problems of agriculture remain outstanding: small farm size, an aged and depleted farm population, inadequate farm care, and subsistence operation mainly meant to meet household requirements.

In sum, government efforts to increase agricultural production to match the expanding population and absorb surplus labor have probably been inadequate. The ultimate solution may lie in a reexamination of

Table 10.10. Number of Extension Staff in Relation to the Farming Population
Being Served in the Awka-Nnewi Region, 1982

Local govt. area	No. of extension workers	Estimated no. of farming households per extension worker	% of households reached by an extension worker
Aguata	18	8,600	5.6
Anambra	9	6,500	4.2
Awka	13	4,600	6.8
Idemili	16	5,800	3.8
Ihiala	13	9,300	7.3
Njikoka	15	11,000	6.5
Nnewi	12	10,700	7.1
Onitsha	8	6,200	3.9
Awka-Nnewi region	13	7,838	5.7

Source: Compiled from 1982 field data.

the strategies to get the farmers to follow trends of change. As Richards
(1985) has suggested, agricultural revolution may come about through
an in-depth examination of the methods employed by the traditional
farmers to raise productivity, especially in regions of scanty agricultural
resources.

Consequences of Change

The changing population-land relationship has implications not only for
the environment but also for the socioeconomic conditions of the population. Population pressure exacerbated by poor agricultural resources in
the Awka-Nnewi region provided a stimulus to the adoption of various
practices to raise productivity. These practices have had varying effects
on the environment and its ecological and economic sustainability.

Environmental Consequences

Although some physical properties of soil have been improved by
intercropping, mulching, and rotational bush fallow—practices widely
adopted in the Awka-Nnewi region—the long-term effects of reduced
fallow have probably been played down. Forest clearing, which has
characterized intensive cropping of the pressured land, destroyed the natural ecosystem of the region. Consequently, the incidence of leaching
and erosion has been widespread. Efforts at controlling erosion in the

Awka-Nnewi region are not properly coordinated, and further agricultural intensification without appropriate soil-building measures may spell ecological disaster. The maintenance of soil fertility has not kept pace with the demands made from the region's soil in order to meet food requirements. The period of natural regeneration has been drastically reduced. Also, the suspicion surrounding the use of fertilizer has prevented its wide-scale application as a soil-building element. Perhaps the best hope for continuous cropping lies with the intensification of intercropping, which Richards (1983: 36) has described as one of the great glories of African science. The introduction of wheeled machinery, though, may not offer the best protection for the fragile soil of the region. Evidence from the study shows that the farmers are aware of the possible collapse of the ecological system and strive to treat the soil so as to sustain its productivity.

Economic and Social Consequence

Under conditions of high population pressure on poor agricultural land, intensification of agricultural operations is limited to the extent where the marginal productivity of a farm is less than the minimum level of subsistence. Data on agricultural production and land use in the Awka-Nnewi region are in harmony with the observation that the farming systems are stagnating while efforts are made in other directions to meet the food needs of the households. This, perhaps, gives the impression of a partial farming economy. By adopting intercropping and multicropping techniques, a few varieties of quick-maturing and labor-saving crops, and a combination of some husbandry practices, farmers have been trying to slow down the process of diminishing yields. The economic consequences of these responses include a basic alteration in the system of land tenure in which communal tenure has given way to individualized tenure. Also, land price has risen considerably as more people require it more for living space than for agriculture. The landless population has sought alternatives in a multiplicity of occupations. The money that these migrants send home has been an important part of the household budget for meeting the cost of food and other requirements. About 90 percent of the households interviewed in this study indicated that they received remittances of between ₦10 (U.S. $2.50) and ₦100 (U.S. $25) a month. Although it was not possible to obtain the actual income of the migrants, it can be observed that in most cases, these sums represent a substantial proportion of their monthly earnings. The villagers at home look forward to these remittances to meet their various needs. Therefore, it can be concluded that the income generated through migration mitigates the problems associated with agriculture. This conclusion is reinforced by the fact that the imposition of a 5 percent saving scheme on the state civil servants in Anambra State was abandoned after a year largely because of the impact felt in the areas through reduced remittances from migrants to village households.

It is also important not to neglect the part played by this external income in the provision of social amenities in towns and villages. Such development projects as roads, schools, hospitals and piped water schemes are usually financed by remittances from migrants. At the same time, however, the influx of external income results in a more unequal distribution of income among households. Households depending entirely or mainly on proceeds from agriculture have less cash flow than those receiving remittances. But perhaps the disadvantage of this differential income is outweighed by the role that remittances have played in improving living standards and narrowing the gap in the distribution of income between rural households in the Awka-Nnewi region and their urban counterparts.

The economic plight of households having access to progressively smaller plots of land becomes increasingly severe as the proportion of subsistence income derived from their land decreases. Many times such pieces of land are left underutilized as the owners consider migration and nonfarm activities better alternatives.

Thus, although the changes in agricultural operation introduced in most parts of the Awka-Nnewi region are those principally designed to increase yields, increases in food production are merely inching forward and remaining below the rate of population increase. The fear is that if there are no noticeable improvements in productivity through technology, production expansion may eventually come to a halt. In the Awka-Nnewi region, the limits to this increase may also have been reached. The caloric consumption and nutritional level have not appreciably increased and the incidence of hunger and malnutrition is still significant. Shortage of basic foodstuffs reflects on every aspect of the people's lifestyle.

The net result of the socioeconomic changes has been a restructuring of the region's social organization on an economic basis rather than on traditional kinship relationships. Every effort is geared toward generating the extra income that agriculture cannot provide. Periodic and daily markets provide the economic nexus for activities aimed at improving the living standard (Okafor 1982).

Probability of a Sustained Trajectory of Change

The extremely densely settled "rural" populace of the Awka-Nnewi region is confronted with declining farmland per capita on marginal agricultural soils and is exploring numerous strategies to alleviate food shortages and poverty. The traditional compound-outerfield farm has given way to smaller compound farms with intensive inter- and multicropping. Land and labor inputs and switches in cultigens have greatly enhanced yields, but overall production has not kept pace with population growth. Given the small size of the farms, agriculture cannot be expected to absorb more labor (see Sen 1965), and the number of landless is expected to grow.

A lesson from this case study concerns the multivaried causes and responses in the intensification process different from a linear model set with a closed economy (see Turner et al. 1977). Boserup's (1965) and other demand models may undervalue this complexity, not adequately accounting for situations of agricultural stagnation. Once the latter conditions arise, the types of responses may extend far beyond agriculture per se, as is the case in Awka-Nnewi.

The immediate trajectory of change in the region may be largely nonagricultural. Udo (1971: 429) has argued that "since division of labour and occupational and crop specialization are necessary features of a modern progressive economy, nothing is inherently wrong in a rural area that imports some or even all its food requirements so long as it is able to pay for them." This trajectory will solve some problems and create many others. Nigeria, for example, does not feed itself, and the abandonment of agriculture by any region certainly will not help this situation. Also, a subsistence tie to the land remains a part of much of the African heritage, the loss of which will not come easily, even if it were appropriate.

Solutions include migration to urban areas and less crowded rural areas. It is questionable whether urban areas can provide sustained opportunities for rural migrants. Others argue that this migration acts as a "brain drain" in that the more active population that might develop the rural region tend to be migrants. Yet others have suggested a redistribution of the population across the region (Floyd 1965; Udo 1971). This option is beset with numerous institutional barriers such as land ownership and may only be a stopgap measure, given population growth rates.

These options do not appear to provide a lasting solution to food and hunger problems in the region. Perhaps a better approach would be to emphasize the improvement of the intensive compound gardening that is already underway, focusing on manuring, composting, and fertilizing and building on the skills of smallholder cultivators. This would be complemented, if not superseded, by nonfarm activities, such as those that are underway. The coexistence of the two sectors of activities holds the key. Furthermore, the riverine zone can be fully developed to rice cultivation; the potential here may be great enough to offset the deficit productions throughout the remainder of the region.

However, no lasting solution seems probable without a decreased population growth rate and, perhaps, an enforced policy to achieve it. The government has recently voted a policy of only four children per female, but the details of enforcement have not been determined.

References

Abalu, G. O. I. 1976. "A Note on Crop Mixture under Indigenous Conditions in Northern Nigeria." *Journal of Development Studies* 12: 7–18.

Aluko, S. A. 1965. "How Many Nigerians: An Analysis of Nigeria's Census Problems, 1901–1963." *Journal of Modern African Studies* 3: 371–92.

Anambra State Ministry of Finance and Economic Development. 1977. Estimated population of Anambra State by LGAs, 1st ed. Enugu: ASMFED.

Boserup, E. 1965. *The Conditions of Agricultural Growth.* Chicago: Aldine.

Buchanan, K. M., and J. C. Pugh. 1955. *Land and People in Nigeria.* London: London University Press.

Chubb, L. T. 1961. *The Ibo Land Tenure.* Ibadan: Ibadan University Press.

Dike, K. O. 1956. *Trade and Politics in the Niger Delta, 1830–1865.* London: Oxford University Press.

Federal Office of Statistics. 1952–53, 1963. *Census of Nigeria.* Lagos: Federal Office of Statistics.

Floyd, B. N. 1965. "Soil Erosion and Deterioration in Eastern Nigeria: A Geographical Appraisal." *Nigerian Geographical Journal* 8: 33–44.

———. 1969. *Eastern Nigeria: A Geographical Review.* London: Macmillan.

Forde, D., and G. I. Jones. 1950. *The Ibo and Ibibio-Speaking Peoples of South-Eastern Nigeria,* London: Faber and Faber.

Grossman, D. 1968. "Migratory Tenant Farming in Northern Igboland in Relation to Resource Use." Ph.D. dissertation, Columbia University.

Grove, A.T. 1951. *Land Use and Soil Conservation in Parts of Onitsha and Owerri Provinces.* Geological Survey of Nigeria Bulletin, No. 2. Zaria: Gaskiya Corporation.

Harrison-Church, R.J. 1974. *West Africa.* New York: Longman.

Igbozurike, U.M. 1971. "Ecological Balance in Tropical Agriculture." *Geographical Review* 61: 519–29.

Jefferys, M.D.W. 1931. The Awka Report. Manuscript.

Jones, W.O. 1959. *Manioc in Africa.* Stanford, Calif.: Stanford University Press.

Lagemann, J. 1977. *Traditional African Farming Systems in Eastern Nigeria.* Munich: Weltforum Verlag.

Martin, S.M. 1988. *Palm Oil and Protest: An Economic History of the Ngwa Region, South-Eastern Nigeria, 1800–1980.* Cambridge: Cambridge University Press.

Mohr, E.C.J. 1944. *The Soils of Equatorial Regions,* trans. R. Pendleton. Ann Arbor, Mich.: J.W. Edwards.

Norman, D.W. 1974. "Rationalizing Mixed Cropping under Indigenous Conditions: The Example of Northern Nigeria." *Journal of Development Studies* 27: 3–21.

Obihara, G.H. 1961. "The Acid Soils of Eastern Nigeria." *Nigerian Scientist* 1: 57–64.

Ofomata, G.E.K. 1976. Conserving the Scarce Land of Southeastern Nigeria. Conference paper on Land Policy, NISER, Ibadan, University of Ibadan.

———, ed. 1975. *Nigeria in Maps: Eastern States.* Benin City: Ethiopia Publishing House.

Okafor, F.C. 1979a. "Labour Shortage in Nigerian Agriculture." *Labor Capital and Society* 12: 108–22.

———. 1979b. "Small Farmers and the Extension Service in Southeastern Nigeria." *Journal of Administration Overseas* 7: 43–48.

———. 1982. "The Dynamics of Change in the Rural Marketing System of Southeastern Nigeria." *Malaysian Journal of Tropical Geography* 6: 40–49.

———. 1986. "The Adaptive Strategies of Smallholders in Parts of Southeastern Nigeria: Implications for Agricultural Planning." *Journal of Rural Studies* 2: 117–26.

Olusanya, P.O. 1975. "Population Growth and Its Components." In *Population Growth and Socio-Economic Change in West Africa,* ed. J.C. Caldwell et al. New York: Columbia University Press.

Richards, P. 1983. "Ecological Change and the Politics of African Land Use." *African Studies Review* 26: 1–72.

———. 1985. *Indigenous Agricultural Revolution: Ecology and Food Production in West Africa.* London: Hutchinson.

Ruthenberg, H., ed. 1968. *Smallholder Farming and Smallholder Development in Tanzania.* Munich: Weltforum Verlag.

Sen, A. K. 1965. "The Choice of Agricultural Techniques in Underdeveloped Countries." *Economic Development and Cultural Change* 13: 69-79.

Shaw, T. 1970. *Igbo-Ukwu: An Account of Archaeological Discoveries in Eastern Nigeria.* London: Oxford University Press.

Trewartha, G. T., and W. Zelinsky. 1954. "Population in Tropical Africa." *Annals of the Association of American Geographers* 34: 135-62.

Turner, B. L. II, R. G. Hanham, and A. V. Portararo. 1977. "Population Pressure and Agricultural Intensity." *Annals of the Association of American Geographers* 67: 384-96.

Udo, R. K. 1971. "Food-Deficit Areas of Nigeria." *Geographical Review* 61: 853-64.

―――. 1975. *Migrant Tenant Farmers of Nigeria.* Lagos: African University Press.

11 / The Intensification of Peri-Urban Agriculture: The Kano Close-Settled Zone, 1964–1986

Michael Mortimore

A large area around Kano in northern Nigeria has high rural population densities and long-established, intensive smallholder agriculture. This is notwithstanding a semiarid climate with variable rainfall and poor soils. The population is growing (although the rate is uncertain) and metropolitan Kano, with a population of over a million, is expanding rapidly. A conventional view of the relations between population growth, urban expansion, and ecology might expect evidence of stress in the agricultural system. On the contrary, this system exhibits stable characteristics. It is based on three interactive components (crops, farm trees, and livestock). Indigenous management is directed toward sustainability, and indigenous small-scale technologies provide a sound basis for further improvements in productivity. Economic diversification at the household level provides supplementary income.

Longitudinal studies of change in African conditions suffer from a scarcity of data and problems of continuity, compatibility, and completeness. For the present study, the baseline is a field survey carried out in Ungogo District, 10 km north of Kano, in 1964 (Mortimore and Wilson 1965).[1] My living in or near Kano for the following two decades permitted an informal monitoring of change, but having transferred my intensive field investigations further north since the 1970s, I have to draw on studies by others for more recent data, in particular, Hill (1977) and Amerena (1982),[2] and by my colleagues in the Kano Rural Energy Research Project (Cline-Cole et al. 1987). I also make use, for comparative purposes, of field studies carried out at greater distances from Kano, both within and outside the Close-Settled Zone (CSZ). The time frame for this study is two decades, 1964–86, but where the opportunity arises, trends will be viewed in longer perspective. Such a perspective is employed by Watts (1983), on the basis of archival sources relating to Hausaland. However, the objectives of the present study are more limited both theoretically and spatially.

The Kano CSZ was originally defined on the basis of the preliminary returns of the census of 1962 as having rural population densities in excess of 141/km² (350/mi²). It extends 65 to 95 km from metropolitan Kano, asymmetrically disposed about a NW/SE axis and roughly coincident with the boundaries of major soil groups (fig. 11.1). Settlement is characteristically dispersed in nuclear or extended family compounds on or near dispersed farm holdings (fig. 11.2). Compact or nucleated settlements, associated with the power base of precolonial fiefholders, were rare, but since 1950, some planned villages have been formed by the resettlement of dispersed villages or ward administrative units. Road communications are strongly radial from Kano, and seven-day markets, few in relation to the population, are supplemented by smaller registered and unregistered night, roadside, or neighborhood markets, small shops, fixed or peripatetic retailers, and networks of inter-house trade (Hill 1971). Few markets are large. Eighty-four percent of the surface area is under annual rain-fed cultivation or perennial irrigated cultivation along the banks of rivers or (occasionally) near wells.

The inner or peri-urban zone has a radius of about 30 km, the effective limit of a day trip to the city by donkey or on foot. Intensive rural-urban interaction long preceded the colonial era. During the 1960s, the principal components of this interaction were firewood, manure, and other trade goods. The advent of the minibus in the 1970s extended the range and frequency of personal mobility among low-income earners and intensified urban interventions in the peri-urban zone, especially land acquisition, its transfer to residential and other urban uses, and commuting, particularly near roads.[3] Within the administrative boundary of metropolitan Kano, physical development is controlled by the Urban Development Board; therefore, parasitic developments occur just outside it.[4] The peri-urban zone is now a mosaic of rural and urban residential and land-use patterns.

The further Kano region has lower population densities. It is the economic hinterland of Kano and extends hundreds of kilometers into neighboring states of Nigeria and adjacent countries, especially Niger. In much of this region, the percentage of arable land has been estimated to range from 35 to 65, and there are protected forest reserves, extensive woody fallows, and some uncultivable areas. Settlement patterns are

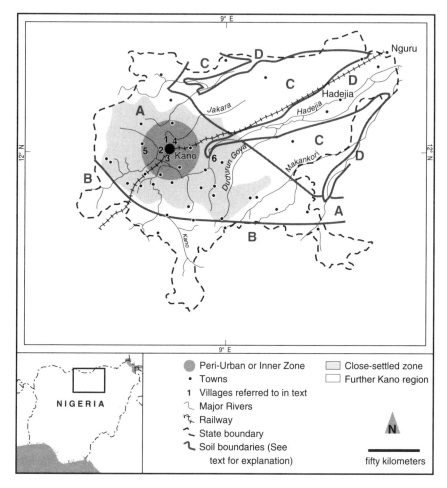

Fig. 11.1. Kano close-settled zone and soil groups. Reproduced from B.S. Hoyle, ed., *Spatial Aspects of Development*, p. 131. Copyright 1974 by John Wiley & Sons. Reprinted by permission of John Wiley & Sons, Ltd.

more variable, markets more numerous (in relation to the population), cattle production more important (relative to farming), and the major towns larger than the tributary towns of the CSZ. The dynamics of the CSZ cannot be divorced from this wider region.

Environment—Rainfall

Mean annual rainfall at Kano (1906–85) is 822 mm, distributed in a rainy season of five months at most (May–September), and normally

Fig. 11.2. Vertical air photo of a part of the Kano close-settled zone 20 km northeast of metropolitan Kano, 1981 (enlarged from scale 1:25,000). Note a compact village and dispersed compounds among the characteristically rectangular small fields at different stages of cropping and weeding. Farm trees appear as black dots, vegetated field boundaries as dark lines, pathways as white lines, and cattle tracks as diffuse dark stripes. Reproduced with the permission of the Director of Federal Surveys, Nigeria.

characterized by a pronounced peak in August. Average rainfall diminishes northward. Rainfall events may be brief, intense, and localized, causing sheetwash on exposed surfaces, rill or gully erosion on steeper slopes, and short-lived flooding in depressions. Major droughts occurred in 1905, 1913, 1926, and 1942. Two relatively wet decades preceded the great drought of 1972–74, and the persistence of drought thereafter was reflected in a progressive decline of the thirty-year means from 104 percent of the long-term mean in 1931–60 to 99 percent in 1941–70 and 97 percent in 1951–80 (Mortimore 1989: 140). There were major droughts in 1983 and 1984. But in 1988, after a slow start, rainfall was higher than for many decades, and there were heavy falls and extensive flooding.

Surface and Groundwater

The Kano River and its tributaries form a part of the Lake Chad drainage basin. Until their regimes were altered by the construction of dams, their flow was conspicuously seasonal, their beds wide and sandy for much of the period November–May. The smaller rivers Gari, Tomas, and Jakara, after following the regional slope northeastward, disappear by seepage and evaporation. Wells are the principal sources of domestic water, and the depth of the water table at the end of the dry season (May) in 1964 was 12 to 15 m around Kano, rising during the rains. Levels fell during the drought of 1972–74, but subsequently, groundwater remained accessible at shallow depth throughout the inner CSZ. The wells are generally sited on interfluves, but water is much closer to the surface (1–2 m) in the stream beds, though beyond the reach of most crops without irrigation.

Soils

The soils of the CSZ (A on fig. 11.1) are classified as brown and reddish-brown soils of arid and semiarid regions or inceptisols (see Jones and Wild 1975); they developed on wind-transported dune sands overlying the granitic Basement Complex. They are not intrinsically fertile and support an open Sudan savanna woodland under natural conditions. They are superior to the Chad Formation dune soils (C on fig. 11.1), but they are lighter to cultivate than the heavier but richer ferruginous tropical soils (B on fig. 11.1). They have 14.6 percent clay and silt (compared with 10.9 percent for C, and 32.1 percent for B). Their carbon content is 0.23 percent (compared with 0.15 percent and 0.54 percent), and their infiltration rate is 2.3 (compared with 6.5 and 0.2).[5] Seasonally flooded valley floors normally have grey hydromorphic soils, possessing a relatively high clay fraction and carbon content (D on fig. 11.1). Such lowland or *fadama* soils are quite distinct from upland soils, whose principal variable property is the depth to the lateritic horizon.

Soil erosion is most serious along valley sides where the steepest slopes occur, gullies working back from the river banks along footpaths, and cultivation furrows. The sandy nature of the drift cover facilitates erosion, not only by easing the removal of the soil by surface runoff but also by providing little resistance to the undercutting of stream banks.

Pests and Pathogens

No catalogue of pests and pathogens has been compiled for the CSZ. A rapid diagnostic survey of a farming system 130 km northeast of Kano identified a long and varied list affecting the main crops (Abalu et al. 1983).[6] All others paled into insignificance when rosette disease struck groundnuts in 1975, continuing its depredations in subsequent years. Bird damage to grain (especially bulrush millet) caused by *Quelea quelea* or other species, is heavy in some years. Grasshoppers (notably *Oedaleus senegalensis*) may appear in huge numbers when the rainfall favors their breeding cycle. Their impact is greatest when grass is scarce and the young grain shoots are attacked, and they may also attack the immature grain at the end of the season. Locust invasions are less frequent. Granivorous rodents may steal grain, frustrating planting.

Nature of Population Change

There is no reliable series of census data for Nigeria. Under- and over-counting affected the censuses of 1952–53 and 1963. The census of 1973 was canceled, and that of 1991 was not available for the present study. The canceled results of 1962 provide a baseline.

Population Structure

Demographic surveys were carried out in three villages of Ungogo District (within 10 km of the north edge of metropolitan Kano) in 1964 (Mortimore and Wilson 1965) and in six villages affected by compensation payments on the new campus of Bayero University (within 13 km of the west edge) in 1977 (Stokes 1978) (table 11.1). The populations enumerated were 5,949 and 6,532. This comparison of two populations separated by thirteen years in time and 10 km in space, although very rough because of the sources of possible error, indicates comparable population structures.[7] In Dorayi (5 km southwest of Kano), Hill (1977: 89) reported that 39 percent of the population were children under 14–16 years in 1972; and in two villages north and west of Kano, Amerena (1982: 96) found that 64 and 69 percent of men had one wife.

Population Growth

The data of 1964 do not permit estimates of fertility or reproduction rates. A comparison between the village data from the sample census of 1931, the censuses of 1952 and 1962, and the field study of 1964 suggested overall rates of increase of 1.8 percent (1931–52), 3.8 percent (1952–62) and 0.45 percent (1962–64). But it is widely believed that undercounting occurred in 1931 and again in 1952. The discrepancy between the second and third periods throws doubt on the reliability of the census data for 1962, at least for these villages.[8] For Kano Province (now Kano State), the censuses of 1952 and 1962 suggest a rate of increase of 2.6 percent a year (Mortimore 1974: 135), although a higher estimate of 2.8 to 2.9 percent is available (Green 1970).[9] Somewhat slower rates of growth in rural areas are indicated by urban rates of 7 to 9 percent (10.5 percent of the province's population of 4.3 million was then urbanized).

In Ungogo District, a decline in growth was recorded from 2.2 percent (1931–52) to 1.2 percent (1952–62) (Mortimore 1968). This unexpected and unusual development lends support to the view that outmigration must have been important. No trustworthy census data are available for the peri-urban zone after 1962.[10] Hill (1977: 91–92) estimated the annual rate of growth of the population of Kumbotso District to have been 0.5 to 1 percent between 1932 and 1971. This estimate makes allowance for undercounting in the District Reassessment Report of 1932 (from 40,200 to 60,000) and for underrecording in the tax returns of 1971 (from 62,335 to 81,000).[11] Speculative as it is, her argument provides a warning against assuming a high growth rate derived from estimates of the rate of natural increase, as yet without demonstration, in the CSZ.

Population Density

The average density of the residential population in the three Ungogo villages was 353/km² in 1964, although marked variations existed at microscale, and in Ungogo District as a whole, it was 244/km² according to the census of 1962. Given that 84 percent of the area was under culti-

Table 11.1. Population Structure in 1964 and 1977[a]

	1964 (three Ungogo villages)	1977 (three Bayero University villages)[b]
Age structure (percent of population)		
Children	30.4 (0–10 yrs)	41.0 (0–14 yrs)
Reproductive	67.2 (11–60 yrs)	57.2 (15–64 yrs)
Elderly	2.4 (over 60 yrs)	1.8 (over 64 yrs)
Males per 100 females		
Age 71+	85	114
61–70	105	164
51–60	126	132
41–50	100	142
31–40	121	101
21–30	74	68
11–20	46	82
0–10	117	106
All	83	96
Marriage		
Percent of married men having one wife	65	61
Household size		
Persons per household	8.1	8.5

Sources: Mortimore and Wilson 1965 (Ungogo District villages); Stokes 1978 (Bayero University villages).

[a]The figures are approximate. There are many sources of possible error, including: inaccurate age estimation (digital preference, age advancement of married girls, forgetfulness); withholding of information about certain individuals (tax fears); constant short-term movements; and conducting of some interviews away from the home (in the 1977 survey).

[b]Two of Stokes' villages are excluded.

vation, the amount of arable land available per head was 0.24 ha in the villages and 0.36 in the district as a whole (Mortimore and Wilson 1965: 93). Among a sample of 11 family holdings surveyed in 1964, ranging from 15 residents on a holding of 0.61 ha (0.04 ha/person) to 35 residents on one of 13.4 ha (3.38 ha/person), the average cultivated holding was 4.1 ha, and the average amount of cultivated land per person was only 0.23 ha. (Mortimore and Wilson 1965: 51).

The lack of population data after 1964 renders any subsequent estimate of population density in Ungogo speculative.[12] If the rate of natural increase since 1962 were assumed to be 2.9 percent (see note 10) and migration zero, the average density in the district in 1988 would be 495/km^2 (1,282/mi^2). Such an increase does not appear probable from informal observations. Hill (1977: 88–92) gives population data for Dorayi in 1972. She reports a total population of 3,499, a male:female ratio of 101, and a density of 540/km² (1,400/mi²), higher than any hitherto estimated for the CSZ. She attributed this high figure to the proximity of Dorayi to Kano City,[13] and "to our ability (unlike that of official enumerators) to *repeat* our population counts—which yielded successively higher figures before they finally stabilized" (Hill 1977: 77; my emphasis). Unless movements between enumerations were compensated for, this procedure would approximate a de jure enumeration, whose results are not compatible with those of a de facto count of persons actually present at the time of the census, subject as it may nevertheless be to undercounting. This would explain the achievement of a balanced male:female ratio, which is rare in rural Hausaland; short-term mobility is widespread in rural Hausa communities.

Frustrating as it is, the only conclusion that can be safely made is that average densities in the inner CSZ approached 250/km² in the early 1960s (locally, 350/km²) and may exceed 500/km², if locally, in the late 1980s. Interesting as an accurate assessment would be, the density now has little economic significance owing to the importance of nonfarming incomes and the impossibility—except by painstaking research—of unravelling the complexities of individual claims to land.

Migration

A quiescent picture of migration obtained from the survey of 1964 (Mortimore and Wilson 1965) leaves the imbalance in the age-sex structure of the Ungogo villages unexplained. The method used to elicit information on migration must be assumed to have been too superficial.[14] Hill's thorough study in Dorayi in 1972 (1977: 146–51) revealed that 239 men had left the village, whose departures, if spread evenly over the preceding twenty-five years, would have amounted to an annual rate of migration of 1 to 2 percent (cf. her estimate for the rate of population growth of 0.5 to 1 percent). The largest group (97) had moved into Kano City and would perhaps have been much larger had not urban employment opportunities in casual, unskilled work been within walking distance of home. A large number (57) had left without trace of their whereabouts, and a similar number (61) had spread among destinations elsewhere in Kano or other Hausa emirates. There were no reported instances of migration for farming.

Like the Ungogo villages, Dorayi reported little dry-season migration (*cin rani*). In 1979–80, only 1 percent of those interviewed by Amerena (1982: 191–95, 249ff.) in the peri-urban village of Takurza (7 km north of Kano) migrated for the dry season, but 20 percent in Doka (23 km west of Kano) travelled to Lagos, Kaduna, and Kano, principally for unskilled jobs. The incidence of cin rani had risen there from 12 percent in 1969 to peaks of 30 percent in 1973 and 1976. Drought was a recruiting agent, those taking part for the first time in 1972 or 1973 nearly doubling the numbers. It is clear that the difference between the two villages was due to the availability of urban employment opportunities within walking distance of Takurza. Amerena did not investigate long-term outmigration.

During the 1970s and 1980s the demand for rented accommodation in metropolitan Kano generated increased building activity in the peri-urban zone. Where land is under the control of local government authorities (i.e., outside the domain of the Urban Planning Board), the regulation of its acquisition under customary tenure is lax, and economic and political pressure on landholders to sell may be considerable. Adjacent to major peri-urban sources of employment (such as the university), the pace of speculative land acquisition and development may be spectacular (Main and Cline-Cole 1987). On the northwest side of the city such development now extends more than 15 km. This shows that the conversion of the peri-urban zone from a rural to a suburban economic base, scarcely noticeable in 1964, is now proceeding apace.

The overall picture is clear. The CSZ as a whole grew historically by inmigration as well as natural increase, owing to the political and commercial attraction exerted by Kano City. As the supply of land became exhausted, net inmigration changed—not later than the 1940s—into net male outmigration, which has reduced the rate of population growth in the inner CSZ. A brake on the rate of such outmigration has been exercised since around 1970 by the possibility of commuting to urban employment from the peri-urban zone; and in locations along major roads, speculative building for rental now attracts increasing numbers of inmigrants. Neither natural increase nor migration has yet been quantified. Dry-season circulation is not important within commuting range of metropolitan Kano, but it assumes great significance outside the peri-urban zone and, independently of demographic factors, it intensified as a consequence of the loss of farm incomes from drought in the years after 1971.

Nature of Agricultural Change

The two main farming systems—upland and fadama systems—are differentiated on the basis of topography and land use. A land-use map of 75 km² in Ungogo District, based on air photography (1962, scale 1:4,800) indicated that 79.6 percent of the area was then under annual (upland) cultivation, 4.2 percent under seasonally irrigated, perennial (lowland or fadama) cultivation, and 7.5 percent was degraded scrub woodland used for grazing and woodcutting (Mortimore and Wilson 1965: 19–24). These proportions are still representative of the inner CSZ. By contrast, at a distance of 69 km northeast of Kano (just outside the CSZ), where fadama is lacking and rotational fallowing is practiced on upland, cultivation occupied only 45.2 percent, and woodland, scrub and grassland (including fallows) 53.4 percent. The population densities for the two districts (Ungogo and Ringim) were 244/km² and 116/km² in 1962, according to the census (Mortimore 1970).

The Annual (Upland) System

The annual upland system was based in 1964 on the four major crops: guinea corn, bulrush millet (short- and long-season varieties), cowpea, and groundnuts. Cassava was a minor crop, and sweet potatoes, sorrel, and some vegetables might be grown in compound gardens. Crop production was carried out in conjunction with the planting, protection, and harvesting of economic trees (such as *Acacia* spp., *Adansonia digitata*, *Parkia biglobosa*, and *Ziziphus* spp.), the maintenance of live hedges and field boundaries (notably *Lawsonia inermis* and *Andropogon gayanus*), and the management of small livestock (goats, sheep, fowls) and donkeys.

The System in 1964

The technical base of the system was described in the following terms (Mortimore and Wilson 1965: 45–50). Manure was applied to unprepared fields before or shortly after planting, with a peak of activity in March (toward the end of the dry season). Planting took place after the first heavy rain, using the long-handled seedhoe and the help of women and children. Millet was usually planted first, guinea corn second, and groundnuts or cowpeas third, making up a variety of interplanting patterns using the furrows between the previous years' ridges where the manure had been spread and moisture had collected. Manure might be heaped at the feet of the growing plants. If groundnuts were grown alone, the soil would be first hoed into large flat-topped ridges using the heavy ridging hoe. Weeding was carried out within ten to fourteen days of planting, and twice more later in the season. The first weeding was done with the light weeding hoe and subsequently ridges were built up around the plants using the ridging hoe. Ridging supports the tall grains and facilitates drainage during the August rainfall peak. Weeding created the greatest demand for male labor during the agricultural year (women and girls did not normally participate). Harvesting of the early millet started in September by cutting off the heads with the cutlass and leaving the stems in the ground until the guinea corn and late millet were ready in October or November. The stalks were cut and laid in the furrows to dry, and the heads removed in bundles to the granaries. The residues provided fodder, construction materials, and fuel or were burned in the fields. Groundnuts were lifted in October or November, dried in stacks, and the nuts then removed for sale (shelled or unshelled); the residues were valuable fodder. Cowpeas were picked during the same months, traditionally by the women, and the leaves also retained as fodder. Cassava remained in the ground until needed but had to be protected from free-grazing livestock by earth banks or fences.

Sheep and goats were kept in small numbers in almost every compound, grazing freely during the dry season, but they were kept inside and fed on collected grasses and fodder during the wet season, or grazed under supervision on such grazing land as still existed. They were killed periodically for ceremonies or festivals, but their principal value was as a capital asset, saleable in times of food shortage. Donkeys were more valuable and less commonly owned. They were normally kept in or close to the house and fed on fodder; their purpose was trade and local transport, especially of firewood and manure. Most families possessed a few fowls.

All the trees growing on the farmed parkland had economic uses either for firewood—which might be obtained by lopping or by felling—or for harvesting marketable crops every year and emergency or regular foods. The species were selected from the natural flora or introduced from other ecological zones north or south, over a long period of time. They grew typically at densities of 8 to 10/ha, added variety to the diet, and provided stand-by foods in times of famine.

Much of this description of the system as it was observed in 1964 applies equally well in 1988, as far as informal observations over two decades suggest.[15] However, pronounced variations occur between localities and also between years, the variable pattern of rainfall generating much divergence from the chronology given above. The principal change variables will now be isolated briefly, though few quantitative answers can be extracted from the information available.

Labor

The markedly seasonal pattern of farm labor inputs has not changed, though whether labor is in surplus or deficit on a given holding during the growing season depends, as always, on the specific land:labor ratio. The smaller holdings had surplus labor in 1964 even at the height of the weeding season; the surplus was channeled into nonfarm occupations or into laboring for others. Assuming an optimal land:labor ratio (under conditions of hand technology and seasonal rainfall) of one adult male to 2 ha, only two of eleven sampled holdings—and they the largest—did not then have surplus labor.[16] Hill (1977: 103, 168) considers that there was a labor surplus of more than 100 percent in Dorayi in 1972: ". . . individual men, especially poorer men, spend less and less time on cultivation as the population increases"; and the supply of farm labor far exceeded the demand for it. Therefore, on intuitive (because of population growth) and empirical grounds it is reasonable to suppose an accentuating labor surplus in the CSZ, although the position is variable according to the time of the year.

Labor hiring is commonly believed to have increased, but there is no hard evidence for it. Wage rates increased by at least 1,000 percent between 1964 and the 1980s (from 3 shillings or N0.30 to more than N 3.00 per working day—about 6.30 to 14.30 hours).[17] Amerena (1982: 148) reported that 52 percent of the farmers in peri-urban Takurza and 42 percent in the outer CSZ village of Doka hired labor and that more money (N86 in Takurza, N57 in Doka) was spent per farmer per year on this than on other inputs (N25 and N16 respectively). The figures (N86 cf. N25 in Takurza; N57 cf. N16 in Doka) suggest some degree of labor intensification on larger farms over and above family labor but not very much—say, seventeen working days/year in Doka and twenty-eight in Takurza. Since the institution of hired laboring (*kwadago*) transfers labor from smaller to larger holdings, any increase in its incidence might suggest a corresponding increase in capitalization in farming and heightening inequality in the size distribution of landholdings.

Fixed Capital

Fixed capital, other than that created by labor (such as granaries, fences, or ditches), is still rare except on farms belonging to wealthy persons (often city residents), where poultry or cattle fattening are carried on. Draught animals and mechanical cultivation are still rare and are restricted to such farms. Most farmers work with a small assemblage of locally smithed hand implements worth little more than ₦10/ha in 1964 or ₦50/ha in the 1980s (see note 17). They cannot acquire either the capital to purchase a plow team or the land necessary to make its operation economic; fodder is also scarce and costly.

By no means new to the CSZ, capitalist farmers are increasing in number as part of a general trend in northern Nigeria (Labaran 1987), attracted by rising food prices and land values and by the ease of acquiring land under customary tenure by privileged persons. This trend represents a threat to the long-term security of smallholders in the CSZ, unless restrictions are placed on the transfer of land. On the other hand, increased capitalization should facilitate the adoption of new high-yielding technologies, when available.

Farm Inputs

Fertilizers were purchased at subsidized prices for use on groundnuts in 1964 but rarely on other crops. In 1979, 67 percent of farmers purchased fertilizers in Doka (Amerena 1982: 148) but bought little—about a bag apiece. Observations indicate that it was being used quite widely on grain crops in the 1980s. But organic manure is preferred, if available; all farmers (unless compelled by poverty to sell their animals or their manure) used it both in 1964 and in 1979.[18] Average applications were 4.1 t/ha in the 1962–63 and 1963–64 seasons, though much higher at 6.5 t/ha, on one sample of eleven holdings (Mortimore and Wilson 1965: 48, 53). Part of the manure was purchased: on the sample holdings, expenditure averaged ₦3.30/ha. In addition, manure was produced domestically. Donkey loads cost ₦0.05 in Kano City and were exported to the inner CSZ at the rate of 140 to 185 t/day in the dry seasons of 1965 and 1969 (Mortimore 1972), its distribution in space diminishing with distance.[19] Among Amerena's respondents in 1979, almost all used manure; but only farmers in the peri-urban village spent significantly on it.[20] Other purchased inputs (herbicides, pesticides) continue to be rather rare, although mention should be made of the fact that many farmers still buy seed in the planting season.

Recent data on farm inputs have not been found. Therefore, the question of whether intensification—particularly through fertilization—has continued cannot be answered. All that can be stated is that there is no evidence for any decrease either in farm inputs or in the labor used in their application—especially for organic manure.

Frequency of Cultivation

There has been no change in the index of cultivation frequency since 1964 (1964 = 100). There is no unused cultivable land, barring accidents that may prevent a farmer from working his land. Gowers estimated in 1913 that about one-third of the land was fallowed under grass each year. No reports of fallowing since then are known to me. Since the growing season is very short (five months or less), any further increase in the cropping index will depend on the introduction of irrigation to upland soils. This is beyond the technical resources of small-scale agriculture but has been achieved on the Government's Kano River Irrigation Project (Baba 1989).

Crops

Table 11.2 analyzes changes in cropping strategies by means of a crude comparison of the frequencies of farmers growing each crop in Ungogo District in 1964 and in Doka and Takurza in 1979–80. The main trends that may be tentatively discerned are a weakening in the position of groundnuts and cowpeas and the virtual disappearance of cassava. However, these changes were not caused by population changes or ongoing intensification; quite the reverse. Northern Nigeria's export groundnut crop (over a million tons in 1967) was destroyed by drought in 1973 and rosette disease in 1975; subsequently the diminished output was entirely diverted to the local market by higher prices. Continued vulnerability to drought and disease has dramatically reduced its importance, especially north of Kano (lat. 12° N). The decline of the cowpea (an alternative both as a revenue earner and as a source of nitrogen in the

Table 11.2. Frequency of Main Crops in the Inner CSZ, 1962–63 and 1979–80 (% of farmers planting)

Crop	Ungogo District 1962–63 (1)	Doka, 1979 (2)	Takurza, 1979 (3)	Average (2 and 3)
Cassava	common	0	0	0
Cowpeas	75	26	68	47
Groundnuts	>90	78	52	65
Guinea corn	>90	100	98	99
Millet, early	75	27	87	57
Millet, late	75	41	27	34

Sources: Mortimore and Wilson 1965: 53f.; Amerena 1982: 150f.

cropping mixture) in Doka was due to alternative opportunities available in local dry-season market gardening. However, output of this crop fluctuates widely from year to year. Cassava was eliminated by drought risk. A shift from late to early millet, and from guinea corn to early millet, which is believed to have occurred farther north, is not apparent from these figures, which of course take no account of the area sown.

Livestock

Cattle were rarely seen in 1964 and still are not, except for workbulls and small fattening or dairy herds owned by capitalist farmers. Their cost, since the great drought of 1972–74, and their need for purchased fodder, continue to put them beyond the reach of the poor.[21] As Hendy (1977) showed, the distribution of cattle and of small livestock is inversely related in the CSZ, the first correlating negatively, and the second positively with the density of the human population, who use small livestock for savings and milking and feed them on crop residues and foliage. Every family aspired to own sheep or goats (Hill 1977: 82–83), but still livestock ownership fell in the drought of 1972–74. Absolute losses through sales or death were high, the proportion of nonowners increased, and prices first collapsed, then inflated. The mean number of sheep and goats per family in five villages in northern Kano State, for example, fell from 6.7 in 1972 to 2.9 in 1974 (Mortimore 1989: 52, 59). But breeding cycles are short, and numbers later recovered. In the CSZ, Amerena (1982: 148) reported that in Doka, 83 percent of her respondents owned goats and 69 percent sheep; in Takurza, 75 percent owned goats and 68 percent sheep; and the mean number of animals in 1980 ranged from 3.4 to 5.5. This fragmentary evidence is consistent with the hypothesis that small livestock occupy an undiminished place in the farming system, notwithstanding the recurrence of drought and rising costs of fodder.

The donkey population, on the other hand, did not recover from the drought. Hill (1977: 82–83) estimated that there were two donkeys for every three married men in Dorayi in 1972; and their use in the manure trade was as essential then as in 1964. But in 1979–80, only 8 percent of Amerena's farmers in Doka owned donkeys. In Takurza the figure was 34 percent—unusually high, as shown by the fact that in the dry season of 1982–83, the number of donkeys entering and leaving Kano had fallen to 6 percent of the numbers counted in the 1960s (Cline-Cole et al. 1990: 36). The substitution of motor transport for the donkey—one may hire a "pickup" to deliver city manure even to remote farms—was certainly one factor accounting for the change.

Trees

Notwithstanding the obvious resemblance between the farmed parkland of the CSZ today and descriptions of it written in the nineteenth century, Trevallion (1966), on the basis of projected urban fuelwood demand, predicted the virtual disappearance of wood stocks by the 1980s, and Eckholm et al. (1984), evidently without benefit of a visit to the area, asserted that the agricultural system and wood-stock management were on the point of collapse. The facts are quite otherwise (Cline-Cole et al. 1990).

Economic trees on a holding of 13.5 ha surveyed in 1964 numbered 94 at an average density of seven trees/ha. Nine species were identified, and the estimated harvest value per tree ranged from ₦0.25 to ₦1.20, excluding firewood (Mortimore and Wilson 1965: 60). Apart from the unusually large size of the holding, these results are representative. Harvests tended to coincide with the dry season (January–May) and to make a significant contribution to family budgets. The latest evidence from air photography of a part of both inner and outer CSZ shows that the density of trees on farmed parkland increased by 23 percent between 1972 and 1981, from 10 to 12 trees/ha, notwithstanding the occurrence of several droughts when both natural mortality (especially *Acacia albida*) and woodcutting pressure were at a maximum.

In 1964, it was estimated that 25 percent of wood cut from trees in Ungogo District was sold, the rest being consumed as domestic fuel or used in construction. In 1983, a survey of woodcutting practice in Rimin Gado District (50 km west of Kano) concluded that 39 percent of woodcutters marketed wood. In 1964, most of the wood sold formed the inward component of a system of rural-urban, donkey-borne trade whose main outward component was manure for the fields. Surveys in 1965 and 1969 indicated daily imports at the height of the dry season of 120 to 125 tons of firewood and exports of 140 to 185 tons of manure (Mortimore 1972). In 1983, a comprehensive survey of traffic flows revealed that donkey-borne traffic in firewood had fallen to a mere 6 percent of its former volume, and even making generous allowance for the replacement of donkeys by motor pickups, the inner CSZ was supplying only 15 to 20 percent of its former wood and not more than 2 percent of total urban estimated demand.

Since 1952, when the donkey trade supplied almost all urban demand, urban consumption had risen by about 800 percent, average household use having remained more or less constant. Whence the balance? The answer lies in the extension of the fuelwood hinterland of metropolitan Kano to the further Kano region, helped by improved transport infrastructure and subsidized motor fuel. Woodcutting from farm trees and fallows is an increasingly important source of income, but more important are the activities of large-scale entrepreneurs who operate in distant woodland areas, attracted to the trade by the high prices and steady demand in the urban fuelwood market.

The significance of this for the farmed parkland of the inner CSZ is that producer resistance has evidently transferred urban market pressure from the multiple-use agroforestry system of the CSZ to the further Kano region. Farmers in the CSZ plant and protect trees, even as official sanctions against the cutting of trees are weakening. The alternative uses of such trees are valued as highly as they were in 1964, and the preferred fuelwood trees are those with few such uses. Wood management, cutting, and use are the subjects of a comprehensive body of ethnoscientific practice that is rational from a conservation standpoint.

Outputs

Crop-yield estimates obtained for the years 1962 and 1963 were considered to err on the conservative side, and there are no more recent data available to permit an evaluation of trends.[22] Livestock, similarly, have not been subjected to compatible output investigations, and even less is known of tree crops, except for firewood. It is, therefore, impossible to estimate the trends in output over the last two decades. All that can be said is that lacking any evidence of the withdrawal of labor, it must be assumed that yields are maintaining their relative values.

Conclusion

On the basis of the limited and indirect evidence reviewed, the annual (upland) system of agroforestry with livestock in the Kano CSZ appears to have been stable during the past two decades with regard to most inputs, and there is no evidence of declining output, with the major exception of groundnuts. There is no evidence, either, of the breakdown alleged by some writers. However, it can be safely assumed that the process of intensification has not kept pace with the growth of the residential population. The small scale of most farming enterprises and the low opportunity cost of family labor have inhibited the introduction of labor-saving technologies.

The Perennial (Lowland or Fadama) System

The perennial fadama system is found in river valleys (and adjacent to some wells) and occupies less than 5 percent of the surface area, but its importance is disproportionately large.

The System in 1964

The market-gardening system of Jakara River fadama was described as follows (Mortimore and Wilson 1965: 65–71). The farms were operated in conjunction with upland farms, and produced vegetables for sale in the urban market. Land was worth four times as much as upland, and holdings were small, often 0.1 ha or less. Labor allocation between these farming systems reflected the priority of subsistence production in the rainy season; the major period of activity in the fadama was from February to April. Irrigation by *jigo* (*shaduf*) is time-consuming, and close attention to the growing plants is necessary to ensure good yields. In the wet season, the less-demanding crops such as spinach, maize, and cucumber were planted; flood damage was a common occurrence. The limits of the fadama are determined not by soil characteristics but by water viability. Distance, through excessive percolation, or gradient, necessitating raised aqueducts or excavated plots, cause rapidly diminishing returns for extra labor near the boundary.

Beside seed and labor, agricultural inputs included manure and water. Manure was applied in large quantities, even though the river water contains nutrients, draining as it does most of the old City's sewage. Watering took the greater part of labor inputs, each plot receiving several hours' application at intervals of two to three days. The jigo was cheap to construct and might be owned individually or shared. Irrigation channels admitted water into each subplot of little more than a meter square. Two people, one on the jigo and one with a hoe, were required for efficient operation. They lifted 5,000 liters/hour or more, the equivalent of 24,000 in a 4- to 5-hour irrigation shift. The produce was normally sold to middlemen on the spot. The cultivation frequency index was 200 (assuming two crops/year) but potentially higher (since more than one crop of quick-growing vegetables could be grown in a single season).

Technical Change

There are no known investigations for locations in the CSZ, but Erhabor's (1982) detailed input-output study at Ringim (on the eastern perimeter of the CSZ) in 1978–79 is of much interest, although it provides no direct indication of time trends. Two technical systems were then in use, based on the jigo and on petrol pumps. In the absence of evidence to the contrary, I assume that the operating characteristics and relative costs of the jigo system were similar to those in the inner CSZ.

By the early 1980s, the majority of the jigo appliances in the Jakara fadama had been replaced by pumps.[23] The implications of such a technological transformation are suggested by Erhabor's data from ten pump farmers at Ringim. The pumps involved high capital costs (whereas the jigo, being made from local materials, is extremely cheap), higher total costs, and require more land to realize maximum returns (model experiments indicated 2.56 ha for a pump compared with 1.92 ha for the jigo), although the average area operated was much less (0.83 ha and 0.17 ha respectively). But the pump delivered ten times more water to the field than the jigo at one-third of the unit cost and gave much higher returns to labor and management, more than compensating for its costs.

Two points arising from Erhabor's analysis have major significance for the question of future labor intensification in the CSZ. First, water supply was ranked top among major problems hindering irrigation farming by both jigo and pump farmers. There has been a major extension of the area under small-scale irrigation in northern Nigeria since about 1960, but it is subject to physical limitations. Areas dependent on low-yielding water sources cannot change to the pump system. Second, the problem of labor supply was ranked seventh among jigo farmers but equal first among pump farmers. Model experiments appear to have shown that an average farm, using a jigo with unlimited water, required only one full-time family operator and one part-time hired worker to maximize returns. An average farm with a pump could employ at least two family members. But since the average pump farm is four times larger, it appears that a transformation to pump irrigation has a negative effect on the labor-absorbing capacity of small-scale irrigation.[24]

Nature of Other Changes

Environmental Change

It is impossible, without ambiguity, to pin down the environmental consequences of demographic and agricultural changes. The assumption that the effects of management on the ecosystem can be easily disentangled from those of autonomous environmental change, particularly in the rainfall regime, has actually impeded an analytical understanding of desertification (Mortimore 1989). Contradictory evidence can be discerned in the hydrological, woodland, grassland, farmland, and morphodynamic subsystems in the Nigerian semiarid zone. This evidence cannot be reviewed here. But with regard to the CSZ, work recently undertaken or in progress provides some pointers to critical questions of environmental change.

Rainfall

The evidence of a drier rainfall regime since the 1960s (table 11.3) indicates that drought years should be expected to occur with greater frequency than they did before the drought of 1972–74. Droughts are unpredictable (as far as farmers are concerned), both on a yearly and on

Table 11.3. Monthly Distribution of Rainfall at Kano (June–September), 1906–85

Time period	June	July	August	September
1906–85 average (mm)	115.3	201.1	294.7	126.9
1906–25	102.3	211.2	329.3	139.7
1926–45	119.7	197.6	305.3	135.6
1946–65	130.8	220.8	313.7	129.2
1966–85	108.4	174.9	230.4	103.3
1906–85 average (%)	100	100	100	100
1906–25	88.7	105.0	111.7	110.1
1926–45	103.8	98.3	103.6	106.8
1946–65	113.4	109.8	106.4	101.8
1966–85	94.0	87.0	78.0	81.4
Percentage change from 1946–65 to 1966–85	−19	−23	−28	−21

Source: Mortimore 1989: 143.

a monthly basis; they are uneven in space, so that rainfall is deficient somewhere in almost every year; and it should be noted that *average* rainfall in the 1980s would have been regarded as a significant negative departure in the 1960s. These facts exert considerable pressure on farming and other land-use systems to evolve adaptive strategies in the medium or shorter term. It now appears possible that persistent drought has contributed as much to environmental degradation in the semiarid zone as suboptimal land use.

Water Erosion

Methods are still being developed for measuring rates of water erosion in savanna environments, and no regional assessment is available for the CSZ. Ahmed (1987), basing his studies on earlier work by Ologe (1972) and Olofin (1984), estimates erosion rates from 1.1 to 6.9 mm/year on different landform systems in the Hadejia-Jama'are basin. The greater part of the cultivated CSZ probably falls near the lower end of this range, having slopes of less than 2° and sandy, freely draining soils. The most serious erosion (as noted above) is found on steeper slopes adjacent to river valleys, especially where the hydrological regime has been affected by such activities as gravel digging or dam construction (Olofin 1984). Conspicuously eroded granite and quartzite hills, carrying a degraded scrub woodland, may testify to the antiquity of soil erosion in the area.[25]

Wind Erosion and Deposition

Despite the visible impact of local dust storms on exposed arable land, it is probable that the soils of the CSZ are net importers of inorganic material via the agency of the Harmattan. McTainsh (1987) has argued that the conditions under which the aeolian drift soils were formed were essentially the same as those governing the behavior of the Harmattan today. Mean weekly deposition of dust at Kano ranged from 3 to 7 gm/m² during the months of October–April in the years 1978–84 (McTainsh 1980; Mortimore 1989: 150).[26] The dust contains significant quantities of trace and major elements whose total annual deposition has been stated to exceed the amounts removed by an average crop of guinea-corn (Beavington and Cawse 1978).[27] However, before net deposition and its implications for soil fertility can be estimated at the regional scale, a method has to be found of separating locally remobilized from imported dust.[28]

Soil-Nutrient Status

The relative contributions of natural weathering, dust deposition, nitrogen fixation by plants, organic-matter additions from plant residues, animal droppings and manuring, and chemical fertilizers have not been estimated for the upland soils of the CSZ. Investigations into the contribution of manuring are in hand. Meanwhile, it should be noted that because both annual cultivation and manuring have been practiced for at least one hundred years, and manure inputs are not thought to be declining, alarm over the nutrient status of upland soils under indigenous management is premature.

Under irrigated management the position is different. Large-scale irrigation has been introduced to both upland and lowland soils in several projects in the CSZ. On the Tomas Irrigation Project (40 km north of Kano), Daniel (1987) found evidence of deterioration in both physical and chemical soil properties between 1970 and 1984–85. Continuous irrigation had washed out the fine fractions. The pH had risen, and so had exchangeable sodium, whereas the amounts of exchangeable calcium, magnesium, and potassium had fallen. Organic-matter content also had fallen. These changes were observed throughout the topographic profile. It is not known whether they are representative of other projects, in particular the Kano River Project where 60,000 ha of upland soils may eventually be brought under irrigation. The logic of irrigation development at the inception of these schemes was to introduce perennial cultivation to densely populated areas restricted by a seasonal rainfall regime to one cycle of cultivation each year (Mortimore 1974). Failure to achieve a stable soil-management regime would have grave long-term implications and would be reprehensible in view of the fact that indigenous management, according to all available evidence, achieved some degree of stability, even under the pressure of demographic growth.

Change and Stress in Land Tenure and Supply

In 1964 a cadastral survey was made of one village in Ungogo District, and the results were compared with a farm-boundary survey made in 1932.[29] During those three decades, the number of separately occupied plots in the 181 ha surveyed increased by 42 percent to 185. The number of landholders also increased from 95 to about 115. During the same period, the cultivated area was increased by the clearance of 10.5 ha of marginal scrubland in depressions. Of all the plots registered in 1932, 41 percent had been subdivided by 1964, whereas only 16 percent had been consolidated with adjacent holdings. Thus, subdivision gained at the expense of consolidation. Fragmentation also increased. The average plot decreased in size by 22 percent, whereas the average holding decreased by less than 11 percent (Mortimore 1967). These changes were considered to show the impact of demographic pressure on the operation of a cycle of subdivision and consolidation adjusted to the normal growth and subdivision of families (fig. 11.3). As a man increases his wealth he attempts to increase the size of his holding by purchase (*saye*) of adjoining plots or if these are not available, distant ones. His sons, on marriage or before, receive by gift (*kyauta*) parts of the father's holding (numbered 11–14 on fig. 11.3). On such a farm (*gayauna*) they grow market crops independently, while continuing to work under the father's direction on the main farm and thereby contributing to the family food supply. On the death of the father, Shari'a law provides for the division of the inheritance (*gado*) among male heirs, who in turn attempt to increase the size of their holdings by purchase and, where possible, to consolidate fragmented plots.[30]

Such a cyclical model may describe reality no more often than among Chayanov's (1966) Russian peasants. The *gandu* or extended family-based farming unit (see Hill 1972, Goddard 1973, Wallace 1978), though normal in the CSZ, may not be universal even when demographically feasible.[31] Not all wealthy family heads could ensure that

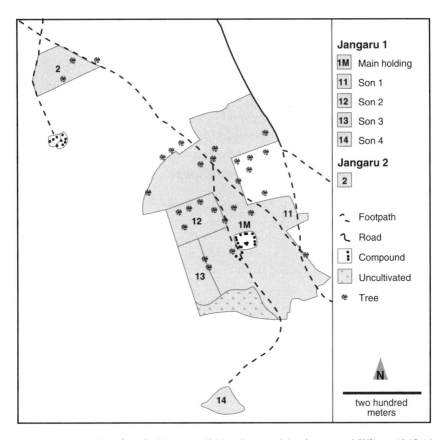

Fig. 11.3. Landholdings in Ungogo, 1964. Source: Mortimore and Wilson 1965:46.

they themselves would have sons (even by taking extra wives), whereas family fertility could easily run ahead of the economic capacity to expand one's holding. The second holding (no. 2 on fig. 11.3) was operated by a nuclear family with several young children, whose head was too poor to expand his holding and diversified into weaving instead.

Hill (1977: 96–99, 121–22, 124–27) attempted an analysis of the effect of population pressure on land distribution by comparing Batagarawa in Katsina with Dorayi in the CSZ, whose population density was estimated to exceed that of Batagarawa by a factor of six. The use of Batagarawa (200 km northwest in a lower-rainfall zone) as a proxy for Dorayi in the 1930s is debatable, and the comparison was further constrained by excluding a number of small plots from the Dorayi survey,[32] and by limiting the Batagarawa survey to manured fields (cultivated annually), leaving out bush farms, which are also important (see Hill 1972). Nevertheless, the conclusions are interesting. Inequality in landholding was found to be equally pronounced in both samples, in the sense that the top 5 percent of farmers owned about 20 percent and the top 15 percent owned about 45 percent of the land in both places; but it was more pronounced in Dorayi in the sense that about 33 percent owned less than 0.4 ha (compared with 10 percent in Batagarawa), and there were some virtually landless men. In Dorayi, a greater willingness on the part of richer farmers to loan plots (*aro*) to the poor partly compensated for this inequality, although not fully in the case of the poorest of all.

In Dorayi, the average size of plots was said to have decreased substantially within living memory to 0.5 ha in 1972, as the result of subdivision on inheritance. This may be compared with a decrease in Ungogo from 1.3 ha in 1932 to 1 ha in 1964; however, it is not certain that the definitions of the plot used in each place are compatible.[33] The trend is the same, though Hill's method could not assess the strength of the countervailing processes of acquisition and consolidation.

The price of farmland in Ungogo had risen 400 to 800 percent in the twenty years before 1964 (from little more than ₦5/ha to ₦20–40/ha, see Note 17). The history of one plot of 0.4 ha is indicative. It changed hands for ₦4 in 1927, and ₦10 in 1934. Less than half of it was sold in 1954 for ₦16 (the balance being taken over by the government on payment of compensation equivalent to ₦20). By 1964, the smaller part was considered to be worth more than ₦40 (over ₦200/ha: Mortimore and Wilson 1965: 52). In Dorayi, land was worth about £60/acre (₦300/ha) in 1972, but in 1930 "may have been a little higher than in Batagarawa, say £2 to £3 per acre" (₦10–15/ha; Hill 1977: 99).

Most previous work on land tenure in Hausaland and administrative practice (for example, when compensation payments are made) proceeds from the assumption that plots are subject to the exclusive use rights of individuals (usually men), including trees growing on them. Indeed, it is sometimes thought that landholding rights are equivalent to freehold because of an apparent absence of constraints on the right to sell. This assumption is incorrect, because customary rights (and transfers) are subject to the ultimate recognition of the State Governor who administers all land on behalf of the community. It does, however, reflect the sharp distinction separating the individualized customary tenure of Hausaland from communal forms of tenure operating in some other parts of the country. Such individualization is sometimes taken as evidence of population pressure, but in northern Nigeria it has more to do with the impact of Shari'a law, which has all but eliminated communal tenure in long-established Muslim areas.

A penetrating study of land tenure dynamics in 91 ha of farmland at Hurumi, situated 50 km southeast of Kano, in 1975–76 by Ross (1987) has taken the analysis of land tenure to a greater depth. It indicates that the rights to land may be much more complex and that the relations between the ownership and operation of farmland may also be very intricate. The background to this study is one of increasing land scarcity in an area of high and rising population density in the outer CSZ. The amount of land sold was found to be declining in response to its scarcity. (Reluctance to part with land rights is widely reported in the CSZ and contributes to the inflation of land values.) Delayed inheritance claims were widespread; 66 percent of inherited plots were subject to additional claims by persons other than the recognized owner. Such dormant claimants included both women and departed migrants. Such sharing, rather than final subdivision, of use rights constrains further fragmentation. As an attempt to secure access to land by increasing numbers of people, it is described by Ross as involution.[34] It may constrain the growth of absolute landlessness.

Land circulation is a means whereby ownership rights may be adjusted to the economic demand for land where there is unconformity. In this area, Ross found that circulation within the village involved 30 percent of the persons included in the study. Only sixteen farmed solely the land they owned; twenty-eight farmed only land they did not own, fifty-two supplemented their own land with land belonging to others; twenty-one received use rights that they then assigned to others. In addition, as mentioned above, absentees might claim rights. Such complexities warn against an oversimplified view of land tenure, particularly in areas affected by large-scale irrigation (Baba 1975; Wallace 1980; Morris 1981; Orogun 1986). There seems no reason why Ross's findings should not also be indicative of the inner CSZ, where an even higher population density may be expected to accentuate the demand for sharing ownership rights and redistributing operating rights, as well as city residents' interests in acquiring additional farm land.

Household Self-Sufficiency in Grain

Given the evidence of environmental uncertainty and of high and mounting land scarcity, the question of household self-sufficiency in food grains is obviously critical. Hill (1977: 117–38) estimated that with an average yield of 561 kg/ha (500 lb/acre) of grain per year and an average per capita consumption in a mixed population of men, women, and children of 164 kg/year (1 lb of threshed grain per day), more than three-quarters of Dorayi's households had less than the 0.3 ha (0.7 acres) necessary to achieve self-sufficiency in food grain. In Ungogo in 1964, only two of a small sample of ten households were self-sufficient, and the average amount of farmland per capita was 0.23 ha (0.36 in the district as a whole). Of six representative household budgets detailed, four included substantial expenditures on grain. These households were all heavily committed to nonfarming occupations (Mortimore and Wilson 1965: 82-86, 98). Using a higher figure for average grain requirements per capita (218 kg/year), Amerena (1982: 153) reported that in Takurza, 53 percent of households produced less than half, 25 percent more than half, and 22 percent all of or more than their requirements; in Doka, the corresponding percentages were 36, 38 and 26.[35]

These estimates provide no ground for concluding a time trend, but they do put beyond doubt the fact that the inner CSZ, and probably the outer as well, have been deficient in food-grain production for at least three decades and that only a minority of households normally achieve self-sufficiency. Lacking any evidence of rising yields, it is reasonable to conclude from continuing demographic growth—even if slow—that self-sufficiency in grain has diminished for an increasing proportion of households.

Economic Diversification

Given widespread deficits in food grain, economic strategies in the nonfarming sector are critical. This can be shown at the beginning of our time frame from family budgets compiled in Ungogo in 1964, one of which is reproduced in table 11.4. All the budgets except this one spent more on food than on all other items combined. Yet productive resources were diverted from food-grain production to groundnuts. This cultigen was grown by nearly every family and on about half the total number of plots. Groundnut sales, however, did not generally finance food purchases. Usually output was sold immediately after the grain harvest to pay taxes, leaving a very small surplus, which might be used for paying off debts. Woodcutting, weaving, matmaking, laboring, vegetable trading, and the sale of crop residues were used to pay for grain and other food purchases later in the year. Gifts and loans played a significant part in all budgets.[36] Animals were sold. Women had their own

Table 11.4. Sample Budget, Ungogo District, 1964[a]

Item	Percent of total annual expenditure	Main source of income
Clothing	2.8	
Community tax[b]	3.3	Sale of groundnuts
Debt repayment	1.1	
Firewood	2.9	
Festivals, ceremonies	2.1	Help from relatives
Food		
Weekly purchase of grain, meat, cassava, cowpea cake, kola, etc.	32.0 ⎫	Profits from weaving; farm laboring (5 days at ₦0.30)
	⎬ 47.5	
Five bags of grain	15.5 ⎭	
House repairs	0.3	
Kerosene	1.8	
Weaving materials	38.2	Sale of weaving
Total (₦135.98)[c]	100	

Source: Mortimore and Wilson 1965: table 29.

[a]The head of a family of two wives and three children; occupations farming and weaving; wives have their own income and expenditure but are not expected to have to contribute to food purchases.

[b]Community tax was abolished in Kano State in 1979.

[c]See note 17.

sources of income from such activities as food selling, spinning, straw working, and trading (Mortimore and Wilson 1965: 79–87). Nonfarming activity peaked in the dry season but continued throughout the year especially for those undersuppplied with land. Incomes ranged widely.

In rural Hausaland, a commitment to earning cash incomes is neither new nor solely a consequence of population growth. However, table 11.5 provides evidence suggesting that dependence on cash incomes (rows 1, 2) increased with proximity to Kano (3), population density (4), the intensity of agriculture (5, 6), and land scarcity (7, 8, 9). Proximity to metropolitan Kano correlates with density and amplifies opportunities for earning such income (Mortimore 1970).

Amerena (1982: 155–202) provides a detailed analysis of income sources in the peri-urban village of Takurza and the rural village of Doka in 1979–80. Only 15 percent of Takurza farmers and 48 percent of Doka farmers sold groundnuts, and their average output was 4 to 5 bags (compared with 8 in Ungogo in 1964). But they had not (apparently) moved into grain sales—3 and 7 percent respectively admitted selling grain.[37] Doka farmers had moved, to some extent, into tomato and

Table 11.5. Some Comparisons between Central and Outlying Villages in the Kano CSZ, 1964

	Center (3 Ungogo villages)	Periphery (4 villages)
1. Percent of family holdings growing 5 or more bags of groundnuts, 1962	32	9
2. Percent of families having significant nonfarming income	100	48
3. Distance from metropolitan Kano (km)	8	60
4. Population density (persons/km²)	235	170
5. Percent of land under cultivation	85	45[a]
6. Percent of holdings applying 2.5 t/ha or more of manure	64	24
7. Average size of holding (ha)	1.4	2.6
8. Average number of adult males per holding	1.4	2.2
9. Percent of holdings partly or wholly purchased	31	24

Source: Goddard et al. 1975.
[a] One village only.

onion production under irrigation (65 percent sold one or both of these crops), and Takurza farmers were moving out of agriculture. The pattern is shown in table 11.6.

Whereas the Doka farmers distributed themselves relatively evenly between categories, those of Takurza capitalized heavily on their proximity to metropolitan Kano, notably by taking up trade in building sand and by commuting to urban formal-sector employment, especially in the airport nearby. The pattern, therefore, is consistent with expectations based on the variation in distance from Kano.[38] Amerena concludes (1982: 313) that involvement in nonfarming occupations in Takurza, with its greater population pressure, was higher than in Doka with its larger farms.

Hill (1977: 167–68) classifies the nature of nonfarming occupations open to the poor as follows: (1) working for wages (farm laboring, assisting craftsmen, cutting wood); (2) transportation for payment (by headloading or with donkeys); (3) collecting and selling free goods (such as fodder grass, wild foods, earth for building); (4) craftwork (cornstalk beds, woodwork); (5) small-scale trading; (6) Koranic teaching or selling charms; and (7) service (domestic servants, messengers, washermen). This range has not changed significantly since 1964, and few offer full-time work or secure incomes for more than a few days at a time.

Diversification into nonfarming occupations extends logically into circulation or permanent migration. Several categories of spatial mobility are traditionally recognized: dry-season circulation to paid work elsewhere, trading itineration, permanent migration, and disappearance (Olofson 1976). The loss of land rights and even shame may attach to irrevocable migrants (Hill 1977: 143–45). The inner CSZ has attracted inmigration during its history (such as the nineteenth-century kola traders described by Lovejoy 1976), and the income-earning opportunities available in metropolitan Kano still provide an alternative to outmigration. Mobility is resorted to more readily by young men, men with brothers (who can look after their interest), or men with a personal history of mobility. However, food shortages in years of drought drive many more into short-term circulation. Mobility forms one element of a structure of alternative opportunities that has to be re-assessed every harvest time (Mortimore 1982).

Price Behavior

Foodstuff trading in Nigeria—as in most West African countries—is not subject to government price control. The behavior of guinea corn, millet, and cowpea prices, which are recorded (if erratically) by officials in the major urban markets, needs to be understood in terms of drought-induced scarcities, the market operations of traders (some of them large), and general inflation. Between 1970 and 1984–85, the average prices recorded for guinea corn and millet in Kano State increased by 2,000 percent (from around ₦50/t to around ₦1,000: Mortimore 1989: 91). Their astonishing upward progression assumed a cyclical pattern with short-lived troughs in 1975–76, 1979–80, 1982–83, and 1985–86. Cowpea prices increased by 2,500 percent in the same period (from ₦ 70–80/t to ₦2,000). In view of the widespread need of households to purchase grain, already evident in 1964, maximizing subsistence output continues (not surprisingly) to be the prior objective of family farms in the CSZ.

The value of tree crops appears to have increased in line with general inflation, but no data can be cited. Firewood, cut systematically from farm trees and used domestically or sold, increased in market value by about 500 percent between 1964 and 1983 (from ₦0.20 per bundle of about 22 kg to ₦1.00; [Cline-Cole et al. 1987: 182]). The value of livestock increased by about 1,000 percent during the same period: a goat worth about ₦3-4 in 1964 might be sold for ₦30-40 in the 1980s. Thus the real values of output, whether for consumption or sale, of the three

Table 11.6. Nonfarming Incomes in the Kano CSZ, 1979–80 (% of respondents)

	Takurza (inner CSZ)	Doka (outer CSZ)
Crafts	1	17
Transport and trading	51[a]	28
Services, and miscellaneous	41[b]	33[c]
Total	93	78
Dry-season circulation	1	20
Wives with income sources	48	78

Source: Amerena 1982: 155–202.
[a]Sand (for building) and firewood trading accounted for 25 of 52 respondents.
[b]Formal-sector jobs in Kano accounted for 23 of 42 respondents.
[c]Koranic teachers/healers accounted for 15 of 45 respondents. Such activity is traditionally associated with circulation.

linked components of the farming system—crops, trees, and livestock—were maintained.

During the two decades, the price of hired labor inflated by about 1,000 percent (from ₦0.30/day to at least ₦3.00). The latter figure corresponds roughly to the lowest rates paid in the urban informal sector (though laborers were commonly reported to earn ₦5.00/day), and may be compared with the federal minimum wage of ₦20/month. Low-paid government workers' pay increased by about 500 percent.

Inadequate though the price information is, the relativities between the principal input (labor) and outputs seem to have remained constant enough to maintain the economic viability of the system. There was no reason for the withdrawal of labor from production or to alter the balance between the three elements—crops, trees, livestock—of the system. The tendency for food-grain prices to set the pace of general inflation provides a basis for continuing labor intensification.

The 1970s saw a national policy of unrestricted food imports (notably wheat and sugar) and of public-sector interventions in the form of infrastructural developments (especially dams on major and minor rivers, constructed by both federal and state governments) and of integrated rural development schemes funded jointly with the World Bank. The linkages between these macroeconomic policies and the status of the agricultural sector have been explored by Wallace (1981), Andrae and Beckman (1985), Watts (1987), and others. Since it is far from clear what specific implications such developments had for the CSZ, they will not be pursued here. Moreover, it should be observed that since the devaluation of the naira in 1986, the economic context of the agricultural sector has fundamentally changed.[39]

Inequality and Welfare

Hill (1977: 100) argues that in Dorayi, economic inequality is less marked than it was in 1900, when the economy was based on long-distance trade, crop sales, and farm slavery. Inequality between individuals is disguised by the common practice of intergenerational co-residence; the scarcity of land perpetuates the *gandu* and the extended-family residence, because sons are unable to strike out on their own. On the other hand, the existence of a massive labor surplus in farming, and the difficulty of obtaining alternative income, generates an underclass or proletariat in the countryside, land-hungry if not landless, and sharing with the urban poor a common dependence on casual, insecure, and short-term employment. The poor may enter an individual impasse in which they have less manure to apply to their farms and so obtain lower yields to labor; must sell grain at glut prices; have unremunerative nonfarm occupations; have no time to farm because of their need for cash; have to sell land; have insufficient land to set their sons to work; and are not creditworthy. But extreme poverty also occurred in Batagarawa, where land was plentiful; so "there is not necessarily a close relationship between population density and the incidence of severe impoverishment" (Hill 1977: 164).

However, proletarianization in the sense of dispossession from the land has occurred where urban expansion, preceded by the compulsory acquisition of land by the state government, has made incursions into the peri-urban zone. Such an area is the new university campus (Main and Cline-Cole 1987). Compensation payments below the market value of land, the scarcity of alternative land, and the influence of speculators in bidding up land prices have effectively dispossessed some landholders and transformed them into urban wage laborers.[40]

There are three indicators of the direction of change. First, the Kano River Irrigation Project (30–40 km south) has created an enclave of relative prosperity, and increased inequality in terms of incomes and landholdings (Baba 1989). But despite claims that the project increased landlessness (Wallace 1980), there is little evidence that this is occuring yet (Orogun 1986). Such irrigation schemes further marginalize pastoralists who depend on access to valley grazings and unrestricted movement during the dry season (Binns and Mortimore 1989). Second, the Kano State Agricultural and Rural Development Authority, partly funded by the World Bank, is introducing agricultural-improvement packages to farmers throughout the state. These are centered on new technologies for raising output per hectare. Elsewhere, such programs have increased inequality between the larger and smaller farmers, the smaller often failing to benefit from the program (Mabogunje and Gana 1981). Third, intensified market pressure on farming systems must increase the likelihood of social inequality, in view of the fluidity of customary land tenure, which tends to facilitate the redistribution of unregistered farm holdings from the economically weak to the strong (Mortimore 1987b). But resistance to landlessness may lead to even smaller holdings and multiple claims to land.

Notwithstanding the arrival of universal primary education in 1976 (a policy whose inception and continuation have been fraught with difficulty: Bray 1981), the election of a state administration with a populist agenda in 1979 (some of whose goals continued to receive assent after the return to military rule in 1984), and public investments in dams, boreholes and other projects, no evidence has come to hand of a significant improvement in the quality of life of the generality of the inhabitants of the CSZ. Drought and the decline of oil revenues have seen to that. In the contemporary context of deteriorating standards of education and health care, stagnating wage levels, public-sector retrenchments, withdrawal of fuel subsidies and scarcities of imports, such evidence is unlikely to emerge. In practice, it is impossible to decouple the effects of such macroeconomic variables from those of population pressure on poverty and welfare.

Trajectories

The conventional wisdom of doomsday literature postulates runaway population growth, increasing pressure on land resources, declining yields, ecological degradation, and the breakdown of primary production systems. But degradation and breakdown are not characteristics of the Kano CSZ, even though environmental constraints are limiting. Evidence has been given for the ecological and economic stability of this system. It has three interactive components and is not restricted to crop production as often supposed in discussions of "the race between population and food." These components are crops, trees, and livestock. Their

Table 11.7. Trajectories of Change

Trajectory	Primary productivity per hectare	Income trend per capita	Ecological outcome
PI_1	Absolute decline compounded by population growth	Cumulative decline	Cumulative degradation: "domesday"
PI_2	Constant	Decline, at the rate at which population grows	Arrested degradation
PI_3	Rising: slower than the rate of population growth	Slow decline	Unstable intensification: failing to "keep up" with population growth
PI_4	Rising: equal to the rate of population growth	Constant	Stable intensification
PI_5	Rising: faster than the rate of population growth	Rising	Progressive intensification: "green revolution"

interdependence is an operational solution to the need to achieve the most efficient use of land and biotic resources, and it has developed over a long period of experimentation and adaptation, during which labor inputs per hectare have tended to rise with the growth of the residential population. The future trajectory of this system is likely to offer continuity with its past history.[41]

Five alternatives appear possible. In the following schema (table 11.7), real prices are assumed constant, and the growth of the residential population (i.e., population growth net of permanent outmigration) is assumed to be more than zero. Real primary income per capita (PI) is the sum of subsistence and marketed output from the crop, farm tree, and livestock enterprises.

Real income per capita from nonfarming or alternative income sources (AI) has three possible trajectories: AI_1 declining; AI_2 stable; AI_3 increasing. During this period in question (1964–86), the Kano CSZ, on the basis of the evidence reviewed here, appears to be described by the terms $PI_2 + AI_2$. That is, an ecologically and economically stable system of primary production became less capable of supporting a growing residential population, and this burden has shifted progressively to alternative sources of income. This hypothesis requires empirical testing.

If the system of primary production is viewed in isolation, a reduction in the price (or improvement in availability) of land-saving technologies will accelerate a transition to a higher-yield trajectory. However, viewed in the context of diversification, the opportunity cost of labor will have crucial significance.[42] It is wrong to assume that the only constraint to further intensification in a region subject to rising population is technology. However, the allocation of labor between primary production and alternative income opportunities, including those incurring mobility, has received rather little attention in the CSZ. How it is done, both at the level of the family or individual and at the level of the region, and the rationale for labor-allocation decisions, will continue to exercise a strong influence on the course of development.

Notes

I am grateful for the thoughtful comments of Polly Hill and Ken Swindell on a draft of this chapter.

1. Unfortunately, this survey was rapid and superficial. The data are subject to a margin of error.

2. The interpretations I shall make on the basis of their work remain, of course, my responsibility.

3. Subsidized fuel prices (about half the world price after 1973) and imported Japanese minibuses combined with the effects of the oil boom (1970–78) to increase personal mobility.

4. Planning machinery and enforcement procedures could not cope adequately with the demand for land and physical development within the metropolitan area. Beyond the boundary, local authorities exercised an easy-going regime.

5. We derived these data from analyses carried out in 1962–64 by R. A. Pullan, G. M. Higgins, and K. Klinkenberg and cited in Mortimore (1968).

6. These were as follows (Abalu et al. 1983: 35–37): pests included, on millet, headworm (*Raghuva* spp.), stem borer (*Acigora ignefusalis*), black ants (*Messor galla*); and on cowpea, green leafhoppers (*Empoasoxa* spp.). Diseases included on millet, *Striga hermontheca*, downy mildew; on guinea corn, argot, smut, leaf spot, and anthracnose; and on cowpea, *Septovia* leaf spot and *Striga gesneroides*.

7. In 1952, the census recorded 95 males per 100 females in Ungogo District, 95 in Kano Division, and 95 in Kano State (then a province). About 150 km west, in Malumfashi District in 1974–77, a demographic survey of over 40,000 people gave 95 males per 100 females (Bradley et al. 1982a, 1982b).

8. There had been disruptions caused by airport construction and the resettlement of some of the affected persons in the survey villages.

9. Baba (1975: 64) calculated the average rate of increase in Kura District (30–40 km south of Kano) between 1950–51 and 1970–71 as 2.2 percent by using tax-assessment records.

10. The results of the Malumfashi District study (see n. 7), the first large-scale demographic study in the Sudan Zone of Nigeria, indicate a gross fertility rate of 22.1 percent, a crude birth rate of 5.5 percent, a crude death rate of 2.6 percent, and a crude rate of natural increase of 2.9 percent. To transpose such rates to the CSZ, however, would ignore the possibility of significant variation.

11. The first adjustment is based on the assumed omission of unmarried youths from the count of 1932 and the second on the difference of 30 percent between Hill's own enumeration (1972) and the 1971 tax returns for a part of the Dorayi area. The official figure for Kumbotso District in 1971 (62,335) is lower than the preliminary census figure for 1962 (65,844).

12. Baba (1975: 59) calculated the average density in Kura District as 231/km^2 in 1970–71 by using tax-assessment records.

13. Dorayi is a name given to an area containing several administrative villages southwest of Kano City wall and adjacent to Bayero University. Such proximity is expected to affect residential density positively.

14. The migration survey was based on the assumption of a de jure household whose absent members could easily be identified. Such a model is inappropriate. There may be reasons for withholding information about departed male migrants.

15. These observations were generated by continuous residence in the area, research in other locations in the CSZ, supervised student research, and field classes.

16. Hill (1977) suggests 2 ha (5 acres) per adult male on the basis of her findings in Batagarawa, near Katsina; in the more extensive system on the sandier soils of northeast Kano State, the figure is 3 ha (Mortimore 1989).

17. The use of local currency (naira) units is retained, because international currency equivalents varied during the period of analysis. In the early 1980s, the naira (N) was worth about U.S. $1.50, but it was devalued from 1986 to $0.25 and less. The naira was introduced in 1972 at N2 = £ 1, and earlier values expressed in pounds have been converted in the text to naira at this rate.

18. In conditions of drought, farmers consider that soil temperatures may be raised unacceptably by manure. This risk is believed to be even greater with chemical fertilizers.

19. Old Kano City had a large population of sheep and goats (12,000 according to tax returns, probably an undercount), numerous horses and donkeys, compound sweepings, and excavated pit latrines.

20. By 1979, the dominant means of transport had changed from the donkey to the motor pickup and two grades had replaced one; for a lower price, one could buy city refuse, in which organic material is liberally diluted with tin cans and polythene bags. Such material has to be laboriously sorted and

burned before application of the manure to the fields. (Such operations were seen by Hill in 1971.)

21. The titled class, and a proportion of ordinary farmers, are of Fulani descent and predisposed to cattle as a form of investment. The contradiction between cattle ownership and the scarcity of fodder in the CSZ is resolved by sending them to graze elsewhere for much of the year. Locally, concentrations of cattle may occur (see Hill 1977: 93–94).

22. The only methodological alternative to survey questionnaires is direct measurement, which may be unacceptable on grounds of cost and because of the level of interference necessitated in private farm operations. Even the World Bank projects in northern Nigeria have found reliable yield data hard to obtain.

23. By 1977, pumps commanded an estimated 1,072 ha in Kano State, compared with 2,736 ha under jigo irrigation (Erhabor 1982: 26).

24. It seems probable that many of the pump farms in the Jakara fadama are smaller than the optimal size. Erhabor points out that farmers may switch from less labor- and water-intensive crops (such as pepper) to crops that are more so (such as tomato and onion) in order to employ additional family labor.

25. Although never cultivated, the woodland was heavily cut for charcoal production in the thousands of iron smelters that litter their lower slopes (P.J. Darling, personal communication).

26. Measurements were made 9 m above ground level by using bowls of distilled water, which was then evaporated.

27. These samples were obtained at a rural location 56 km south of Kano by using a collector 1.5 m above the ground, and the elements were determined by instrumental neutron-activation analysis.

28. According to McTainsh (1984), a primary deposition rate of $96t/km^2$ could have generated a mantle of loessic soils 3m thick during the past 40,000 years.

29. The survey of 1932 formed a part of the Revenue Survey carried out in the home districts of Kano Emirate and was undertaken by teams of surveyors trained to use the Hausa language in Ajami script (MacBride 1938). The survey of 1964 used air photography (1962, scale 1:4,800), and title was determined in the field by the Village or Ward Head in the presence of witnesses.

30. Farmers in Dorayi might even retire from farming in favor of their sons.

31. Hill (1977: 99–101) argues that it is exceptionally common in the CSZ because of the difficulty in a land-scarce situation for sons to set up on their own.

32. The scale of the air photographs used did not permit identification of very small plots.

33. In Mortimore (1967), a plot was defined as contiguous farmland owned by one person irrespective of whether it was further subdivided by internal boundaries (visible on air photographs).

34. This term Hill considers inappropriate (1977: 98).

35. This coefficient was based on my consumption estimates in a lower-density area outside the CSZ (Mortimore 1988: 86–88).

36. Not least that of the Village Head, for whom they exceeded his official allowance! The Head also stored part of his grain crop until the price rose. But he, too, purchased grain.

37. Shame may attach to selling the contents of the family granary, which in any case are private.

38. The significance of incomes is difficult to assess owing to the wide range reported and possible reluctance to give accurate information. The estimated average earnings from agriculture and from nonfarm sources respectively were N123 and N974 in Takurza and N184 and N1,026 in Doka.

39. It was widely believed that low farm incomes (compared with the expected rewards of urban employment) caused a labor shortage that contributed to the decline in agricultural production that is supposed to have taken place from the 1970s to 1985. Since then, urban recession and high food prices have reversed the position.

40. The absorptive capacity of Kano's urban informal sector, on which such landless or land-hungry peri-urban residents rely, was adversely affected by the government's war on discipline (Stage 4: Environmental Sanitation), which attempted to sweep away street trading in 1984.

41. In treating the system as an aggregate, of course, nothing can be said of the distributional aspect, which is arguably more relevant to the incidence of poverty.

42. Even on the highly profitable Kano River Project, it was found that surplus family labor had been overestimated by the planners, and during the irrigation season there is much labor hiring from outside.

References

Abalu, G.O.I., et al. 1983. *Exploratory Survey of the Farming Systems of North-Eastern Kano State, Nigeria.* Working Paper 4. Samaru, Nigeria: Department of Agricultural Economics and Rural Sociology, Institute for Agricultural Research.

Ahmed, K. 1987. "Erosion Hazard Assessment in the Savanna: The Hadejia-Jema'are River Basin," In *Perspectives on Land Administration and Development in Northern Nigeria*, ed. M. Mortimore, E.A. Olofin, R.A. Cline-Cole, and A. Abdulkadir, pp. 234–50. Kano: Department of Geography, Bayero University.

Amerena, P.M.J. 1982. "Farmers' Participation in the Cash Economy: Case Studies of Two Settlements in the Kano Close-Settled Zone of Nigeria." Ph.D. dissertation, University of London.

Andrae, G., and B. Beckman. 1985. *The Wheat Trap*. London: Zed Books.

Baba, J. M. 1975. "Induced Agricultural Change in a Densely Populated District, Impact of the Kano River Irrigation Project." Ph.D. dissertation. Ahmadu Bello University, Zaire.

———. 1989. "The Problem of Rural Inequality on the Kano River Project, Nigeria." In *Inequality and Development: Case Studies from the Third World*, ed. K. Swindell, J. M. Baba, and M. Mortimore. London: Macmillan.

Beavington, F., and P. A. Cawse. 1978. "Comparative Studies of Trace Elements in Air Particulate in Northern Nigeria." *Science of the Total Environment* 10: 239–44.

Binns, J. A., and M. Mortimore. 1989. "Time, Ecology and Development in Kano, Nigeria." In *Inequality and Development; Case Studies from the Third World*, ed. K. Swindell, J. M. Baba, and M. Mortimore. London: Macmillan

Bradley, A. K., et al. 1982a. "Malumfashi Endemic Diseases Research Project XIX. Demographic Findings: Population Structure and Fertility." *Annals of Tropical Medicine and Parasitology* 76: 381–91.

———. 1982b. "Malumfashi Endemic Diseases Research Project XX. Demographic Findings: Mortality." *Annals of Tropical Medicine and Parasitology* 76: 393–404.

Bray, T. M. 1981. *Universal Primary Education in Nigeria. A Study of Kano State*. London: Routledge and Kegan Paul.

Chayanov, A. V. 1966. *The Theory of Peasant Economy*. Homewood, Ill.: American Economic Association.

Cline-Cole, R. A.; J. A. Falola; H. A. C. Main; M. J. Mortimore; J. E. Nichol; and F. D. O'Reilly. 1990. *Wood Fuel in Kano*. Tokyo: United Nations University Press.

Daniel, M. B. 1987. "The Significance of Post-Implementation Monitoring in Land Development Projects." In *Perspectives on Land Administration and Development in Northern Nigeria*, ed. M. Mortimore, E. A. Olofin, R. A. Cline-Cole, and A. Abdulkadir. Kano: Bayero University, Department of Geography.

Eckholm, E., et al. 1984. *Firewood: The Energy Crisis That Won't Go Away*. London: Earthscan.

Erhabor, P. O. 1982. *Efficiency of Resource Use under Small-Scale Irrigation Technology in Nigeria*. Technical Report 148. West Lafayette, Ind.: Purdue University Water Resources Research Center.

Goddard, A. D. 1973. "Changing Family Structures among the Rural Hausa." *Africa* 73: 207–18.

Goddard, A. D., M. Mortimore, and D. W. Norman. 1975. "Some Social and Economic Implications of Population Growth in Rural Hausaland." In *Population Growth and Socio-Economic Change in West Africa*, ed. J. C. Caldwell et al., pp. 321–38. New York: Columbia University Press.

Gowers, W. F. 1913. *Kano Province Annual Report for 1913*. Kaduna: Nigerian National Archives.

Green, L. 1970. *Population Models for National Planning*. Ibadan: Nigerian Institute for Social and Economic Research.

Hendy, C. R. C. 1977. *Animal Production in Kano State and the Requirements for Further Study*. Land Resource Report 21. Tolworth: Ministry of Overseas Development, Land Resources Division.

Hill, P. 1971. "Two Types of West African House Trade." In *The Development of Trade and Markets in West Africa*, ed. C. Meillassoux. Oxford: Oxford University Press.

———. 1972. *Rural Hausa. A Village and a Setting*. Cambridge: Cambridge University Press.

———. 1977. *Population, Prosperity and Poverty. Rural Kano 1900 and 1970*. Cambridge: Cambridge University Press.

Jones, M. J., and A. Wild. 1975. *Soils of the West African Savanna. The Maintenance and Improvement of Their Fertility*. Technical Communication 55. Harpenden, U.K.: Commonwealth Agricultural Bureaux, Commonwealth Bureau of Soils.

Labaran, A. 1987. "Land Appropriation for Capitalized Farming in the Sokoto Region: Some Preliminary Findings." In *Perspectives on Land Administration and Development in Northern Nigeria*, ed. M. Mortimore, E. A. Olofin, R. A. Cline-Cole, and A. Abdulkadir. Kano: Bayero University, Department of Geography.

Land Resources Division. 1972. *The Land Resources of North-Eastern Nigeria*. Tolworth: Ministry of Overseas Development, Land Resources Division.

———. 1979. *The Land Resources of Central Nigeria*. Tolworth: Ministry of Overseas Development, Land Resources Division.

Lovejoy, P. E. 1976. *Caravans of Kola*. Zaria: Ahmadu Bello University Press.

Mabogunje, A. L., and J. A. Gana. 1981. *Rural Development in Nigeria: Case Study of the Funtua Integrated Rural Development Project, Kaduna State, Nigeria*. Geneva: United Nations Centre for Regional Development.

MacBride, D. F. H. 1938. "Land Survey in the Kano Emirate, Northern Provinces, Nigeria." *Journal of the Royal African Society* 37: 75–91.

McTainsh, G. 1980. "Harmattan Dust Deposition in Northern Nigeria." *Nature* 286: 587–88.

———. 1984. "The Nature and Origin of the Aeolian Mantles of Central Northern Nigeria." *Geoderma*. 33: 13–37.

———. 1987. "Desert Loess in Northern Nigeria." *Zeitschrift für Geomorphologie* 31(2): 145–65.

Main, H. R. C., and R. A. Cline-Cole. 1987. "Land-Related Processes in Peripheral Capitalist Societies: Metropolitan Kano's Western Peri-Urban Fringe." In *Perspectives on Land Administration and Development in Northern*

Nigeria, ed. M. Mortimore, E. A. Olofin, R. A. Cline-Cole, and A. Abdul-kadir. Kano: Bayero University, Department of Geography.

Morris, J. 1981. "Agrarian Structure Implications for Development. A Kano (Nigeria) Case Study." *Oxford Agrarian Studies* 10: 44–69.

Mortimore, M. 1967. "Land and Population Pressure in the Kano Close-Settled Zone, Northern Nigeria." *The Advancement of Science* 23(118): 677–88.

———. 1968. "Population Distribution, Settlement and Soils in Kano Province, Northern Nigeria 1931–62." In *The Population of Tropical Africa*, ed. J. C. Caldwell, and C. Okonjo. London: Longman.

———. 1970. "Population Densities and Rural Economies in the Kano Close-Settled Zone, Nigeria." In *Geography and a Crowding World*, ed. W. Zelinsky, L. A. Kosinski, and R. M. Prothero. Oxford: Oxford University Press.

———. 1972. "Some Aspects of Rural-Urban Relations in Kano, Nigeria." In *La Croissance Urbaine en Afrique Noire et à Madagascar*, ed. P. Vennetier. Paris: Centre National de la Recherche Scientifique.

———. 1974. "The Demographic Variable in Regional Planning in Kano State, Nigeria." In *Spatial Aspects of Development*, ed. B. S. Hoyle. Chichester, U.K.: Wiley.

———. 1982. "Framework for Population Mobility: The Perception of Opportunities in Nigeria." In *Population Redistribution in Africa*, ed. J. I. Clarke and L. A. Kosinski. London: Heinemann.

———. 1987a. "Shifting Sands and Human Sorrow: Social Response to Drought and Desertification." *Desertification Control Bulletin* 14: 1–14.

———. 1987b. "The Lands of Northern Nigeria: Some Urgent Issues." In *Perspectives on Land Administration and Development in Northern Nigeria*, ed. M. Mortimore, E. A. Olofin, R. A. Cline-Cole, and A. Abdulkadir. Kano: Bayero University, Department of Geography.

———. 1989. *Adapting to Drought. Farmers, Famines and Desertification in West Africa*. Cambridge: Cambridge University Press.

Mortimore, M., and J. Wilson. 1965. *Land and People in the Kano Close-Settled Zone*. Occasional Paper 1. Zaria: Ahmadu Bello University, Department of Geology.

Olofin, E. A. 1984. "Some Effects of the Tiga Dam on Valley Side Erosion in Downstream Reaches of the River Kano." *Applied Geography* 4(4): 321–32.

Olofson, H. 1976. "Yawon Dandi: A Hausa Category of Migration." *Africa* 46: 1–15.

Ologe, K. O. 1972. "Gullies in the Zaria Area: A Preliminary Study of Headscarp Recession." *Savanna* 77: 55–67.

Orogun, B. T. 1986. "Land Administration on the Kano River Project." M.Sc. thesis, Bayero University, Kano.

Pullan, R. A. 1974. "Farmed Parkland in West Africa." *Savanna* 3(2): 119–52.

Ross, P. 1987. "Land as a Right to Membership: Land Tenure Dynamics in a Peripheral Area of the Kano Close-Settled Zone." In *State, Oil and Agriculture*, ed. M. Watts. Berkeley: University of California, Institute of International Studies.

Stokes, S. 1978. "A Comparative Study of Rural Population Structures in Hausaland, Northern Nigeria." *Savanna* 7(2): 151–62.

Trevallion, B. W. 1966. *Metropolitan Kano. Twenty-Year Development Plan 1963–1983*. Kano: Newman Neame, for the Greater Kano Planning Authority.

Wallace, T. 1978. "The Concept of *gandu*: How Useful Is It in Understanding Labour Relations in Rural Hausa Society?" *Savanna* 7(2): 137–50.

———. 1980. "Agricultural Projects and Land in Northern Nigeria." *Review of African Political Economy* 17: 59–70.

———. 1981. "The Challenge of Food: Nigeria's Approach to Agriculture 1975–80." *Canadian Journal of African Studies* 15: 239–58.

Watts, M. 1983. *Silent Violence, Food, Famine and Peasantry in Northern Nigeria*. Berkeley: University of California Press.

12 / Beyond Intensification

Goran Hyden, Robert W. Kates,
and B. L. Turner II

We began this endeavor by linking fact with speculation. The *fact* is that most of sub-Saharan Africa has skyrocketing population growth accompanied by rather slow or marginal growth in agriculture. As a result, per capita food production has been falling throughout much of the subcontinent, although the extent of this decline is unclear. Marginal environments, usually semiarid zones with major cycles of drought, have been invaded for cultivation or for intensified livestock production, in most cases leading to land degradation. Where these changes have been associated with warfare or drought, major food shortages and famines have been the consequence. The *speculation* was that population growth per se is not necessarily the cause of all of these problems; indeed, in many cases it may lead to their solution. As Boserup (1965) argues, population growth is a prerequisite both for agricultural growth, particularly through the intensification process, and, ultimately, for a shift from production for local consumption to a more diversified economy with an increase in the overall material standard of living. Demand, in this case primarily from population needs, drives agricultural and economic development (Boserup 1981; also Hayami and Ruttan 1985).

We did not attempt to address empirically and in detail such far-ranging and complex linkages throughout the subcontinent. Our decision, therefore, was to concentrate on the first link—the relationship between population and agricultural growth—but to tackle it in such a way as to generate insights about the subsequent facets of the Boserup argument, emphasizing economic diversification and well-being. This was done by focusing on the relationship as it has been played out in select areas of the subcontinent with traditions of dense rural population and intensive agriculture. In this sense, our approach is that of the "natural experiment" in that we could make observations but could not control the varied influences on the relationship in question. Experts on these places and relationships were asked to make assessments of the population-agriculture linkage and also encouraged to elaborate on its broader socioeconomic impacts.

We feel vindicated in our use of this approach for the examination of the principal questions of this study. The case studies themselves, spanning the east and west of the continent, are quite variable, providing multiple views, for example, of the forest regions of Nigeria or the highlands of East Africa. Because we did not control the range of variables that affect agricultural growth, we illuminated a number of important lessons that might not have been highlighted otherwise. The participation of senior scholars with long and intimate knowledge of the study areas generated an impressive amount of interesting and important data and provided historical depth that help us understand current trends. These studies thus deepen and complement recent cross-sectional research on the subject (see Pingali, Bigot, and Binswanger 1987). Surely, there are gaps in the data sets and variability in the authors' interpretations that limit our ability to answer many questions. But by illuminating the understudied and misunderstood roles of population growth, our findings have both practical and theoretical implications.

Comparative Findings

A summary of the principal findings in the various case studies is the basis from which we build our overall assessments. The critical features of each case are summarized in table 12.1: the values assigned to each feature have been reviewed by the case study authors.

In all but one of our cases (Bushenyi), the population densities of the areas in question, or portions thereof, approach or exceed 200 people/km². Four of the cases (Kano, Imo State, Awka, and Kisii) exceed densities of 500 people/km². What is more, the population of each area continues to grow.

Intensities of agriculture in these zones are also high and increasing, almost every case approaching or exceeding annual cultivation. These levels of cropping frequencies have been achieved everywhere primarily by major increases in labor (amount per hectare) and by modest increases in capital inputs (monetary investment). Increased labor is needed for more frequent weeding and other procedures and for major outlays in creating "resource" capital, largely through land or water transformations, such as irrigation, ridging, terracing, tree planting, and wetland conversion. Farmers in almost all sites have experimented with and use new cultigens and biotechnic inputs, such as pesticides and fertilizers, which constitute the majority of monetary investments. Mechanization, however, is almost absent in the areas. The Kano case is the principal exception in that mechanical water pumps have proliferated there.

These increased inputs have led to intensified outputs in every case. Cropping frequency continues to increase everywhere, with the exception of Kano. Yields are improving at seven sites, declining in Imo State, remaining stable in Kano, and varying in Meru, owing to the expansion of agriculture onto lower and drier adjacent land. Also, significant land expansion complementing intensification is taking place in six of the cases.

As a result, at least eight of the ten cases involve increases in total agricultural production. Production is apparently decreasing only in the Awka-Nnewi case, and stabilizing in Kano, even with growth in irrigation. Significant market production is occurring everywhere. Market production as a proportion of all agriculture is increasing in half the cases, stable in four, and decreasing only in the Kano area.

Not only has agricultural production risen at almost all sites and the marketed proportion has increased or remained stable in the majority, but other forms of economic diversification are increasing everywhere, including household enterprises and local off-farm employment. In addition, outmigration, primarily of adult males, is occurring almost everywhere. This absent "household" labor results in monetary and other remittances to the areas in question, although their impacts on cultivation per se may be marginal, as we discuss later.

The use of new cultigens has led not only to increased yields of production but to substantial dietary changes as well. In almost all of the sites, major dietary shifts have taken place in response to population growth, substituting less-demanding, higher-yielding, or greater-density foods for traditional ones. Thus cassava has replaced yams in West Africa, and bananas and white potatoes have replaced finger millet in Ruhengeri and Bushenyi. Of course, this follows a long tradition in sub-Saharan Africa of substituting for traditional crops, such as occurred with the introduction of maize and groundnuts (see Miracle 1966). Most recently this has involved the growth of cassava production. Although there is little doubt that these shifts have been economically and calorically wise, they have also involved, given the conditions in which the farmers must operate, the decline in production of crops that have been adapted to particular African environments.

Table 12.1. Case Study Comparison

Variables	Nigeria Jos Plateau	Nigeria Kano Close-Settled Zone	Nigeria Imo State	Nigeria Ngwa-Igbo	Nigeria Awka-Nnewi	Tanzania Usambara Mountains	Rwanda Ruhengeri District	Kenya Meru District	Kenya Kisii District	Uganda Bushenyi District
Population										
Density (per sq. mile)	90–300	+500	200–1000	–230	525	190	367–418	190	+500	+158
Input intensification										
Change in labor (workdays/ha)	+	+	+	+	+	+	+	?	+	?
Monetary investment	+	+	+	+	+	?	+	+	+	+
Surface transformation	√√	√√	√√	√√	√√	√√	√√	√√	√√	√√
New cultigens	√√	√	√√	√√	√√	√√	√√	√√	√√	√√
Mechanization	x	mwp	x	x	x	x	x	x	x	x
Biotechnic	√√	√	√	√	√	√	√√	√√	√	√
Output intensification										
Cropping frequency	80–100	+100	100–14	+100–33	?	+100	+100	+100(hl)	?	100–?
Change in cropping frequency	+	=	+	+	+	+	+	+	+	+
Change in kg/ha	+	=	–	+	+	+	+	±	+	+
Land expansion	√√	x	√√	x	x	√	√√	√√	x	√√
Agricultural production										
Change in total	+	=	+	+	–	+	+	+	+	+
% devoted to market	√√	√√	√√	√√	√	√	√√	√√	√√	√√
Change in % market	+	–	+	=	=	=	=	+	+	+

Economic diversification									
Livelihood changes	√	√√	√√	√√	+	+	+	√√	+
Migration	+	+	+	+	+	+	+	+	−
Well-being (changes in)									
Food/nutrition	=	=	?	?	−	+	±	=	=
Material	+	=	?	?	?	+	±	=	+
Social differentiation	√	+	?	+	+	√	?	?	+
Gender roles	=	=	?	+	+	√	+	?	?
Environmental									
degradation	√(?)	=	+	+	±	+	√√	+/=	√

Codes: + increase; − decrease; = constant; ± variable; √√ yes, major/significant; √ minimal; x no; ? no data; mwp mechanized water piper; hl highland zone of case study.

Definition of variables (if needed);

% market = % of agricultural produce intended for sale.

Kg/ha = total output per plot per year (yield).

Agricultural surplus = amount of food and/or materials beyond subsistence needs or wants.

Land expansion = extending cultivation into lands not previously cultivated.

Surface transformation = structural changes in land surface for cultivation (e.g., tie-ridging), deforestation, and afforestation.

Biotechnic = HYV and other such cultivars, chemical fertilizers and pesticides, and so on.

Livelihood changes = move to economic activities other than agriculture.

Therefore, overall, the basic population-agriculture relationship proposed in the induced-intensification model—that increasing population is associated with agricultural output per unit area and time—seems to be operating or to have operated in these areas, supporting the conclusions of earlier studies in this vein (Netting 1968; Gleave and White 1969; Vermeer 1970; and, more recently, Pingali, Bigot, and Binswanger 1987). Exceptions seem to follow the general conditions found elsewhere that intercede in the basic relationship (see "Constraints" below).

Our case studies, in conjunction with other works, demonstrate the resilience of African farmers in general in the face of pressures on production and their ability; thus far they have responded to these pressures through some land expansion, economic diversification, and dietary change, and primarily through increased labor directed mainly to indigenous land and plant improvements. They also indicate that quite high levels of population density may be accommodated in many parts of the subcontinent before agriculture involutes or stagnates. This conclusion is particularly significant because our high-density, high-intensity cases represent such a range of environmental conditions. They are not confined to river basins, wetlands, or high altitude or high-quality agricultural soils.

Therefore, with regard to the first link in our speculation, we conclude that substantial increases in the overall low population densities of sub-Saharan Africa can be matched by increases in agriculture, even in areas that are relatively poorly endowed for cultivation. That the population density thresholds for these areas will vary, as will the ability to respond to different rates of population growth, is obvious, but there is little doubt that agricultural production can grow and that much of this growth will be associated with population pressures.

There is greater variability with regard to the second facet of our speculation: that increasing population also spawns diversification in labor, promotes market-oriented production, encourages capital investment in agriculture and adoption of modern technology, and, generally, leads to the emergence of a multisectoral economy in which per capita food production and material well-being improve. Economic diversification is on the rise in all cases. Much of the diversification involves outmigration of male laborers, however, and investments from this labor seem to be made primarily outside of agriculture. Therefore, the agricultural sector is increasingly maintained by intensified uses of "remaining" labor, particularly female labor. Characteristic of these changes is the growth of local trade and/or sale in basic foods as food crops replace "export" crops. Thus, there is evidence that the rural populace is working longer hours to feed itself and for the market, although commodity production as a share of total production has apparently stabilized or slightly decreased in five areas.

Much more scattered data are available for other dimensions of the diversification thesis. Increases in food availability or improvement in general material well-being (recognizing that not all individuals or households benefit equitably) as a result of the "spinoffs" of intensification are apparent in four cases (Jos, Ngwa, Ruhengeri, and Bushenyi). Improvements in well-being have occurred in parts of Meru and, in the recent past, in Kisii. Demand-led development is exemplified in the Jos case, where a "frontier" or open land has been used for major market cultivation of great benefit to local farmers; a similar scenario is also reported from Bushenyi, although there it appears to be associated with much more obvious social stratification. In Ngwa the adoption and sale of cassava, the expansion of oil palm production, and urban migration enabled the Ngwa farming system to support a dense population at a rising standard of living. Intensification of market practices has benefitted those with farms in the highlands of Meru, but economic diversification has not been able to accommodate all those needing farm land. As a result, a dry, lowland frontier has been invaded, one to which the Meru farmer is, as yet, not well adapted and that should be used for purposes other than farming. Intensive market gardening and diversification are responsible for stable levels of food availability and material well-being in Kano and Kisii. In Ruhengeri, a deliberate government policy of intensifying subsistence production seems to be a major factor behind small increases in food availability but with no apparent major improvements in material well-being beyond that.

Decreases in food availability, or well-being, were identified from some of the "forest belt" cases from Nigeria and from the Usambara Mountains. Increasingly, food has to be imported from other regions of the country to support the extremely large populations of the forest belt, and economic diversification has not been sufficient in Imo State or Awka-Nnewi to offset the impacts of rapid growth in such large populations. In two cases in the forest belt of Nigeria, the possibility of locally expanding food availability through the cultivation of rice in the river beds was noted. A decrease in food availability is also reported for Usambara, although the circumstances there are quite different. Customary land-tenure arrangements as well as macroeconomic policies and infrastructural inadequacies have apparently combined to create a condition that makes it more difficult for people to obtain enough food than in the past.

A legitimate—but not easily answered—question relates to the effects of the introduction of new cultigens and subsequent dietary changes that replace traditional dietary elements. Does the loss of such elements as, for example, yams in Nigeria or millet in Rwanda result in diminished nutritional or cultural well-being? Or is it that as starchy roots, tubers, or fruits replace favored foods, other widely marketed foods add sufficient diversity and varied nutrients to compensate for any nutritional and cultural losses incurred?

The other variables that we have used to measure well-being are even more difficult to assess than food and material wealth. Understandably, our authors (all but one male) tended to assess such issues as social or gender differentiation, or environmental degradation differently, seeing them through their own perspectives and expectations of change. Thus, for example, reduced fallow was seen by some authors as "soil mining" with the loss of fertility characterizing environmental degradation, whereas others required physical signs of enhanced erosion to draw similar conclusions. Nevertheless, with some allowance for this variability, it is possible to summarize some conclusions.

Social differentiation is on the increase in the seven cases reporting, taking the form of increasing discrepancies in access to land and other resources. This process seems to be most pronounced in Bushenyi, where customary land tenure is giving way to new forms and commodity production is increasing. It is significant, however, that none of our cases provide evidence of "proletarianization"—people removed from the land in the interest of more efficient production. The poor continue to have formal rights to land owned by relatives, even if they do not exercise that right.

Similarly, gender roles are changing significantly in a majority of the cases (and we suspect at least minor changes everywhere). Primarily, these changes represent the now well-documented impacts of male migration on the female-headed households left behind, households still dependent on subsistence agriculture (Callear 1982; Palmer 1985; Mazambani 1990). In other cases, however, these changes involve the move of males only into cash cropping, hence increasing the female's subsistence responsibilities, and the development of household enterprises in which women may be engaged. Gender issues impinging on African agriculture are wide ranging and important, as the recent literature has emphasized (see Carney 1988). This is illustrated in the Usambara case where much-needed land improvement for agriculture has been stymied, in part, because women would thereby lose subsistence access to improved lands.

In contrast to the major publicity given to the massive environmental degradation in Africa—a problem recognized as early as the 1950s (Shantz and Turner 1958) and that has indeed substantially increased since—our case studies indicate that degradation of a severity that destroys agriculture does not necessarily follow from high population pressures or intensive cultivation. This conclusion is tempered by the variability in our authors' perception of environmental degradation. As described above, they differ, for example, in their perception of the impacts of reduced fallow, a condition that has taken place everywhere. But severe environmental degradation seems to be associated with agriculture only in three circumstances: (1) extreme rural densities (e.g., +500 people/km^2) where economic diversification has not been able to substitute adequately for the increasing population (e.g., Nigeria's forest-belt cases); (2) physically or biologically vulnerable areas, such as the escarpment underlain by friable sandstone in the Awka-Nnewi region or the "marginal" frontier lands (arid zones historically dominated by pastoralists) recently colonized by landless farmers (e.g., the lowland Meru case); and (3) where socioeconomic organization impedes the implementation of needed conservation strategies (e.g., Usambara Mountains). Relatively stable environmental conditions are noted for most of the highland cases of eastern Africa, for the Jos Plateau, and for the Kano area, despite large populations and, with the exception of the Jos Plateau, despite long-term, intensive cultivation. This is not to say that environmental problems, including degradation, are not important in these areas; after all, intensive cultivation relying on major human-produced inputs typically is associated with some forms of degradation. Rather, farmers in these areas have managed their lands, even under severe pressures, in a manner that has permitted sustained use to date. These observations indicate that where farmers have extensive knowledge about the environment that they manage, perceive that their capital and managerial investment is in their own interest, and have a socioeconomic organization facilitating this management, environmental problems can be confronted successfully.

Conditions Favoring Agricultural Success

Although our findings are variable and incomplete in some dimensions, the case studies demonstrate that Africans can subsist and, more rarely, improve their well-being through agriculture in conditions of very high densities. Several conditions are associated with these successes; the more of them are present, the greater the likelihood that farmers will prosper beyond subsistence. They are favored agricultural environments, promising economic locations, commitment to regions of refuge and, perhaps, deep attachment to homeland, and supportive socioeconomic organization and structures.

Favored Environments

The notion of "favored" agricultural environments is a tricky one, because, as noted in chapter 1, all agricultural environments are a product of their physical condition (natural stock) and its modification by the farmer. Few environments, if any, require no modifications; virtually all offer various constraints or resistance to cultivation, particularly intensive cultivation. Favored environments, then, are those that offer the least resistance to production or can be altered or transformed to reduce resistance at minimal costs. Typically, although not always, such environments attract farmers, are intensively used, and, if managed properly, yield well.

Most of the East African cases have relatively good soils and stable rainfall by African standards. The major exception is the lowland area of Meru, which is arid. In Nigeria, the Jos Plateau suffers from occasional drought, whereas the arid Kano area regularly experiences inadequate rainfall; however, both areas have relatively good soils, and the Close-Settled Zone has access to an aquifer for irrigation. In contrast, the forest-belt cases present good rainfall qualities, although these areas contain relatively marginal soils. All else being equal, where precipitation and soils have been less constraining, the current conditions of production remain good or stable (Ruhengeri, Bushenyi, Kisii, highland Meru, and Jos), and where irrigation has offset inadequate precipitation, stable conditions also exist (Kano).

Promising Locations

Such locations are those that provide economic benefits beyond their environmental condition, excluding, of course, locations selected for specific agricultural development projects, which are not considered in this volume. These favored locations are those that benefit the farmer in high-density areas in the current socioeconomic conditions of the subcontinent, primarily those that provide easy access to markets for produce, to capital inputs, and alternative economic opportunities. Market access is especially facilitated by near-urban locations or adequate infrastructures, especially transportation networks. Near-urban locations favor the development of market gardening, with its relatively high returns, as appears in the Kano Close-Settled Zone, in parts of Kisii, Meru, Ruhengeri, and Bushenyi, and in the three Nigerian forest-belt cases. Market access through transportation networks is relatively well developed in all cases, save lowland Meru and, until recently, Usambara.

With qualifications, then, our cases lend some support to the conclusions of Pingali and colleagues (1987: 4) that market access is associated with intensification or its ability to support high-density settlement, because it enables rural households to diversify economically without large-scale migration (e.g., Meru and Kisii), setting into motion the flow of goods and services. It is recognized, however, that market access must also be accompanied by socioeconomic and political or policy conditions that allow the farmer to take advantage of it. This has been the case in Jos Plateau, with major development occurring; it has not been the case in the Usambara Mountains, where stagnation in agriculture has followed.

Regions of Refuge and Deep Attachment

Agriculture on Ukara and Ukerewe islands (Lake Victoria) has apparently ebbed and waned in the past, as its inhabitants were either restricted to the islands or expanded onshore (Kollmann 1899; Ludwig 1968). These islands, perhaps more marginal for cultivation than the mainland, were regions of refuge in which the population felt secure and invested in landscape modifications to sustain intensive agriculture. Historically, the general principle behind regions of refuge apparently has operated elsewhere in sub-Saharan Africa, with significant impacts on intensification (see Cohen and Toland's 1988 discussion of containment).

The principle is clear for instances such as the islands mentioned and where people seeking refuge actually migrate to new locations. In other cases, people occupying historical core lands have been restricted in their expansion, surrounded by equally powerful neighbors. The "fringe" or contact zones between some agriculturalists and pastoralists groups in eastern Africa are a case in point. The case of the Ibos in eastern Nigeria may be a more modern example. The buildup of extreme land pressures there in the 1950s and 1960s led to major movements of Ibos elsewhere, which, coupled with other factors, contributed to the Biafran War (1967–70), leading to a reversal of these movements and further contributing to the intensification of agriculture there.

Another type of self-containment that has impacts on agriculture is the strong attachment to homelands exhibited throughout sub-Saharan Africa. Although it is difficult to disentangle the role of "attachment" in a cultural sense (e.g., burial) from the economic security and other roles that homelands provide, it does affect agriculture, although in varying ways. The Usambara case suggests that the input intensification required for sustained output is in part stymied by homeland claims from households that are not fully committed to agriculture but have sought economic opportunities outside the agricultural sector. Remittances may intensify cultivation—as in Meru and Kisii—where these flows are to male-headed households with good agricultural lands, in which case improvements are worthwhile economic investments.

Supportive Socioeconomic Organization and Structures

This study has focused primarily on the inner workings of the population-intensification relationship by accepting the larger macroeconomic and political conditions as a given and without examining in any depth their impacts on the relationship. As noted in chapter 1, this emphasis was followed because of the greater attention given elsewhere (see Bernstein et al. 1990) to socioeconomic organization and structure (or macrotheory). As such, the influences of macrostructures, both economic and political, on agriculture are not detailed in our case studies. In general, however, they provide several insights that have bearing on these issues.

The Jos Plateau and Kisii cases illustrate the general positive impacts on agricultural growth and economic diversification when resource-allocation rules, government policy, and functioning factor markets favor agriculture. Particularly important have been flexible local tenure rules and arrangements in supporting the growth of farms in size and number as indicated by the Jos and Kisii cases. Land improvements have been facilitated by security in tenure, along with factor markets that provide outlets for production and marketing arrangements that provide for reasonable producer prices.

The policy frameworks under which intensification takes place obviously are important. The neoliberal economic position—that of many of the major international development and funding agencies—favors frameworks that promote markets under conditions of lessened control, whereas alternative positions—those followed by some national governments—have favored frameworks promoting local food production and self-sufficiency. Both positions can claim some successes and many failures. Most of the examples of sustained food production and well-being provided involve movement into market cultivation of some kind and economic diversification. Nevertheless, the Ruhengeri case demonstrates the positive impacts of policies emphasizing smallholder self-sufficiency over large-scale market cultivation.

Combined with the larger African experience in policies of "free markets" and of radical alternatives (see Johnston 1989 on Kenya and Tanzania), our studies suggest to us that success in high-density regions is largely associated with conditions of flexibility that have allowed the positive aspects of economic diversification and marketing to be "balanced" with the needs and demands of subsistence of the African farmer. We stress flexibility, because customary rules for resource allocation and household security, the very circumstances of the households, and the options for intensification, marketing, and diversification differ throughout Africa. Thus, we are more cautious than Pingali and his colleagues (1987) who suggest that economic diversification always helps to improve food availability and material well-being in the countryside. To us, it appears to be one important element that must be balanced with others.

Such observations are, of course, truisms. But in the heated polemics and exchanges over African development and agriculture, these simple points are sometimes lost.

Constraints to Further Intensification

Identifying the immediate constraints to further intensification in the high-density zones is a somewhat easier task than that undertaken above. This is so because multiple paths and circumstances can lead to regions of dense settlement and intensive cultivation. Once these rather high levels of land and agricultural pressures have been reached (and several of the cases examined here involved rural densities that are extremely high by world standards), similar problems emerge. Two of these—technological limitations and environmental degradation—are common to all intensive agricultural situations. Three are, in part, particularly acute in Africa: inadequate market development, customary resource allocation, and withdrawal of needed labor.

Technological Limitations

Large-scale mechanization is not necessarily appropriate for labor-based, intensive agriculture (for Africa, see Pingali, Bigot, and Binswanger 1987). Individual household plots tend to be relatively small and spatially fragmented. In many cases, labor is abundant and hence cheap, and usually laborers would have minimal opportunities for employment if displaced by machines. But beyond this, the level of "intermediate" technology that has been adopted, such as hand tractors or improved seed, is surprisingly low.

Farmers in all our case studies remain primarily hoe cultivators, although animal traction is emerging in some areas. Many possess rich traditions of creating resource-capital inputs, such as tie-ridging and alley cropping. Biotechnic inputs are used throughout the cases, but again sporadically. Some studies (see Goldman 1987) have shown that smallholder farmers in Africa have sophisticated knowledge in their use of pesticides to protect their crops. The same might be said of fertilizers and improved cultivars as well, especially in Kenya. Our case studies, however, suggest that farmers shy away from major use of such inputs because of their costs, in the case of fertilizers and pesticides, and because the use of many improved cultivars is not worthwhile without irrigation, which is poorly developed throughout the cases, save that for horticultural activities in the Kano area. With local currency devaluations in all the case study countries, these inputs are likely to remain prohibitively expensive for the average smallholder in the future.

How severe are these technological limitations in sub-Saharan Africa? At least two contrasting opinions have been presented: one optimistic, the other more cautious. The first argues that Africa can feed itself—or certainly improve its current state—without much new technology or agricultural knowledge (see Rocheleau, Weber, and Field-Juma 1988). The challenge, Richards (1985) has argued, is to develop and improve upon existing peasant knowledge. The second view sees further technology as essential but questions its availability and then the ability to use it, even if available. Apparently, no new technologies are waiting "on the shelf" to be adopted (Herdt 1988). This may be so in part because until recently, the international research centers designed to create biotechnology have devoted relatively little attention to African agriculture and crops (Eicher 1988). Even though breakthroughs may be possible, few are likely to be available to smallholders in the next decade. Moreover, Lele and Stone (1989) argue that any technological changes in sub-Saharan Africa will not have full impact unless they are matched by other policy changes and focused on regions that are most likely to realize their potential—high-density and high-agricultural-quality zones.

Our case studies indicate that African farmers have adapted indigenous technologies and crops more than they have adopted new technological packages and have made incremental changes to their land capital rather than wholescale transformations. The result has led to incremental intensification and productivity growth. These choices occur because risk-averse strategies are followed and because of the considerable constraints farmers face. They select measures that they believe they can afford and manage, and many of these involve off-farm activities. Our evidence suggests that, to date, these approaches have been relatively successful in the high-density zones, but for the most part, the recent trends in yields and overall land productivity indicate that they may have reached or may be reaching their limits.

The challenge in the technological field, then, is twofold: to develop appropriate innovations for African agriculture, and to "stretch" farmers' readiness and ability to use these innovations. As to the innovations themselves, Eicher (1988), among others, argues that much further research and funding are needed, not only for field technologies but also for the institutions that facilitate and sustain the adoption of such innovations. Many economists argue that adoption can be facilitated by price incentives for farmers and by a shift in trade terms in favor of agriculture. Although it is hard to argue with this prescription, it would be wrong to assume that this problem can be reduced to one of incentives alone. The African farm is not always a male-headed, single-family unit, and the complexity of farm-unit types would seem to require multiple incentives.

Indeed, the data from Imo pose an additional issue of the indigenous capacity to manage innovation. The large sample size of villages studied exhibits considerable variation in the creation and adoption of innovations: for example, group rotation in Ukwa, wet-rice cultivation in Uboma, or agroforestry in Mbaise. The studies also show that even when relatively similar environments and culture are present, innovations do not move easily from region to region. This leads to our question of whether local groups can manage more than a single set of novel techniques at a time. Having made such a choice preempts the adoption of other innovations, thus limiting their spread.

Inadequate Market Development

Adequately functioning markets in sub-Saharan Africa are rare for both purchased inputs and the disposal of produce. Economists view this problem as a major constraint to the subcontinent's development (Collier 1988; World Bank 1989).

Our case studies strongly confirm that improved well-being arising from the population-intensification relationship has been associated with the development of local markets. They have facilitated economic diversification and have generally helped reduce farmer dependence on distant markets for export crops and public marketing boards involved as intermediaries. The emergence of local markets in densely populated areas also has enabled part of the farming population to engage in nonagricultural occupations. Therefore, as suggested by Hyden (1980), markets take on a particularly important role in areas characterized by high population density.

These high-density areas, however, cannot carry the load of economic development alone. They must be complemented by improved performance in other areas or sectors of the economy. For instance, as people in southeastern Nigeria become increasingly market dependent and buy more of their food, other parts of the country or the region will need to produce the necessary surplus to feed them. This requires an adequate infrastructure, both economic and physical. There must be dependable transportation networks, including organizational structures that deliver reliable and honest services between the producer and the consumer. In three of the countries represented in this volume—Kenya, Nigeria, and Rwanda—much of this infrastructure is in place. In the other two—Tanzania and Uganda—it has been disrupted by antimarket policies or civil disturbances. Also, where population is less dense and more dispersed, as in Tanzania, Zambia, and Mali, the infrastructure that keeps markets going is more difficult to sustain. Wherever it breaks down, it tends to cause crop losses, in part because both storage and transport are inadequate.

Farmers resist participating in markets that do not serve their interests or when opportunities outside of agriculture are perceived to be better (see Carney 1988). Whether they live in high-density regions or not, African farmers' response to agriculture depends on where they see opportunities that best serve their larger needs and wants. The various strategies designed to involve the African farmers in the market have often failed to take into account distinctive African circumstances, such as community and kin obligations and the poor development of security mechanisms beyond them, gender responsibilities and constraints, and resource allocation.

Overall, market development is threatened today less from within than from without Africa. The African farmer engages in contracts for production or directly competes with subsidized first-world production and large-scale agribusiness both in the world economy and within the internal markets of sub-Saharan Africa. Commodity prices have declined in Africa in recent years, severely stressing the income of specific groups and of national economies as a whole.

Customary Resource Allocation

Rules of resource allocation can facilitate or constrain agricultural growth. They become a constraint in any society or economy where change is very rapid, and the needs promoting agricultural growth come in conflict with the objectives of allocation rules. In the contemporary world, this conflict is particularly accentuated where indigenous economies are encircled and penetrated by capitalist or socialist economies. These conflicts have been particularly acute throughout Africa.

Much of the economic literature (see Levi and Havinden 1982: 81–86) concludes that given the current conditions in Africa, nonprivate forms of land tenure, whether communal or collective, do not work. Our studies suggest that for two interrelated reasons, the situation is more complex. Throughout Africa, land tenure is still largely a nonpublic, clan, or lineage matter. In this respect, Africa differs from Europe and Asia, where land tenure was decided on by either feudal landlords or corporate villages as peasants gained autonomy from these landlords. Furthermore, according to widespread customs, every member of a social unit (family, lineage or clan) is guaranteed the right to subsistence. To be sure, not everybody exercises this right in terms of access to land, but pressure to subdivide farms is likely to remain high as long as population growth is rapid. Although the customary land-tenure system is beginning to give way, it is not clear that it will disappear altogether.

Our case studies again show mixed results about agricultural intensification linked to resource-allocation rules. The Usambara case study illustrated such a conflict, with negative impacts on agricultural growth. In this case, the conflict is over the "unimproved" land to which women have rights and "improved" lands that become the domain of males usually engaged in commodity production. Local male farmers are apparently willing to expend efforts in much-needed land improvements, principally erosion control, thus increasing production. They are challenged by women who would not only lose access to land but probably witness the conversion of improved land to grow market crops rather than subsistence crops. The result, as reported in our case study, is a stagnation in agricultural growth.

Although Usambara represents an obvious case, others in our study mention or are undergirded by more subtle conflict. They corroborate the resilience of indigenous land-tenure institutions observed by a recent major study of land-tenure systems in sub-Saharan Africa (Downs and Reyna 1988) but also suggest that Africans are at a turning point with respect to their relationship to land. It is no longer a free good; access to it is becoming more restricted; some people are acquiring large amounts of it, whereas others are losing what little they had; and the means of exploiting it are changing. Moreover, it is no longer the sole occupation of the household, nor are the decisions about its use primarily in the hands of its "owners." Increasingly, day-to-day decisions about all facets of agriculture are being made by females, in most cases under conditions in which access to land is invested in males. This contradiction, inherent in the lowland Meru context and in those of the Nigerian forest belt, is one that must be resolved adequately if agriculture is not to stagnate.

Land tenure, then, must be considered a key institutional factor in agricultural development in sub-Saharan Africa. Some governments in Africa have tried to overcome these constraints by "modernizing" land-tenure regulations. Two broad approaches have been followed: one capitalist, the other socialist. Land registration and land consolidation in the hands of individual owners were the hallmarks of the Kenyan land reform that began in the wake of the Mau Mau rebellion in the late 1950s. The significance of this reform is the extent to which it has been "indigenized" (Okoth-Ogendo 1976). Family and lineage members retain claims to the land. The prevalent pattern, then, is one of "concentration without privatization," as Berry (1988) calls it. In Kenya, as in other parts of the subcontinent, there are multiple rights to particular pieces of land. These rights may be held simultaneously but are often transacted separately by the same or different people. As a result, some rights may be concentrated, whereas others are not. In Bushenyi, land was not legally privatized but made available for leasehold, essentially allowing for privatizing through ninety-nine-year leases. Johnston (1989), citing agricultural success in Kenya in contrast to Tanzania, notes that Kenya, by allowing government officials to acquire and control land, even sometimes by abusing their positions, created an entrepreneurial class with a vested interest in stimulating and modernizing agriculture.

The socialist approach has been attempted in several countries but perhaps most systematically in Tanzania. Between 1967 and 1976 rural people were initially encouraged and subsequently forced to engage in cooperative or collective production. Although it was carried out under the guise of *ujamaa*—a Swahili concept for familyhood—the concept of collective tenure by a village, as opposed to by the clan, was foreign to the local population. Reform has been modified by local customs. The collectivist ambition has failed and been abandoned, largely because of the peasants' silent opposition (see Scott 1985; Lipton 1989). Individual households have been allowed to expand their holdings beyond the plots they were initially allocated. Tenure rights are reverting to lineages and clans. Access to resources, then, depends on nonmarket criteria, notably the establishment and reaffirmation of advantageous connections within acceptable social formations, a phenomenon that Hyden (1980) elsewhere refers to as the "economy of affection."

The major conclusion to be drawn from this discussion is that direct state intervention to alter patterns of land control is fraught with difficulties. Land reforms are always hard to carry out. The interesting thing about such efforts in Africa is that resistance does not necessarily come from a class of well-endowed landholders but from multiple and intractable systems of family-related land rights among smallholders. State intervention in these systems may temporarily redefine the conditions of access to land, and new struggles over rights may ensue. It is unlikely, however, that government policy is going to bring about either land concentration or land redistribution in sub-Saharan Africa in the foreseeable future.

In this perspective, population growth is likely to prove as effective as anything else in changing land-tenure patterns. Our case studies indicate that the high-density areas have accommodated population pressure by incorporating systems of multiple rights. The existence of multiple—and often vaguely defined—rights, however, causes much stress in society. Disputes over such rights are on the increase in high-density areas, as illustrated by Shipton (1988) for the Luo in western Kenya. Attempts of local communities to cope with these tensions may turn out to be an important determinant of change in rules of access to land resources in the rural areas of sub-Saharan Africa.

Withdrawal of Needed Labor

In the absence of any major changes in the capitalization of the farms and the technologies used, African farming is bound to remain labor intensive. In general, there is no evidence that rural-to-urban labor migration has necessarily halted the overall intensification of agriculture in the cases examined here. It alone has not been a sufficient condition to give rise to stagnation or involution, although individual households may have been so affected. In contrast, the broader consequences of this migration for economic diversification and well-being is less clear, producing both negative and positive results.

The negative effects of such outmigration depend on at least two factors. The first is who in the family moves. Whether it is the male head of the household—the breadwinner—or his son makes a difference. The son is likely to leave less of a gap than his father. The son commonly has no direct management responsibilities in the household. The father's absence is more problematic. Although he has a great stake in the land in the sense of property or resource rights, he is often not a worker of it or physically dependent on it. He often provides labor in relation to only specific crops—typically those grown for cash—or specific tasks, most likely heavy-labor ones. Whether or not he contributes labor to agriculture, he is, as long as he remains on the farm, its "manager." This is his principal role in many cases. His presence on the farm is often the key element that determines the investment in capital improvements and market cultivation.

Neither the growing literature on intrahousehold processes (see Guyer 1981; Moock 1986; Carney 1988) nor our case studies provide evidence of a general rule of intensification following the departure from the farm of the male head. In some cases, wives, given a chance, are able to undertake agricultural improvements in the absence of the husband. In others, circumstances do not allow them to do so. In any event, migration leads to role adjustments that often result in new conflicts between husband and wife (or wives) and father and son. These factors are probably as significant to the development of agriculture in sub-Saharan Africa as are purely technical or ecological considerations.

The second factor influencing the effects of outmigration on agriculture is whether household members remit money or not and, if they do, whether such funds are used for farm development. These remittances are often made as compensation for absent labor, a reciprocal act that has been widely documented throughout Africa (see Caldwell 1969; Spiegel 1981). The money, however, is often too little for capital investments. Many times it is specifically earmarked for other purposes, notably paying school or hospital fees for family members or other relatives. Even when it is being used in agriculture, its role may be controversial, as indicated by the Usambara case.

The effects of male migration seem to present regional and local differences. They are reported to be worst in southern Africa for two related reasons: Africans typically farm the more marginal lands to which they were relegated during colonial times; and the urban migrants are more proletarianized there than elsewhere. A recent study among the Shona of eastern Zimbabwe shows that remittances are invested in agriculture so as to lead to intensification, sustainability, and increased rewards only on those male-headed farms in better environments where "real" benefits are realized, usually in commodity crops (Mazambani 1990). Yet another study in Zambia suggests that the real impacts of the migrant are felt through economic diversification that occurs once urban-derived savings have been accumulated and the migrant returns home (Chanda 1986). The effects of migration seem less harmful in West Africa, as suggested by the literature. For example, Richards (1986) shows that when male heads of household return to their farms from extended stays elsewhere, agriculture benefits. In East Africa, the pattern is more mixed. For instance, urban migration does not seem to have impeded agricultural development among the Kikuyu in Kenya's Central Province, but it has had little positive effect on farm development among the Luo in Nyanza Province.

Our case studies tend to confirm the mixed impacts of male migration. It is difficult to argue that agriculture can effectively absorb all labor in the zones of extremely high density, or that further intensification would adequately reward the labor expended. It is clear, however, that many households have diminished agricultural production and display inadequate land improvements largely owing to the absence of male labor. In this respect, overall agricultural growth may have been stymied. The critical issue, of course, is the total impact on the household income and living standards that follows from the migration. This impact appears to be mixed in both the short and the long run.

Environmental Degradation

An important conclusion is that agricultural intensification is not necessarily accompanied by severe environmental degradation. Contrary to much conventional wisdom that portrays the African smallholders as wrecking their physical resources, particularly in the face of land-intensive conditions, the farmers included in this study have made considerable investments in resource-based capital, thereby protecting their farms from major environmental deterioration and the negative impacts on intensification and production that usually follow.

Despite this, the case studies include examples of declining soil fertility and increasing erosion, affecting yields and overall land productivity. As noted, these problems appear to be accentuated in those cases where other constraints and conditions have inhibited land improvements (e.g., Usambara); where cultivation practice has apparently approached its limits, given soil and water resources (e.g., the forest belt of Nigeria); or where physical and biological constraints make the region particularly vulnerable (e.g., Awka-Nnewi and the lowlands of Meru). In these cases, environmental degradation could be offset or controlled by the application of appropriate technology if the farmers had access to it or perceived a reward for using it. If the environmental problems in some of these areas are not confronted soon and if agriculture continues to use land at its current frequency, then acute damage to both the environment and the well-being of the people may follow.

These mixed results give rise to an important lesson. In much of the continent, African farmers have the knowledge and skills to intensify agriculture without excessive environmental impact on yields. (The landscape, of course, is transformed, but then this is so in all cultivation, particularly in intensive cultivation.) However, with continued rapid growth in demand as higher levels of agricultural intensity are reached, indigenous technologies must be balanced with new (biotechnic) ones, particularly in regard to soil-nutrient conservation.

Sustainable Development Potential

Our case studies demonstrate that African farmers have shown great ingenuity in coping with growing population pressures on their land; they have been able to sustain themselves, even if sometimes only marginally, through combinations of household labor arrangements and agricultural strategies that do not cut off future options in either. But what are the prospects that these same farmers or their children will continue to sustain themselves in the face of continued rising density? We do not pretend that we have any firm answers; indeed our authors vary considerably in their degree of optimism for the future. But, based on an assessment by the participants in the Gainesville conference, we suggest that sustainable development at such high densities is possible when African farmers can intensify with significant returns to increased inputs; intensify without marked environmental degradation; expand into adjacent land; diversify into high-value, marketable crops and other activities; and export some labor and receive remittances without undermining agriculture.

Our assumption is that the more of these options farmers have at their disposal, the greater the prospect for viable development and that some of these options are more available outside the densely settled areas.

Focusing on our case studies, the future prospects are somewhat brighter for the highland than for the lowland areas, as indicated in table 12.2. The Jos Plateau and the East African cases (with the exception of Usambara) constitute an "optimistic" cluster. Less optimism is warranted for the lowland cases in southeastern Nigeria and lowland Meru, with the exception of locales where possibilities for river-based rice irrigation may enhance local agriculture. Kano appears to be a "neutral" case in this regard.

The Jos Plateau and Kisii appear to be the places where intensification, expansion, and diversification have served the local population best and where there are prospects for coping with continued population growth for some time to come. Bushenyi may be a similar case. The future of much of its population, however, will depend on finding land elsewhere: the land frontier has been closed not only by population growth but also by privatizing and fencing land holdings. Incidentally, Bushenyi is the only place where privatization and consolidation of holdings are reported to be prevalent. In Ruhengeri and Meru, future viability depends on the ability of people to expand into adjacent land (as farmers or laborers) and on improved markets and land-conservation measures.

Assuming that groundwater resources are not indiscriminately tapped in the Kano area, the prospects for viable intensive gardening by irrigation appear to be good.

Socioeconomic conditions in the Usambara Mountains have apparently constrained land inputs, thus encouraging environmental degradation on steep slopes and diversification into crops other than those already produced. In principle, agricultural growth is still possible through intensification and diversification in the mountains themselves and through expansion into adjacent lowland areas. However, it is not clear that either option is viable in southeastern Nigeria with the exception, as stated already, of Imo, where cultivation of rice in riverine and wetland environments provides a new opportunity. There, as in the Usambara Mountains, involution or stagnation is already a serious problem.

Although participants in the Gainesville conference varied considerably in their assessment of future prospects for each individual area, there was general agreement that the six areas with higher land quality (Bushenyi, Kisii, Kofyar, Meru, Ruhengeri, and Usambara) have more options. Their agricultural base is stronger. For the most part, they not only feed their own people but also export food and other commodity crops. Economic diversification into off-farm activities is not a matter of life and death as it may be for a growing number of people in less-favorable environments (Awka-Nnewi, Imo, Ngwa, and Kano). The margins for intensification are narrower in these areas, and the future well-being of their occupants is particularly tied to the successful performance of other sectors in the economy. Although intensification has served these areas well in the past, the prospects for agricultural growth in the future are limited.

In conclusion, we reiterate our mixed message. African smallholders have shown great resilience in adapting their agricultural systems to the larger socioeconomic conditions in the face of high population pressure and unprecedented population growth. And, because this resilience has not necessarily been related to favorable environmental conditions, there is good reason to suppose that major increases in agriculture might be expected in many of the areas of the subcontinent that remain relatively sparsely used. There is even evidence that further agricultural improvements and, perhaps, stable-to-increasing well-being may be experienced in some of the densely settled areas. This said, there is also evidence that several of the densely settled zones will probably not be able to intensify

Table 12.2. Summary of Trajectories toward Sustainable Agriculture by Case Study

Trajectory	Nigeria Jos Plateau	Nigeria Kano Close-Settled Zone	Nigeria Imo State	Nigeria Ngwa-Igbo	Nigeria Awka-Nnewi	Tanzania Usambara Mountains	Rwanda Ruhengeri District	Kenya Meru District	Kenya Kisii District	Uganda Bushenyi District
Agriculture continues to intensify with significant returns to increased inputs	+	+	−	−	−	−	+	±	+	+
Agriculture continues to intensify without marked environmental degradation	+	+	−	−	−	−	+	±	−	+
Agriculture is expanding lands under cultivation	+	−	+	±	±	+	+	±	−	+
Diversification in marketed crops or economic activities continues	+	+	+	+	+	−	+	+	+	+
Labor outmigration does not undermine agriculture	±	+	+	±	±	−	+	±	+	+

Codes: + yes; − no; ± varies or neutral.

agriculture much further and that well-being is increasingly tied to economic diversification.

The Role of Population

Population growth cannot be ignored. It serves as one of the major driving forces behind changes, both positive and negative, in today's Africa and even more so in the future. Neither socioeconomic nor technical constraints alone determine the subcontinent's fate. As population inevitably increases in sub-Saharan Africa, a much better understanding is required of how Africans respond to such growth. To consider this response, we return to the theoretical expectations of chapter 1, considering first how the major traditions have addressed agrarian change in European history and then how they explain agrarian stagnation in Africa today. Briefly repeating (from fig. 1.1), neo-Malthusians see unchecked population as ultimately negatively affecting agricultural growth and well-being. Neo-Marxists consider current socioeconomic conditions (markets and capitalism) as suppressing such growth and largely ignore the role of population. Neoliberal economists also downplay population but see the market as the mechanism in which a large population can prosper. Finally, Boserupians believe that agricultural intensification and, ultimately, economic diversification can follow from population growth, particularly in sparsely populated agrarian economies.

Agrarian Change in Europe

To place this discussion in perspective, it is important to remember that Africa was irrelevant or very marginal to the evolution of views about population-agriculture relationships until Boserup's thesis began to have an impact. European history has been the principal source of inspiration. But even with reference to European agrarian history, some traditions have been more influential than others. The theoretical debate about population versus economy in this context has been dominated by neo-Malthusians and neo-Marxists.

A Malthusian line has been taken by Postan (1966) in England and LeRoy-Ladurie (1966) in France who have argued that changes in the growth of the population in Medieval Europe were largely responsible for shifts in agricultural profits, real incomes for the mass of the population, and migration. Thus, times when the population was rising, as in the thirteenth, sixteenth, and early seventeenth centuries, were accompanied by rising prices and growing agricultural profits but also by low real incomes for the majority of the population. By contrast, when population was falling or stationary, agricultural profits were low, but mass incomes were relatively high. Under conditions of low-level agricultural organization and techniques, and low levels of investment in agriculture, they argue, population fluctuations are the determinant of changes in economic performance.

Against this model, Marxian theory emphasizes the market and ensuing commercialization as the key variables for understanding the breakthrough from a "traditional economy" to relatively self-sustaining economic development in Europe. The destruction of serfdom and the short-circuiting of the emerging predominance of small-peasant property and its replacement by capitalist class relations are the principal elements in this transformation (Braudel 1973; Wallerstein 1974). Using England as the prime empirical reference for their argument, advocates of this school suggest that it was the emergence of the classical landlord–tenant–wage labor structure that made possible the transformation of agricultural production in that country. Brenner (1976), for example, argues that the peasants' failure to establish freehold control over the land enabled the landlords to engross, consolidate, and enclose: to create large farms and lease them to capitalist tenants who could afford to make the necessary capital investments. This change in class relations was indispensable for agrarian advance, which, in this perspective, is predicated upon significant inputs of capital, involving the introduction of new technologies and a larger scale of operation.

Brenner (1976) and others recognize that peasant production was capable of improvement, but they argue that in and of itself it cannot provide the agrarian basis for economic development. Small-scale farming, for instance, could be very effective with certain industrial crops like flax, as well as with viticulture, horticulture, and dairying. But this sort of agriculture brings about increased yields through the intensification of labor rather than through greater efficiency of a given unit of labor input. It is in this sense that, according to adherents of the Marxian theory, improvement of peasant agriculture does not produce "development." But neither does capitalism in the long run; in their perspective, it generates its own contradictions and lays the foundation for its own destruction.

This brief detour into European agrarian history invites the following comments: both these theories are exceedingly pessimistic. One suggests that humankind has no control over its own destiny, the other that the destiny humankind sets for itself is apocalyptic. European history confronts both these interpretations in examining how societies resolved these issues in ways different from what was predicted. To understand fully the complexity of change in European history, it is necessary also to incorporate the more optimistic scenarios of neoliberal economics and of Boserup's population-driven themes.

This reference to divergent interpretations of agrarian change in Europe also serves the purpose of illustrating how academic discourse tends to be dominated by a few perspectives at the expense of others. In the social sciences, there are almost always endless numbers of possible explanations of a given phenomenon, but only a select few typically command attention at any given time. One theoretical tradition tends to become the dominant, if only temporarily. While it occupies center stage, other traditions are forced into the back seats. These are being increasingly called upon when the prevailing theme has exhausted its explanatory potential or when changing empirical circumstances render it less relevant. This is when the discourse experiences a "paradigmatic shift," to use Thomas Kuhn's language.

Agrarian Stagnation in Africa

Social science explanations of African development in the past two decades have been largely attentive to "economy" rather than "population." In the 1970s, the dominant theoretical tradition was neo-Marxist, depending quite heavily on a crude class analysis. The premise was that international capitalism had already penetrated Africa enough to make class relations the prime determinants of change. In the 1980s, it has been generally recognized that this kind of class analysis offers little promise in a subcontinent where social stratification has yet to crystallize into genuine class relations. Peasant producers in sub-Saharan Africa simply are not subject to the same kind of squeeze by a class of landlords as was in the case of the critical period of agricultural transformation in Europe. Neo-Marxist class analysis was partly replaced in the 1980s by two competing approaches: a neoliberal approach that emphasizes the role of monetary and other forms of incentives to spur development (Timmer, Falcon and Pearson 1983; Johnston 1989); and a "revisionist" neo-Marxist school that stays loyal to economy as the major independent variable but shifts its focus to questions of ecological regulation and household-labor processes (see Watts 1983, 1989; Blaikie 1984).

The neoliberal renaissance cannot be understood in terms of the perceived theoretical shortcomings of the neo-Marxist paradigm only. It has also been formed by disappointments experienced throughout the subcontinent with pervasive state intervention in the economy that, among other things, led to depressed prices for agricultural goods relative to manufactures and services, discouraged increased agricultural production, and reduced farmers' real incomes.

Therefore, neoliberal development economists have not found it difficult to build up a strong argument for a significant reduction of state intervention in the domestic economy. Such a step, they maintain, enables a system of incentives conducive to agricultural expansion to emerge and permits the dissemination of improved agricultural technology (World Bank 1981; Timmer, Falcon and Pearson 1983). Others, although not disagreeing with this assumption, are ready to defend select state intervention in the form, for example, of agricultural price supports and increased investments in rural infrastructure and agricultural research (Eicher 1982; Johnston 1989; Lele and Stone 1989).

The problem with this argument is that it tends to assume that prices, extension services, and infrastructure are the primary variables mediating between household income-generating strategies on the one hand and aggregate economic policies and performance on the other. As our case studies suggest, Africa's agriculture is still not fully market based, and many of the assumptions underpinning this argument simply do not apply in the subcontinent. This is why we also believe that the "induced-innovation" theory (Hayami and Ruttan 1985) requires modification in the study of African agriculture, to be perhaps merged with the kind of "indigenous induced innovation" inherent in Boserup's scheme and its elaborations (see the discussion on induced intensification in chapter 1). The point is that, owing to the large proportion of subsistence cultivation, commodity production is not yet sufficiently strong to drive institutional innovation adequately according to the induced-innovation model and that most African smallholders have not yet reached that threshold of production in which such innovation could be adopted.

The "revisionist" school abandons the simplistic form of European-style class relations to examine the situational logic of household-resource managers. In this perspective, questions of ecological regulation are shaped by property rights and by the social relations of production. Differential patterns of access and control over resources operating at levels from global to household determine the capacity of individuals, households, or groups to manage their resource-based capital. If, for instance, peasant farmers are driven to exploit their own environment detrimentally, the explanatory variable is a "reproduction squeeze" imposed by other exploitative forces—people are driven into hardship by the perceived dynamics of a capitalist economy.

The household focus implicit in this approach complements political ecology by illustrating the great diversity of labor organization that exists in rural Africa today and how struggles arise around work as a result of agricultural intensification. Some of these struggles are located in the conjugal realm, specifically over the customary rights, responsibilities, and obligations linking labor claims and property rights in the marriage agreement. Other conflicts are generational, such as, for example, those between elders and juniors or fathers and sons. The main point, Berry (1985, 1988) has underscored, is that the household is not necessarily a cohesive decision-making unit.

We find ourselves partly in agreement with both the neoliberals and the neo-Marxists as their arguments have evolved in the 1980s. Where we depart is in the interpretation of the role of population. In neither analysis does population act as either a prime or a mediating agent of change (but see Lele and Stone 1989). In fact, what is striking about the whole development debate in Africa is the subsidiary position accorded demographic variables. There are at least three reasons for this intellectual blind spot.

The first is that in a subcontinent where progress in the twentieth century has centered on effective incorporation into the global economy, economic variables have taken on a special significance, regardless of whether theory has been used to promote or oppose this process. The second is that for policy analysts, economic variables are seen as more manipulable than demographic ones. Thus, in a climate characterized more by political impatience than by the delivery of improved material well-being, theories stressing economy over population found an easier market. The notion that "development is the best contraceptive" reigned in the 1970s and still has its supporters among both policy analysts and theorists. The third reason is that demography has been side-tracked by those for whom population means essentially issues of fertility control.

Unlike the situation in other regions of the world, there really has not been debate about how far and in what way demographic factors in sub-Saharan Africa determine development in general and agriculture in particular. They have been either totally ignored or interpreted only in a neo-Malthusian fashion (see McNamara 1984).

Underlying these specifics is the long tradition of hostility between neo-Marxist and neo-Malthusian thought. These date back to the origins of the respective ideologies: Malthus's responses to the policy issues of his day, and Marx's interpretation of Malthus as a class justification for further immiseration of the poor (for a review, see Dupâquier 1983). Rare indeed have been efforts to bring together Marx and Malthus by focusing on societal forces of production and on the domestic economy's forces of reproduction, such as Harris's (1979) cultural materialism. These differences have been exacerbated in the African intellectual tradition by its early post-independence, neo-Marxist roots and by the origins of neo-Malthusian views almost entirely in the industrialized west and north. The neo-Malthusian views clash with traditional economic necessity in peasant households for large families and with the complementary notion that having many children is a sign of status and respect in society.

Studies of the kind contained in this volume help create a much-needed balance between contending approaches to the study of African development. They suggest that population growth is an independent driving force for change or is synergistic with others. It plays an independent role in the constantly shifting dialectic between society and land-based resources and also within classes and groups within society (Blaikie and Brookfield 1986: 17), the turf that political economists have chosen as their home ground. The same applies to the neoliberal focus on economic incentives in reshaping behavior. In both traditions, the economic variables have been stressed to the exclusion of other variables, notably demographic ones.

Let us return for a moment to the agrarian history of Europe. When a "reproductive squeeze" was imposed on the peasantry by the landlords or the state, it resulted in calculated changes in demographic behavior. Farmer family size changed in response to economic trends. In this respect class analysts of European history seem to be right in suggesting that exploitative relations were the independent variable. The "squeeze" was real. Peasants had virtually no alternative but to respond to the conditions imposed upon them by more powerful classes.

This scenario is not borne out for sub-Saharan Africa by our case studies. Surely, the conditions for a "reproductive squeeze" are emerging with higher population density, but it is questionable whether they should be portrayed as singularly determinant. Land alienation and concentration in the hands of a small group of landlords is still the exception rather than the rule in the subcontinent. Although we admire the finesse with which much of the microanalysis of household-labor processes is being carried out, there is a risk that, in the absence of competing theories, the explanatory powers of this type of studies are exaggerated. The argument made by both Postan (1966) and LeRoy-Ladurie (1966) in their explanation of agrarian change in Europe seems hypothetically as valid to Africa as anything else: under conditions of traditional agricultural organization, techniques, and low levels of investment in agriculture, demography is a major change determinant in economic performance.

Therefore, there are good reasons why the autonomy of the demographic variables should be taken seriously, particularly in the African context. Caldwell's (1976) pioneering work on demographic and fertility behavior in the subcontinent has been followed among others by Frank and McNicoll's (1987) (see also Lee et al. 1988). Their recent work indicates that there are few limits on fertility in the typical rural African household. Patriarchal authority, risk of divorce and property loss, and the need for future security generate positive fertility incentives for women. From the male perspective, the effects of additional children are diffuse: female offspring confer bridewealth advantages; paternity confers prestige; and tangible support can be gleaned in old age from children.

This "new" demography emphasizes the difference in family structure between sub-Saharan Africa on the one hand and Europe, America, and Asia on the other (although many of these elements are found elsewhere). It suggests a different dynamic of fertility management than in the rest of the world. And, above all, it proposes that the kind of conflicts that we have been accustomed to think of as determined by economic variables are in fact population driven.

If the population variable is so important, where do our case studies suggest that Africa stands between Malthus and Boserup? We have already concluded that population growth has been associated with agricultural intensification in Africa as elsewhere, which we have interpreted as evidence that population is a major driver of intensification. With regard to improvements in material well-being, however, we are more ambivalent. We do not have enough evidence to suggest that Malthusian considerations can be ignored altogether. Borrowing from Herlihy (Newman et al. 1990), we are ready to describe the African situation in terms of a "Malthusian deadlock." African societies have continued to accommodate rising numbers of people in spite of adverse conditions. Neither the famines of the 1970s and the 1980s nor the deteriorating world economic conditions during the same period have had much impact on the demographic curve. Many Africans have doubtless gone hungry, but populations have continued to grow rapidly.

This pattern resembles Europe in the fourteenth century when its population reached a then stunning size and famines were widespread and recurrent. It suffered under a Malthusian deadlock that might well have persisted indefinitely had not the plague broken it and paved the way for a profound reorganization of the European economy.

We do not suggest that the factors at play in contemporary Africa are the same and that a plague (AIDS?) would facilitate renewed economic development. What we are proposing, however, is that, beyond the field of demography, demographic variables be taken much more seriously by theorists and policy analysts alike. As our studies have confirmed, population growth in Africa has both positive and negative consequences. Population as much as—if not more than—economy seems to drive what is happening there. Therefore, it is time that the population variable be given the prominence it deserves in the study of African development in general, and of agricultural growth in particular.

Policy Implications

What are the policy messages that may be derived from this survey and from our interpretations of the results? Following from our initial population survey, there are many more areas in Africa already with population densities equally high or higher than those examined in this volume. Furthermore, with the rate of population growth prevailing in sub-Saharan Africa, the number of such areas is growing rapidly. Thus the insights gleaned from this study have implications for an increasing number of other areas in the subcontinent.

A message of practical consequence is that not all outcomes of high levels of population density in sub-Saharan Africa are negative. In certain cases, farmers have been able to keep pace with population growth through agriculture and economic diversification. Economic and environmental deterioration has not always followed population growth, because changing population needs generate new social dynamics that change behavior.

A second message is that, for the future, the critical link is between intensification and material well-being. Our examples indicate that this link is still weak, the main reason being that most African smallholders have not found (or been provided with) the technological breakthrough that rapidly shifts production to new levels on a per capita basis, and given this shift, that produces sufficient market rewards. There appears to be a cap on per capita production by following indigenous strategies alone, in spite of the innovations of local farming. Thus greater attention to the development of suitable technologies for the African experience is needed.

A third message is that, as long as population growth continues at high levels in the current economic climate, the intensification process is likely to generate increased production of "nonbasic" commodities as opposed to staple foods. Such commodities, obtained in perennial tree and shrub crops, horticulture, and dairying, are currently of much higher market value than are staples, and the smallholder responds to this value in the context of complementary-subsistence production. Therefore, other locations must be found for the production of staples to feed nonfarmers and some rural populations. In some cases, the food in question will need to be imported from other regions of the world.

A fourth message is that the policy lessons are likely to differ according to the specific character of the high-density area. Here we identify three different types, each of which has its own policy implications.

1. *Near-urban areas* are high-density, high-intensity places that are within relatively close proximity of major markets, that have particularly high demands for horticultural products and that offer many nonmigrant, off-farm economic activities. Here the policy needs seem to be: to keep both factor and consumer markets functioning well; to increase attention to horticultural activities; and to emphasize the development and role of small-town activities associated with the major market.

2. *Frontier areas* are "open lands" (or underutilized lands) immediately adjacent to high-density high-intensity locales into which population is spreading. Two types of open lands are recognized: those relatively marginal and those favored for agriculture. Marginal lands are prone to major environmental degradation under rapid settlement, in part because they tend to be settled by economically marginal households that do not have the labor or capital to cope adequately, and in

part because such lands often involve relatively new environmental experiences of which the farmers in question do not have an adequate knowledge. The policy implication here would appear to emphasize less rapid settlement and to encourage extensive means of land use. Interestingly, there remain good agricultural lands in sub-Saharan Africa that are relatively sparsely settled and that are attracting population; such colonization will increase with disease control. Presumably, this movement should be encouraged with emphasis on the development of an infrastructure that facilitates agricultural development, notably roads, and on functioning markets.

3. *Isolated areas* are high-density, high-intensity locales that have poorly developed infrastructures and weak markets, in part because of their geographical setting and, therefore, have weak interregional and international linkages. Policy prescriptions here, presuming no immediate developments that would alter the isolation, include promoting land-based capital improvements and land-conservation technologies; preserving access to those lands in which agriculture might extend (e.g., wetlands); and encouraging the growth of intraregional markets.

Finally, it would appear that the principle of comparative advantage, following Lele and Stone (1989), is a good one for intervention policy interested in increasing agriculture in general. We differ from these two authors in the emphasis placed on the inherent fertility of land in determining comparative advantage because of the anthropogenic nature of perception of farmland quality and because of the important locational issues discussed.

As many more agricultural districts in Africa approach densities similar to our studies (greater than 200 persons/km²), we can reject with some confidence an expectation of Malthusian collapse. There will be a cushion of intensification, diversification, and dietary change sufficient to provide for the immediate subsistence needs of the greater population, but a better life will not spontaneously follow. Beyond the intensification of agriculture solely from the labor and ingenuity of small farmers, there is need for social relationships that encourage, techniques that make possible, and incentives that reward agrarian-based development.

References

Bernstein, H., B. Crow, M. Mackintosh, and C. Martin, eds. 1990. *The Food Question: Profit versus People?* London: Earthscan.

Berry, Sara. 1985. *Fathers Work for Their Sons*. Berkeley: University of California Press.

———. 1988. "Concentration without Privatization? Some Consequences of Changing Patterns of Rural Land Control in Africa." In R. E. Downs and S. P. Reyna, eds., *Land and Society in Contemporary Africa*. Hanover, N.H.: University of New England Press.

Blaikie, Piers. 1984. *The Political Economy of Soil Erosion*. London: Longman.

Blaikie, Piers, and H. C. Brookfield. 1986. *Land Degradation and Society*. London: Methuen.

Boserup, E. 1965. *The Conditions of Agricultural Growth*. Chicago: Aldine.

———. 1981. *Population and Technological Change*. Chicago: University of Chicago Press.

Braudel, Fernand. 1973. *Capitalism and Material Life 1400–1800*. New York: Harper & Row.

Brenner, Robert. 1976. "Agrarian Class Structure and Economic Development in Pre-Industrial Europe." *Past and Present* 70: 30–75.

Caldwell, J. S. 1969. *African Rural-Urban Migration: The Movement to Ghana's Towns*. New York: Columbia University Press.

———. 1976. "Toward a Restatement of Demographic Transition Theory." *Population and Development Review* 2: 321–66.

Callear, D. 1982. *The Social Culture Factors Involved in Production by Small Farmers in Wedza Communal Area, Zimbabwe, on Maize and Its Marketing*. Report Studies RRD 17. Paris: UNESCO, Division for the Study of Development.

Carney, J. 1988. "Struggles over Crop Rights and Labour within Contract Farming Households in a Gambian Irrigation Rice Project." *Journal of Peasant Studies* 15: 334–49.

Chanda, R. 1986. "Relations between Migration and Rural Resource Management and Development in the Sanfya Area, Zambia." Ph.D. dissertation, Clark University.

Cohen, Ronald, and Judith Toland, eds. 1988. *State Formation and Political Legitimacy*. New Brunswick, N.J.: Transaction Books.

Collier, Paul. 1988. "Contractural Constraints upon the Process of Labour Exchange in Rural Kenya." *International Labour Review* 128: 754–68.

Downs, R. E., and S. P. Reyna, eds. 1988. *Land and Society in Contemporary Africa*. London: Methuen.

Dupâquier, J., ed. 1983. *Malthus Past and Present*. New York: Academic Press.

Eicher, Carl. 1982. "Facing Up to Africa's Food Crisis." *Foreign Affairs* 61:151–74.

———. 1988. Sustainable Institutions for African Agricultural Development. Paper for seminar on The Changing Dynamics of Global Agriculture: Research Policy Implications for National Agricultural Research Systems,

ISNAR, CTA and DSE, Feldafing, Federal Republic of Germany, 22–28 Sept.

Frank, Odile, and Geoffrey McNicoll. 1987. "An Interpretation of Fertility and Population in Kenya." *Population and Development Review* 13: 209–44.

Gleave, M. B., and H. P. White. 1969. "Population Density and Agricultural Systems in West Africa." In *Environment and Land Use*, ed. M. F. Thomas and G. W. Whittington. London: Methuen.

Goldman, Abe. 1987. Agricultural Innovation in Three Areas in Kenya. Unpublished paper presented at the Annual Meeting of the Association of American Geographers, Portland, Oreg.

Guyer, Jane. 1981. "Household and Community in African Studies." *African Studies Review* 24: 87–138.

Hayami, Y., and V. Ruttan. 1985. *Agricultural Development: An International Perspective*. Baltimore, Md.: Johns Hopkins University Press.

Harris, M. 1979. *Cultural Materialism: The Struggle for a Science of Culture*. New York: Random House.

Herdt, Robert. 1988. Increasing Crop Yields in Developing Countries. Paper presented at the 1988 Meeting of the American Agricultural Economics Association.

Hyden, Goran. 1980. *Beyond Ujamaa in Tanzania: Underdevelopment and an Uncaptured Peasantry*. Berkeley: University of California Press.

Johnston, Bruce F. 1989. "The Political Economy of Agricultural Development in Kenya and Tanzania." *Food Research Institute Studies* 21: 205–64.

Kollmann, P. 1899. *The Victorian Nyanza*. London: Swan.

Lee, R. D., W. B. Arthur, A. C. Kelly, G. Rodgers, and T. N. Srinivasan, eds. 1988. *Population, Food and Rural Development*. Oxford: Clarendon Press.

Lele, Uma, and S. B. Stone. 1989. Population Pressure, the Environment, and Agricultural Intensification: Variations on the Boserup Hypothesis. Managing Agricultural Development in Africa (MADIA) Symposium.

LeRoy-Ladurie, E. 1966. *Les Paysans de Languedoc*, 2 vols. Paris: Sevpen.

Levi, J., and M. Havinden. 1982. *Economics of African Agriculture*. Harlow, UK: Longman.

Lipton, Michael. 1989. *New Seeds and Poor People*. Baltimore: Johns Hopkins University Press.

Ludwig, H. D. 1968. "Permanent Farming on Ukara." In *Smallholder Farming and Smallholder Development in Tanzania: Ten Case Studies*, ed. H. Ruthenberg. London: Hurst

McNamara, Robert. 1984. "Time Bomb or Myth: The Population Problem." *Foreign Affairs* (Summer): 1107–131.

Mazambani, D. 1990. "Labor Migration Impacts on Communal Land. Agriculture in Zimbabwe: Case Studies from Manicaland Province." Ph.D. diss., Clark University.

Miracle, M. 1966. *Maize in Tropical Africa.* Madison: University of Wisconsin Press.

Moock, J., ed. 1986. *Understanding Africa's Rural Households and Farming Systems.* Boulder, Colo.: Westview Press.

Netting, R. McC. 1968. *Hill Farmers of Nigeria. Cultural Ecology of the Kofyar of the Jos Plateau.* Seattle: University of Washington Press.

Newman, L. F., A. Boegenhold, D. Herlihy, R. W. Kates, and K. Raaflaub. 1990. "Agricultural Intensification, Urbanization and Hierarchy." In *Hunger in History: Food Shortage, Poverty, and Deprivation,* ed. L. F. Newman. Oxford: Basil Blackwell.

Okoth-Ogendo, H. W. O. 1976. "African Land Tenure Reform." In *Agricultural Development in Kenya,* ed. J. Heyer, J. Maitha, and W. Senga. Nairobi: Oxford University.

Palmer, I. 1985. *Women's Roles and Gender Differences in Development: The Impact of Male Out Migration on Women in Farming.* West Hartford, Conn.: Kumarian.

Pingali, P., Y. Bigot, and H. P. Binswanger. 1987. *Agricultural Mechanization and the Evolution of Farming Systems in Sub-Saharan Africa.* Baltimore: Johns Hopkins University Press.

Postan, M. M. 1966. *The Cambridge Economic History of Europe.* Cambridge: Cambridge University Press.

Richards, Paul. 1985. *Indigenous Agricultural Revolution. Ecology and Food Production in West Africa.* London: Hutchinson.

———. 1986. *Coping with Hunger: Hazard and Experiment in an African Rice Farming System.* London: Allen and Unwin.

Rocheleau, D., F. Weber, and A. Field-Juma. 1988. *Agroforestry in Dryland Africa.* Nairobi: International Council for Research in Agroforestry.

Scott, J. C. 1985. *Weapons of the Weak: Everday Forms of Peasant Resistance.* New Haven: Yale University Press.

Shantz, H. L., and B. L. Turner. 1958. *Photographic Documentation of Vegetation Changes in Africa over a Third of a Century.* Tucson: University of Arizona, College of Agriculture Report 169.

Shipton, Parker. 1988. "The Kenyan Land Tenure Reform: Misunderstanding in the Public Creation of Private Property." In *Land and Society in Contemporary Africa,* ed. R. E. Downs and S. P. Reyna. Hanover, NH: University of New England Press.

Spiegel, A. 1981. "Rural Differentiation and the Diffusion of Migrant Labour Remittances in Lesotho." In *Black Villagers in an Industrial Society,* ed. P. Mayer. Cape Town: Oxford University Press.

Timmer, C. P., W. P. Falcon, and S. R. Pearson. 1983. *Food Policy Analysis.* Baltimore: Johns Hopkins University Press.

Vermeer, D. 1970. "Population Pressure and Crop Rotational Changes among the Tiv of Nigeria." *Annals of the Association of American Geographers* 67: 384–96.

Wallerstein, I. 1974. *The Modern World System: Capitalist Agriculture and the Origins of the European World Economy in the Sixteenth Century.* New York: Monthly Review Press.

Watts, Michael. 1983. *Silent Violence: Food, Famine and Peasantry in Northern Nigeria.* Berkeley: University of California Press.

———. 1989. "The Agrarian Crisis in Africa: Debating the Crisis." *Progress in Human Geography.* 13: 1–41.

World Bank. 1981. *Accelerated Growth in Sub-Saharan Africa.* Washington, D.C.: The World Bank.

———. 1989. *Sub-Saharan Africa: From Crisis to Sustainable Growth.* Washington, D.C.: The World Bank.

GLOSSARY ✦

Aerial yam	*Dioscorea bulbifera*
Aro	Loan (in present context, of land)
Avocado	*Persea americana*
Banana	*Musa acuminata, M. balbisiana, M. paradisiaca, M. sapientum* (also Ensete family)
Barley	*Hordeum vulgare*
Beans	*Phaseolus vulgaris, P. iunatus*
Breadfruit	*Treculia africana*
Bunds	Earthen embankments built to check erosion
Cabbage	*Brassica oleracea capitata*
Cardamom	*Elettaria cardamomum*
Carrot	*Daucus carota (*var. *sativus)*
Cashew nuts	*Anacardium occidentale*
Cassava	*Manihot utilissima, M. esculenta*
Castor	*Ricinus communis*
Cherry tomato	*Lycopersicon esculentum*
Chili pepper	See pepper
Cin rani	Dry season or short-term circulation
Coconut	*Cocos nucifera*
Cocoyam	*Colocasia antiquorum, C. esculenta, Xanthosoma sagittifolium*
Coffee	*Coffea arabica, C. canephora*
Cotton	*Gossypium* spp.
Cowpea	*Vigna unguiculata*
Dwang or Hausa potato	*Coleus dysentericus*
Dwarf walls	Small or short walls built around plots to check erosion or ward off animals
Early crops	Rapidly maturing cultigens grown as a check against poor yields or loss of major staples
Eggplant (*bringal*)	Solanum melongena, var. *esculentum*

Egusi melon	*Citrullus colocynthis*
Fadama	Seasonally flooded or waterlogged depression or river floodplain
Field capacity	Stage at which soil can hold no more moisture and excess converts to runoff
Gado	Inheritance (in present context, of land)
Gandu	Large extended family-based farm, or a cooperative farming unit operated by two or more men under the direction of the father or senior brother
Garri	Cassava flour
Gourd	*Lagenaria vulgaris*
Gram	Black, *Phaseolus mungo*; green, *P. aureus*
Grapefruit	*Citrus paradisi*
Groundnut	*Arachis hypogaea*
Guava	*Psidium guajava*
Guinea corn	*Sorghum bicolor*
Haricot bean	*Phaseolus vulgaris*
Harmattan	Dry, dust-laden wind experienced in West Africa during the dry season
Hyacinth or black bean	*Dolichos lablab*
Immigration cells	Favored locations for migrants because of presumed economic opportunities
Jigo	Hand-operated, counterpoised water lift or *shaduf*
Kale (*Sukuma wikli*)	*Brassica oleracea* var. *acephala*
Kwadago	Wage labor, usually on a daily basis
Kyauta	Gift (in present context, of land)
Lemon	*Citrus limon*
Lettuce	*Lactuca sativa*
Lima bean	*Phaseolus lunatis*
Maize	*Zea mays*
Mango	*Mangifera indica*
Millets	*Pennisetum typhoideum* (bulrush); *Eleusine coracana* (finger); *Setaria italica* (foxtail or Italian)
Miraa	*Catha edulis*

Muati	August rains in Usambara Mts.
Ngemo	Work parties where friends and relatives are fed (in Usambara Mts.)
Ng'waka	March–May rains and name of farming cycle at that time (Usambara Mts.)
Nyika	Farming zone located below 650 m in Usambara Mts.
Oil palm	*Elaeis guineensis*
Onion	*Allium* spp.
Orange	*Citrus sinensis*
Papaya	*Carica papaya*
Passion fruit	*Passiflora incarnata (edulis)*
Pea	*Pisum sativum*
Pear	*Pyrus* spp.
Pepper	*Capsicum annuum*
Pigeon pea	*Cajanus cajan*
Pineapple	*Ananas comosus*
Plantain	*Musa paradisiaca*
Plum	*Prunus* spp.
Potatoes (also Irish)	*Solanum tuberosum*
Pumpkin	*Cucurbita pepo*
Pyrethrum	*Chrysanthemum cinerariifolium*
Rice	*Oryza* spp.
Rosette disease	A groundnut disease of which *Aphis craccivora* is the vector. Present in northern Nigeria for many years, the disease became endemic in 1975.
Savanna, derived	Conversion of forest into grassland owing to burning for agricultural and other activities
Saye	Purchase (in present context, of land)
Shambaai	Farming zone located above 1,000 m in Usambara Mts.
Sisal	*Agave sisalana*
Soak-away pits	Small holes dug around plots to drain excessive water
Sorghum	*Sorghum vulgare (S. bicolor?)*

Sugarcane	*Saccharum officinarum*
Sunflower	*Helianthus annuus*
Sweet potato	*Ipomoea batatas*
Taro	*Colocasia antiquorum (C. esculenta* var. *antiquorum?)*
Tea	*Camellia sinensis*
Telfairia or fluted pumpkin	*Telfairia occidentalis*
Tobacco	*Nicotiana tabacum*
Tomato	*Lycopersicon esculentum (L. lycopersicon?)*
Tsetse fly	*Glossina* spp., carries trypanosomiasis (nagana disease), especially a problem in the forest-vegetation zone
Velvet bean	*Mucuna sloanei (deeringiana?)*
Vui	October–December rains in Usambara Mts.
Vuu or *rizga*	*Coleus dazo*
Wattle	*Acacia mearnsii*
Wave-bedding technique	(Also tie-ridging) construction of earthen ridges across slope to inhibit erosion
Wheat	*Triticum aestivum*
Yam	*Dioscorea* spp.: three-leaved yam, *D. dumetorum*; yellow yam, *D. cayenensis*; white yam, *D. rotundata (D. alata?)*
Yam bean	*Sphenostylis stenocarpa (Pachyrrhizus erosus, P. tuberosus?)*

CONTRIBUTORS

FRANK E. BERNARD is professor of geography and environmental studies at Ohio University.

STEVEN FEIERMAN is professor of history at the University of Florida.

ROBERT E. FORD is assistant professor of geography, Utah State University.

ABRAHAM C. GOLDMAN is assistant professor of geography, University of Florida.

GORAN HYDEN is professor of political science, University of Florida.

NELSON KASFIR is professor of government, Dartmouth College.

ROBERT W. KATES is distinguished scientist/scholar, George Perkins Marsh Institute, Clark University.

SUSAN MARTIN is lecturer, History of West Africa, School of Oriental and African Studies, University of London.

MICHAEL MORTIMORE is senior research associate, Department of Geography, University of Cambridge and an independent consultant on African drylands development.

ROBERT Mc.C. NETTING is professor of anthropology, University of Arizona.

FRANCIS C. OKAFOR is professor of geography and regional planning, University of Benin.

H. W. O. OKOTH-OGENDO is professor of Public Law and director, Centre for African Family Studies, Nairobi.

JOHN O. OUCHO is associate professor, Population Studies Research Institute, University of Nairobi.

GLENN DAVIS STONE is assistant professor, Department of Anthropology, Columbia University.

M. PRISCILLA STONE is program director, African Studies, Social Science Research Council.

B. L. TURNER II is director, George Perkins Marsh Institute, and professor of geography, Clark University.

INDEX ✦